Open-Source Property

Casebook

Who-hoop!

www.opensourceproperty.org

Build Author: Christopher Cotropia

Build Date: October 2018

Table of Contents

Part I: Foundations

Found and Stolen Property

Finders keepers, losers weepers?

Armory v. Delamirie

(1722) 1 Strange 505, 93 Eng. Rep. 664 (K.B.)

The plaintiff being a chimney sweeper's boy found a jewel and carried it to the defendant's shop (who was a goldsmith) to know what it was, and delivered it into the hands of the apprentice, who under pretence of weighing it, took out the stones, and calling to the master to let him know it came to three halfpence, the master offered the boy the money, who refused to take it, and insisted to have the thing again; whereupon the apprentice delivered him back the socket without the stones. And now in trover against the master these points were ruled:

1. That the finder of a jewel, though he does not by such finding acquire an absolute property or ownership, yet he has such a property as will enable him to keep it against all but the rightful owner, and consequently may maintain trover.

2. That the action well lay against the master, who gives a credit to his apprentice, and is answerable for his neglect.

3. As to the value of the jewel several of the trade were examined to prove what a jewel of the finest water that would fit the socket would be worth; and the Chief Justice directed the jury, that unless the defendant did produce the jewel, and shew it not to be of the finest water, they should presume the strongest against him, and make the value of the best jewels the measure of their damages: which they accordingly did.

Questions

1. One way of describing the holding of *Armory* is that it sets out the rights of finders. Suppose that the "rightful owner" of the jewel, Lord Hobnob, had shown up in the shop while the chimney-sweep and the apprentice were arguing over the jewel. Who would have been entitled to the jewel? If the chimney-sweep is not the "rightful owner," why does he still win the case? What kind of interest does he have in the jewel?

2. A second way of describing of describing the holding of *Armory* is that it illustrates "relativity of title." As between the plaintiff and the defendant, the party with the relatively better claim to title wins, even if their title is in some sense defective in an absolute sense. Relativity of title is intimately connected to the idea of "chains of title": competing claimants to a piece of property each do their best to trace their claims back to a rightful source. What is the source of the chimney-sweep's claim to the jewel? And the jeweler's? Does this explain the outcome of the case? What result if the jeweler had proven that he had signed a contract to purchase the jewel from Lord Hobnob but that Lord Hobnob had lost the jewel before delivering it?

3. A third way of describing the holding of *Armory* is that it rejects the jeweler's attempt to assert a *jus tertii* (Latin for "right of a third party") defense. The defendant cannot defeat the plaintiff's otherwise-valid claim to the jewel by arguing that a third party – Lord Hobnob – has an even better claim. Put differently, we might say that "as against a wrongdoer, possession is title." *Jeffries v. Great W. Ry. Co.*, (1856) 119 Eng. Rep. 680, 681 (Q.B.). Does this narrowing of focus to the parties before the court make sense?

Here is one way to think about it. Suppose that Lord Hobnob shows up in court while *Armory* is being argued and explains that the jewel slipped from his finger while he was strolling in Lincoln's Inn Fields. Who is entitled to the jewel? What if Lord Hobnob shows up and explains that he tossed the jewel aside in the mud, saying "I have become tired of this bauble; it bores me and I no longer wish to have it." What if he explains that he handed it to the chimney-sweep, saying "I wish you to have this jewel; may it serve you better than it has me." But recall that in the actual case, Lord Hobnob was nowhere to be found; no one even knew his identity. Does it matter to the outcome of *Armory v. Delamirie* how the jewel passed from Lord Hobnob's hands to the chimney-sweep's?

If you are still not convinced, consider this. If the jeweler could set up Lord Hobnob's title to show that the chimney-sweep's title was defective, would the chimney-sweep be entitled to present evidence that Lord Hobnob's title was defective, say because Lord Hobnob stole the jewel from a visiting Frenchman in 1693? Cutting off inquiry into third parties' claims also helps cut off inquiry into old claims. Can you see why this might be an appealing choice for a system of property law?

4. We are not quite done with Lord Hobnob. Consider the remedy the plaintiff obtains: an award of the value of the jewel, rather than the jewel itself. This is in effect a forced sale of the jewel, which the defendant can keep after paying the plaintiff's damage award. *Now* who owns the jewel? What if Lord Hobnob shows up now? Can he also bring trover, and if so, will the jeweler be forced to pay out a second time? In fact, why is Paul de Lamerie, the goldsmith whose name the court mangles, on the hook for his apprentice's wrongdoing? What if the apprentice pocketed the jewel and never turned it over to the master?

5. About that damage award. Why is the jury instructed to presume that the jewel was "of the finest water?" (i.e. highest quality)?

Other Variations on *Armory*

Just how far does the holding of *Armory v. Delamirie* ("That the finder of [property], though he does not by such finding acquire an absolute property or ownership, yet he has such a property as will enable him to keep it against all but the rightful owner") go? Consider three nineteenth-century cases about lost lumber. Are they required by *Armory*? Consistent with *Armory*? Consistent with each other? Which is most persuasive?

In *Clark v. Maloney*, 3 Del. 68 (1840), the plaintiff found ten logs floating in a bay after a storm. He tied them up in the mouth of a creek, but they (apparently) got free again and the defendants (apparently) found them floating up the creek. *Held*, the plaintiffs were entitled to the logs:

> Possession is certainly prima facie evidence of property. It is called *prima facie* evidence because it may be rebutted by evidence of better title, but in the absence of better title it is as effective a support of title as the most conclusive evidence could be. It is for this reason, that *the finder of a chattel, though he does not acquire an absolute property in it, yet has such a property, as will enable him to keep it against all but the rightful owner.* The defence consists, not in showing that the defendants are the rightful owners, or claim under the rightful owner; but that the logs were found by them adrift in Mispillion creek, having been loosened from their fastening either by accident or design, and they insist that their title is as good as that of the plaintiff. But it is a well settled rule of law that the loss of a chattel does not change the right of property; and for the same reason that the original loss of these logs by the rightful owner, did

not change his absolute property in them, but he might have maintained trover against the plaintiff upon refusal to deliver them, so the subsequent loss did not divest the *special* property of the plaintiff. It follows, therefore, that as the plaintiff has shown a special property in these logs, which he never abandoned, and which enabled him to keep them against all the world but the rightful owner, he is entitled to a verdict.

In *Anderson v. Gouldberg*, 53 N.W. 636 (Minn. 1892), the defendants took ninety-three logs from the plaintiff's mill. The defendants claimed that the plaintiff had cut the logs on their land, but the plaintiff replied (and a jury agreed) that he had actually cut the logs by trespassing on the land of a third party. *Held*: the plaintiff was entitled to the logs:

> Therefore the only question is whether bare possession of property, though wrongfully obtained, is sufficient title to enable the party enjoying it to maintain replevin against a mere stranger, who takes it from him. We had supposed that this was settled in the affirmative as long ago, at least, as the early case of *Armory v. Delamirie*, so often cited on that point. When it is said that to maintain replevin the plaintiff's possession must have been lawful, it means merely that it must have been lawful as against the person who deprived him of it; and possession is good title against all the world except those having a better title. Counsel says that possession only raises a presumption of title, which, however, may be rebutted. Rightly understood, this is correct; but counsel misapplies it. One who takes property from the possession of another can only rebut this presumption by showing a superior title in himself, or in some way connecting himself with one who has. One who has acquired the possession of property, whether by finding, bailment, or by mere tort, has a right to retain that possession as against a mere wrongdoer who is a stranger to the property. Any other rule would lead to an endless series of

unlawful seizures and reprisals in every case where property had once passed out of the possession of the rightful owner.

Anderson states what is overwhelmingly the majority rule. Seven years after *Anderson*, North Carolina took the opposite course. In *Russell v. Hill*, 34 S.E. 640 (N.C. 1899), two different people held what appeared to be state grants to the same tract of land, and the plaintiff cut timber on the land with the wrong one's permission. While the logs were floating in a river, the defendants – unconnected with either of the purported landowners – took them away and sold them. *Held*: the defendants were entitled to the logs (internal quotation marks omitted):

> In some of the English books, and in some of the Reports of our sister states, cases might be found to the contrary, but that those cases were all founded upon a misapprehension of the principle laid down in the case of *Armory v. Delamirie*. There a chimney sweep found a lost jewel. He took it into his possession, as he had a right to do, and was the owner, because of having it in possession, unless the true owner should become known. That owner was not known, and it was properly decided that trover would lie in favor of the finder against the defendant, to whom he had handed it for inspection, and who refused to restore it. But the court said the case would have been very different if the owner had been known.

Is this an accurate reading of *Armory*? The court also expressed concern about the defendant's potential liability to the true owner:

> It is true that, as possession is the strongest evidence of the ownership, property may be presumed from possession. ... But if it appears on the trial that the plaintiff, although in possession, is not in fact the owner, the presumption of title inferred from the possession is rebutted, and it would be manifestly wrong to allow the plaintiff to recover the value of the property; for the real owner

may forthwith bring trover against the defendant, and force him to pay the value the second time, and the fact that he paid it in a former suit would be no defense. Consequently trover can never be maintained unless a satisfaction of the judgment will have the effect of vesting a good title in the defendant.

Is the fear of double liability sufficient reason to allow the defendant to escape liability entirely? Based on a review of the court records in the case, John V. Orth writes that the true owner in *Russell v. Hill* was "no bodiless abstraction but had in fact a name and identity: [Fabius Haywood] Busbee, one of the state's leading lawyers, a man well known to every member of the supreme court that decided the case." John V. Orth, Russell v. Hill *(N.C. 1899): Misunderstood Lessons*, 73 N.C. L. REV. 2031, 2034 (1995). Does this help explain *Russell?*

Professor Orth, arguing for a middle ground between *Anderson* and *Russell,* argues that *Armory* should protect only prior possessors who took the property in good faith: "A technical wrongdoing, such as an innocent trespass, as the source of possession should not disable the possessor from securing judicial protection against an unauthorized taking, but a willful trespass at the root of title should. Plaintiff in *Russell,* in other words, deserved a new trial at which to show, not his title, but his *bona fides*" Id. at 2060. Is this a better rule?

Bridges v. Hawkesworth
21 L.J. Q.B. 75 (1851)

June 19 and November 26.

Trover — Lost Property — Rights of Finder.

The place in which a lost article is found does not constitute any exception to the general rule of law, that the finder is entitled to it as against all persons except the owner.

The plaintiff, having picked up from the floor of the shop of the defendant a parcel containing bank-notes, handed them over to the defendant to keep till the owner should claim them. They were advertised by the defendant, but no one appearing to claim them, and three years having elapsed, the plaintiff requested the defendant to return them, tendering the costs of the advertisements, and offering an indemnity. Upon the defendant's refusal, an action was brought in the county court, and judgment given for the defendant : —

Held, on appeal, reversing the judgment below, that the plaintiff was entitled to the notes as against the defendant.

THIS was an appeal against a decision of the judge of the County Court of Westminster. The following facts appeared upon the case stated and signed by the judge : — In October, 1847, the plaintiff, who was town traveller to Messrs. Rae & Co., called at Messrs. Byfield & Hawkesworth's on business, as he was in the habit of doing, and as

Bridges *v.* Hawkesworth.

he was leaving the shop he picked up a small parcel which was lying upon the floor. He immediately shewed it to the shopman, and opened it in his presence, when it was found to consist of a quantity of Bank of England notes, to the amount of 65*l.* The defendant, who was a partner in the firm of Byfield & Hawkesworth, was then called, and the plaintiff told him he had found the notes, and asked the defendant to keep them until the owner appeared to claim them. The defendant caused advertisements to be inserted in *The Times* newspaper, to the effect that bank notes had been found, and the owner might have them on giving a proper description and paying the expenses. No person having appeared to claim them, and three years having elapsed since they were found, the plaintiff applied to the defendant to have the notes returned to him, and offered to pay the expenses of the advertisements, and to give an indemnity. The defendant had refused to deliver them up to the plaintiff, and an action had been brought in the County Court of Westminster in consequence of that refusal. The case also found that the plaintiff, at the time he delivered over the notes to the defendant, did not intend to divest himself of any title that he might have to them. The judge had, upon these facts, decided that the defendant was entitled to the custody of the notes as against the plaintiff, and gave judgment in his favor accordingly. It was to review this decision that the present appeal had been brought.

Gray, Heath with him, for the appellant. The plaintiff, by finding the notes in question, acquired a title to them against the whole world, except the true owner. *Amory* v. *Delamirie*, 1 Str. 504; 1 Smith's L. C. 151. Having found them, he delivered them to the defendant for a special purpose only, and never intended to part with his property therein. The judge appears to have decided the case upon the ground that they were found in the house of another; but that makes no difference. If they had been found in the highway, they would have been the property of the finder, except as against the true owner; and yet the highway is the private property of some one, subject to the right of the public to pass over it. Suppose they had been found in the yard of the defendant, then they could be lawfully retained as against him; he might have had an action of trespass for entering the yard, but not any action founded on the possession of the goods. How did the defendant acquire any property therein? The mere fact of the notes having been dropped on the floor of his shop did not give it to him.

[PATTESON, J. If one enters a cab, and takes away a parcel left there by a former passenger, the property might be laid in the cab-owner in an indictment for the felony.

WIGHTMAN, J. If the notes had been left on a chair, and the customer coming in had merely lifted them off, would they have become his property? They were not lost in the ordinary sense of the term, but were there in *conspectu omnium*. You say that any one taking possession of them, although they were, in one sense, in the possession of the shopkeeper, acquires a title to them, except as against the true owner.]

Bridges *v.* Hawkesworth.

Yes. Perhaps an indictment would lie for stealing the goods of a person unknown; but here the owner of the shop, not having taken possession, could not lay the property in himself.

[PATTESON, J. Is there any instance of indicting a person for stealing the goods of a person unknown? If the owner be unknown, could felony be committed in respect of the goods? There might probably be an indictment for a robbery of a person unknown.]

The man who first picked up the notes would be the finder, even although the owner of the shop should first see them. Puffendorf, (lib. 4, c. 6, s. 8,) shews that the bare seeing, or the knowing where lost goods are, is not sufficient.

[WIGHTMAN, J. You must go further, and shew that their being in the shop of the defendant makes no difference. Blackstone says, that whatever movables are found on the face of the earth belong to the first occupier.]

That would be so where no owner appears; it would be the same, as between the finder and the rest of the world, as if there were no owner. Blackstone, (1 Com. 296,) speaking of treasure-trove, says, " Such as is casually lost or unclaimed, still remains the right of the fortunate finder." That was an express authority for the general rule; and if the other side contended that the notes being found in a man's house made any difference, it lay upon them to establish that proposition.

[PATTESON, J. In Puffendorf, (lib. 4, c. 6, s. 13,) it is said, " He who hath hidden treasure in another's ground, without acquainting the lord of the soil, is judged to have slipped his opportunity; . . . but if the ground belongs to another, then the finder seems engaged by his conscience to inquire, at least indirectly, of him concerning the matter; because, without this, it cannot certainly be known but that the money was laid there by the master of the place only for the greater security, or by some person else with his privity and consent." From which it would appear, that if it were laid there without the consent or privity of the owner of the soil, he would not be entitled to it. These notes were certainly not intrusted to the defendant — they were lost.]

By the law of nature, a finder acquires property by taking possession of the goods found, and those cases in which the property is given to the state or to particular individuals are exceptions upon the law of nature. In *Reg.* v. *Kerr*, 8 Car. & P. 176, it was held, " that a servant who had found some bank notes in her master's house ought to have inquired of him whether they were his or not." Those were her master's notes, which brought the facts within the rule laid down by Pufendorf where the owner of property is known. It therefore does not apply to this case. But if the other side were right, the servant would be equally guilty of felony whether they were her master's notes or not. They must put it upon the ground of a special property in the owner of the house; and if so, the servant would be guilty of felony whether she made inquiry as to the true owner or not; but a finder is not guilty of larceny where he has no reasonable opportunity of knowing the owner, because the articles

COURT OF QUEEN'S BENCH, 1851. 427

Bridges *v.* Hawkesworth.

found belong to him, whatever may be his intention at the time of taking them.

[PATTESON, J. If goods were found in an inn, it would be different. There a special property is vested in the innkeeper by reason of his liability. In *Merry* v. *Green*, 7 M. & W. 623, it was held, that there might be property in a person of goods, although he did not know of its existence. There a bureau was bought at an auction, and a purse of money was found in a secret drawer therein; and it was held that it belonged to the seller although he knew nothing of it. That and *Cartwright* v. *Green*, 8 Ves. 405, appear to be the nearest to the present case.]

In *Merry* v. *Green* the money was not lost — it was entirely inclosed in a chattel belonging to the seller; here the loss and the finding are stated in the case. The defendant, to have any right, must have indicated his intention to take possession before the other did. If the shopkeeper had placed it on one side until he found the owner, it would have been different; but here the plaintiff is the finder. As to the notes being found in the shop, that reduces it merely to a question of degree; a shop is more private than a field, a field more private than a highway; but the fact of the articles found being upon the soil of another does not prevent them from becoming the property of the finder. The defendant had not made himself liable to the true owner. *Isaack* v. *Clark*, 2 Bulst. 312, shews, " that when a man doth find goods, he is bound to answer him that hath the property." The defendant received the notes only for the purpose of advertising them, and restoring them to the true owner, if he should appear. [He also cited *Sutton* v. *Moody*, 1 Ld. Raym. 250.]

Heath offered to address the court on the same side, but it was decided that only one counsel could be heard on each side.

Hake, for the respondent. The plaintiff could not acquire property in these notes by merely picking them up; and if he could, he had in this case divested himself of that property by handing them over to the defendant, thereby making him the principal in the matter, and investing him with the responsibility of a finder. The notes, if they were in truth the property of a customer, came into the shop by leave of the owner of the shop. Dig., lib. 41, De Acq. Re. Dom., tit. 1.

[PATTESON, J. That assumes that they are deposited intentionally; in which case there can be no doubt whatever.]

Savigny, in his celebrated treatise on the Law of Possession, translated by Sir Edward Perry, s. 18, states that the principle of the rule is easily to be discovered The maxim is, " Vacua est quam nemo detinet." Here the *jus detentionis* was in the defendant, and there was no vacancy of possession. If the goods had been of larger bulk, the owner of the house might have distrained them damage faisant, and no one could have taken them from his custody. If a scintilla of a dominion might be exercised by the shopkeeper, they could not vest in the finder.

[PATTESON, J. Savigny speaks of money buried in the land; but how is it if it be in my house? The expression, "If I know where it is, I possess it, without the act of taking it from its place of concealment," p. 163, note (*e*), seems to make the question of property turn upon a mere chance.]

That doubt is answered by the case of *Merry* v. *Green.* In many instances property is held to belong to the owner of the soil, though he does not know of it, as in the case in Lord Raymond. In *Toplady* v. *Stalye*, Sty. 165, ROLLE, C. J., says, "If cattle be stolen, and put into my ground, I may take them damage faisant." If the owner could not take them away, how could a stranger do so? Anon. 1 Bulst. 96. In the Year Book, 12 Hen. 8, 9, it is said, "that the owner of a forest is the owner of the wild creatures therein *ratione loci.*" In *Reg.* v. *Kerr*, PARKE, B., asks, "What if I drop a ring, is my servant to take it away?" Suppose my guest loses his ring, is the servant finding it at liberty to keep it? Has not the owner of the house a right to take it from him?

[WIGHTMAN, J. In that case there would be no question about the property.]

If, in *Armory* v. *Delamirie*, the sweep had been employed to sweep a chimney, and having entered a house for that purpose, had picked up a jewel therein, he could not have claimed it. In the case of a wreck the lord, before seizure, has a constructive possession. In *Smith* v. *Milles*, 1 T. R. 480, ASHURST, J., says, "The right is in the lord, and a constructive possession, in respect of the thing being within the manor of which he is lord."

[PATTESON, J. That is a manorial right and does not apply to any other person.

WIGHTMAN, J. In the preface to Savigny a difficulty is suggested in the passage quoted from Mr. Bentham:—"A street porter enters an inn, puts down his bundle upon the table, and goes out; one person put his hand upon the bundle to examine it, another puts his to carry it away, saying, 'It is mine.' The innkeeper runs to claim it, in opposition to them both. The porter returns, or does not return. Of these four men, who is in possession of the bundle?"]

In that case the innkeeper has the property *ratione loci et impotentiæ.* The parcel cannot fly away. In *Isaack* v. *Clark*, Lord Coke says the finder has it in his election to take the goods or not into his custody. Did the plaintiff take to himself the charge of these notes, or make himself liable for the advertisements?

[WIGHTMAN, J. If the plaintiff had merely shewed them to the defendant, and said he would keep them, could the defendant have sued him for them?]

Yes; by reason of their being found in the house he had a constructive possession, and also something less than a possession — a *jus detentionis. Burn* v. *Morris*, 4 Tyr. 485, shews that the defendant was responsible to the true owner. In the case of *Swans*, 7 Rep. 17 b., Lord Coke says that a possessory right is obtained in wild animals *ratione loci et impotentiæ* — that is, so long as they do not or cannot fly away. The reason of these decisions is given by Savigny, p. 163, "A movable becomes connected with an immovable without, never

Bridges v. Hawkesworth.

theless, being incorporated with it." *Semayne's case*, 5 Rep. 93, shews that a house protects all goods lawfully there; and it is to be inferred that it displaces all right in a finder. The maxim of the civil law is, " Si in meam potestatem pervenit, meus factus sit." Savigny, p. 169, comments upon it—" Possession of a thing may be acquired simply by the fact of its having been delivered at one's own residence, even though we are absent from the house at the time."

[WIGHTMAN, J. There they were directed to the house: here, if the finder had put the notes into his own pocket, the owner of the shop would not have known of them. If you can put any case where the goods came into the house without the knowledge of the owner of the house, it would be in point.]

[PATTESON, J. If property is intentionally in my house, it is certainly in my possession.]

There is a distinction between property obvious on the surface of the soil and what is buried. In the former case it is supposed that it will be seen by the owner or his servants; but if it is buried, the next owner is as likely to find it as the former one, Savigny, 169. The passages in Blackstone cited on the other side put the question upon the intention of the true owner to come back and claim the goods. By our old law goods were to be delivered to justices; and in Deut. c. 22, we read, " Goods found should be kept near where they are lost." In *Reg.* v. *Thurborn*, 2 Car. & K. 831, it was held, that to prevent the taking of goods from being larceny, it is essential that they should be taken in such a place and under such circumstances as that the owner would be reasonably presumed to have abandoned them. In 5 Rep. 109 a, it is said, " If one steal my goods and throw them into the house of another, they are not waifs." So in Com. Dig. " Waif." This case is undistinguishable from one where goods are left at an inn, and the relation of landlord and guest has ceased; if the goods are then stolen, the innkeeper is not liable. The act of taking possession of the notes by the plaintiff did not render him chargeable to the true owner, nor confer a property upon him. Dig., lib. 41, tit. 1, De Acq. Re. Dom.; *May* v. *Harvey*, 13 East, 197. If no engagement be exacted to redeliver, the party delivering cannot sue while the trust remains open. The defendant may set up a *jus tertii*; he is liable to the true owner, and ought not to be liable to two in respect of one interest. He advertised that the notes could be had at his shop, and incurred liability for the advertisements. [He also cited *Ogle* v. *Atkinson*, 5 Taunt. 759; and *Templeman* v. *Case*, 10 Mod. 24.]

Gray, in reply, cited Savigny, 170—" Every case of possession is founded on the state of consciousness of unlimited physical power." *Cur. adv. vult.*

November 26. PATTESON, J., now delivered the following judgment:—The notes which are the subject of this action were incidentally dropped, by mere accident, in the shop of the defendant, by the owner of them. The facts do not warrant the supposition that they

430   COURT OF QUEEN'S BENCH, 1851.

Bridges v. Hawkesworth.

had been deposited there intentionally, nor has the case been put at all upon that ground. The plaintiff found them on the floor, they being manifestly lost by some one. The general right of the finder to any article which has been lost, as against all the world, except the true owner, was established in the case of *Armory* v. *Delamirie*, which has never been disputed. This right would clearly have accrued to the plaintiff had the notes been picked up by him outside the shop of the defendant; and if he once had the right, the case finds that he did not intend, by delivering the notes to the defendant, to waive the title (if any) which he had to them, but they were handed to the defendant merely for the purpose of delivering them to the owner, should he appear. Nothing that was done afterwards has altered the state of things; the advertisements inserted in the newspaper, referring to the defendant, had the same object; the plaintiff has tendered the expense of those advertisements to the defendant, and offered him an indemnity against any claim to be made by the real owner, and has demanded the notes. The case, therefore, resolves itself into the single point on which it appears that the learned judge decided it, namely, whether the circumstance of the notes being found inside the defendant's shop gives him, the defendant, the right to have them as against the plaintiff, who found them. There is no authority in our law to be found directly in point. Perhaps the nearest case is that of *Merry* v. *Green*, but it differs in many respects from the present. We were referred, in the course of the argument, to the learned works of Von Savigny, edited by Chief Justice Perry; but even this work, full as it is of subtle distinctions and nice reasonings, does not afford a solution of the present question. It was well asked, on the argument, if the defendant has the right, *when* did it accrue to him? If at all, it must have been antecedent to the finding by the plaintiff, for that finding could not give the defendant any right. If the notes had been accidentally kicked into the shop, and there found by some one passing by, could it be contended that the defendant was entitled to them from the mere fact of their being originally dropped in his shop? If the discovery had never been communicated to the defendant, could the real owner have had any cause of action against him because they were found in his house? Certainly not. The notes never were in the custody of the defendant, nor within the protection of his house, before they were found, as they would have been had they been intentionally deposited there; and the defendant has come under no responsibility, except from the communication made to him by the plaintiff, the finder, and the steps taken by way of advertisement. These steps were really taken by the defendant as the agent of the plaintiff, and he has been offered an idemnity, the sufficiency of which is not disputed. We find, therefore, no circumstances in this case to take it out of the general rule of law, that the finder of a lost article is entitled to it as against all persons except the real owner, and we think that that rule must prevail, and that the learned judge was mistaken in holding that the place in which they were found makes any legal difference. Our judgment, therefore, is, that the plaintiff is entitled to these notes as against the defendant; that the judgment of

Grange v. Trickett.

the court below must be reversed, and judgment given for the plaintiff for 50*l.* Plaintiff to have the costs of appeal.[1]

Judgment accordingly.

South Staffordshire Waterworks Co. v. Sharman

2 Q.B. 44 (896)

Vol. XLIV.   [Aug. 8, 1896.]   THE WEEKLY REPORTER.   653

HIGH COURT.   SOUTH STAFFORDSHIRE WATERWORKS CO. v. SHARMAN.   HIGH COURT.

Appeal dismissed with costs, and judgment for the Crown.

Solicitors for the appellants, *H. Becher*, for *Simons & Sons*, Pontypridd.

Solicitor for the respondent, *Solicitor of Inland Revenue.*

Q. B. Div.
(Lord Russell of Killowen, }
C.J., and Wills, J.)   May 12.

SOUTH STAFFORDSHIRE WATERWORKS CO. v. SHARMAN. (a.)

Detinue—Finding of goods—Title of finder—Rings found in pool—Title of owner of pool as against finder.

Where an owner of land has a de facto possession of the land and an actual control over the same, a chattel found upon or beneath such land is presumed to be in the possession of the owner of the land, who can claim possession of the chattel from the finder.

Appeal by the plaintiffs from the Lichfield County Court.

The action was an action of detinue to recover two gold rings, as the property of the plaintiffs, found by the defendant in the Minster Pool, Lichfield, while the defendant was in the plaintiffs' employment. The plaintiffs claimed the return of the rings or £5 for their value, and £1 damages for their detention.

The plaintiffs were the freeholders of the land covered by the Minster Pool, situate near the Cathedral, Lichfield.

The defendant was employed by the plaintiffs, with about forty other labourers, to clean out the pool, and while the defendant was so employed he found in the mud from the bottom of the pool the two gold rings in question. The plaintiffs demanded the rings, but the defendant refused to deliver them up, but he afterwards placed the rings in the hands of the police, with whom they remained a considerable time. The police endeavoured to find the original owner, but failed to do so, and they afterwards handed the rings back to the defendant from whom they had received them.

The plaintiffs then demanded the rings from the defendant, but the defendant refused to deliver them up, and the present action of detinue was then brought.

It was proved as a fact that there was no special contract between the plaintiffs and the defendant as to giving up any articles that might be found.

For the plaintiffs the cases of *Reg.* v. *Rowe*, 7 W. R. 236, 28 L. J. M. C. 128, and *Elwes* v. *Brigg Gas Co.*, 35 W. R. 192, 33 Ch. D. 562, were cited, and it was contended that the present case was governed by the principles acted upon in those two cases, and the plaintiffs also relied on Pollock and Wright on Possession, pp. 40-41.

The defendant relied on *Armory* v. *Delamirie*, 1 Sm. Lead. Cas., 10th ed., p. 343, and *Bridges* v. *Hawkesworth*, 21 L. J. Q. B. 75.

The learned county court judge decided, on the authority of *Armory* v. *Delamirie* and *Bridges* v. *Hawkesworth*, that the defendant had a good title against all the world except the true owner, and he gave judgment for the defendant with costs, with leave to appeal on the terms that the plaintiffs should pay the defendant's costs in any event.

The plaintiffs appealed.

(a) Reported by Sir SHERSTON BAKER, Bart., Barrister-at-Law.

W. Wills, for the plaintiffs.—The learned judge was wrong in finding for the defendant. The plaintiffs were the freeholders of this land, and they had not only the possession, but the *de facto* control over the pool and the contents of the pool. Everything found in the pool was therefore presumptively in the possession of the plaintiffs. *Armory* v. *Delamirie* does not apply to such a case as this, nor does *Bridges* v. *Hawkesworth* apply, as there the bundle of notes was found in a part of the shop to which customers had a right to go. The principles applicable are those laid down in *Reg.* v. *Rowe*, where a piece of iron found in a canal was held to be presumptively the property of the canal company; in *Elwes* v. *Brigg Gas Co.*, where a prehistoric boat found in the soil was held to be in the possession of the freeholder of the soil. [He was stopped.]

Disturnal, for the defendant.—I admit that if there is a *de facto* control over the place where the article is found the article presumably belongs to the person who has such control. Here, as in *Bridges* v. *Hawkesworth*, there was no actual or *de facto* control by the plaintiffs over the pool or the contents of the pool. The principle therefore laid down in *Bridges* v. *Hawkesworth* applies to this case, as well as the same principle laid down in *Armory* v. *Delamirie*. The onus is on the plaintiffs, and they have not discharged that onus, and have not shown that the mere ownership of land proves a presumptive ownership of every chattel found on the land.

He also referred to *Reg.* v. *Clinton*, Ir. Rep. 4 C. L. 6, 18 W. R. C. L. Dig. 29; and *Brew* v. *Haren*, Ir. Rep. 11 C. L. 198, 25 W. R. Dig. 248.

Lord RUSSELL OF KILLOWEN, C.J.—In this case I think the learned judge was wrong, and his judgment must be reversed. The case raises an interesting question. It is no doubt correct that before the plaintiffs can succeed they must show that they had a *de facto* control over this particular *locus in quo* and its contents. Can it be said that this pool and its contents were under the control of the plaintiffs? I think they were under the control of the plaintiffs, just as the iron found in the canal in *Reg.* v. *Rowe*. I think that the principles on which this case ought to be decided are well laid down in Pollock and Wright on Possession, p. 41: "The possession of land carries with it in general, by our law, possession of everything which is attached to or under that land, and, in the absence of a better title elsewhere, the right to possess it also; and it makes no difference that the possessor is not aware of the thing's existence. So it was lately held concerning a prehistoric boat imbedded in the soil. It is free to anyone who requires a specific intention as part of *de facto* possession to treat this as a positive rule of law. But it seems preferable to say that the legal possession rests on a real *de facto* possession, constituted by the occupier's general power and intent to exclude unauthorized interference." That passage is entirely applicable to this case, and it shows the difference between the present case and some of the cases referred to on behalf of the defendant, of things thrown away into a public place or into the sea, where there was not in anyone a real *de facto* possession or a general power and intent to exclude unauthorized interference. *Bridges* v. *Hawkesworth* is a case standing by itself and on its own special grounds, and I think it was rightly decided. There a person had dropped a bundle of banknotes in a shop—in the part of the shop that was open to the public; and it was held that a customer who came in and picked up the bundle was entitled to the notes as against the shopkeeper, and the real ground of the decision is that given by Patteson, J.: "The notes never were in the

654   **THE WEEKLY REPORTER.**   [Aug. 8, 1896.]   **Vol. XLIV.**

HIGH COURT.   REG. v. LILLYMAN.   HIGH COURT.

custody of the defendant" (the shopkeeper) "nor within the protection of his house before they were found." The general principle seems to be this, that where there is possession of a house or land with a manifest intention to exercise control over it, and with actual control over the particular *locus in quo*, then if a chattel is found on it by a servant or a stranger the presumption is that the thing found belongs to the owner.

For these reasons I think the judgment must be for the plaintiffs.

WILLS, J.—I entirely agree.

Appeal allowed.   Judgment for the plaintiffs.

Solicitors for the plaintiffs, *Burton, Yeates, & Hart,* for *Johnson, Barclay, Johnson, & Rogers,* Birmingham.

Solicitors for the defendant, *Nelson & Son,* for *H. S. Chinn & Son,* Lichfield.

at all; and, secondly, that even if the fact of a complaint having been made was admissible, the particulars of it could not be elicited in the examination in chief. I overruled both objections, and the complaint with full particulars was deposed to by the witness. The jury found the prisoner guilty on the first count only. That, however, does not affect the question we have to decide, because, although to establish guilt upon that count it was not essential to prove want of consent, yet, as the girl had emphatically stated that whatever was done was against her will, the reason which, in our opinion, as it will appear, made the complaint evidence upon the second and third counts were equally applicable to the first. It is necessary, in the first place, to have a clear understanding as to the principles upon which evidence of such a complaint, not on oath, nor made in the presence of the prisoner, nor forming part of the *res gestæ,* can be admitted.

Hannah v. Peel

1 K.B. 509 (1945)

HANNAH *v.* PEEL.   1945

Trover—Detinue—Possession—Chattel found on land never occupied by freeholder—Owner of chattel unknown—Right of finder.

June 11, 13.

Birkett J.

The defendant was the owner of a house which he had never himself occupied. While the house was requisitioned, the plaintiff, a soldier, found in a bedroom used as a sick-bay, loose in a crevice on the top of a window frame, a brooch, the owner of which was unknown. There was no evidence that the defendant had any knowledge of the existence of the brooch before it was found by the plaintiff; but the police to whom the plaintiff handed the brooch

1945

HANNAH
v.
PEEL.

to ascertain its owner, delivered it to the defendant who claimed it as being on premises of which he was the owner.

Held, that the plaintiff, as finder, was entitled to the possession of the brooch as against all others than its owner.

Bridges v. *Hawkesworth* (1851) 21 L. J. (Q. B.) 75 ; 15 Jur. 1079, followed.

South Staffordshire Water Co. v. *Sharman* [1896] 2 Q. B. 44 and *Elwes* v. *Brigg Gas Co.* (1886) 33 Ch. D. 562, distinguished.

ACTION tried by Birkett J.

On December 13, 1938, the freehold of Gwernhaylod House, Overton-on-Dee, Shropshire, was conveyed to the defendant, Major Hugh Edward Ethelston Peel, who from that time to the end of 1940 never himself occupied the house and it remained unoccupied until October 5, 1939, when it was requisitioned, but after some months was released from requisition. Thereafter it remained unoccupied until July 18, 1940, when it was again requisitioned, the defendant being compensated by a payment at the rate of 250*l*. a year. In August, 1940, the plaintiff, Duncan Hannah, a lance-corporal, serving in a battery of the Royal Artillery, was stationed at the house and on the 21st of that month, when in a bedroom, used as a sick-bay, he was adjusting the black-out curtains when his hand touched something on the top of a window-frame, loose in a crevice, which he thought was a piece of dirt or plaster. The plaintiff grasped it and dropped it on the outside window ledge. On the following morning he saw that it was a brooch covered with cobwebs and dirt. Later, he took it with him when he went home on leave and his wife having told him it might be of value, at the end of October, 1940, he informed his commanding officer of his find and, on his advice, handed it over to the police, receiving a receipt for it. In August, 1942, the owner not having been found the police handed the brooch to the defendant, who sold it in October, 1942, for 66*l*., to Messrs. Spink & Son, Ltd., of London, who resold it in the following month for 88*l*. There was no evidence that the defendant had any knowledge of the existence of the brooch before it was found by the plaintiff. The defendant had offered the plaintiff a reward for the brooch, but the plaintiff refused to accept this and maintained throughout his right to the possession of the brooch as against all persons other than the owner, who was unknown. By a letter, dated October 5, 1942, the plaintiff's solicitors demanded the return of the brooch

1 K. B.   KING'S BENCH DIVISION.   511

from the defendant, but it was not returned and on October 21,   1945
1943, the plaintiff issued his writ claiming the return of the   HANNAH
brooch, or its value, and damages for its detention. By his   *v.*
defence, the defendant claimed the brooch on the ground that   PEEL.
he was the owner of Gwernhaylod House and in possession
thereof.

   Scott Cairns for plaintiff. The plaintiff, as the finder of this
brooch, is entitled to its possession as against all persons other
than the owner, who is unknown : *Armory* v. *Delamirie* (1).
The case of *Bridges* v. *Hawkesworth* (2) is precisely in point,
for in that case the finder of a parcel of bank-notes found it on
the floor of a shop. The defendant here had no knowledge of
the existence of the brooch, as the shopkeeper in *Bridges* v.
Hawkesworth (2) had no knowledge of the existence of the parcel
of banknotes. As Professor A. L. Goodhart pointed out in his
" Three Cases on Possession," in " Essays in Jurisprudence
" and the Common Law " (1931), at pp. 76-90, Mr. Justice
O. W. Holmes, Sir Frederick Pollock and Sir John Salmond all
consider the decision in *Bridges* v. *Hawkesworth* (2) to be
correct ; Mr. Justice Holmes on the ground that " the
" shopkeeper, not knowing of the thing, could not have the
" intent to appropriate it, and, having invited the public to his
" shop he could not have the intent to exclude them
" from it " (3) ; Sir Frederick Pollock on the lack of *de* facto
control by the shopkeeper (4) ; and Sir John Salmond on the
absence of the animus possidendi (5). Lord Russell of
Killowen C.J., in *South Staffordshire Water Co.* v. *Sharman* (6)
said that the ground of the decision in *Bridges* v. *Hawkes-*
worth (2) as was pointed out by Patteson J. was that the notes,
being dropped in the public part of the shop, were never in the
custody of the shopkeeper, or " within the protection of his
" house." But that was not so, since Patteson J. said in the
earlier case that the county court judge, whose decision was
appealed, was mistaken in holding that the place in which the
parcel of notes was found made any difference (7). In *South*
Staffordshire Water Co. v. *Sharman* (6) the defendant while

(1) (1722) 1 Str. 505.   Possession in the Common Law,
(2) (1851) 21 L. J. (Q. B.) 75 ;   at p. 37 and seq.
15 Jur. 1079.   (5) Jurisprudence (9th ed.)
   (3) The Common Law (1881) 381-2.
at p. 222.   (6) [1896] 2 Q. B. 44, 47.
   (4) Pollock and Wright on   (7) 21 L. J. (Q. B.) 78.

1945

HANNAH
v.
PEEL.

cleaning out, under the plaintiffs' orders, a pool of water on their land, found two rings in the mud at the bottom of the pool. It was held that the plaintiffs were entitled to the possession of the rings. It is a sufficient explanation of that case that Sharman, as the servant or agent of the water company, though he was the first to obtain the custody of the rings, obtained possession of them for his employers, the water company, and could claim no title to them for himself. It may be that a man owns everything which is attached to or under his land : see *Elwes* v. *Brigg Gas Co.* (1). But a man does not of necessity own or possess a chattel which is lying unattached on the surface of his land. The defendant did not know of the existence of this brooch and had never exercised any kind of control over it. The plaintiff, therefore, as its finder, is entitled to its possession.

Binney for defendant. The defendant was entitled to the possession of the brooch because, when it was found, it was on his land. Lord Russell of Killowen C.J. said in *South Staffordshire Water Co.* v. *Sharman* (2) : " The general principle seems " to me to be that where a person has possession of house or " land, with a manifest intention to exercise control over it and " the things which may be upon it or in it, then, if something is " found on that land, whether by an employee of the owner or " by a stranger, the presumption is that the possession of that " thing is in the owner of the locus in quo." If that statement of law is correct, the defendant here should succeed. The owner of this land does not lose his right to the chattels found on or in it by letting the land : *Elwes* v. *Brigg Gas Co.* (1). The brooch here was found in a crevice of masonry and the facts are similar to those in *South Staffordshire Water Co.* v. *Sharman* (2). In neither case did the owner of the land know of the existence of the thing found. *Bridges* v. *Hawkesworth* (3) can be distinguished on the ground that the parcel of notes was found in a part of the shop to which the public had access—in effect they were found in a public place. If *Bridges* v. *Hawkesworth* (3) is not distinguishable, it has been overruled by *South Staffordshire Water Co.* v. *Sharman* (2) and *Elwes* v. *Briggs Gas Co.* (1).

Cur. adv. vult.

June 13. BIRKETT J. There is no issue of fact in this case

(1) (1886) 33 Ch. D. 562.   (3) 21 L. J. (Q. B.) 75 ; 15 Jur.
(2) [1896] 2 Q. B. 44, 47.   1079.

1 K. B.   KING'S BENCH DIVISION.   513

between the parties. As to the issue in law, the rival claims   1945
of the parties can be stated in this way : The plaintiff says :   ―――――
" I claim the brooch as its finder and I have a good title against   HANNAH
" all the world, save only the true owner." The defendant   PEEL.
says : " My claim is superior to yours inasmuch as I am the   ―――――
" freeholder. The brooch was found on my property,   Birkett J.
" although I was never in occupation, and my title, therefore,
" ousts yours and in the absence of the true owner I am
" entitled to the brooch or its value." Unhappily the law on
this issue is in a very uncertain state and there is need of an
authoritative decision of a higher court. Obviously if it could
be said with certainty that this is the law, that the finder of a
lost article, wherever found, has a good title against all the
world save the true owner, then, of course, all my difficulties
would be resolved ; or again, if it could be said with equal
certainty that this is the law, that the possessor of land is
entitled as against the finder to all chattels found on the land,
again my difficulties would be resolved.   But, unfortunately,
the authorities give some support to each of these conflicting
propositions.

In the famous case of *Armory* v. *Delamirie* (1), the plaintiff,·
who was a chimney sweeper's boy, found a jewel and carried it
to the defendant's shop, who was a goldsmith, in order to know
what it was, and he delivered it into the hands of the apprentice
in the goldsmith's shop, who made a pretence of weighing it
and took out the stones and called to the master to let him
know that it came to three-halfpence. The master offered the
boy the money who refused to take it and insisted on having the
jewel again. Whereupon the apprentice handed him back the
socket of the jewel without the stones, and an action was
brought in trover against the master, and it was ruled " that
" the finder of a jewel, though he does not by such finding
" acquire an absolute property or ownership, yet he has such·
" a property as will enable him to keep it against all but the
" rightful owner, and consequently may maintain trover."
The case of *Bridges* v. *Hawkesworth* (2) is in process of becoming
almost equally as famous because of the disputation which has
raged around it. The headnote in the Jurist is as follows :
" The place in which a lost article is found does not constitute
" any exception to the general rule of law, that the finder is
" entitled to it as against all persons except the owner."

(1) 1 Str. 505.   (2) 21 L. J. (Q. B.) 75 ; 15 Jur.
                                           1079.

1945

HANNAH
v.
PEEL.

Birkett J.

The case was in fact an appeal against a decision of the county court judge at Westminster. The facts appear to have been that in the year 1847 the plaintiff, who was a commercial traveller, called on a firm named Byfield & Hawkesworth on business, as he was in the habit of doing, and as he was leaving the shop he picked up a small parcel which was lying on the floor. He immediately showed it to the shopman, and opened it in his presence, when it was found to consist of a quantity of Bank of England notes, to the amount of 65*l.* The defendant, who was a partner in the firm of Byfield & Hawkesworth, was then called, and the plaintiff told him he had found the notes, and asked the defendant to keep them until the owner appeared to claim them. Then various advertisements were put in the papers asking for the owner, but the true owner was never found. No person having appeared to claim them, and three years having elapsed since they were found, the plaintiff applied to the defendant to have the notes returned to him, and offered to pay the expenses of the advertisements, and to give an indemnity. The defendant refused to deliver them up to the plaintiff, and an action was brought in the county court of Westminster in consequence of that refusal. The county court judge decided that the defendant, the shopkeeper, was entitled to the custody of the notes as against the plaintiff, and gave judgment for the defendant. Thereupon the appeal was brought which came before the court composed of Patteson J. and Wightman J. Patteson J. said : " The notes which are " the subject of this action were incidentally dropped, by mere " accident, in the shop of the defendant, by the owner of them. " The facts do not warrant the supposition that they had been " deposited there intentionally, nor has the case been put at " all upon that ground. The plaintiff found them on the floor, " they being manifestly lost by someone. The general right of " the finder to any article which has been lost, as against all the " world, except the true owner, was established in the case of " *Armory* v. *Delamirie* (1) which has never been disputed. " This right would clearly have accrued to the plaintiff had the " notes been picked up by him outside the shop of the defendant " and if he once had the right, the case finds that he did not " intend, by delivering the notes to the defendant, to waive " the title (if any) which he had to them, but they were handed " to the defendant merely for the purpose of delivering them " to the owner should he appear." Then a little later : " The

(1) 1 Str. 505.

" case, therefore, resolves itself into the single point on which it
" appears that the learned judge decided it, namely, whether
" the circumstance of the notes being found inside the defen-
" dant's shop gives him, the defendant, the right to have them
" as against the plaintiff, who found them." After discussing
the cases, and the argument, the learned judge said : " If the
" discovery had never been communicated to the defendant,
" could the real owner have had any cause of action against
" him because they were found in his house ? Certainly not.
" The notes never were in the custody of the defendant, nor
" within the protection of his house, before they were found,
" as they would have been had they been intentionally
" deposited there ; and the defendant has come under no respon-
" sibility, except from the communication made to him by the
" plaintiff, the finder, and the steps taken by way of advertise-
" ment. . . . We find, therefore, no circumstances in this case
" to take it out of the general rule of law, that the finder of a lost
" article is entitled to it as against all persons except the real
" owner, and we think that that rule must prevail, and that the
" learned judge was mistaken in holding that the place in which
" they were found makes any legal difference. Our judgment,
" therefore, is that the plaintiff is entitled to these notes as
" against the defendant."

It is to be observed that in *Bridges* v. *Hawkesworth* (I) which
has been the subject of immense disputation, neither counsel
put forward any argument on the fact that the notes were
found in a shop. Counsel for the appellant assumed through-
out that the position was the same as if the parcel had been
found in a private house, and the learned judge spoke of " the
" protection of his " (the shopkeeper's) " house." The case
for the appellant was that the shopkeeper never knew of the
notes. Again, what is curious is that there was no suggestion
that the place where the notes were found was in any way
material ; indeed, the judge in giving the judgment of the
court expressly repudiates this and said in terms " The learned
" judge was mistaken in holding that the place in which they
" were found makes any legal difference." It is, therefore,
a little remarkable that in *South Staffordshire Water Co.* v.
Sharman (2), Lord Russell of Killowen C.J. said : " The case
" of *Bridges* v. *Hawkesworth* (I) stands by itself, and on special
" grounds ; and on those grounds it seems to me that the

1945
_____
HANNAH
v.
PEEL
_____
Birkett J.

(I) 21 L. J. (Q. B.) 75 ; 15 Jur.   (2) [1896] 2 Q. B. 47.
1079.

1945

HANNAH
v.
PEEL

Birkett J.

" decision in that case was right. Someone had accidentally
" dropped a bundle of banknotes in a public shop. The shop-
" keeper did not know they had been dropped, and did not in
" any sense exercise control over them. The shop was open
" to the public, and they were invited to come there." That
might be a matter of some doubt. Customers were invited
there, but whether the public at large was, might be open to
some question. Lord Russell continued: " A customer
" picked up the notes and gave them to the shopkeeper in
" order that he might advertise them. The owner of the notes
" was not found, and the finder then sought to recover them
" from the shopkeeper. It was held that he was entitled to
" do so, the ground of the decision being, as was pointed
" out by Patteson J., that the notes, being dropped in the
" public part of the shop, were never in the custody of the
" shopkeeper, or ' within the protection of his house '."
Patteson J. never made any reference to the public part of the
shop and, indeed, went out of his way to say that the learned
county court judge was wrong in holding that the place where
they were found made any legal difference.

    Bridges v. *Hawkesworth* (1) has been the subject of consider-
able comment by text-book writers and, amongst others,
by Mr. Justice Oliver Wendell Holmes, Sir Frederick Pollock
and Sir John Salmond. All three agree that the case was rightly
decided, but they differ as to the grounds on which it was
decided and put forward grounds, none of which, so far as I
can discover, were ever advanced by the judges who decided
the case. Mr. Justice Oliver Wendell Holmes wrote (2):
" Common law judges and civilians would agree that the finder
" got possession first and so could keep it as against the shop-
" keeper. For the shopkeeper, not knowing of the thing, could
" not have the intent to appropriate it, and, having invited the
" public to his shop, he could not have the intent to exclude
" them from it." So he introduces the matter of two intents
which are not referred to by the judges who heard the case.
Sir Frederick Pollock, whilst he agreed with Mr. Justice
Holmes that *Bridges* v. *Hawkesworth* (1) was properly
decided wrote (3): " In such a case as *Bridges* v.
" *Hawkesworth* (1), where a parcel of banknotes was dropped

(1) 21 L. J. (Q. B.) 75 ; 15 Jur.   (3) Possession in the Common
1079.   Law (Pollock and Wright) at p. 39.
    (2) The Common Law (1881)
at p. 222.

" on the floor in the part of a shop frequented by
" customers, it is impossible to say that the shopkeeper has any
" possession in fact.   He does not expect objects of that kind
" to be on the floor of his shop, and some customer is more
" likely than the shopkeeper or his servant to see and take them
" up if they do come there."   He emphasizes the lack of de
facto control on the part of the shopkeeper.   Sir John Salmond
wrote (1) : " In *Bridges* v. *Hawkesworth* (2) a parcel of bank-
" notes was dropped on the floor of the defendant's shop,
" where they were found by the plaintiff, a customer.· It was
" held that the plaintiff had a good title to them as against the
" defendant.   For the plaintiff, and not the defendant, was the
" first to acquire possession of them.   The defendant had not
" the necessary animus, for he did not know of their existence."
Professor Goodhart, in our own day, in his work " Essays
" in Jurisprudence and the Common Law " (1931) has put
forward a further view that perhaps *Bridges* v. *Hawkesworth* (2)
was wrongly decided.   It is clear from the decision in *Bridges*
v. *Hawkesworth* (2) that an occupier of land does not in all cases
possess an unattached thing on his land even though the true
owner has lost possession.

With regard to *South Staffordshire Water Co.* v. *Sharman* (3),
the first two lines of the headnote are : " The possessor of land is
" generally entitled, as against the finder, to chattels found on
" the land."   I am not sure that this is accurate.   The facts
were that the defendant Sharman, while cleaning out, under
the orders of the plaintiffs, the South Staffordshire Water
Company, a pool of water on their land, found two rings
embedded in the mud at the bottom of the pool.   He declined
to deliver them to the plaintiffs, but failed to discover the real
owner.   In an action brought by the company against Sharman
in detinue it was held that the company were entitled to the
rings.   Lord Russell of Killowen C.J. said (4) : " The plaintiffs
" are the freeholders of the locus in quo, and as such they have
" the right to forbid anybody coming on their land or in any
" way interfering with it.   They had the right to say that their
" pool should be cleaned out in any way that they thought fit,
" and to direct what should be done with anything found in the
" pool in the course of such cleaning out.   It is no doubt right,
" as the counsel for the defendant contended, to say that the

1945

HANNAH
v.
PEEL.

Birkett J.

(1) Jurisprudence (9th ed.) 382.   (3) [1896] 2 Q. B. 44.
(2) 21 L. J. (Q. B.) 75 ; 15 Jur.   (4) Ibid. 46.
1079.

1945
───────
HANNAH
v.
PEEL.
───
Birkett J.

" plaintiffs must show that they had actual control over the
" locus in quo and the things in it ; but under the circum-
" stances, can it be said that the Minster Pool and whatever
" might be in that pool were not under the control of the
" plaintiffs ? In my opinion they were. . . . The principle on
" which this case must be decided, and the distinction which
" must be drawn between this case and that of *Bridges* v.
" *Hawkesworth* (1), is to be found in a passage in Pollock and
" Wright's ' Essay on Possession in the Common Law,' p. 41 :
" ' The possession of land carries with it in general, by our law,
" ' possession of everything which is attached to or under that
" ' land, and, in the absence of a better title elsewhere, the
" ' right to possess it also '."   If that is right, it would clearly
cover the case of the rings embedded in the mud of the pool,
the words used being " attached to or under that land."
Lord Russell continued : " ' And it makes no difference that the
" ' possessor is not aware of the thing's existence . . . . It is
" ' free to anyone who requires a specific intention as part of a
" ' de facto possession to treat this as a positive rule of law.
" ' But it seems preferable to say that the legal possession rests
" ' on a real de facto possession constituted by the occupier's
" ' general power and intent to exclude unauthorized inter-
" ' ference.' That is the ground on which I prefer to base my
" judgment. There is a broad distinction between this case and
" those cited from Blackstone. Those were cases in which a
" thing was cast into a public place or into the sea—into a place,
" in fact, of which it could not be said that anyone had a real de
" facto possession, or a general power and intent to exclude
" unauthorized interference."   Then Lord Russell cited the
passage which I read earlier in this judgment and continued :
" It is somewhat strange "—I venture to echo those words—
" that there is no more direct authority on the question ; but
" the general principle seems to me to be that where a person
" has possession of house or land, with a manifest intention to
" exercise control over it and the things which may be upon
" or in it, then, if something is found on that land, whether
" by an employee of the owner or by a stranger, the presumption
" is that the possession of that thing is in the owner of the locus
" in quo."   It is to be observed that Lord Russell there is
extending the meaning of the passage he had cited from
Pollock and Wright's essay on " Possession in the Common
" Law," where the learned authors say that the possession of

(1) 21 L. J. (Q. B.) 75 ; 15 Jur. 1079.

" land carries with it possession of everything which is attached
to or under that land.   Then Lord Russell adds possession of
everything which may be on or in that land.   *South Staffordshire Water Co.* v. *Sharman* (1) which was relied on by counsel
for the defendant, has also been the subject of some discussion.
It has been said that it establishes that if a man finds a thing
as the servant or agent of another, he finds it not for himself,
but for that other, and indeed that seems to afford a sufficient
explanation of the case.   The rings found at the bottom of the
pool were not in the possession of the company, but it seems
that though Sharman was the first to obtain possession of them,
he obtained them for his employers and could claim no title
for himself.

The only other case to which I need refer is *Elwes* v. *Brigg
Gas Co.* (2), in which land had been demised to a gas company
for ninety-nine years with·a reservation to the lessor of all
mines and minerals.   A pre-historic boat embedded in the soil
was discovered by the lessees when they were digging to make
a gasholder.   It was held that the boat, whether regarded as a
mineral or as part of the soil in which it was embedded when
discovered, or as a chattel, did not pass to the lessees by the
demise, but was the property of the lessor though he was
ignorant of its existence at the time of granting the lease.
Chitty J. said (3) " The first question which does actually arise
" in this case is whether the boat belonged to the plaintiff at
" the time of the granting of the lease.   I hold that it did,
" whether it ought to be regarded as a mineral, or as part of the
" soil within the maxim above cited, or as a chattel.   If it was
" a mineral or part of the soil in the sense above indicated, then
" it clearly belonged to the owners of the inheritance as part
" of the inheritance itself.   But if it ought to be regarded as a
" chattel, I hold the property in the chattel was vested in the
" plaintiff, for the following reasons."   Then he gave the
reasons, and continued : " The plaintiff then being thus in
" possession of the chattel, it follows that the property in the
" chattel was vested in him.   Obviously the right of the
" original owner could not be established ; it had for centuries
" been lost or barred, even supposing that the property had
" not been abandoned when the boat was first left on the spot
" where it was found.   The plaintiff, then, had a lawful
" possession, good against all the world, and therefore the

1945
HANNAH
v.
PEEL.

Birkett J.

(1) [1896] 2 Q. B. 44.   (3) Ibid. 568.
(2) 33 Ch. D. 562.

1945

HANNAH
v.
PEEL

Birkett J.

" property in the boat.   In my opinion it makes no difference,
" in these circumstances, that the plaintiff was not aware of
" the existence of the boat."

A review of these judgments shows that the authorities are
in an unsatisfactory state, and I observe that Sir John Salmond
in his book on Jurisprudence (9th ed., at p. 383), after referring
to the cases of *Elwes* v. *Brigg Gas Co.* (1) and *South Staffordshire
Water Co.* v. *Sharman* (2), said : " Cases such as these, however,
" are capable of explanation on other grounds, and do not
" involve any necessary conflict either with the theory of
" possession or with the cases already cited, such as *Bridges*
" v. *Hawkesworth* (3).   The general principle is that the first
" finder of a thing has a good title to it against all but the true
" owner, even though the thing is found on the property of
" another person," and he cites *Armory* v. *Delamirie* (4) and
Bridges v. *Hawkesworth* (3) in support of that proposition.
Then he continues : " This principle, however, is subject to
" important exceptions, in which, owing to the special cir-
" cumstances of the case, the better right is in him on whose
" property the thing is found," and he names three cases as the
principal ones : " When he on whose property the thing is
" found is already in possession not merely of the property,
" but of the thing itself ; as in certain circumstances, even
" without specific knowledge, he undoubtedly may be."   The
second limitation Sir John Salmond puts is : " If anyone finds
" a thing as the servant or agent of another he finds it not for
" himself, but for his employer."   Then : " A third case in
" which a finder obtains no title is that in which he gets
" possession only through a trespass or other act of wrong-
" doing."   It is fairly clear from the authorities that a man
possesses everything which is attached to or under his land.
Secondly, it would appear to be the law from the authorities I
have cited, and particularly from *Bridges* v. *Hawkesworth* (3),
that a man does not necessarily possess a thing which is lying
unattached on the surface of his land even though the thing is
not possessed by someone else.   A difficulty however, arises,
because the rule which governs things an occupier possesses
as against those which he does not, has never been very clearly
formulated in our law.   He may possess everything on the land
from which he intends to exclude others, if Mr. Justice Holmes

(1) 33 Ch. D. 562.   (3) 21 L. J. (Q. B.) 75 ; 15 Jur.
(2) [1896] 2 Q. B. 44.   1079.
                                          (4) 1 Str. 504.

1 K. B.   KING'S BENCH DIVISION.   521

is right ; or he may possess those things of which he has a de facto control, if Sir Frederick Pollock is right.

There is no doubt that in this case the brooch was lost in the ordinary meaning of that term, and I should imagine it had been lost for a very considerable time. Indeed, from this correspondence it appears that at one time the predecessors in title of the defendant were considering making some claim. But the moment the plaintiff discovered that the brooch might be of some value, he took the advice of his commanding officer and handed it to the police. His conduct was commendable and meritorious. The defendant was never physically in possession of these premises at any time. It is clear that the brooch was never his, in the ordinary acceptation of the term, in that he had the prior possession. He had no knowledge of it, until it was brought to his notice by the finder. A discussion of the merits does not seem to help, but it is clear on the facts that the brooch was " lost " in the ordinary meaning of that word ; that it was " found " by the plaintiff in the ordinary meaning of that word, that its true owner has never been found, that the defendant was the owner of the premises and had his notice drawn to this matter by the plaintiff, who found the brooch. In those circumstances I propose to follow the decision in *Bridges* v. *Hawkesworth* (1), and to give judgment in this case for the plaintiff for 66*l*.

Judgment for plaintiff.

Solicitors for plaintiff : *Slaughter & May.*
Solicitors for defendant : *Rooper & Whately.*

(1) 21 L. J. (Q. B.) 75 ; 15 Jur. 1079.

C. G. M.

1945

HANNAH
v.
PEEL

Birkett J.

McAvoy v. Medina
93 Mass. (11 Allen) 548 (1866)

TORT to recover a sum of money found by the plaintiff in the shop of the defendant.

[I]t appeared that the defendant was a barber, and the plaintiff, being a customer in the defendant's shop, saw and took up a pocket-book which was lying upon a table there, and said, "See what I have found." The defendant came to the table and asked where he found it. The plaintiff laid it back in the same place and said, "I found it right there." The defendant then took it and counted the money, and the plaintiff told him to keep it, and if the owner should come to give it to him; and otherwise to advertise it; which the defendant promised to do. Subsequently the plaintiff made three demands for the money, and the defendant never claimed to hold the same till the last demand. It was agreed that the pocket-book was placed upon the table by a transient customer of the defendant and accidentally left there, and was first seen and taken up by the plaintiff, and that the owner had not been found. ...

DEWEY, J.
It seems to be the settled law that the finder of lost property has a valid claim to the same against all the world except the true owner, and generally that the place in which it is found creates no exception to this rule.

But this property is not, under the circumstances, to be treated as lost property in that sense in which a finder has a valid claim to hold the same until called for by the true owner. This property was voluntarily placed upon a table in the defendant's shop by a customer of his who accidentally left the same there and has never called for it. The plaintiff also came there as a customer, and first saw the same and took it up from the table. The plaintiff did not by this acquire the right to take the property from the shop, but it was rather the duty of the defendant, when the fact became thus known to him, to use reasonable care for the safe keeping of the same until the owner should call for it. In the case of *Bridges v. Hawkesworth*, 7 Eng. Law & Eq. R. 424, the property, although found in a shop, was found on the floor of the same, and had not been placed there voluntarily by the owner, and the court held that the finder was entitled to the possession of the same, except as to the owner. But the present case more resembles that of *Lawrence v. The State*, 1 Humph. (Tenn.) 228, and is indeed very similar in its facts. The court there take a distinction between the case of property thus placed by the owner and neglected to be removed, and property lost. It was there held that "to place a pocket-book upon a table and to forget to take it away is not to lose it, in the sense in which the authorities referred to speak of lost property."

We accept this as the better rule, and especially as one better adapted to secure the rights of the true owner.

In view of the facts of this case, the plaintiff acquired no original right to the property, and the defendant's subsequent acts in receiving and holding the property in the manner he did does not create any.

Questions

1. In *Lawrence v. State*, on which *McAvoy* relies, the customer did come back for his lost pocketbook containing $480 in bank notes, which he had left on a table while the barber went out to make change. To quote the court: "The barber left the shop to get the bill changed, and, a fight occurring in the streets, the [customer's] attention was arrested thereat and he left the shop, his pocket-book lying on the table." When he returned, the barber "denied all knowledge of the pocket-book" but then "expended [the bank notes] in the purchase of confections, etc." A criminal prosecution for grand larceny followed, and the barber argued that the pocketbook had been lost because larceny only applies when the defendant takes property from the possession of the victim. The

court held that because the pocketbook on a table was merely **mislaid**, rather than "lost," it was still within the customer's "constructive possession." First of all, is this plausible? And second, is this a good fit for the facts of *McAvoy*?

2. By way of contrast, in *Bridges v. Hawkesworth*, which *McAvoy* distinguishes, the plaintiff found a small parcel on the floor of the defendant's shop and immediately showed it to the defendant's employee. The parcel contained bank notes; the plaintiff "requested the defendant to deliver them to the owner." Three years later, with no owner having returned, the court held the plaintiff as finder was entitled to the notes. "If the notes had been accidentally kicked into the street, and then found by someone passing by, could it be contended that the defendant was entitled to them, from the mere fact of their having been dropped in his shop? ... Certainly not. The notes were never in the custody of the defendant, nor within the protection of his house before they were found, as they would have had they been intentionally deposited there, and the defendant has come under no responsibility." First, what do you make of the *Bridges* court's argument that the shopkeeper's entitlement to the notes should turn on whether he would have been held responsible to the true owner for losing them? And second, is this any better a fit for the facts of *McAvoy*?

3. What do you make of the argument that awarding the pocket-book to the shopkeeper is "one better adapted to secure the rights of the true owner?"

4. In addition to lost and mislaid property, there is also abandoned property: property which the owner has voluntarily relinquished with no intent to reclaim. Since abandoned property is again unowned, the usual rules of first possession apply. (As you have

seen, these rules themselves are not as simple as "first possessor wins."). How easy is it to tell the three apart? Why?

5. In *Benjamin v. Lindner Aviation*, 534 N.W.2d 400 (Iowa 1995) in which an airplane inspector found $18,000 in cash inside the wing of an airplane in 1992 while the plane was parked in his employer's hangar for maintenance. The money, which consisted primarily of $20 bills dating to the 1950s and 1960s, was in two four-inch packets wrapped in handkerchiefs and tied with string and then wrapped again in aluminum foil. The packets were inserted behind a panel on the underside of the plane's wing; the panel was secured with rusty screws that had not been removed in several years. The inspector, the employer, and the bank that owned the plane (after repossessing it from a prior owner who had defaulted on a loan) all made claims to the money. Was it lost, mislaid, or abandoned, and who was entitled to it?

6. Another category sometimes mentioned in the found-property caselaw is treasure trove: money, gold, or silver intentionally placed underground, which is found long enough later that it is likely the owner is dead or will never return for it. At common law in England, treasure trove belonged to the King. Most American states now treat treasure trove like any other found property. Is this a sensible rejection of an archaic and pointless quirk of the common-law, or was there something to the doctrine?

7. In *Hannah v. Peel*, [1945] K.B. 509, the British government requisitioned Gwernhaylod House in 1940 for use during World War II and paid the owner, Major Hugh Edward Ethelston Peel £250 per year. The house had been conveyed to Major Peel in 1938 but it was unoccupied from then until when it was requisitioned. Duncan Hannah, a lance-corporal with the Royal Artillery, was

stationed in the house and was adjusting a blackout curtain in August 1940 when he found something loose in a crevice on top of the window-frame. It turned out to be a brooch covered in cobwebs and dirt; he informed his commanding officer and then turned it over to the police. Two years later, the police gave it to Major Peel, who sold it for £66. Lance-Corporal Hannah sued and was awarded the value of the brooch. The court discussed numerous cases, including *Bridges v. Hawkesworth* and *South Staffordshire Water Co. v. Sharman*, [1896] 2 Q.B. 44, which awarded two rings found by a workman embedded in the mud at the bottom of a pool to the company that owned the land. From them, it extracted a rule that "a man possesses everything which is attached to or under his land." Since Major Peel "was never physically in possession of these premises" and hence had no "prior possession" of the brooch, Lance-Corporal Hannah was entitled to it as a finder. Is this possession-based approach a better way of analyzing found-property cases than the categorical lost-vs-mislaid American approach exemplified by *McAvoy*? Or is *Hannah* an oddball outlier driven by the court's desire to do right by a wartime serviceman "whose conduct was commendable and meritorious," especially as against an absentee landlord from the local gentry?

Adverse Possession

Few doctrines taught in the first year of law school make a worse first impression than adverse possession. Adverse possession enables a non-owner to gain title to land (or personal property, but we will focus here on land) after the expiration of the statute of limitations for the owner to recover possession. That sounds bad, and the thought of "squatters" becoming owners gets its share of bad press. But historically the doctrine has performed, and continues to serve, important functions.

The basic requirements, if not their wording and application, are common from state to state. As one treatise summarizes, an adverse possessor must prove possession that is:

(1) hostile (perhaps under a claim of right);

(2) exclusive;

(3) open and notorious;

(4) actual; and

(5) continuous for the requisite statutory period.

16 POWELL ON REAL PROPERTY § 91.01. States routinely add to the list. California law, for example, requires that

> the claimant must prove: (1) possession under claim of right or color of title; (2) actual, open, and notorious occupation of the premises constituting reasonable notice to the true owner; (3) possession which is adverse and hostile to the true owner; (4) continuous possession for at least five years; and (5) payment of all taxes assessed against the property during the five-year period.

Main St. Plaza v. Cartwright & Main, LLC, 124 Cal. Rptr. 3d 170, 178 (Cal. App. 2011) (citations and quotations omitted).

A.   Adverse Possession Rationales

But why allow adverse possession? One court summarized the doctrine's history and purposes as follows:

> ... a brief history of adverse possession may be of assistance. After first using an amalgamation of Roman and Germanic doctrine, our English predecessors in common law later settled upon statutes of limitation to effect adverse possession. See Axel Teisen, *Contributions of the Comparative Law Bureau*, 3 A.B.A. J. 97, 126, 127, 134 (1917). In practice, the statutes eliminated a rightful owner's ability to regain possession after the passing of a certain number of years, thereby vesting de facto title in the adverse possessor. For example, a 1623 statute of King James I restricted the right of entry to recover possession of land to a period of twenty years. Essentially, in England, the "[o]riginal policy supporting the development of adverse possession reflected society's unwillingness to take away a 'right' which an adverse possessor thought he had. Similarly, society felt the loss of an unknown right by the title owner was minimal." William G. Ackerman & Shane T. Johnson, Comment, *Outlaws of the Past: A Western Perspective on Prescription and Adverse Possession*, 31 Land & Water L. Rev. 79, 83 (1996)....

> In the United States, although the 1623 statute of King James I "came some years after the settling of Jamestown (the usual date fixed as the crystalizing of the common law in America), its fiat is generally accepted as [our] common law. Hence 'adverse possession' for 20 years under the common law in this country passes title to the adverse possessor with certain stated

qualifications." 10 *Thompson on Real Property* § 87.01 at 75. Today, all fifty states have some statutory form of adverse possession ....

....Courts and commentators generally ascribe to "four traditional justifications or clusters of justifications which support transferring the entitlement to the [adverse possessor] after the statute of limitations runs: the problem of lost evidence, the desirability of quieting titles, the interest in discouraging sleeping owners, and the reliance interests of [adverse possessors] and interested third persons." Thomas W. Merrill, *Property Rules, Liability Rules, and Adverse Possession*, 79 Nw. U. L. Rev. 1122, 1133 (1984). Effectively, our society has made a policy determination that "all things should be used according to their nature and purpose" and when an individual uses and preserves property "for a certain length of time, [he] has done a work beneficial to the community." Teisen, 3 A.B.A. J. at 127. For his efforts, "his reward is the conferring upon him of the title to the thing used." Id. Esteemed jurist Oliver Wendell Holmes, Jr. went a step further than Teisen, basing our society's tolerance of adverse possession on the ideal that "[a] thing which you have enjoyed and used as your own for a long time, whether property or an opinion, takes root in your being and cannot be torn away without your resenting the act and trying to defend yourself, however you came by it." O Centro Espirita Beneficente Uniao Do Vegetal v. Ashcroft, 389 F.3d 973, 1016 (10th Cir. 2004) (quoting Oliver Wendell Holmes, Jr., *The Path of the Law*, 10 Harv. L. Rev. 457, 477 (1897)).

Regardless of how deeply the doctrine is engrained in our history, however, courts have questioned "whether the concept of adverse possession is as viable as it once was, or whether the concept always squares with modern ideals in a sophisticated, congested, peaceful society." *Finley*, 160 Cal. Rptr. at 427. Commentators have also opined that, along with the articulated benefits of adverse possession, numerous disadvantages exist including the "infringement of a landowner's rights, a decrease in value of the servient estate, and the encouraged [over]exploitation and [over]development of land. In addition, they ... [include] the generation of animosity between neighbors, a source of damages to land or loss of land ownership, and the creation of uncertainty for the landowner."* Ackerman, 31 Land & Water L. Rev. at 92. In reality, "[a]dverse possession '[i]s nothing more than a person taking someone else's private property for his own private use.' It is hard to imagine a notion more in contravention of the ideals set forth in the U.S. Constitution protecting life, liberty and property." Ackerman, 31 Land & Water L. Rev. at 94-95 (quoting 2 C.J.S. Adverse Possession § 2 (1972)).

Although this Court duly recognizes its role as the judicial arm of government tasked with applying the law, rather than making law, it is not without an eyebrow raised at the ancient roots and arcane rationale of adverse possession that we apply the doctrine to this modern property dispute.

Cahill v. Morrow, 11 A.3d 82, 86-88 (R.I. 2011). Do you share the court's skepticism? Consider the rationales discussed above against the following case.

Tieu v. Morgan
265 P.3d 98 (Ore. App. 2011)

HADLOCK, J.

The parties dispute ownership of a strip of land that runs parallel to defendants' driveway. Plaintiff, who owns residential property adjoining that strip of land, filed suit seeking (1) a declaration that he owns the

---

* [*Eds.*—The modifications to the quotation from Ackerman are ours, not the court's.]

disputed strip and (2) an injunction prohibiting defendants from trespassing on that property. Defendants counterclaimed, asserting that they acquired the disputed strip through adverse possession, and subsequently moved for summary judgment on that counterclaim. The trial court granted defendants' motion and entered a judgment declaring that defendants had acquired the strip through adverse possession. Plaintiff appeals, and we affirm....

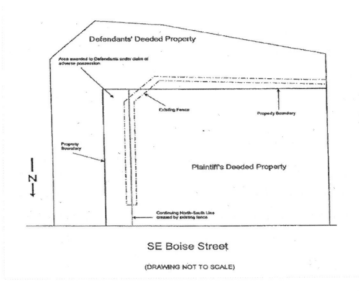

The two parcels subject to this appeal are adjoining residential tax lots in a Portland subdivision. Tax lot 3100 is rectangular, with its north side fronting Southeast Boise Street. Tax lot 3200 is a flag lot that is situated largely south of lot 3100; its driveway (the "flagpole") runs north from the main portion of the lot (the "flag") to Southeast Boise Street, parallel to the eastern edge of lot 3100. The disputed three-foot-wide strip lies between lot 3200's driveway and lot 3100. Defendants own lot 3200. Plaintiff owns lot 3100 and also is the record owner of the disputed strip.

A north-south stretch of fence on plaintiff's property runs along the western boundary of the disputed strip, parallel to defendants' driveway. The fence starts roughly halfway down the driveway from Southeast Boise

Street, running south, then turns 45 degrees to the southwest, cutting off the southeast corner of lot 3100, then makes another 45-degree turn before continuing west, roughly following the east-west boundary between lots 3100 and 3200. The diagonal portion of the fence that cuts the corner of lot 3100 includes a gate wide enough to accommodate a boat trailer. As noted, the disputed three-foot-wide strip lies between defendants' driveway and the north-south fence on lot 3100; its practical effect is to widen the "flagpole" portion of lot 3200.

The fencing that separates the two properties has existed for decades. As of 1984, the two lots were owned by Robert Stevens, who installed most of the fencing that year, including about half of the north-south stretch located west of lot 3200's driveway. In 1994, Robert Stevens sold lot 3200 to his son, James Stevens, believing that the deed he conveyed to James included all property on the east side of a north-south line defined by that portion of the fence, *i.e.*, the disputed strip. Although he never specifically discussed the issue with his father, James also believed that his purchase of the flag lot included the disputed strip along his driveway. James explained that he had "no reason to know—to think [that the fence] would be in the wrong location."

During the four years that James owned the flag lot, he granted Robert permission to occasionally use James's driveway and the disputed strip, so that Robert could drive a large vehicle and boat trailer through the diagonal gate into Robert's back yard. In 1996, James installed a sewer line in the center of the disputed strip, running all the way from Southeast Boise Street to the house on lot 3200. When James later put lot 3200 on the market, he advertised it as having a "fully fenced yard," based on his belief that his ownership included the disputed strip.

James sold lot 3200 to defendants in 1998. The lot was not surveyed in conjunction with that sale; nor did the parties to the sale discuss the lot's recorded boundaries, review paperwork or maps, or perform any investigation specifically related to that subject.

Defendants have made use of the disputed strip since they purchased lot 3200. Defendant Francine Morgan runs a daycare business from her home, and parents regularly use the disputed strip when dropping off and picking up their children. In 1999, defendants extended the fence paralleling the strip north by roughly 40 feet, choosing not to extend the fence all the way to Southeast Boise Street after Robert suggested that they leave that area unfenced to accommodate maneuvering large vehicles in and out of their driveways. Defendants have laid gravel and bark dust on the disputed strip a number of times and have maintained the fence by replacing posts and fence boards. While Robert still owned lot 3100, he specifically asked defendants' permission each time he wanted to use the disputed strip to access or move his boat, and defendants granted that permission.

Plaintiff bought lot 3100 from Robert in early 2006. Before purchasing the property, plaintiff had it surveyed and learned that the north-south fence was not located on the deeded boundary between lots 3100 and 3200. A survey pin marking the recorded boundary was placed at that time. Plaintiff claims that he told defendant Francine Morgan soon after the survey was completed that he planned to move the fence to the deeded property line within two years. According to plaintiff, Francine neither disputed plaintiff's right to move the fence nor claimed ownership of land between the survey marker and the fence. Defendants deny that such a conversation occurred.

In 2008, plaintiff attempted to remove the north-south portion of the fence. After defendants protested, plaintiff initiated this action, seeking a declaration that he owned the disputed strip. As noted, defendants asserted in a counterclaim that they had acquired the strip through adverse possession. The trial court ultimately granted summary judgment to defendants, ruling that the undisputed facts established that defendants had acquired the disputed strip through adverse possession.…

ORS 105.620 codifies the common-law elements of adverse possession, requiring a claimant to prove by clear and convincing evidence that the claimant or the claimant's predecessors in interest maintained actual, open, notorious, exclusive, hostile, and continuous possession of the property for ten years. In addition to those common-law elements, the statute also requires the claimant to have had an honest belief of actual ownership when he or she entered into possession of the property.

Plaintiff makes arguments related to each of the statutory elements, first claiming that defendants did not establish actual, open, notorious, exclusive, or continuous possession of the entire disputed strip. We recently summarized what proof is required to satisfy those elements of an adverse-possession claim:

> "The element of actual use is satisfied if a claimant established a use of the land that would be made by an owner of the same type of land, taking into account the uses for which the land is suited. To establish a use that is open and notorious, plaintiffs must prove that their possession is of such a character as to afford the owner the means of knowing it, and of the claim. The exclusivity of the use also depends on how a reasonable owner would or would not share the property with others in like circumstances. A use is continuous if it is constant and not intermittent. The required constancy of use, again, is determined by the kind of use that would be expected of such land."

Stiles v. Godsey, 233 Or. App. 119, 126, 225 P.3d 81 (2009) (internal quotations and citations omitted).

Here, the land in question is a three-foot-wide strip, covered mostly with gravel or bark dust, adjacent to a narrow driveway. Defendants and their predecessor have used the strip as an extension of that driveway since 1994, both to accommodate wide vehicles and to provide additional loading room for defendant Francine Morgan's daycare clients. That use is consistent with ownership and with the land's character. Moreover, that use was "open" and "notorious," particularly when considered together with James's act of locating his sewer line on the strip and, later, defendants' maintenance of and improvements to the fence. Finally, defendants and their predecessor used the strip continuously from 1994 (when James bought the lot) to at least 2006 (when plaintiff bought lot 3100 from Robert), *i.e.*, for longer than the statutory 10-year adverse-possession period. Thus, the undisputed facts establish defendants' actual, open, notorious, exclusive, and continuous use of the property.

Plaintiff's contrary argument rests on the fact that the disputed strip is not completely separated from his residential lot by a fence; he emphasizes that the fence at issue does not extend all the way to Southeast Boise Street, but starts partway down the driveway.... Here, even though the fence does not extend to the street, it adequately defines the entire disputed strip, indicating that it is separate from the land that abuts it to the west.

Plaintiff also contends that defendants' use of the disputed strip was not "exclusive" because Robert sometimes used the property even after the fence was built. But adverse-possession claimants are allowed the freedom to allow others to occasionally use their property, in the manner that neighbors are wont to do, without thereby abandoning their claim. In this case, Robert asked permission of defendants and their predecessors each time that he used the disputed strip; that permissive use was consistent with defendants' ownership of the land and does not defeat their claim to it.

We also reject plaintiff's argument that defendants' use of the disputed strip was not "hostile" because, he claims, defendants had a conscious doubt regarding the property line. Under ORS 105.620(2)(a), a claimant "maintains 'hostile possession' of property if the possession is under claim of right or with color of title." A "claim of right" may be established through proof of an honest but mistaken belief of ownership, resulting, for example, from a mistake as to the correct location of a boundary. The mistaken belief must be a "pure" mistake, however, and not one based upon "conscious doubt" about the true boundary. Furthermore, ORS 105.620(1)(b) requires that the claimants (or their predecessors) have had an "honest belief" of actual ownership that (1) continued through the vesting period, (2) had an objective basis, and (3) was reasonable under the circumstances.

In *Mid-Valley Resources, Inc. v. Engelson*, 170 Ore App 255 (2000), we concluded that the defendants had failed to establish pure mistake about the location of a boundary line because one of the defendants had a conscious doubt on that subject. That *Mid-Valley* defendant had testified that she had not known where the property line was when she was a child, and she still did not know at the time of trial whether a particular fence was located on that boundary. That defendant's uncertainty about the property line's location defeated the defendants' adverse-possession claim.

Here, by contrast, the undisputed evidence clearly establishes that defendants and their predecessor, James, always believed that the fence marked the north-south line between lots 3200 and 3100. James assumed when he bought lot 3200 in 1994 that the fence was on the property line, and he perpetuated that belief in defendants by telling them, when they bought the property, that it was "fully fenced." Robert, then the record owner of the disputed strip, confirmed those mistaken beliefs when he did not object to installation of the sewer line, to defendants' use of the strip, or to defendants' extension of the fence. No evidence in the record supports plaintiff's assertion that defendants had a "conscious doubt" about whether the fence was actually located on the line separating their property from plaintiff's. Defendants did suggest in their depositions that they had not given much thought to the property line's location until the dispute arose with plaintiff. Read in context, however, those statements simply confirm defendants' *certainty* that the property line was the same as the fence line; the statements do not indicate that defendants had any conscious doubt as to the boundary's location.

Moreover, no evidence calls into question the reasonableness of defendants' belief that they owned the disputed strip. That strip of land is small in relation to the size of lots 3200 and 3100, it regularly has been used as an extension to the width of an existing driveway, it is well suited to that purpose, and it is partly fenced off from plaintiff's property. Under the circumstances, defendants' belief that they owned the disputed strip was reasonable.

In sum, the undisputed evidence establishes clearly and convincingly that defendants and their predecessor, James, had an "honest belief" that the disputed strip was part of lot 3200 and that they continuously maintained actual, open, notorious, exclusive, and hostile possession of that strip for well over 10 years, from 1994 at least until plaintiff bought lot 3100 in 2006.[16] We conclude that defendants' adverse-possession claim to the disputed strip vested in 2004, giving them title and extinguishing any claim that plaintiff might otherwise have had to that land.

Notes and Questions

1. Does the result in *Tieu* jibe with the rationales for adverse possession recited in the note preceding it? Which ones? *Cahill* suggests that these rationales are less relevant today than in the

---

[6] We reject plaintiff's argument that defendants cannot satisfy the 10-year adverse-possession period by tacking their possession to that of James. An adverse-possession claimant may tack his possessory interests to those of a predecessor "if there is evidence that the predecessor intended to transfer whatever adverse possessory rights he or she may have acquired." Fitts v. Case, 243 Ore App 543, 549, 267 P3d 160 (2011). Here, James clearly intended his transfer of lot 3200 to defendants to include the disputed strip, given his belief that the fence marked the boundary line and his advertisement of lot 3200 as "fully fenced."

past. Do you agree? Should the defendants in *Tieu* have been without recourse?

2. *Tieu* involves an error in a conveyance. The parties' predecessors in interest thought they had bargained to transfer land that they didn't. This is a common source of adverse possession litigation. Other recurring fact patterns include mistaken deed descriptions, surveying errors, and accidental encroachments by neighbors. Adverse possession claims may also follow the souring of relationships, perhaps between cotenants or one involving permissive land use. None of these cases necessarily involve bad faith actors; although the doctrine may indeed be applied in favor of the mere trespasser, depending on the jurisdiction's interpretation of the state of mind required to satisfy the "hostility" element. We will discuss this issue further below.

3. Title based on adverse possession is as good as any. To think through the implications of that observation, imagine the following facts. Neighbor A mistakenly builds a fence on her neighbor's land and gains title to the enclosed land by adverse possession. Neighbor B then notices the encroachment and demands that A move the fence. She agrees, but changes her mind two years later and rebuilds it. B sues for trespass. Who wins?

4. **Open and notorious possession**. Whatever its merits, adverse possession is strong medicine. The doctrine therefore provides safeguards to prevent a title owner from losing her property without adequate notice by, for example, requiring that the possession be open and notorious—it has to be the kind of act that an owner would notice.

But even overt acts may not be obvious threats to ownership rights. A fence on someone else's property certainly seems open and notorious, but what if it is just an inch or two over the border? What about the three-foot incursion at issue in *Tieu*? What if it had been built while the plaintiff was in occupation of his lot? Do we expect owners to commission surveys anytime a neighbor builds near the property line?

For some courts, the answer is no. *Mannillo v. Gorski*, 255 A.2d 258, 264 (N.J. 1969), for example, holds that minor encroachments are not open and notorious without actual knowledge on the part of the title owner. But where would that leave an innocent encroacher, whose trespass may be costly to remedy? In *Mannillo*, the court balked at placing the trespasser, whose steps and concrete walk extended 15 inches into the plaintiffs' property, at her neighbor's mercy.

It is conceivable that the application of the foregoing rule may in some cases result in undue hardship to the adverse possessor who under an innocent and mistaken belief of title has undertaken an extensive improvement which to some extent encroaches on an adjoining property. In that event … equity may furnish relief. Then, if the innocent trespasser of a small portion of land adjoining a boundary line cannot without great expense remove or eliminate the encroachment, or such removal or elimination is impractical or could be accomplished only with great hardship, the true owner may be forced to convey the land so occupied upon payment of the fair value thereof without regard to whether the true owner had notice of the encroachment at its inception. Of course, such a result should eventuate only under appropriate circumstances and where no serious damage would be done to the remaining land as, for instance, by rendering the balance of the parcel unusable or no longer capable of being built upon by reason of zoning or other restrictions.

Id.[2] Is this result—a forced transaction in which the innocent trespasser becomes the owner, but must pay—the best accommodation of the relevant interests? If the true owner wasn't on notice of the incursion, why can she be forced to surrender her land, even for payment?

---

[2] As *Manillo*'s resort to equity shows, adverse possession is not the only way to address boundary disputes. Other options include the equitable doctrine of acquiescence, *see, e.g.*, Hamlin v. Niedner, 955 A.2d 251, 254 (Me. 2008) ("To prove that title or a boundary line is established by acquiescence, a plaintiff must prove four elements by clear and convincing evidence: (1) possession up to a visible line marked clearly by monuments, fences or the like; (2) actual or constructive notice of the possession to the adjoining landowner; (3) conduct by the adjoining landowner from which recognition and acquiescence, not induced by fraud or mistake, may be fairly inferred; and (4) acquiescence for a long period of years[.]"); the doctrine of agreed boundaries, Finley v. Yuba Cnty. Water Dist., 160 Cal. Rptr. 423, 428 (Cal. App. 1979); estoppel, *see, e.g.*, Douglas v. Rowland, 540 S.W.2d 252 (Tenn. App. 1976), and laches. *See generally* L. C. Warden, *Mandatory injunction to compel removal of encroachments by adjoining landowner*, 28 A.L.R.2d 679 (Originally published in 1953) (discussing factors influencing issuance of an injunction).

Laches raises a conceptual difficulty, as it seems to cover some of the same ground as adverse possession. Laches is an equitable defense analogous to the legal defense provided by a statute of limitations: if a plaintiff unreasonably delays in bringing suit and the defendant is prejudiced by the delay, laches will bar the suit as a matter of equity. But if an owner tries to recover land within the limitations period, doesn't that imply that there has been no unreasonable delay? Clanton v. Hathorn, 600 So. 2d 963, 966 (Miss. 1992) (observing that the adverse possession statute "would seem to occupy the field"); Kelly v. Valparaiso Realty Co., 197 So. 2d 35, 36 (Fla. Dist. Ct. App. 1967) (where adverse possession was unavailable due to failure to pay taxes on the land "we do not feel that equity can be invoked to circumvent the statutory law of adverse possession"); *see generally* 27A Am. Jur. 2d Equity § 163 ("Only rarely should laches bar a case before the statute of limitations has run."). *But see* Pufahl v. White, No. 2050-S, 2002 WL 31357850, at *1 (Del. Ch. Oct. 9, 2002) (although laches claim cannot lead to title, the "laches defense may, however, be applicable to the plaintiffs' request to enjoin the defendants to remove the encroachment").

5. **Adverse possession and the property owner.** State-to-state variation about whether encroachments need to be obvious may reflect a deeper question about the purpose of adverse possession. Some authorities view the doctrine as having an object of punishing inattentive owners who sleep on their rights. If so, then perhaps it makes sense to require an incursion to be sufficiently obvious that a property owner would not need to conduct a survey to determine the existence of a violation.

   But should sleeping owners be the target of the doctrine? Are property owners who fail to assert their rights also less likely to develop their property (or sell it to someone who will)? And if that is the underlying end, are there any problems with using adverse possession doctrine as a means to it?

6. **Adverse possession as reward.** The reciprocal view—that adverse possession exists to reward the possessors—has two flavors. One is externally focused. The possessor, by putting the land to productive use, "has done a work beneficial to the community." Axel Teisen, 3 A.B.A. J. 97, 127 (1917). The other is more internal:

   > A thing which you have enjoyed and used as your own for a long time, whether property or an opinion, takes root in your being and cannot be torn away without your resenting the act and trying to defend yourself, however you came by it. The law can ask no better justification than the deepest instincts of man. It is only by way of reply to the suggestion that you are disappointing the former owner, that you refer to his neglect having allowed the gradual dissociation between himself and what he claims, and the gradual association of it with another.

Oliver Wendell Holmes, *The Path of the Law,* 10 HARV. L. REV. 457, 477 (1897). Do either of these views resonate? What does this rationale tell you about what the state of mind of the adverse possessor should be?

7. **Third-party interests.**

> The statute has not for its object to reward the diligent trespasser for his wrong nor yet to penalize the negligent and dormant owner for sleeping upon his rights; the great purpose is automatically to quiet all titles which are openly and consistently asserted, to provide proof of meritorious titles, and correct errors in conveyancing.

Henry W. Ballantine, *Title by Adverse Possession,* 32 HARV. L. REV. 135, 135 (1918) (footnotes omitted). By providing stability to existing property arrangements after the passage of time, adverse possession simplifies transactions by relieving purchasers and mortgagees of the risk that they are dealing with title founded on a long-ago mistake or trespass. The doctrine is a healing mechanism that realigns possession and paperwork when they've gotten too badly out of sync. The benefit extends to the legal system as well by relieving courts of the need to delve into the details of long-forgotten events.

8. **Adverse possession's information function.** Adverse possession also enables rights that exist as a matter of custom (e.g., "the Smiths always farm that strip of land") to receive legal status. A banker in a distant city may not understand (or trust) allocations based on local understandings, but that doesn't matter if the claims

are translated into recordable title.[3] The land may now serve as the object of a sale or collateral for a loan for an expanded audience, enhancing its value. Adverse possession's role in converting informal understandings into formal rights illustrates law's ability to facilitate the aggregation and dissemination of information across society. Can you think of others?

9. **Tacking.** What happens if a series of possessors occupy a property, but none of them are present long enough for the limitations period to run? *Tieu* notes in passing the concept of tacking, which enables a succession of adverse possessors to collectively satisfy the statutory period. The usual approach is to allow tacking so long as the successive possessors are in "privity": a relationship in which the prior possessor knowingly and intentionally transfers whatever interest she holds to the subsequent possessor. *See, e.g.,* Stump v. Whibco, 715 A.2d 1006 (N.J. Super. Ct. App. 1998) ("Tacking is generally permitted "unless it is shown that the claimant's predecessor in title did not intend to convey the disputed parcel.") (citations and quotation omitted). So the clock continues to run if one possessor sells or leases the occupied land, but there is no privity if one trespasser wanders onto the lot after another leaves (or worse, dispossesses the earlier trespasser by force).

Recall the question of whether adverse possession doctrine is more properly focused on rewarding deserving possessors or punishing

---

[3] "Quiet title" suits perform this function. They are actions that establish the claimant's title to land and foreclose the ability of others to contest it. Although quiet title suits are not necessary to gain rights under adverse possession doctrine, they are very important to adverse possessors. Do you see why? If you cannot answer the question, ask yourself whether you would ever buy property from an adverse possessor.

inattentive owners. Does the U.S. approach to tacking shed light on our answer? The English view is to allow tacking without privity. *Cf.* James Ames, LECTURES ON LEGAL HISTORY 197 (1913) ("English lawyers regard not the merit of the possessor, but the demerit of the one out of possession. The statutes of limitation provide . . . not that the adverse possessor shall acquire title, but that the one who neglects for a given time to assert his right shall thereafter not enforce it.").

10. **Adverse possession and the environment.** An underlying premise of the rationales discussed above is that land should be used. For an argument that this tilt makes adverse possession doctrine environmentally harmful, *see* John G. Sprankling, *An Environmental Critique of Adverse Possession,* 79 CORNELL L. REV. 816, 840 (1994) (arguing that "American adverse possession law is fundamentally hostile to the private preservation of wild lands" and proposing exemption to doctrine for privately held wild lands).

B.   "Hostility" and Intent

Adverse possession requires possession that is "hostile" and, often, "under a claim of right." Hostility is not animosity. "Hostile possession can be understood as possession that is opposed and antagonistic to all other claims, and that conveys the clear message that the possessor intends to possess the land as his or her own." 16 POWELL ON REAL PROPERTY § 91.01[2]. The requirement thus prevents permissive occupancy from ripening into ownership; a lessor need not worry that the tenant will claim title by adverse possession. *See, e.g.,* Rise v. Steckel, 652 P.2d 364, 372 (1982) ("[T]he ten-year statutory period for adverse possession did not begin to run until defendant asserted to plaintiff that he was possessing the property in his own right, rather than as a tenant at sufferance."). A "claim of right," sometimes called claim of title,[4] means that the possessor is holding the property as an owner would. This could be seen as synonymous with the hostility requirement, but not all jurisdictions treat the concept this way. The Powell treatise states that the predominant view in the United States is that good faith is not required for adverse possession, 16 POWELL § 91.01[2], but as you may have already noticed in the *Tieu* case above, intent often matters.

Cahill v. Morrow
11 A.3d 82 (R.I. 2011)

INDEGLIA, J.

The property in dispute is located on Gooseberry Road in the Snug Harbor section of South Kingstown, Rhode Island. Identified as lot 19 on assessor's plat 88-1, the land is sandwiched between lot 20, currently owned by Cahill, and lot 18, formerly coowned by members of the Morrow family. Morrow is the record owner of the subject property, lot 19.

In 1969, Morrow's husband, George Morrow, purchased lot 19, and the same year George and his brothers jointly purchased lot 18. At the time of lot 19's purchase, it was largely undeveloped, marked only by a preexisting clothesline, grass, and trees. Since that time, the Morrows have not improved or maintained lot 19, but have paid all property taxes assessed to it. As such, instead of vacationing on their lot 19, the Morrows annually spent two weeks in the summer at the cottages on the adjacent lot 18. During these vacations, the Morrow children and their cousins played on lot 19's grassy area. Around 1985, the Morrows ceased summering on Gooseberry Road,[3] but continued to return at least once a

---

[4] Which is not the same thing as "color of title," as discussed below.

[3] In 1991, George Morrow and his joint-owner brothers sold lot 18.

year to view the lot. Morrow stopped visiting lot 19 in October 2002, after her husband became ill, and she did not return again until July 2006.

In 1971, two years after George Morrow purchased lot 19, Cahill's mother bought the land and house designated as lot 20 as a summer residence. Between 1971 and 1975, Cahill and her brother did some work on lot 19. They occasionally cut the grass, placed furniture, and planted trees and flowers on it.

Cahill's mother passed away in 1975, and in 1977, after purchasing her siblings' shares, Cahill became the sole record owner of the lot 20 property. Once she became lot 20's owner, Cahill began living in the house year-round. From that time through 1991, she and her boyfriend, James M. Cronin, testified that they continued to mow lot 19's grass on occasion. In addition, she hung clothing on the clothesline, attached flags to the clothesline pole, used the picnic table, positioned a bird bath and feeder, and planted more flowers and trees. Cahill placed Adirondack chairs on lot 19 and eventually replaced the clothesline and picnic table. In 1987, Cahill held the first annual "cousins' party" allowing her relatives free rein with respect to her property and lot 19 for playing, sitting, and car parking. She also entertained friends and family on lot 19 during other summer days. Mary Frances McGinn, Cahill's cousin, likewise recalled that lot 19 was occupied by Cahill kindred during various family functions throughout this time period. Cahill admitted that she never objected to neighborhood children using lot 19, however.

During the period of 1991 through 1997, Cahill testified that she planted more flowers and trees, in addition to cutting the grass occasionally. Cahill also stored her gas grill and yard furniture on the lot and had her brother stack lobster pots for decorative purposes. In 1991 or 1992, she began hosting the annual "Cane Berry Blossom Festival," another outdoor event that used both her lot and lot 19 as the party venue. Like the other gatherings, the festival always took place on a day during a warm-weather month. In 1997 or 1998, she installed a wooden border around the flower beds.

On July 22, 1997, Cahill wrote to George Morrow expressing an interest in obtaining title to lot 19. In the 1997 letter, Cahill stated: "I am interested in learning if your narrow strip of property is available for sale. If so, I would be interested in discussing purchasing it from you." Cahill continued: "If there is a possibility that you would like to sell it, could you please either call me or send me a note?" Cahill did not receive a response.

In the "late 1990s," though Cahill is unclear whether this occurred before or after the 1997 letter, a nearby marina sought permission to construct and elevate its property. Cahill attended the related zoning board hearings and expressed her concerns about increased flooding on lot 19 due to the marina elevation. She succeeded in having the marina developer grade part of lot 19 to alleviate flooding. Additionally, Cahill instituted her own trench and culvert drainage measures to divert water off of lot 19 and then reseeded the graded area. By Cahill's own admission, however, her trenching and reseeding work occurred in 1999 or 2000.

Subsequent to 2001, the new owners of lot 18[5] stored their boat on lot 19 and planted their own flowers and small trees on the property. In 2002, when the town (with approval from George Morrow) erected a stone wall and laid a sidewalk on the Gooseberry Road border of lot 19, Cahill loamed and planted grass on that portion of the lot. Also in 2002, Cahill asked Morrow's two sisters on separate occasions whether George Morrow would be interested in selling lot 19. The Morrows gave no response to her 2002 inquiries. In 2003, George Morrow passed away.

After making her third inquiry concerning the purchase of lot 19 in 2002, Cahill testified, she continued using the property in a fashion similar to

---

[5] In approximately 2001, new owners purchased lot 18 from the Morrow brothers' successor.

her prior practice until December 2005, when she noticed heavy-machinery tire marks and test pits on the land. Thereafter, she retained counsel and authorized her attorney to send a letter on January 10, 2006 to Morrow indicating her adverse possession claim to a "20-foot strip of land on the northerly boundary" of lot 19. According to a survey of the disputed property, however, the width of lot 19 from the northerly boundary (adjacent to Cahill's property) to lot 18 is 49.97 feet and therefore, more than double what Cahill originally claimed in this letter. Nonetheless, on April 25, 2006, Cahill instituted a civil action requesting a declaration that based on her "uninterrupted, quiet, peaceful and actual seisin and possession" "for a period greater than 10 years," she was the true owner of lot 19 in its entirety. On July 25, 2007, the trial justice agreed that Cahill had proved adverse possession under G.L. 1956 § 34-7-1 and vested in her the fee simple title to lot 19....

In Rhode Island, obtaining title by adverse possession requires actual, open, notorious, hostile, continuous, and exclusive use of property under a claim of right for at least a period of ten years.

Here, the trial justice recited the proper standard of proof for adverse possession and then found that Cahill had

> "met her burden of establishing all of the elements of an adverse possession claim to lot 19 by her and her mother's continuous and uninterrupted use of the parcel for well in excess of ten years. She maintained the property, planted and improved the property with shrubs, trees, and other plantings, sought drainage control measures, and used the property as if it were her own since 1971. She established that use not only by her own testimony, but as corroborated by other witnesses, photographs, and expert testimony relative to the interpretation of aerial photographs."

At trial, as here on appeal, Morrow argued that Cahill's offers to purchase the property invalidated her claim of right and the element of hostile possession. To dispose of that issue, the trial justice determined that "even assuming that [Cahill's] inquiry is circumstantial evidence of her knowledge that George Morrow, and subsequently Margaret [Morrow], were the legal title holders of [lot] 19, that does not destroy the viability of this adverse possession claim." The trial justice relied upon our opinion in *Tavares*, 814 A.2d at 350, to support his conclusion. Recalling that this Court stated in *Tavares* that "even when the claimants know they are nothing more than black-hearted trespassers, they can still adversely possess the property in question under a claim [of] right to do so if they use it openly, notoriously, and in a manner that is adverse to the true owner's rights for the requisite ten-year period," the trial justice found that Cahill's outward acknowledgement of Morrow's record title did not alone "negate her claim of right." He further found that "even if somehow the expression of interest in purchasing lot 19, made initially in 1997, stopped the running of the ten[-]year period under * * * § 34-7-1, the evidence was overwhelming that [Cahill] and her predecessor in title had commenced the requisite ten-year period beginning in 1971."

On appeal, Morrow challenges the trial justice's legal conclusion that Cahill's offers to purchase lot 19 did not extinguish her claim of right, hostile possession, and ultimately, the vesting of her title by adverse possession. Morrow also contends that the trial justice erred in finding that Cahill's testimonial and demonstrative evidence was sufficient to prove adverse possession under the clear and convincing burden of proof standard. We agree that as a matter of law the trial justice failed to consider the impact of Cahill's offers to purchase on the prior twenty-six years of her lot 19 use. As a result, we hold that this failure also affects his factual determinations.

1. 1997 Offer-to-Purchase Letter

In *Tavares*, this Court explained that "requir[ing] adverse possession under a claim of right is the same as requiring hostility, in that both terms simply indicate that the claimant is holding the property with an intent that is adverse to the interests of the true owner." *Tavares*, 814 A.2d at 351 (quoting 16 Powell on Real Property, § 91.05[1] at 91-28 (2000)). "Thus, [we said] a claim of right may be proven through evidence of open, visible acts or declarations, accompanied by use of the property in an objectively observable manner that is inconsistent with the rights of the record owner." Here, the first issue on appeal is how an offer to purchase has an impact on these elements....

...[I]n *Tavares*, 814 A.2d at 351, with regard to "establishing hostility and possession under a claim of right," we explained that "the pertinent inquiry centers on the claimants' *objective manifestations* of adverse use rather than on the claimants' *knowledge* that they lacked colorable legal title." (Emphases added.) Essentially, *Tavares* turned on the difference between the adverse possession claimant's "knowledge" regarding the owner's title and his "objective manifestations" thereof. In that case, the adverse-possession claimant surveyed his land and discovered "that he did not hold title to the parcels in question." After such enlightenment, however, the claimant objectively manifested his claim of ownership to the parcels by "posting no-trespass signs, constructing stone walls, improving drainage, and wood cutting." This Court explained that simply having knowledge that he was not the title owner of the parcels was not enough to destroy his claim of right given his objective, adverse manifestations otherwise. In fact, we went so far as to state that "even when claimants know that they are nothing more than black-hearted trespassers, they can still adversely possess the property in question under a claim of right to do so if they use it openly, notoriously, and in a manner that is adverse to the true owner's rights for the requisite ten-year period." This statement is legally correct considering that adverse possession does not require the claimant to make "a good faith mistake that he or she had legal title to the land." 16 Powell on Real Property § 91.05[2] at 91-23. However, to the extent that *Tavares*'s reference to "black-hearted trespassers" suggests that this Court endorses an invade-and-conquer mentality in modern property law, we dutifully excise that sentiment from our jurisprudence. !

In the case before this Court, Cahill went beyond mere knowledge that she was not the record owner by sending the offer-to-purchase letter. As distinguished from the *Tavares* claimant who did not communicate his survey findings with anyone, Cahill's letter objectively declared the superiority of George Morrow's title to the record owner himself. *See also* Shanks v. Collins, 1989 OK 115, 782 P.2d 1352, 1355 (Okla. 1989) ("A recognition by an adverse possessor that legal title lies in another serves to break the essential element of continuity of possession.").

In the face of this precedent, Cahill contends that the trial justice accurately applied the law by finding that an offer to purchase does not automatically negate a claim of right in the property. While we agree that this proposition is correct with respect to offers made in an effort to make peace in an ongoing dispute, we disagree that this proposition applies in situations, as here, where no preexisting ownership dispute is evident.... Her offer was not an olive branch meant to put an end to pending litigation with the Morrows. Rather, it was a clear declaration that Cahill "wanted title to the property" from the record owner. By doing so, she necessarily acknowledged that her interest in lot 19 was subservient to George Morrow's....

Accordingly, the trial justice erred by considering any incidents of ownership exhibited by Cahill after the 1997 letter to George Morrow interrupted her claim....

2. The Impact of Cahill's Offer to Purchase on her Pre-1997 Adverse-Possession Claim

Furthermore, we also conclude that the trial justice should not have assumed that even if Cahill's "inquiry is circumstantial evidence of her knowledge that George Morrow, and subsequently [Morrow], were the legal title holders of [lot] 19, that does not destroy the viability of this adverse possession claim." We agree that an offer to purchase does not automatically invalidate a claim already vested by statute, but we nonetheless hold that the objective manifestations that another has superior title, made after the statutory period and not made to settle an ongoing dispute, are poignantly relevant to the ultimate determination of claim of right and hostile possession during the statutory period....

3. Questions of Fact Remain

Despite the significant deference afforded to the trial justice's findings of fact, such findings are not unassailable. Here, we find clear error in the trial justice's conclusion that "even if somehow the expression of interest in purchasing [lot] 19, made initially in 1997, stopped the running of the ten[-]year period * * * the evidence was overwhelming that [Cahill] and her predecessor in title had commenced the requisite ten-year period beginning in 1971." Given our opinion that some of Cahill's lot 19 activities cannot be considered because of the time frame of their occurrence, we disagree that the trial record can be classified as presenting "overwhelming" evidence of adverse possession.

.... On remand, the trial justice is directed to limit his consideration to pre-1997 events and make specific determinations whether Cahill's intermittent flower and tree planting, flag flying, clothesline replacing, lawn chair and beach-paraphernalia storing, and annual party hosting are adequate. Furthermore, given our ruling today, the trial court must evaluate the nature of Cahill's and her predecessor's twenty-six-year acts of possession in the harsh light of the fact that Cahill openly manifested the existence of George Morrow's superior title on three occasions....

FLAHERTY, J., dissenting.
.... Simply put, I do not agree that the correspondence between plaintiff and defendant in which plaintiff offers to purchase defendant's interest in lot 19 is the smoking gun the majority perceives it to be. As is clear from a fair reading of plaintiff's testimony, she believed that she owned the property as a result of her longtime use of and dominion over it. But her testimony also demonstrates that she drew a crisp distinction between whatever ownership rights she may have acquired and record title, which she recognized continued to reside in the Morrows.... Even if that letter were as significant as the majority contends, there is no doubt that it was sent after the statutory period had run. It is beyond dispute that plaintiff's correspondence could not serve to divest her of title if she had already acquired it by adverse possession.... There certainly was credible evidence for the trial justice to find that plaintiff had used the property as her own for well over twenty years before she corresponded with Mr. Morrow in 1997....

Dombkowski v. Ferland
893 A.2d 599 (Me. 2006)

DANA, J.
....Although "some courts and commentators fail to distinguish between the elements of *hostility* and *claim of right,* or simply consider *hostility* to be a subset of the *claim of right* requirement[,] *see, e.g., Johnson v. Stanley,* 96 N.C. App. 72, 384 S.E.2d 577, 579 (1989)[,] ... under Maine law, the two elements are distinct." *Striefel,* 1999 ME 111, P13 n.7, 733 A.2d at 991.

"'Hostile' simply means that the possessor does not have the true owner's permission to be on the land, and has nothing to do with demonstrating a heated controversy or a manifestation of ill will, or that the claimant was in any sense an enemy of the owner of the servient estate." *Id.* P13, 733 A.2d at 991 (quotation marks and citation omitted). "Permission negates the element of hostility, and precludes the acquisition of title by adverse possession." *Id.* "'Under a claim of right' means that the claimant is in possession as owner, with intent to claim the land as [its] own, and not in recognition of or subordination to [the] record title owner." *Id.* P14, 733 A.2d at 991 (quotation marks omitted).

Under Maine's common law, as part of the claim of right element, we have historically examined the subjective intentions of the person claiming adverse possession. *See Preble v. Maine C. R. Co.,* 85 Me. 260, 264, 27 A. 149, 150 (1893). Under this approach, which is considered the minority rule in the country, "one who by mistake occupies ... land not covered by his deed with no intention to claim title beyond his actual boundary wherever that may be, does not thereby acquire title by adverse possession to land beyond the true line." *Preble,* 85 Me. at 264, 27 A. at 150; *see also McMullen,* 483 A.2d at 700 ("[If] the occupier intend[s] to hold the property only if he were in fact legally entitled to it[, the] occupation [is] 'conditional' and [cannot] form the basis of an adverse possession claim."). The majority rule in the country is based on *French v. Pearce,* 8 Conn. 439 (1831), and recognizes that the possessor's mistaken belief does not defeat a claim of adverse possession. [The court then interpreted legislation to overrule Maine precedents and allow mistaken possession to meet the claim of right requirement.]

Notes and Questions

1. **Doctrine v. practice.** Richard Helmholz has argued that though adverse possession doctrine generally does not require the adverse possessor to plead good faith, judicial practice is to disfavor those who know they are trespassing compared to those acting out of a good faith mistake. Richard H. Helmholz, *Adverse Possession and*

Subjective Intent, 61 WASH. U. L. Q. 331, 332 (1983). Is *Cahill* an example of this dynamic?

In recent decades, state legislatures have increasingly demanded good faith on the part of the possessor (the Oregon statute in *Tieu* requiring honest belief in ownership, for example, was passed in 1989). *See* 16 POWELL ON REAL PROPERTY § 91.05 (collecting examples).

2. Should good faith be required? And if so, what is good faith? Is it an honest belief about the facts on the ground (e.g., whether the fence builder is correct that his fence is on the right side of the boundary line)? Or is it an attitude about one's potential adversary (a willingness to move the fence if wrong)? Either view creates evidentiary difficulties.

    Even when good faith is not part of the analysis as a formal matter, Helmholz argues that judges and juries often cannot help but "prefer the claims of an honest man over those of a dishonest man." Helmholz, *supra*, at 358. Might this be a satisfactory middle ground? Are there advantages to having courts officially ignore intent while applying a de facto bar to the bad faith possessor when there is evidence of dishonesty? Or is it problematic to have legal practice depart from official doctrine?

    Perhaps another way to reconcile the benefits of adverse possession with the distaste for bad faith possessors would be to allow dishonest possessors to keep the land, but pay for the privilege. Thomas W. Merrill, *Property Rules, Liability Rules, and Adverse Possession*, 79 NW. U. L. REV. 1122, 1126 (1984) (suggesting "requiring indemnification only in those cases where the [true owner] can show that the [adverse possessor] acted in bad faith.").

As Merrill notes, a California appellate court required such payment in a case concerning a prescriptive easement (which is similar to adverse possession except that it concerns the *right to use* someone else's land rather than its ownership), only to be overturned by the state supreme court. *Id.* (discussing Warsaw v. Chicago Metallic Ceilings, Inc., 676 P.2d 584 (Cal. 1984)). The proposal may remind you of the *Manillo* case discussed above. How does it differ?

3. A minority of states, as Dombkowski indicates, require adverse possessors to prove their subjective intent to take the land without regard to the existence of other ownership interests. This is sometimes referred to as the "aggressive trespass" standard: "I thought I did not own it [and intended to take it]." Margaret Jane Radin, *Time, Possession, and Alienation,* 64 WASH. U. L.Q. 739, 746 (1986) (brackets in the original). Is there a reason to prefer it? Lee Anne Fennell argues for a knowing trespass requirement that requires the adverse possessor to document her knowledge:

> [A] documented knowledge requirement facilitates rather than punishes efforts at consensual dealmaking. One of the most definitive ways of establishing that a possessor knew she was not the owner of the disputed land is to produce evidence of her purchase offer to the record owner. Currently, such an offer often destroys one's chance at adverse possession because it shows one is acting in bad faith if one later trespasses; one does far better to remain in ignorance (or pretend to) and never broach the matter with the record owner. Under my proposal, such offers would go from being fatal in a later adverse possession action to being practically a prerequisite. As a result, it would be much more likely that any resulting adverse possession

claim will occur only where a market transaction is unavailable. A documented knowledge requirement would also reduce litigation costs and increase the certainty of land holdings. Actions or records establishing that the trespass was known at the time of entry, necessary if the possessor ever wishes to gain title under my approach, would serve to streamline trespass actions that occur before the statute has run. Moreover, an approach that refuses to reward innocent mistakes would be expected to reduce mistake-making.

Lee Anne Fennell, *Efficient Trespass: The Case for "Bad Faith" Adverse Possession*, 100 Nw. U. L. Rev. 1037, 1041-44 (2006) (footnotes omitted). One's position on these matters may depend on which scenarios one believes are most common in adverse possession cases and adjust the state of mind required to include or exclude them accordingly. Should the state of mind required depend on the context? A state might, for example, require good faith for encroachments, but bad faith or color of title if the possessor seeks to own the parcel as a whole. Is this a good idea?

C. Finer Points of Adverse Possession Law

1. **Actual and Continuous Possession.** Adverse possessors are not required to live on the occupied property, what matters is acting like a true owner would. That use, however, must be continuous, not sporadic. *Compare, e.g.,* Lobdell v. Smith, 690 N.Y.S.2d 171, 173 (N.Y. App. Div. 3d Dep't 1999) (although undeveloped land "does not require the same quality of possession as residential or arable land," no adverse possession where claimant "seldom visited the parcel except to occasionally pick berries or hunt small game"), *with* Nome 2000 v. Fagerstrom, 799 P.2d 304, 310 (Alaska 1990)

(claimants of a rural parcel suitable for recreational and subsistence activities "visited the property several times during the warmer season to fish, gather berries, clean the premises, and play.... That others were free to pick berries and fish is consistent with the conduct of a hospitable landowner, and undermines neither the continuity nor exclusivity of their possession."). Regular use of a summer home may constitute continuous use. *See, e.g.,* Nechow v. Brown, 120 N.W.2d 251, 252 (Mich. 1963).

2. **Color of title.** Claim of title, an intent to use land as one's own, is distinct from color of title, which describes taking possession under a defective instrument (like a deed based on a mistaken land survey). States often apply more lenient adverse possession standards to claims made under color of title. *Compare, e.g.,* Fl. St. § 95.16, *with id.* § 95.18. Why do you think that is?

   Entry under color of title may also affect the scope of the land treated as occupied by the adverse possessor. 2 C.J.S. *Adverse Possession* § 252 ("Adverse possession under color of title ordinarily extends to the whole tract described in the instrument constituting color of title."). *But see* Wentworth v. Forne, 137 So. 2d 166, 169 (Miss. 1962) ("In brief, when the land involved is, in part, occupied by the real owner, the adverse possession, even when this possessor has color of title, is confined to the area actually possessed.").

3. **Adverse possession by and against the government.** Although government agencies may acquire title by adverse possession, the general rule is that public property held for public use is not subject to the doctrine. Why do you think that is?

4. **Disabilities**. The title owner of land may be subject to a disability (e.g., status as a minor, mental incapacity) that may extend the time to bring an ejectment action against an unlawful occupant. States generally spell out such exceptions by statute.

5. **A Moving Target.** States vary their adverse possession rules to take into account a variety of factors (e.g., claim under color of title, payment of property taxes, enclosure or cultivation of land, etc.). These factors may change with the times. In the aftermath of the financial crisis, for example, reports of trespassers occupying foreclosed, vacant properties with the goal of acquiring title via adverse possession prompted renewed attention to the doctrine. Florida enacted legislation that requires those seeking adverse possession without color of title to pay all outstanding taxes on the property within one year of taking possession and disclose in writing the possessor's identity, date of possession, and a description of the property sufficient to enable the identification of the property in the public records. Local officials are then required to make efforts to contact the record owner of the property. Fl. St. § 95.18. The form created under the statute is reprinted below. Are measures like these useful? Consider the problem of "zombie foreclosures." A property may be vacant because the owners received a notice of foreclosure and left. Sometimes the lenders never complete the foreclosure process, perhaps to avoid the costs that come with ownership of the property. Title therefore remains with the out-of-possession owners, who remain responsible for taxes, association fees, and the like. What outcome should adverse possession law seek to promote in such cases?

**RETURN OF REAL PROPERTY IN ATTEMPT TO ESTABLISH
ADVERSE POSSESSION WITHOUT COLOR OF TITLE**
Section 95.18, Florida Statutes

DR-452
R. 07/13
Provisional
Effective 01/14

**DEPARTMENT
OF REVENUE**

**THIS RETURN DOES NOT CREATE ANY INTEREST
ENFORCEABLE BY LAW IN THE DESCRIBED PROPERTY**

For residential structures, a person who occupies or attempts to occupy a residential structure solely by claim of adverse possession prior to making a return, commits trespass under s. 810.08, F.S. A person who occupies or attempts to occupy a residential structure solely by claim of adverse possession and offers the property for lease to another commits theft under s. 812.014, F.S.

COMPLETED BY ADVERSE POSSESSION CLAIMANT

The person claiming adverse possession (claimant) must file this return with the property appraiser in the county where the property is located as required in s. 95.18(1), F.S.

Name of claimant(s)			
Mailing address		Phone	
		Parcel ID, if available	
		☐ the property claimed is only a portion of this parcel ID	
Date of filing		Date claimant entered into possession of property	

Legal description of property claimed
Must be full and complete. If the property appraiser cannot identify the property from the legal description, you may be required to obtain a survey.

Fields will expand online, or you may add pages.

This property has been: (Check all that apply.)	☐ protected by substantial enclosure	☐ cultivated, maintained, or improved in a usual manner

Describe your use of the property, in detail below.

Dates of payments of any outstanding taxes or liens levied by the state, county or municipality:

Under penalty of perjury, I declare that I have read the foregoing return and that the facts stated in it are true and correct. I further acknowledge that the return does not create any interest enforceable by law in the described property.

Signature of claimant(s) _____

_____

State of Florida
County of _____
This instrument was sworn to and subscribed before me on _____ by _____,
personally known to me or who produced _____ as identification.

_____
Signature and seal, notary public

COMPLETED BY PROPERTY APPRAISER

Received in the office of the property appraiser of _____ County, Florida, on _____.
A signed copy of this return has been delivered to the claimant(s). A copy will be sent to the owner of record.

_____   _____
Signature, property appraiser or deputy   Date

TO THE OWNER OF RECORD

A tax payment made by the owner of record before April 1 the year after the taxes were assessed will have priority over a payment made by the claimant. An adverse possession claim will be removed if the owner of record or tax collector furnishes a receipt to the property appraiser showing payment of taxes by the owner of record during the period of the claim. (S. 95.18, F.S.)

This return is a public record and may be inspected by any person under s. 119.01, F.S.

Part II: Interests

Estates and Future Interests

A. Introduction

All land under the dominion of the English crown is held "mediately or immediately, of the king"—that is, the crown has "radical title" to all land under its political dominion. William the Conqueror declared that all land in England was literally the king's property; everyone else had to settle for the privilege of holding it for him—the privilege of *tenure* (from the Norman French word "tenir"—to hold). Tenurial rights were intensely personal in early feudal society: the right to hold land was a

Homage Ceremony
Source: JAMES HENRY BREASTED & JAMES HARVEY ROBINSON, 1 OUTLINES OF EUROPEAN HISTORY 399 (1914).

privilege granted by the crown in exchange for an oath of allegiance and a promise of military service by the tenant—the oath of homage. The word homage derives from the French word *homme*—literally "man"—precisely because the ceremony surrounding the oath created not only the right of tenure, but a political and military relationship between "lord and man."[5] In exchange for the tenant's loyal support, or *fealty*, the lord warranted the tenant's right to hold a plot of land, called a fief, or *fee*.

---

[5] The ceremony of homage, recorded by the 13th-century jurist and ecclesiastic Henry de Bracton, required the tenant to come to the lord in a public place, and there "to place both his hands between the two hands of his lord, by which there is symbolized protection, defense and warranty on the part of the lord and subjection and reverence on that of the tenant, and say these words: 'I become your man with respect to the tenement which I hold of you ... and I will bear you fealty in life and limb and earthly honour ... and I will bear you fealty against all men ... saving the faith owed the lord king and his heirs.' And immediately after this [to] swear an oath of fealty to his lord in these words: 'Hear this, lord N., that I will bear you fealty in life and limb, in body, goods, and earthly honour, so help me God and these sacred relics.'" 2

Acceptance of this form of military tenure obligated the tenant to provide a certain number of knights when called on by the king, and the land held by the tenant was supposed to provide sufficient material support to enable him to meet this military obligation. Sometimes, by the process of *subinfeudation*, the King's direct tenants (or "tenants-in-chief") could spread this burden around by in turn accepting homage from other, lesser nobles and freemen, each of whom would be responsible to the tenant-in-chief for a portion of the tenant-in-chief's obligation to provide knight-service. The tenants-in-chief thereby became "mesne lords" in their own right ("mesne" being Norman French for "middle" or "intermediate"). There could be several layers of mesne lords (i.e., "land lords") in the feudal hierarchy, at the bottom of which were "tenants in demesne" ("demesne" being Norman French for "domain" or "dominion")—who actually held the land rather than subinfeudating it further. Of course, holding land did not mean one actually worked it; a tenant in demesne often left the cultivation and productive use of land to those of lower social status. These could be "villeins"—serfs legally bound to the land by birth—or "leasehold" tenants—a leasehold being a right to hold land for a term of years in exchange for payment of rent in cash or (more often) kind, and of lesser status than the "freehold" estate held by feudal tenants tracing their rights up the feudal pyramid to the crown.

Because a feudal tenant's land rights were intimately connected to this web of personal, political, and military relationships, there was no logical reason why the tenant ought to be free to transfer those rights to anyone else—and good reason for the lords to resist such alienation of the fee by their tenants. Indeed, fees could be forfeited to the lord for the tenant's

Bracton Online 232 http://bracton.law.harvard.edu/Unframed/English/v2/232.htm. The Anglo-Saxon Chronicle contains a remarkable and much-debated passage in which William the Conqueror is said to have held court at Salisbury twenty years into his reign, and there summoned and taken direct oaths of homage and fealty from every landowner "of any account" in the whole of England. *See* H. A. Cronne, *The Salisbury Oath*, 19 HISTORY 248 (1934); J.C. Holt, *1086*, in COLONIAL ENGLAND, 1066-1215, at 31 (1997).

breach of the homage relationship or commission of some other "felony," and on the tenant's death it was not clear that his family members had the right to inherit the fee. The king was assumed to have the right to retake the fee and re-grant it to a preferable new tenant upon his displeasure with or the death of the old tenant (it was his land, after all). Within a century, however, the dynastic ambitions of the baronage compelled King Henry I to concede (in his Coronation Charter of 1100) that a recently deceased baron's heir could redeem his fee upon payment of "a just and lawful relief"—i.e., a payment of money to the crown, as a kind of inheritance tax. Under the principle of primogeniture that took hold in England around this time, the lord's heir was his eldest son; landowners were not free to choose who would take over their tenancy after their death. Thus, subject to the payment of a relief, the fee became *descendible*—capable of being inherited from one generation to the next—and the grant of a descendible tenancy by the crown was now made not "to Lord Hobnob," but "to Lord Hobnob *and his heirs.*" To this day, the latter phrase remains the classic common-law formula for creating the broadest interest in land that the law will recognize: the *fee simple absolute.*

Descendibility of the fee simple having been settled early in the history of English land law, the broader question of full alienability took several more centuries to work out. The history of medieval English land law is a history of tenants trying to secure their families' wealth and power by expanding alienability and evading tenurial obligations to their lords and the crown, while the crown and higher nobility tried to adapt the law to preserve their status and prevent such evasions. There is a dialectical quality to this history. For example: for complicated reasons subinfeudation quickly came to present a greater threat to the economic interests of the higher ranks of the feudal hierarchy than simple substitution of one tenant for another. Thus, in 1290 the Statute of Quia Emptores banned subinfeudation. But in doing so it validated substitution, and with it the practice of selling an entire fee in exchange for money during the life of the tenant. Similarly, in 1536, at the insistence of King Henry VIII, the Statute of Uses abolished many clever schemes adopted by tenants to use intermediaries to direct the disposition of real property interests after death and to put those interests outside the reach of the law courts (and of the crown's feudal authority). But in doing so, the statute validated one type of flexible property arrangement we have come to know as a *trust*. Moreover, the removal of the primary mechanism lawyers had developed to meet tenants' demand for intergenerational planning was sufficiently unpopular that Henry felt compelled to consent to the enactment of the Statute of Wills in 1540—finally permitting tenants to pass their legal estates in land by will rather than being at the whim of the rule of primogeniture. Finally, since the 16th century, primogeniture has given way to a more complex system of default inheritance rights for various relatives of the deceased who leaves no will; these rights are designed to try to approximate what legislatures think the *decedent* would have wanted, not necessarily what is best for the government. This set of default rights comprises the law of *intestate succession*, which we will discuss in a separate unit (or which you may study in a separate course on trust and estates law).

Various other statutes and common-law developments over the centuries culminated in the system of possessory estates and future interests that were imported into the North American English colonies, and thus into the independent American states (excluding Louisiana). Underlying them all is a fundamental distinction that traces back to the "radical title" asserted by William the Conqueror in 1066: **there is a conceptual difference between the ownership *of land* and the ownership of *a legal interest in that land*.** This distinction remains important to modern property law, and this unit will introduce you to the types of legal interests in land that American law will recognize. In particular, it examines how the common law divides up legal interests in land among successive owners over time.

Before delving into this material, we should warn you that the estates system has limited relevance even for the practicing real estate lawyer of today. The study of estates and future interests remains in property courses for three primary reasons: (1) the estates are still legally valid property interests, and their complexity can therefore can be a danger to lawyers who encounter them and are unfamiliar with them; (2) some of the legal estates and future interests in real property can be usefully extended to *equitable* interests in property held in trust; and (3) the bar examiners are fond of testing aspirant attorneys on future interests— perhaps simply because they are fairly mechanical and therefore highly testable. To be sure, mastering the system of estates and future interests requires considerable exercise of the lawyerly skills of close reading, logical reasoning, and breaking down a big problem into lots of smaller problems. But there are other ways of learning those things, and a contemporary lawyer whose client wanted to divide up interests in property would be courting malpractice by relying on legal estates and future interests in land (which makes the bar examiners' continued affection for them even more baffling). Instead, the modern lawyer should look to the much more flexible law of trusts and to the various forms of business associations—such as corporations—that can own property in their capacity as fictional legal "persons." We discuss these strategies in a separate chapter on trusts and corporate property.

B.   Concepts, Vocabulary, and Conventions

To begin understanding how the law divides up interests in land over time, we begin with the fundamental distinction between **possessory estates** and **future interests**. A **possessory estate** is a legal interest that confers on its owner *the right to present possession* of some thing. A **future interest** is a legal interest *that exists in the present,* but does not entitle the owner to possession until some point *in the future.*

This may sound confusing, but you are probably already familiar with an arrangement that follows this pattern: a lease. A lease is a transaction in which the landlord gives the tenant a possessory estate (a leasehold estate), and *retains* a future interest—the right to retake possession after the lease term ends. This retained future interest—an unqualified right to future possession retained by the party who created the possessory interest that precedes it—is called a **reversion.** (Landlord-tenant relationships are obviously more complicated than this—they entail a number of contractual rights and obligations and are heavily regulated by statutory and decisional law and, in many cases, administrative codes. We cover these relationships more thoroughly in our unit on Landlord and Tenant.)

The idea that both landlord and tenant can have legal interests in the same parcel of land at the same time, even though only one of them has the right to *possess* the land at any given time, is a good introduction to the concept of future interests. If you think about it, you will probably recognize that the basic idea of a lease implies certain rights and powers of a landlord in the leased premises even *during* the term of the lease. The most important one is the reversionary right itself: the right to take possession at some point in the future. That's a right the tenant can't take away, even while the tenant has the right to possession. The landlord might be interested in selling (or mortgaging) this reversionary right, even before the lease ends. And if she does sell or mortgage her interest (which she may, subject to the tenant's interest), the thing sold is not "the property"; it is *the landlord's reversion:* a legal interest in real property *that exists in the present* but will not entitle its holder to *possession* of that real property until some point *in the future.*

When learning about estates and future interests, we will follow some conventions that will simplify our discussion as much as possible. Most of our problems will involve an owner of land transferring some interest in that land to one or more other parties. Following longstanding tradition in the study of Anglo-American property law, we will refer to the parcel of land in question as "Blackacre" (or "Whiteacre," "Greenacre," "Ochreacre," etc. if more than one parcel is at issue). We will refer to the original owner as O, and the other parties as A, B, C, etc.

In addition, there are a variety of technical terms that arise, a few of which you should be familiar with:

- A *grant* or *conveyance* is a transfer of an interest in property. The person making the grant is the *grantor* (or *transferor*); the person receiving the grant is the *grantee* (or *transferee*). If the grant is made during the life of the grantor, it is said to be an *inter vivos* conveyance (literally, "between the living"). If in a will, it is said to be a *testamentary* conveyance. A testamentary conveyance of real property is called a *devise*. A testamentary conveyance of personal property is called a *bequest* (or sometimes a *legacy*).

- When a person dies, they will either have left a valid will or not. A person who dies with a valid will dies *testate*; one who dies without a valid will dies *intestate*. Either way, the dead person can be referred to as a *decedent*. If the decedent did leave a valid will, they may also be referred to as a *testator* if male, or a *testatrix* if female.

- The assets that a decedent owned at her death are collectively referred to as the decedent's *estate*. An estate can sometimes take on the qualities of a legal person—it is not uncommon to say that a certain asset is owned by "the estate of O." The property rights of this fictional legal person are managed by an actual person whose title depends on whether the decedent left a will. The instructions in a will are carried out by an *executor* (if male) or *executrix* (if female), designated as such in the will itself. An intestate estate is disposed of by a court-appointed *administrator* (if male) or *administratrix* (if female).

- The authority of an administrator or executor to dispose of the estate's assets is conferred by a *probate court*. When a valid will is filed with the probate court and deemed valid, the court will *admit the will to probate* (or *probate the will*), and will issue *letters testamentary* to the executor authorizing him to take possession of the estate's assets and dispose of them according to the will's instructions. If the decedent died intestate, the court will issue *letters of administration* to an administrator authorizing him to take possession of the estate's assets and dispose of them according to the laws of intestate succession.

- If the decedent did leave a valid will, it will typically contain instructions for transferring assets to various identified people or entities. The parties receiving the bequests are referred to as the will's *beneficiaries*, *devisees* (for real property), or *legatees* (for personal property). When a decedent passes property by will he or she is said to have *devised* that property. A property interest that the decedent has the power to transfer by will is said to be *devisable*.

- Sometimes a will fails to provide instructions for all the assets owned by the testator at death; in this case the unallocated assets are said to create a *partial intestacy*. When this happens, assets designated in the will are distributed according to the will's terms, while the estate's remaining assets are distributed according to the laws of intestate succession. In order to avoid partial intestacy, it is good practice to include a *residuary clause* in a will, disposing of all the assets of the decedent not devised through specific bequests. Such unenumerated assets are referred to as the *residuary estate*.

- If the decedent did not leave a valid will, her property will pass to her *heirs* (sometimes referred to as *heirs at law*). Heirs are those who are designated by law as successors to property that passes by intestate succession rather than by will. When heirs take such property, they are said to *inherit* it. A property interest that can pass by intestate succession is said to be *descendible*.

- Note that until the decedent actually dies, we don't know who her heirs are; rights of inheritance are allocated only to relatives of the decedent who *survive* her—who are still alive when the decedent dies. Thus, until a property owner dies, her relatives have no legally enforceable rights in her property under the laws of intestate succession. It is sometimes said that such relatives have a mere *expectancy*, and they are sometimes referred to as *heirs apparent*.

- Heirs under intestacy laws are drawn from various categories of relatives. In addition to spouses, there are *issue*: the direct descendants of the decedent (children, grandchildren, great-grandchildren, etc.); *ancestors* (parents, grandparents, great-grandparents, etc.); and *collaterals*: relatives who are not direct ancestors or descendants (siblings, aunts, uncles, nieces, nephews, cousins).

- If a person dies without a will and without any heirs at law, any property in their estate *escheats* to the state, which becomes its owner.

C.   Basic Estates and Future Interests

We will begin by examining two possessory estates—the **fee simple absolute** and the **life estate**—and two future interests (one of which you have already encountered)—the **reversion** and the **remainder**.

1.   The Fee Simple Absolute

The *fee simple absolute* is the most complete interest in land that the law will recognize. When we say that "O owns Blackacre" without any further qualification, what we actually mean is that O owns a *presently possessory fee simple absolute* in Blackacre. The key distinguishing characteristic of the fee simple absolute is that it has no inherent end—it is an estate of *indefinite duration*. It is descendible, devisable, and alienable *inter vivos*; so it can be *transferred* to a new owner, but it cannot be destroyed. At most, it can be carved up into lesser estates and interests for a while, and we will spend most of the rest of this chapter understanding how that happens.

At common law, as previously noted, the fee simple absolute was created by the formula: "to A and his heirs." That formula still works, but in modern usage it is sufficient to simply say "to A," and the use of such language in a conveyance from the owner of a fee simple absolute will be presumed to create a fee simple absolute in A.

2.   The Life Estate

The *life estate* is just what it sounds like: an estate that confers a right to possession for the life of its owner. The owner of a life estate is referred to as a *life tenant*. The life estate terminates by operation of law upon the owner's death (i.e., it ceases to exist). It is created by the formula: "to A for life." Because it must by definition end—we all have to die sometime—any land held by a life tenant must also be subject to a *future interest* in some other person. We'll explore what those future interests might be shortly.

Recall the legal principle of *nemo dat quod non habet* (or *nemo dat* for short), which we encountered in our discussion of good faith purchasers: a grantor cannot convey title to something she doesn't herself own. Following this principle, life estates are alienable *inter vivos* during the life of the life tenant, but obviously not devisable or descendible: they cease to exist upon the death of their owner, so the life tenant's estate has nothing to convey. *Nemo dat* also implies that the owner of an interest in real property cannot convey *more* than their interest; a life tenant cannot convey a fee simple absolute, for example. More to the point, if a life tenant A transfers their life estate to a grantee B, B cannot receive anything more than what A owns: a possessory estate that will terminate by operation of law *when A dies*. Because such an interest is measured by the life of someone other than its owner, it is called a *life estate pur autre vie* (literally, in Law French, "for another life"). A life estate *pur autre vie* can also be created explicitly, as by a grant "to A for the life of B."

We'll hold off on any further illustrative problems at this point, because we still need some exposition of what happens *after* a life tenant dies. The answer, as we've already noted, involves *future interests*.

3.   The Reversion

We encountered the reversion once before, when discussing leases as an introduction to the concept of a future interest. But reversions often arise in non-leasehold contexts too. Consider what happens when A, owning a life estate in Blackacre, dies. A's life estate terminates by operation of law; it simply ceases to exist and disappears. Who "owns" Blackacre now? It seems obvious that *somebody* must have a right to possession of the land, but it seems equally obvious that whoever that somebody is, they had *no right to possession* before A died. Whoever they are, during the term of A's life estate they must have held an interest that would entitle them to take possession at *some point in the future* (that is, a *future interest*).

There are two candidates for such an interest. We will begin with the most basic: the **reversion**. Suppose that O, owning a fee simple absolute in Blackacre, conveys Blackacre "to A for life," and says nothing more? What is the legal effect of this grant?

Based on the formula we just learned, it should be clear that A receives a life estate in Blackacre. But what other effects does the grant have on the legal rights of the parties? Think about the interest O held prior to the conveyance: the fee simple absolute. Remember that a fee simple absolute is an interest of *infinite duration*—it never ends. So when O starts with a possessory interest of infinite duration, and then gives away a life estate—whose duration is limited by a human lifespan—to A, *something was left over*. Specifically, O never gave away the right to possession of Blackacre from the day of A's death to the end of time. Whether meaning to or not, O gave away less of an interest in Blackacre than what he owned, meaning *he still holds some interest*. We call this type of interest—the residual interest left over when a grantor gives away less than they have—a *retained* interest.

This retained interest can't entitle O to possession during A's life—A has the exclusive right to possession as the life tenant. So O's interest must be a *future interest* during the term of A's life estate: an interest that will entitle O to possession *after the natural termination of the life estate*. As we discussed in the example of the lease, we call this kind of future interest a **reversion**. It is a *retained interest in the grantor*—created when a grantor conveys less than his entire interest—that will become possessory by operation of law upon the *natural termination* of the preceding estate. Colloquially, we say that Blackacre "reverts" to O. In some opinions, you will see the holder of a reversion referred to as a "reversioner."

A reversion can of course also be created explicitly, for example, if O conveys Blackacre "to A for life, then to O." In this case, O has explicitly created a life estate in A followed by a reversion in O.

4.   The Remainder

A **remainder** is a type of future interest created in someone *other than* the grantor. The distinguishing characteristic of the remainder is that—like a reversion—it *cannot cut short or divest any possessory estate*. (We will later encounter other future interests that can.) A remainder simply "remains," sitting around and waiting for the natural termination of the preceding possessory estate (be it a life estate or a lease), at which point the remainder will become possessory by operation of law. Suppose that O, owning a fee simple absolute in Blackacre, conveys Blackacre "to A for life, *and then to B*." Again, A would have a life estate, but now O has also affirmatively created a future interest in B. Because the future interest is created in someone *other than* the grantor, it isn't a reversion. And because it cannot cut short A's life estate (note the "and then" language), it must therefore be a **remainder**. Due to the persistence of dated gendered terms in legal discourse, you will often see the holder of a remainder referred to as a "remainderman," even today, regardless of that person's gender.

Future interests get a lot more complicated than this, but you now have enough to begin examining some problems that can arise from even this limited set of interests.

Questions

1. O, owner of a fee simple absolute in Blackacre, conveys Blackacre "to A for life, then to B for life." (Assume that both A and B are alive at the time of the grant.) What is the state of title in Blackacre?

    a. What will be the state of title if A dies, survived by B and O?

    b. What will be the state of title if B dies, survived by A and O?

    c. What will be the state of title if O dies, then A dies, then B dies?

2. What will be the state of title if, while O, A, and B are still alive, B conveys her interest to C?

    a. What will be the state of title if, after B conveys her interest to C, A dies, survived by B, C, and O?

  b. What will be the state of title if, after B conveys her interest to C, C dies, leaving D as his heir, and is survived by A, B, and O?

  c. What will be the state of title if, after B conveys her interest to C, B dies, survived by A, C, and O?

D. Construing Ambiguous Grants

We've recited a few formulas for creating the small number of common-law interests you've encountered. For example, "to A and his heirs" creates a fee simple absolute in A; "to B for life, then to C" creates a life estate in B and a remainder in C. But the actual language of documents conveying legal interests in real property don't always stick to the formula—especially (but unfortunately not exclusively) when they are drafted without the assistance of counsel. Consider the following case.

In the Estate of Dalton Edward Craigen
305 S.W.3d 825 (Ct. App. Tex. 2010)

HOLLIS HORTON, Justice.

We are asked to determine whether the trial court properly interpreted the dispository language in a holographic will. If the will is ambiguous, the applicable rules of will construction yield one result. If the will is unambiguous, the trial court was required to give effect to the express language of the will, and arguably should have reached a different result.

The trial court, in construing the testator's intentions under the will, found "[t]hat it was the intent of the [t]estator to leave his entire estate to his surviving wife in full." The trial court further found "[t]hat there was no intention to leave a life estate to her." In a single issue on appeal, the testator's adult children contend the testator intended to leave a life estate to his wife, and they argue that the remainder of the estate passed to them through the laws of descent and distribution. We find the will is ambiguous and hold that under the appropriate rules of will construction, the trial court properly construed the will. Accordingly, we affirm the judgment.

THE WILL

Dalton Edward Craigen left a holographic will that in its entirety stated:

Last Will & testament
Debbie gets everything till
she dies.
Being of sound mind & this
is my w. last will & testament.
I leave to my Wife Daphne
Craigen all p. real & personal property.
12–17–99 Dalton Craigen

CONTENTIONS OF THE PARTIES

The parties stipulated "[t]hat Debbie and Daphne named in Dalton Craigen's will are one and the same person." Brian Craigen and Sabrina Brumley, Craigen's adult children, argue that the testator's intent under the will is "crystal clear—the testator left everything (all of his real and personal property, his definition of 'everything') to his wife for as long as she lived." According to Brian and Sabrina, the dominant provision of the will (the first sentence) creates a life estate, and the will's third sentence can be harmonized with the will's first sentence by construing the third sentence to define the property that Craigen intended to include in his wife's life estate. Brian and Sabrina ask that we render a judgment in their favor by holding that Daphne received only a life estate under Craigen's will.

Daphne died on January 17, 2009. Yvonne Christian, the independent administratrix of Daphne's estate, argues we should affirm the trial court's judgment. According to Christian, the will is not ambiguous as it reflects Craigen's intent to leave his entire estate to Daphne.

RULES OF CONSTRUCTION

The rules involved in construing wills are well settled. "The primary object of inquiry in interpreting a will is determining the intent of the testator." *Gee v. Read*, 606 S.W.2d 677, 680 (Tex.1980). "The [testator's] intent must be drawn from the will, not the will from the intent." *Id.* We ascertain intent from the language found within the four corners of the will. "In construing the will, all its provisions should be looked to, for the purpose of ascertaining what the real intention of the [testator] was; and, if this can be ascertained from the language of the instrument, then any particular paragraph of the will which, considered alone, would indicate a contrary intent, must yield to the intention manifested by the whole instrument." *McMurray v. Stanley*, 69 Tex. 227, 6 S.W. 412, 413 (1887).

When a will has been drafted by a layperson who is not shown to be familiar with the technical meanings of certain words, courts do not place "'too great emphasis on the precise meaning of the language used where the will is the product of one not familiar with legal terms, or not trained in their use.'" *Gilkey v. Chambers*, 146 Tex. 355, 207 S.W.2d 70, 71 (1947) (quoting 69 C.J. Wills § 1120 (1934)). Instead, in arriving at the meaning intended by the layman-testator, courts refer to the popular meaning of the words the testator chose to use. In summary, the testator's intent, as gathered from the will as a whole, prevails against a technical meaning that might be given to certain words or phrases, unless the testator intended to use the word or phrase in the technical sense.

With respect to the creation of a life estate, no particular words are needed to create a life estate, but the words used must clearly express the testator's intent to create a life estate. A very strong presumption arises that when a person makes a will, the testator intended a complete disposition of his property. "[T]he very purpose of a will is to make such provisions that the testator will not die intestate." *Gilkey*, 207 S.W.2d at 73. When faced with ambiguity, and in applying that presumption, courts generally interpret wills to avoid creating an intestacy.

...In reconciling different parts of a will, the Texas Supreme Court has explained:

> Where, however, the language of one part of a will is not easily reconciled with that used in another, the principal and subordinate provisions should be construed in their due relation to each other, and the intent which is disclosed in the express clause ought to prevail over the language used in subsidiary provisions, unless modified or controlled by the latter. And a clearly expressed intention in one portion of the will will not yield to a doubtful construction in any other portion of the instrument.

Heller v. Heller, 114 Tex. 401, 269 S.W. 771, 774 (1925).

ANALYSIS

A will is ambiguous if it is capable of more than one meaning. Because Debbie and Daphne are in fact the same person, the ambiguity in Craigen's will becomes apparent. Why would Craigen in the first sentence grant his wife a life estate, but then in the concluding sentences bestow upon her all of his property? The resolution of that question by Craigen's children seems reasonable, as the last sentence could be construed to merely describe the property that Craigen intended to include in Daphne's life estate.

On the other hand, Craigen did not mention his children in his will and he made no provisions to expressly benefit them. Moreover, Brian and Sabrina's construction of Craigen's will would, if adopted, allow all of Craigen's property to pass under the laws of intestacy at Daphne's death.

Brian and Sabrina's construction assumes that Craigen, when writing his will, did not intend to completely dispose of his estate. The rule that Craigen did not likely intend to create an intestacy favors the construction of the will that the trial court adopted.

Brian and Sabrina contend that the will gave Daphne a life estate, but Craigen did not utilize those exact words in his will. Although no particular words are needed to create a life estate, the words used must clearly express the testator's intent to create one. In the absence of a remainderman clause, we are skeptical that Craigen used the phrase "till she dies" in a technical sense to create a life estate. Instead, Craigen likely intended to limit Daphne's use of his property; nevertheless, the will manifests an intent that she have his property in fee simple absolute. Consequently, although the first sentence in the will is susceptible to the interpretation that Craigen created a life estate, the will becomes ambiguous when, in the will's third sentence, Craigen expressly names Daphne as the beneficiary of all of his property and he makes no further provision for his estate upon her death.

We conclude that the will is reasonably capable of more than one meaning; therefore, we resort to the rules of construction that apply to ambiguous wills.... Craigen's will can be interpreted to avoid the intestacy certain to result under Brian and Sabrina's construction of the will. The potential intestacy is avoided if the phrase "till she dies" is interpreted as a conditional bequest. The third sentence then functions as intended to give Daphne all of Craigen's property in fee simple. The immediate vesting construction favors Daphne, the sole beneficiary named in Craigen's will. It also affords the phrase "till she dies" a nontechnical meaning.

We decline to apply the presumption that Craigen did not intend to disinherit his children when the will expressly states that Craigen gave all of his real and personal property to Daphne and when Brian and Sabrina offered no evidence regarding Craigen's situation and the circumstances surrounding the execution of the will. Taking the will as a whole, the dominant gift is all of Craigen's real and personal property, and he made that gift to his wife. As this is the dominant clause, Craigen's expressed intention prevails.

We hold that under the appropriate rules of will construction, the trial court correctly construed the will. We overrule the issue and affirm the judgment.

AFFIRMED.

Notes and Questions

1. **Holographic Wills.** A holographic will—a will handwritten by the testator—often presents a particular challenge for courts attempting to interpret it. Indeed, they are thought to be so problematic that about half of American jurisdictions refuse to recognize them as valid wills at all. *See* Stephen Clowney, *In Their Own Hand: An Analysis of Holographic Wills and Homemade Willmaking*, REAL PROPERTY, TRUST AND ESTATE LAW JOURNAL 27 (2008) (arguing that the defects of holographic wills, though real, are overstated). Lay testators attempting to settle their affairs without assistance of counsel often make legal or technical errors of various kinds, including errors of ambiguity such as the one that generated the litigation in *Craigen*.

2. **Presumptions and Rules of Construction.** The court reviews a number of rules of construction applied by courts in construing ambiguous grants. Most jurisdictions have similar rules of construction—sometimes promulgated by statute, other times judge-made. In *Craigen*, two rules in particular do considerable work: the presumption against intestacy and the clear-statement

rule for creation of a life estate. The latter rule is sometimes expressed in other jurisdictions as a presumption in favor of the largest estate the grantor could convey. *See, e.g., White v. Brown,* 559 S.W.2d 938, 939 (Tenn. 1977) (quoting Tenn. C. Ann. § 32-301) ("Every grant or devise of real estate, or any interest therein, shall pass all the estate or interest of the grantor or devisor, unless the intent to pass a less estate or interest shall appear by express terms, or be necessarily implied in the terms of the instrument.").

What justification is there for presuming that an ambiguous grant conveys a fee simple absolute rather than a life estate? Is it any different for the justification underlying the presumption against intestacy? Was *Craigen* an appropriate case for the application of these presumptions?

3. **Finding Ambiguity.** Are you convinced by the court's arguments that the language "till she dies" does not "clearly express the testator's will to create a life estate"? What do you think Dalton Craigen meant by this phrase?

4. **Dueling Presumptions.** The court mentions another rule of construction—the presumption against disinheritance—but declines to apply it. Why? Is its reason for following the presumption against intestacy but declining to follow the presumption against disinheritance persuasive? How is a court to decide when a presumption or other rule of construction applies and when it doesn't?

E.   Present vs. Future: The Doctrine of Waste

Even if we are very clear on the nature and allocation of possessory and future interests in a parcel of land, we soon run into a practical problem:

it can be difficult to protect the value of a future interest while someone else is in possession of the land, acting for most purposes as its owner. What if a life tenant burns down the structures on the parcel? Or decides to undertake a remodeling project that would make the parcel less desirable to future renters? Or fails to do anything about a leaky pipe, leading to a costly mold infestation? What if the possessor uses the property in such a way as to maximize its current value at the expense of its future value—depleting natural resources, wearing out buildings and fixtures without repairing or maintaining them—in ways that can't be recovered? Can it be wrongful—as a matter of property law—for a lawful possessor to use the possessed premises however they wish, for good or for ill?

The common law recognized that it *could* be wrongful for a present lawful possessor to take (or fail to take) certain acts with respect to land in their possession—if those acts affected the ability of a *future* possessor to enjoy their interest when their turn came around. To vindicate the rights of these future interest holders, the common law gave them a private right of action to enjoin, and obtain damages for, the acts and omissions of possessors that permanently decrease the value of the future interest. This was the action for waste.

Jackson v. Brownson
7 Johns. 227 (N.Y. Sup. Ct. 1810)

... THIS was an action of ejectment for a farm in Whitestown. The cause was tried at the Oneida circuit, the 5th June, 1809, before Mr. Justice Yates.

At the trial, the plaintiff gave in evidence the counterpart of a lease, dated the 3d September, 1790, from Philip Schuyler, [6] of Albany, to the defendant, for the premises in question, for the lives of the defendant, his wife, and Samuel Shaw, respectively. The farm contained 133 acres and a

---

[6] [Yes, that Philip Schuyler.—*eds.*]

half. The lease contained various covenants, reservations and conditions, among which was the following: …"And it is further conditioned on the part of the said lessee, that neither the said lessee, his executors, &c., … shall, at any time hereafter, commit any waste."

"And in case the said lessee, his, &c., shall not perform, fulfil, abide by, and keep all and every of the covenants and conditions herein covenanted and conditioned, &c., then in each of the said cases, it shall thenceforth be lawful for the lessor, his, &c., into the whole of the said premises, or into any part thereof, in the name of the whole, to reënter, and the same to have again, repossess and enjoy, as his or their former estate," &c.

The lessors were the heirs of Philip Schuyler; this action was brought to recover the possession of the south half of the premises, on the ground of forfeiture by a breach of the covenant; the lessee or his assigns having committed waste thereon by clearing and draining off the land more than a reasonable and due proportion of the wood. It was admitted that, at the date of the lease, the premises were wild and uncultivated, and covered throughout with a forest of heavy timber.

The plaintiff proved that the defendant occupied the south half of the premises, which were entirely cleared of wood, before the commencement of the suit; and that on the north half occupied by Shaw, the whole was cleared except about six or eight acres, on which more than half the wood and timber had been cut down and removed, before the commencement of the suit.

It was also proved, that a permanent supply of fuel, timber for buildings, and wood for fences, for the use of the demised premises, would require that, at least, thirty acres should have been preserved in wood.

… It was also proved, that about 12 years since, there were 35 acres of land covered with wood and timber on the premises, and about 12 acres of woodland, on that part in the possession of the defendant, only half of which was good for timber, ... that the defendant had cut no wood or timber on the part in his possession, except for fuel, fences, and building for the use of the farm, and which had been gradually cut, ... [that] the defendant had built a house on the premises, which was completed about four years since; and had used the farm in a husbandlike manner, and had carried on more materials for fences than he had taken off; that ... cleared land was of much greater value than land covered with wood and timber; and that good farms in the vicinity of the premises had not reserved more than 12 acres of woodland out of 100 acres....

The judge was of opinion, ... that the gradual clearing of that part in possession of the defendant, ... did not, in law, amount to waste; and he directed the jury to find a verdict for the defendant; and the jury found accordingly.

A motion was made to set aside the verdict and for a new trial, for the misdirection of the judge....

VAN NESS, J.

... It is a general principle, that the law considers every thing to be waste which does a permanent injury to the inheritance. Now, to say that cutting down the wood on almost every acre of the demised premises is not waste, within the spirit and meaning of the covenant in the case, is to say that no waste, by the destruction of wood, can be committed at all. We are bound to give effect to this covenant if we can, but to decide that the facts stated in the case do not constitute waste, would be destroying it almost altogether. That the destruction of the timber is a lasting injury to the reversion cannot be disputed. For this injury the lessors of the plaintiff may, at their election, bring covenant, or enter as for condition broken.

... It is true, that what would in England be waste, is not always so here. The covenant must be construed with reference to the state of the property at the time of the demise. The lessee undoubtedly had a right to fell part of the timber, so as to fit the land for cultivation; but it does not follow that he may, with impunity, destroy all the timber, and thereby essentially and permanently diminish the value of the inheritance. Good sense and sound policy, as well as the rules of good husbandry, require that the lessee should preserve so much of the timber as is indispensably necessary to keep the fences and other erections upon the farm in proper repair. The counsel for the defendant is mistaken when he says that lessees in England are prohibited from cutting wood upon the demised premises altogether; the prohibition, in principle, extends no further, in this respect, there than it does here. In England, that species of wood which is denominated timber shall not be cut down, because felling it is considered as an injury done to the inheritance, and therefore waste. Here, from the different state of many parts of our country, timber may, and must be cut down to a certain extent, but not so as to cause an irreparable injury to the reversioner. To what extent wood may be cut before the tenant is guilty of waste, must be left to the sound discretion of a jury, under the direction of the court, as in other cases.... The principle upon which all these cases were decided is that which I have before stated, namely, that whenever wood has been cut in such a manner as materially to prejudice the inheritance, it is waste; and that is the principle upon which I place the decision of this cause.

...My opinion, therefore, is, that the motion for setting aside the nonsuit, and granting a new trial, ought to be granted.

KENT, Ch. J., and THOMPSON, J., were of the same opinion.

SPENCER, J.
... The land was covered with heavy timber; and, for the use of it, the lessee was to pay a rent. The parties must, therefore, have intended that the lessee should be at liberty to fell the timber to a certain extent, at least, for agricultural purposes.

If the restriction to commit waste would operate to restrain the lessee from the use of the premises, it would be void, as repugnant to the grant. I shall have no difficulty in maintaining that, according to the common law of England, the lessee could not enjoy the land, nor derive any benefit from it, without the commission of waste; and should that point be established, this covenant must be rejected. The general definition of waste is, that it is a destruction in houses, gardens, trees, or other corporeal hereditaments, to the disherison of him in remainder or reversion. It is not every injury to lands that the law considers as waste, nor every act which injures the remainder-man, or the reversioner. To test this supposed waste, by considering the reversioner injured by the acts done, is not warranted by law; and, in point of fact, when the premises were cleared of the timber, cleared land was more valuable than wood land.... I insist that, according to the common law of England, no tenant can cut down timber, &c., or clear land for agricultural purposes; and that the quantity of timber cut down never enters into the consideration whether waste has or has not been committed; but that it is always tested by the fact of cutting timber, without the justifiable excuse of having done it.... A single tree cut down, without such justifiable cause, is waste as effectually as if a thousand had been cut down; and the reason is this, that such trees belong to the owner of the inheritance, and the tenant has only a qualified property in them for shade and shelter.

The doctrine of waste, as understood in England, is inapplicable to a new, unsettled country. ...The rule furnished by the common law is fixed and certain; and the lessor knows what wood he may cut, and for what purposes; but if a covenant not to commit waste is hereafter to be considered as a covenant to leave a sufficient quantity of land in wood, no lessee is safe. If the act of cutting timber on the premises, without the justifiable excuse already stated, was not waste, cutting more or less was immaterial. Under the covenant not to commit waste, we have no right to say some waste might be committed, and other waste might not; the covenant is inapt to the case, and if any remedy exists, it must lie in covenant. I am, therefore, against granting a new trial.

YATES, J., was of the same opinion.

Rule granted.

Notes and Questions

1. What exactly is the dispute between the majority and the dissent? Do they agree on the existence of a remedy for waste under New York law? On the definition of waste? On the applicability of waste doctrine to the lease before the court? On the remedy for waste?

2. Although this case deals with a lease for life—a peculiar hybrid estate that is not recognized in many jurisdictions—the doctrine of waste applies between freehold possessory estate holders and future interest holders just as it applies between leasehold tenants and landlords. Thus, even in the absence of a lease contract, Brownson could have been held liable for damages, or enjoined from felling any further timber, in an action for waste by the reversioners (if the jury concluded that it would indeed be waste for a possessor in Brownson's position to fell such timber).

3. **Forms of Waste.** Waste can be either *voluntary* or *permissive*. Volutnary waste (sometimes called *affirmative* waste) refers to *acts* of the holder of the possessory estate, such as erecting or demolishing a structure, or extracting non-replenishing natural resources. Permissive waste refers to *omisssions* of the holder of the possessory estate, such as failing to pay property taxes, or failure to make needed repairs. Either can support a claim for waste by the owner of a future interest whose rights are permanently devalued as a result. Which form of waste was at issue in *Jackson?*

4. **Theories of Waste.** One commentator argues that *Jackson* was the starting point for a peculiarly American departure from the English doctrine of waste deplored by the dissenters. In this view, "courts created the American law of waste for several reasons: to promote efficient use of resources that the English rule would have inhibited; to advance an idea of American landholding as a republican enterprise, free of feudal hierarchy; and perhaps to advance a belief that a natural duty to cultivate wild land underlay the Anglo-American claim to North America." Jedediah Purdy, *The American Transformation of Waste Doctrine: A Pluralist Interpretation*, 91 CORNELL L. REV. 653, 661 (2006). And indeed, the sensitivity of both opinions in *Jackson* to local conditions, the desirability of converting wild lands to agricultural use, and the sustainability of yeoman farming tend to support this pluralist view.

5. Law-and-economics theorists, in contrast, identify waste doctrine solely with the criterion of efficiency, and particularly the internalization of externalities and mitigation of holdout problems. As Judge Posner puts it: "The incentive of a life tenant is to maximize not the value of the property—that is, the present value of the entire stream of future earnings obtainable from it—but only the present value of the earnings stream obtainable during his expected lifetime. So he will, for example, want to cut timber before it has attained its mature growth even though the present value of the timber would be greater if the cutting of some or all of it were postponed; for the added value from waiting would inure to the remainderman.... [Moreover,] since tenant and remainderman would have only each other to contract with, the situation would be one of bilateral monopoly and transaction costs might be high." To avoid these problems, "[t]he law of waste forbids the tenant to reduce the value of the property as a whole by considering only his own interest in it." Richard A. Posner,

Comment on Merrill on the Law of Waste, 94 MARQ. L. REV. 1095-96 (2011).

A Note on Ameliorative Waste

What if, instead of doing something that *decreases* the value of the future interest, the holder of the possessory estate does something that *increases* the market value of the land, but in doing so changes the premises in ways the future interest holder doesn't like? Such alterations—known as *ameliorative waste*—have generated two types of approaches in the courts.

The first approach, adopted in *Melms v. Pabst Brewing Co.*, 79 N.W. 738 (Wisc. 1899), looks to the effect of the life tenant's actions on the market value of the parcel and whether those actions were necessitated by a change in conditions surrounding the parcel. In *Melms*, the Pabst Brewing Company had torn down an old mansion abutting a brewery it owned, mistakenly believing it owned the lot in fee simple when in fact it owned only the life estate of the widow Melms (the remainder being owned by her children). At the time of the demolition, the neighborhood around the house had become heavily industrialized, and had been re-graded such that the house stood 20-30 feet above street level and was worthless as a residential property. In these circumstances, the court held, whether the act of destroying the mansion and re-grading the lot on which it stood to street level constitutes waste is a question of fact for the jury. The court suggested that such actions will not constitute waste "when it clearly appears that the change will be, in effect, a meliorating change, which rather improves the inheritance than injures it." *Id.* at 739.

The second approach—more consistent with the common-law roots of waste doctrine—holds that *any* material change to real property caused by a lawful possessor without the consent of the holder of the future interest is waste, full stop. This approach informed the decision of the New York Supreme Court in *Brokaw v. Fairchild*, 237 N.Y.S. 6 (Sup. Ct. N.Y. Cty.

1929). In that case, the court refused to allow the life tenant of a stately mansion on New York's Fifth Avenue at 79th Street to tear the mansion down over the objections of the holders of future interests in the lot, even though living in the mansion had become cost-prohibitive and the neighborhood had become a prime location for luxury apartment buildings, which could be built and operated on the site for a substantial profit. The theory underlying this result is that a life tenant has merely the rights of use, not full rights of ownership, and that the holder of the future interest is entitled to take possession of the parcel in substantially the same condition as it existed at the time the future interest was created: "The act of the tenant in changing the estate, and whether or not such act is lawful or unlawful, i.e., whether the estate is so changed as to be an injury to the inheritance, is the sole question involved." *Id.* at 15.

The opinion in *Brokaw* generated a backlash in New York's reform-minded legislature, which enacted a statute redefining waste law along the lines set forth in *Melms*; that statute remains in force today. *See* N.Y. REAL PROP. ACTS. & PROCS. L. § 803. But interestingly, the opinion in *Melms* itself seems to have arisen from a number of questionable factual and legal pronouncements from the Wisconsin courts. The full, fascinating story is recounted in Thomas W. Merrill, Melms v. Pabst Brewing Co. *and the Doctrine of Waste in American Property Law*, 94 MARQ. L. REV. 1055 (2011). As of 2009, the rule of *Melms* was followed in most U.S. jurisdictions, while a small number continued to follow the rule of *Brokaw*. *Id.* at 1083 (citing Gina Cora, *Want Not, Waste Not: Contracting Around the Law of Ameliorative Waste* (Apr. 1, 2009) (Yale Law School Student Prize Papers: Paper 47), http://digitalcommons.law.yale.edu/ylsspps_papers/47).

Which of these two rules do you think is most consistent with the pluralist justifications for waste doctrine described by Professor Purdy? Which do you think is most consistent with the law-and-economics approach? Do either of the rules require some other form of justification, and if so, what might that justification be?

Co-ownership

More than one person can "own" a thing at any given time. Their rights will be exclusive as against the world, but not exclusive as against each other. When conflicts between them develop, or when the outside world seeks to regulate their behavior, we need to understand the nature and limits of their rights.

In this section, we will not address the form of concurrent ownership known as partnership, which we cover separately, though you will see some comparative references to it in the case that follows. Nor will we address corporations (in which ownership can be nearly infinitely divided and is separated from control; see Corporations section). These topics are dealt with in detail in business associations and similar courses. We will also not consider forms of concurrent ownership that are of purely historical interest, such as coparceny.[7] The main types of co-ownership we will consider are (1) tenancy in common, (2) joint tenancy, and (3) tenancy by the entireties, along with a brief look at (4) community property, a particular kind of co-ownership available in some states.

In the late 1980s, a sample of real estate records showed that about two-thirds of residential properties were held in some form of co-ownership. Evelyn Alicia Lewis, Struggling with Quicksand: The Ins and Outs of Cotenant Possession Value Liability and a Call for Default Rule Reform, 1994 Wis. L. Rev. 331; see also Carole Shammas et al., Inheritance in America from Colonial Times to the Present 171-72 (1987) (showing percentage of land held in joint tenancies rising from under 1% in 1890 to nearly 80% in 1960, then dropping to 63% in 1980); N. William Hines, Real Property Joint Tenancies: Law, Fact, and Fancy (51 Iowa L. Rev. 582 (1966) (finding that joint tenancies in Iowa rose from under 1% of

---

[7] A form of ownership only available to female heirs, when there were no male heirs.

acquisitions in 1933 to over a third of farm acquisitions and over half of urban acquisitions in 1964, almost exclusively by married couples); Yale B. Griffith, Community Property in Joint Tenancy Form, 14 Stan. L. Rev. 87 (1961) (study of California counties in 1959 and 1960 finding that married couples held over two-thirds of property as cotenants, 85% of which was as joint tenants).

Given that many justifications for the institution of private property rely on the idea that competing interests in property lead to inefficiency, waste, and conflict, it is perhaps surprising that so much private property is, in practice, owned by more than one person. If communal ownership is so inefficient, why do we recognize so many kinds of co-ownership?

A.   Types of Co-Ownership: Introduction

U.S. v. Craft
535 U.S. 274 (2002)

Justice O'CONNOR delivered the opinion of the Court.
... English common law provided three legal structures for the concurrent ownership of property that have survived into modern times: tenancy in common, joint tenancy, and tenancy by the entirety. The tenancy in common is now the most common form of concurrent ownership. The common law characterized tenants in common as each owning a separate fractional share in undivided property. Tenants in common may each unilaterally alienate their shares through sale or gift or place encumbrances upon these shares. They also have the power to pass these shares to their heirs upon death. Tenants in common have many other rights in the property, including the right to use the property, to exclude third parties from it, and to receive a portion of any income produced from it.

Joint tenancies were the predominant form of concurrent ownership at common law, and still persist in some States today. The common law characterized each joint tenant as possessing the entire estate, rather than a fractional share: "[J]oint-tenants have one and the same interest … held by one and the same undivided possession." Joint tenants possess many of the rights enjoyed by tenants in common: the right to use, to exclude, and to enjoy a share of the property's income. The main difference between a joint tenancy and a tenancy in common is that a joint tenant also has a right of automatic inheritance known as "survivorship." Upon the death of one joint tenant, that tenant's share in the property does not pass through will or the rules of intestate succession; rather, the remaining tenant or tenants automatically inherit it. Joint tenants' right to alienate their individual shares is also somewhat different. In order for one tenant to alienate his or her individual interest in the tenancy, the estate must first be severed – that is, converted to a tenancy in common with each tenant possessing an equal fractional share. Most States allowing joint tenancies facilitate alienation, however, by allowing severance to automatically accompany a conveyance of that interest or any other overt act indicating an intent to sever.

A tenancy by the entirety is a unique sort of concurrent ownership that can only exist between married persons. Because of the common-law fiction that the husband and wife were one person at law (that person, practically speaking, was the husband), Blackstone did not characterize the tenancy by the entirety as a form of concurrent ownership at all. Instead, he thought that entireties property was a form of single ownership by the marital unity. Neither spouse was considered to own any individual interest in the estate; rather, it belonged to the couple.

Like joint tenants, tenants by the entirety enjoy the right of survivorship. Also like a joint tenancy, unilateral alienation of a spouse's interest in entireties property is typically not possible without severance. Unlike joint tenancies, however, tenancies by the entirety cannot easily be severed unilaterally. Typically, severance requires the consent of both spouses, or the ending of the marriage in divorce. At common law, all of the other rights associated with the entireties property belonged to the husband: as the head of the household, he could control the use of the property and the exclusion of others from it and enjoy all of the income produced from it. The husband's control of the property was so extensive that, despite the rules on alienation, the common law eventually provided that he could unilaterally alienate entireties property without severance subject only to the wife's survivorship interest.

With the passage of the Married Women's Property Acts in the late 19th century granting women distinct rights with respect to marital property, most States either abolished the tenancy by the entirety or altered it significantly. Michigan's version of the estate is typical of the modern tenancy by the entirety. Following Blackstone, Michigan characterizes its tenancy by the entirety as creating no individual rights whatsoever: "It is well settled under the law of this State that one tenant by the entirety has no interest separable from that of the other .... Each is vested with an entire title." And yet, in Michigan, each tenant by the entirety possesses the right of survivorship. Each spouse – the wife as well as the husband – may also use the property, exclude third parties from it, and receive an equal share of the income produced by it. Neither spouse may unilaterally alienate or encumber the property, although this may be accomplished with mutual consent. Divorce ends the tenancy by the entirety, generally giving each spouse an equal interest in the property as a tenant in common, unless the divorce decree specifies otherwise....

B.   Tenancy in Common

Tenancy in common is the modern default form of co-ownership, unless a contrary intent is expressed; usually that intent must be in writing. All tenants in common are entitled to possession and use of the property. Only partition, discussed below, results in separate and divided interests.

Tenants in common need not own equal shares. If there is no document or legal rule of inheritance specifying their shares, courts will often look to the contribution of the cotenants to the purchase in order to determine appropriate shares.

1.   Rights and Duties of Tenants in Common

Concurrent owners can generally contract among themselves to allocate the various benefits and burdens of ownership as they see fit. But in the absence of such agreement, there are several default rules regarding the rights and obligations that arise between cotenants of property.

This system of default rules begins with the premise that each cotenant is entitled to all the rights of ownership in the entire co-owned parcel. Thus, for example, cotenants do not necessarily have the right to compromise other cotenants' right to exclude. If one cotenant objects to a police search and the other would allow it, the objecting cotenant prevails. A warrantless search is not allowed unless an exception to the warrant requirement applies. Georgia v. Randolph, 547 U.S. 103 (2006).

The implications of multiple equal and undivided interests in a co-owned parcel become far more complicated with respect to other rights of ownership—particularly the rights of possession and use. If all co-owners are equally entitled to possession and use of the whole parcel, what happens when more than one cotenant decides to assert those rights at the same time? Is it physically possible to put co-equal rights of all concurrent owners into practice? And if not, what if any obligation does a cotenant in possession owe to cotenants out of possession? Consider the following case:

Martin v. Martin
878 S.W. 2d 30 (Ky. Ct. App. 1994)

... Garis and Peggy own an undivided one-eighth interest in a tract of land in Pike County. This interest was conveyed to Garis by his father, Charles Martin, in 1971. Appellees, Charles and Mary Martin, own a life estate in the undivided seven-eighths of the property for their joint lives, with remainder to appellants.

In 1982, Charles Martin improved a portion of the property and developed a four lot mobile home park which he and Mary rented. In July of 1990, Garis and Peggy moved their mobile home onto one of the lots. It is undisputed that Garis and Peggy expended no funds for the improvement or maintenance of the mobile home park, nor did they pay rent for the lot that they occupied.

In 1990, Garis and Peggy filed an action which sought an accounting of their claimed one-eighth portion of the net rent received by Charles and Mary from the lots. The accounting was granted, however, the judgment of the trial court required appellants to pay "reasonable rent" for their occupied lot. It is that portion of the judgment from which this appeal arises.

The sole issue presented is whether one cotenant is required to pay rent to another cotenant. Appellants argue that absent an agreement between cotenants, one cotenant occupying premises is not liable to pay rent to a co-owner. Appellees respond that a cotenant is obligated to pay rent when that cotenant occupies the jointly owned property to the exclusion of his co-owner.

Appellants and appellees own the subject property as tenants in common. The primary characteristic of a tenancy in common is unity of possession by two or more owners. Each cotenant, regardless of the size of his fractional share of the property, has a right to possess the whole.

The prevailing view is that an occupying cotenant must account for outside rental income received for use of the land, offset by credits for maintenance and other appropriate expenses. The trial judge correctly ordered an accounting and recovery of rent in the case sub judice.

However, the majority rule on the issue of whether one cotenant owes rent to another is that a cotenant is not liable to pay rent, or to account to other cotenants respecting the reasonable value of the occupancy, absent an ouster or agreement to pay.

The trial court relied erroneously on Smither v. Betts, Ky., 264 S.W.2d 255 (1954), for its conclusion that appellants were "obligated to pay seven-eighths of the reasonable rental for the use of the lot they occupy." In *Smither*, one cotenant had exclusive possession of jointly owned property by virtue of a lease with a court-appointed receiver and there was an agreement to pay rent. That clearly is not the case before us. There was no lease or any other agreement between the parties.

The appellees reason that the award of rent was proper upon the premise that Garis and [Peggy] ousted their cotenants. While the proposition that a cotenant who has been ousted or excluded from property held jointly is entitled to rent is a valid one, we are convinced that such ouster must amount to exclusive possession of the entire jointly held property. We find support for this holding in Taylor, supra, in which the Court stated at 807-08:

> But, however this may be, running throughout all the books will be found two essential elements which must exist before the tenant sought to be charged is liable. These are: (a) That the tenant sought to be charged and who is claimed to be guilty of an ouster must assert exclusive claim to the property in himself, thereby necessarily including a denial of any interest or any right or title in the supposed ousted tenant; (b) he must give notice to this effect

to the ousted tenant, or his acts must be so open and notorious, positive and assertive, as to place it beyond doubt that he is claiming the entire interest in the property.

We conclude that appellants' occupancy of one of the four lots did not amount to an ouster. To hold otherwise is to repudiate the basic characteristic of a tenancy in common that each cotenant shares a single right to possession of the entire property and each has a separate claim to a fractional share.

Accordingly, the judgment of the Pike Circuit Court is reversed as to the award of rent to the appellees.

Notes and Questions

1. **Recurring conflicts between cotenants**. Rules for cotenant liability are incoherent and unsatisfactory despite centuries of litigated cases. Evelyn Lewis speculates that "cotenant conflicts receive little attention from property law reformers" because they involve "'one-shotters' – parties who rarely litigate, who are predominantly members of the obedient middle-class and who suffer quietly the rules of law they were too unsophisticated to know or consider in advance of the conflict." Evelyn Lewis, *Struggling with Quicksand: The Ins and Outs of Cotenant Possession Value Liability*, 1994 WIS. L. REV. 331.

   Management conflicts can arise easily because, unlike in a trust or a corporation (both forms of joint ownership) there is no one with the legal right to manage the property on behalf of the other owners, and a cotenant who takes on the burden of management is not entitled to be paid for her services to the others. See Combs v. Ritter, 223 P.2d 505 (Cal. Ct. App. 1950). Although each cotenant has the right to possess and benefit from the property, and the duty to pay her share of necessary expenses such as taxes, there is no mechanism for group decision-making. If co-owners can't agree, they may simply have to split – by divorce followed by a transfer to one party or sale in the case of tenancy by the entirety and community property; by severance and partition for joint tenants; and by partition for tenants in common. Short of partition, which involves selling or physically dividing the property, the only assistance the courts offer cotenants is a claim for accounting for rents or profits received by another cotenant, or a claim for contribution for payments of another cotenant's share of taxes, mortgage payments, and necessary maintenance expenses.

2. **Ouster.** Denial of a right to possession constitutes ouster, and the damages are the non-possessing cotenant's share of the rental value of the property. Harlan v. Harlan, 168 P.2d 985 (Cal. Ct. App. 1946) (damages for ouster are rental value).

Evelyn Lewis concludes that, as with adverse possession, the standard for what constitutes an ouster is so manipulable that courts can reach almost any result on any given set of facts. See, e.g., Cox v. Cox, 71 P.3d 1028 (Idaho 2003) (tenant in common was ousted and was entitled to ½ of the fair rental value of the house occupied by her brother when he told her he was selling the house and that she "had better find a place to live"); Mauch v. Mauch, 418 P.2d 941 (Okla. 1966) (cotenants in possession of family farm ousted widowed sister-in-law by telling her they "didn't want to have her on the place" and that she "was not to come back"); but see Fitzgerald v. Fitzgerald, 558 So.2d 122 (Fla. Dist. Ct. App. 1990) (ex-wife didn't oust ex-husband by telling him to leave the family home and that otherwise "she'd call the law").

What if one cotenant denies that the other has any title to the property? Estate of Duran, 66 P.3d 326 (N.M. 2003) (cotenant lived on the property kept silent or gave evasive answers to questions about his use of the property; this was not ouster where he "never expressly told [the other cotenants] that he claimed to own their portions of the property"). Purporting to convey full title to the property is an ouster, since it sets up a claim for adverse possession by the grantee. Whittington v. Cameron, 52 N.E.2d 134 (Ill. 1943).

What if one cotenant seeks to use a portion of the land, and the other prevents her from doing so, perhaps by building a structure on it?

3. **Constructive Ouster.** What if the property is a single-family home and the co-tenants are recently divorced or separated? Hertz v. Hertz, 657 P. 2d 1169 (N.M. 1983) (applying theory of "constructive ouster" to require payment of half of fair rental value); Stylianopoulos v. Stylianopoulos, 455 N.E.2d 477 (Mass. Ct. App. 1983) (divorce constituted ouster, so ex-wife had to pay fair rental value to ex-husband); In re Marriage of Watts, 217 Cal. Rptr. 301 (Ct. App. 1985) (separated spouse must reimburse community for exclusive use of house); Palmer v. Protrka, 476 P.2d 185 (Or. 1970) (if, as a practical matter, the couple can't live together, requiring the cotenant in possession to pay half of fair rental value most closely matches parties' intentions).

Suppose a woman moves out of her family home after being physically assaulted by her husband. The husband begs her to come back, but she refuses. After two years, when their divorce becomes final, the ex-wife sues for half the fair rental value of the house during the two-year period she was out of possession. Should she win? What if, instead of the wife leaving, she ejects the husband and tells him not to come back, and two years later, after she's awarded the house in the divorce, he sues for half the fair rental value of the house during the two-year period he was out of possession? See Cohen v. Cohen, 746 N.Y.S2d 22 (App. Div. 2002) (no right to rent for period during which a court protective order barred cotenant from the property due to his assaultive conduct).

The majority rule is against constructive ouster, in the absence of physical exclusion. See, e.g., Reitmeier v. Kalinoski, 631 F. Supp. 565 (D.N.J. 1986) ("[T]he mere fact that defendant does not wish to live with plaintiff on the premises is of no import. What counts is that she could physically live on the premises.").

Which rule is better? If you were advising a client in a divorce, how would you deal with co-owned property?

What if the property is so small that physical occupation by all cotenants is impracticable? Some courts will also call this a "constructive ouster" of the cotenants out of possession. Capital Fin. Co. Delaware Valley, Inc. v. Asterbadi, 942 A.2d 21 (N.J. Super. Ct. App. Div. 2008) (finding that a bank that was a cotenant through foreclosure with the wife of the defaulting mortgagor was constructively ousted from a single-family home).

4. **Contribution: sharing the costs.** "[T]he protection of the interest of each cotenant from extinction by a tax or foreclosure sale imposes on each the duty to contribute to the extent of his proportionate share the money required to make such payments." 2 AMERICAN LAW OF PROPERTY §6.17. Because failure to pay carrying costs increases the risk that the asset will be lost to all cotenants, every concurrent owner has an obligation to pay her share. *See also* Beshear v. Ahrens, 709 S.W.2d 60 (Ark. 1986) (allowing contribution for mortgage payments and property taxes as "expenditures necessarily made for the protection of the common property").

The majority rule is that cotenants out of possession need not share in the costs of repairs in the absence of an agreement to do so. The idea is that questions "of how much should be expended on repairs, their character and extent, and whether as a matter of business judgment such expenditures are justified," are too uncertain for judicial resolution. 2 AMERICAN LAW OF PROPERTY §6.18. But then, in a partition action, cotenants who pay for repairs will get credit for them – does that make sense? Further, some courts will allow contribution for "necessary" repairs. Palanza v. Lufkin, 804 A.2d 1141 (Me. 2002) (finding contribution towards necessary repairs justified, even though some of the repairs had cosmetic effects). Some jurisdictions require a cotenant to provide her fellow cotenants with notice and opportunity to object to the repairs in order to be entitled to contribution. Anderson v. Joseph, 26 A.3d 1050 (Md. Ct. Spec. App. 2011) (denying contribution for repairs that resulted from "massive flooding" for failure to provide notice).

5. **Accounting: the right to share in profits**. Cotenants who allow others to use the land, whether to exploit resources or to rent, must give other cotenants their shares of any consideration received from the third-party users.

Recall that in at least some contexts one cotenant cannot unilaterally exercise the right to exclude of the other cotenants. But that isn't always true with respect to productive uses of land by third parties with permission of one cotenant. To be sure, in some states, a lease from only one co-owner is void and the lessee can be ejected. But in other states, one cotenant can lease his interest, subject only to a duty to account to the non-leasing cotenants for net profits. Swartzbaugh v. Sampson, 54 P.2d 73 (Cal. Ct. App. 1936). Where there is such a duty, to whom does the lessee owe rent? The answer is that she only owes rent to the leasing cotenant, unless she ousts the other cotenants. Those other cotenants must look to a contribution action against the leasing cotenant.

The usual rule is that cotenants must account for the raw value of resources they extract themselves, but particularly bad misbehavior by a cotenant may lead to an award of the processed value. Kirby Lumber Co. v. Temple Lumber Co. 83 S.W.2d 638 (Tex. 1935) (raw value of timber where timber was taken in good faith); cf. White v. Smyth, 214 S.W.2d 967 (Tex. 1948) (cotenant who mined asphalt without consent from other cotenants had to account for net profits, although he took no more than his one-ninth interest – resource could not be partitioned in kind because the quality and quantity of asphalt varied sharply across the parcel in ways that could not be easily determined; cotenant couldn't take the most easily mined resources for himself and make his own partition).

Absent an ouster, an accounting usually just requires the cotenant to share the actual value received, not the fair market value. Suppose a lease claims to be nonexclusive and to only lease one cotenant's share, and is for half of the fair market rental value of the property. What should happen when the other cotenant seeks an accounting? See Annot., 51 A.L.R.2d 388 (1957). Suppose the lease is made by one cotenant to spite or harm another? Cf. George v. George, 591 S.W.2d 655 (Ark. Ct. App. 1979) (where 99-year lease carried nominal rent and the court found an intent to defraud the cotenant, the lease was set aside).

6. **Tenants in possession; tenants out of possession.** *Martin* applies the majority rule that—absent ouster—a cotenant in possession need not pay anything to cotenants out of possession if she lives on and farms the land, absent an ouster. DesRoches v. McCrary, 24 N.W.2d 511 (Mich. 1946) (no duty of cotenant in

possession to pay rent to other cotenants). Reciprocally, there is generally no ouster if one cotenant requests her share of the fair rental value of the land from the occupying cotenant, and the occupying cotenant denies the request. Von Drake v. Rogers, 996 So. 2d 608 (La. Ct. App. 2008) ("A co-owner in exclusive possession may be liable for rent, but only beginning on the date another co-owner has demanded *occupancy* and been refused.") (emphasis added). But a few cases hold that denying a request for rent constitutes an ouster. Eldridge v. Wolfe, 221 N.Y.S. 508 (1927).

Why might courts have developed a practice of requiring cotenants to account for profits from mining and cutting lumber, but not for profits from their own farming or residential uses of co-owned property? Logically, the cotenant in possession should have to pay – she is receiving a benefit from using the land, the fair market rental value of the property, and the other cotenants are not. As *Martin* itself proves, if she did rent the land to a third party, she would be required to share that benefit with the other co-owners. This rule creates an incentive for the cotenant to stay in possession rather than renting the land out, even if renting to a third party would be more efficient overall.

7. **The relationship between contribution and accounting**. If one cotenant occupies the property, with no ouster, and seeks contribution from the non-occupant for his share of the taxes and insurance, can the non-occupant offset the amounts due by the value of living on the property to the occupant? Many courts say yes. See, e.g., Barrow v. Barrow, 527 So. 2d 1373 (Fla. 1988) (occupant can only recover contribution if non-occupant's proportionate share of expenses is greater than the value of occupying the property); Esteves v. Esteves, 775 A.2d 163 (N.J. Super. Ct. App. Div. 2001) (parents who occupied house for 18

years were entitled to be reimbursed by their son for half of the expenses of mortgage and maintenance, but the son was allowed to set off the amount equal to the reasonable value of the parents' sole occupancy). This view is not strictly consistent with the majority rule that non-ousting tenants are not liable to non-possessing cotenants for rent, because it means that the occupant is essentially paying the non-occupant for being able to live on the land. Is this rule, which will often keep much actual cash from changing hands nonetheless fair?

The minority view is that no defensive offset is available against a cotenant in possession, absent ouster. Yakavonis v. Tilton, 968 P.2d 908 (Wash. Ct. App. 1998); Baird v. Moore, 141 A.2d 324 (N.J. App. Div. 1958) (cotenant out of possession may not offset value of occupation if cotenant's possession is not adverse). Which rule makes more logical sense? More practical sense?

Basically, courts often have enough flexibility to rule in the direction the equities point – finding that contribution is or isn't available. The need to balance the harms from imposition of unexpected costs on cotenants out of possession with the harms to the property's value from negligent co-owners also gives courts flexibility. Ultimately, because partition is always available to cotenants who truly can't agree, it makes sense for courts to point them towards partition if they're fighting over maintenance and repairs.

In *Martin*, when calculating Garis and Peggy's 1/8th share of the "net rent," what expenses should be deducted? Can they be required to pay a share of the costs of developing the mobile home park, such as putting in sewage lines and electrical connections? Note that a cotenant is generally not entitled to contribution from other cotenants for the costs of improving the property (see note

8 below). But, on partition, the improver is entitled to the part of the property that's been improved, or in case of sale to the lesser of (1) the increase in value due to the improvement or (2) the cost of the improvement. Should that rule be applied in an accounting as well?

Lewis suggests that courts use ouster to enagage in the "equitable second-guessing that so often blurs crystalline rules." Compare Spiller v. Mackereth, 334 So. 2d 859 (Ala. 1976) (lock change wasn't ouster), with Morga v. Friedlander, 680 P.2d 1267 (Ariz. Ct. App. 1984) (lock change was ouster). In effect, courts use ouster, plus the majority rule allowing offset of the value of an occupying cotenant's possession in an action for contribution, to nullify the formal rule that any cotenant can occupy the land rent-free, regardless of the size of his or her share, and still seek contribution for necessary expenses.

8. **Quasi-fiduciary duties of good faith.** ~~Cotenants are fiduciaries for each other, at least if they receive their interests in the same will or grant, or through the same inheritance.~~ Poka v. Holi, 357 P.2d 100 (Haw. 1960) (cotenants have fiduciary obligation to give other cotenants adequate notice of adverse claims to the property); but see Wilson v. S.L. Rey, Inc., 21 Cal. Rptr. 2d 552 (Ct. App. 1993) (cotenants who acquire interests at different times by different instruments have no fiduciary relationship).

If one co-tenant buys the property at a tax sale or a foreclosure sale, the title is shared with the other co-tenants: for these purposes, the co-tenant is a fiduciary for the other co-tenants. Johnson v. Johnson, 465 S.W.2d 309 (Ark. 1971); but cf. Stevenson v. Boyd, 96 P. 284 (Cal. 1908) (finding assertion of cotenant's claim barred by laches after four-year delay). However, the purchasing co-tenant can seek contribution from the others, so that they bear their fair share of the cost of removing the lien or mortgage. Why would the courts create such a fiduciary duty? What is the abusive practice that they fear?

9. **Improvements.** Any cotenant has the right to make improvements to the property, but other cotenants are not required to contribute. SeeKnight v. Mitchell, 240 N.E.2d 16 (Ill. Ct. App. 1968) (cotenant couldn't seek contribution for developing and running oil wells, though he could set off necessary operating expenses in other cotentant's action for accounting of his profits); Johnie L. Price, *The Right of a Coteanant to Reimbursement for Improvements to the Common Property*, 18 BAYLOR L. REV. 111 (1966).

In most states, the interests of the improver will be protected if that won't harm the interests of the other cotenants. This usually allows the improver to recoup the added value, if any, resulting from his improvements on partition, or in accounting for rents and profits. Graham v. Inlow, 790 S.W.2d 428 (Ark. 1990). But if improvements fail to pay off, the improver is not compensated – he bears all the risk. A few cases limit recovery to the smaller of the amount of value added by an improvement or its costs. The risk is borne by the improver, but the rewards are shared. Which rule makes more sense?

10. **Waste.** If one cotenant damages the property or harms its value, other cotenants may have claims for waste. While the ordinary remedy for waste is treble damages, courts will normally just hold the tenant in possession accountable for net profits from exploiting the property, as explained above in the discussion of removing timber and similar resources. CASNER, AMERICAN LAW OF PROPERTY, §6.15. What effects does that rule have on the use of land?

Waste claims are correspondingly difficult to win. Davis v. Byrd, 185 S.W.2d 866 (Mo. 1945) (mining by one cotenant isn't waste as long as the other cotenants aren't excluded and the miner doesn't willfully or negligently injure the land); Hihn v. Peck, 18 Cal. 640 (1861) (cotenant may remove valuable timber "to an extent corresponding to [his] share of the estate" without commiting waste); Prairie Oil & Gas Co. v. Allen, 2 F.2d 566 (9th Cir. 1924) (cotenant can produce oil without other cotenants' consent, but cannot exclude other cotenants from exercising the same right). Consider whether time matters: should the standard for what constitutes waste vary depending on whether the other interest-holders have present interests (and could act now to reap their own benefits, albeit at greater cost than waiting) or future interests (and thus can only wait for their ownership interests to attach)?

11. **Adverse possession by cotenants against other cotenants**. Because each cotenant has the right to possession, it can be difficult for one cotenant to possess adversely to another. Under New York law, a cotenant must have exclusive possession for ten years before the statutory adverse possession can even *begin* to run against other cotenants. Myers v. Bartholomew, 697 N.E.2d 160 (N.Y. 1998). After all, the fact that someone else is living on and using the land lacks its ordinary significance to cotenants. Ex parte Walker, 739 So. 2d 3 (Ala. 1999) (cotenant's redemption of property at tax sale in 1934, payment of all property taxes, exclusive possession for over 50 years, demolition of old buildings, and harvesting of timber did not show adverse possession against other cotenants); Tremayne v. Taylor, 621 P.2d 408 (Idaho 1980) ("A cotenant who claims to have adversely possessed the interest of his cotenants must prove that the fact of adverse possession was 'brought home' to the cotenants."); Hare v. Chisman, 101 N.E.2d 268 (Ind. 1951) (husband's sole possession of house after

wife died was not adverse to his cotenants, her heirs, since it "was not an unnatrual act of them to permit their father to occupy this property, collect the income, pay the expense, and enjoy the surplus"); West v. Evans, 175 P.2d 219 (Cal. 1946) (cotenant out of possession must have either actual or constructive notice of hostility; recordation of a deed isn't sufficient notice); Official Code Ga. Ann. §44-6-123 (allowing cotenant to gain title by adverse possession if she "effects an actual ouster, retains exclusive possession after demand, or gives [her] cotenant express notice of adverse possession").

Adverse possession is, however, not entirely impossible in these circumstances. *See* Johnson v. James, 377 S.W.2d 44 (Ark. 1964) (presumption against adversity is even stronger when cotenants are related, though presumption was overcome through sole possession for 36 years, where cotenants knew of a will purportedly granting occupant sole possession and said nothing); McCree v. Jones, 430 N.E.2d 676 (Ill. Ct. App. 1981) (finding in favor of claimant who'd been in possession for thirty years under a quitclaim deed purporting to give title to the entire property).

12. **Intangible assets.** In the U.S., "joint authorship" occurs when two or more authors contribute to the creation of a unitary work of authorship, such as a song with music written by one author and lyrics written by another. (Here, "joint" doesn't mean what it means in real property. There is no right of survivorship, so the ownership rights behave more like what you know as tenancy in common.) Courts have interpreted copyright law to impose a default rule, absent explicit agreement, that each joint author owns an equal share of the resulting work, even if her contribution was substantially less than that of other authors. This rule, which is not mandated by the statute, has led courts to be extremely reluctant to find joint authorship when there is one clear

"dominant" author and someone else seeks to be recognized as a co-author. Because copyrights are intangible, they cannot be partitioned, nor can there be an ouster of one co-author by another. Instead, each co-owner can grant a nonexclusive license to other people to use the work—whether that means putting a song on a record, using a sample of it in a new song, or using it in a television show. This right to license is subject only to a duty to account to the other co-owners for their shares of the resulting profits. An exclusive license requires the agreement of all the co-owners acting together.

Suppose one co-author, angry at her co-author, grants Quentin Tarantino a nonexclusive license to turn their book into a movie for $1, and duly gives her co-author fifty cents. Because of this license, no other moviemaker will buy the rights, fearing competition from Tarantino's movie. Has the licensor committed waste? Would it matter if, instead of acting out of malice, the co-author granted the $1 license because she believed in Tarantino's vision for the film and only a low price would induce him to take on the book as his next project? Do tenancy in common rules work for property that can't be exclusively possessed?

13. **Concluding thoughts: crystals and mud.** Transaction costs – the costs of managing the property and getting cotenants to agree – can be very high among cotenants, as compared to the costs of having a manager with authority to make decisions for the group. (For example, consider the issue of approving a particular tenant who wishes to rent the property and have exclusive possession.) The actively engaged cotenant who rents to a third party gets only some of the gain, but takes most of the risk. After all, if the renter turns into a nightmare who trashes the place, the cotenant who rented the property will be liable for any harm; but the other cotenants might sue to share in any gains that materialize.

Professor Carol Rose argues that courts sometimes impose equitable duties – muddy rules – on parties in order to replicate the results that would have occurred had they trusted each other and behaved fairly and decently towards one another. Thus, our rules about co-ownership are not just rules about economic efficiency, but about how people should behave. *See generally* Carol Rose, *Crystals and Mud in Property Law*, 40 STAN. L. REV. 577 (1988). Does this help you make any sense of the co-ownership rules?

2.   Partition

Delfino v. Vealencis
436 A.2d 27 (Conn. 1980)

ARTHUR H. HEALEY, Associate Justice.

The central issue in this appeal is whether the Superior Court properly ordered the sale, pursuant to General Statutes s 52-500,[1] of property owned by the plaintiffs and the defendant as tenants in common.

The plaintiffs, Angelo and William Delfino, and the defendant, Helen C. Vealencis, own, as tenants in common, real property located in Bristol, Connecticut. The property consists of an approximately 20.5 acre parcel of land and the dwelling of the defendant thereon. The plaintiffs own an undivided 99/144 interest in the property, and the defendant owns a 45/144 interest. The defendant occupies the dwelling and a portion of the

---

[1] General Statutes s 52-500 states: "Sale of Real or Personal Property Owned by Two or More. Any court of equitable jurisdiction may, upon the complaint of any person interested, order the sale of any estate, real or personal, owned by two or more persons, when, in the opinion of the court, a sale will better promote the interests of the owners.... A conveyance made in pursuance of a decree ordering a sale of such land shall vest the title in the purchaser thereof, and shall bind the person entitled to the life estate and his legal heirs and any other person having a remainder interest in the lands; but the court passing such decree shall make such order in relation to the investment of the avails of such sale as it deems necessary for the security of all persons having any interest in such land."

land, from which she operates a rubbish and garbage removal business.[3] Apparently, none of the parties is in actual possession of the remainder of the property. The plaintiffs, one of whom is a residential developer, propose to develop the property, upon partition, into forty-five residential building lots.

In 1978, the plaintiffs brought an action in the trial court seeking a partition of the property by sale with a division of the proceeds according to the parties' respective interests. The defendant moved for a judgment of in-kind partition and the appointment of a committee to conduct said partition. The trial court, after a hearing, concluded that a partition in kind could not be had without "material injury" to the respective rights of the parties, and therefore ordered that the property be sold at auction by a committee and that the proceeds be paid into the court for distribution to the parties.

On appeal, the defendant claims essentially that the trial court's conclusion that the parties' interests would best be served by a partition by sale is not supported by the findings of subordinate facts, and that the court improperly considered certain factors in arriving at that conclusion. In addition, the defendant directs a claim of error to the court's failure to include in its findings of fact a paragraph of her draft findings.

General Statutes s 52-495 authorizes courts of equitable jurisdiction to order, upon the complaint of any interested person, the physical partition of any real estate held by tenants in common, and to appoint a committee for that purpose.[7] When, however, in the opinion of the court a sale of

---

[3] The defendant's business functions on the property consist of the overnight parking, repair and storage of trucks, including refuse trucks, the repair, storage and cleaning of dumpsters, the storage of tools, and general office work. No refuse is actually deposited on the property.

[7] If the physical partition results in unequal shares, a money award can be made from one tenant to another to equalize the shares.

the jointly owned property "will better promote the interests of the owners," the court may order such a sale under s 52-500.

It has long been the policy of this court, as well as other courts, to favor a partition in kind over a partition by sale. ... Due to the possible impracticality of actual division, this state, like others, expanded the right to partition to allow a partition by sale under certain circumstances. The early decisions of this court that considered the partition-by-sale statute emphasized that "(t)he statute giving the power of sale introduces ... no new principles; it provides only for an emergency, when a division cannot be well made, in any other way. The court later expressed its reason for preferring partition in kind when it stated: "(A) sale of one's property without his consent is an extreme exercise of power warranted only in clear cases." Ford v. Kirk, 41 Conn. 9, 12 (1874). Although under General Statutes s 52-500 a court is no longer required to order a partition in kind even in cases of extreme difficulty or hardship; it is clear that a partition by sale should be ordered only when two conditions are satisfied: (1) the physical attributes of the land are such that a partition in kind is impracticable or inequitable; and (2) the interests of the owners would better be promoted by a partition by sale. Since our law has for many years presumed that a partition in kind would be in the best interests of the owners, the burden is on the party requesting a partition by sale to demonstrate that such a sale would better promote the owners' interests.

The defendant claims in effect that the trial court's conclusion that the rights of the parties would best be promoted by a judicial sale is not supported by the findings of subordinate facts. We agree. H⁴D

Under the test set out above, the court must first consider the practicability of physically partitioning the property in question. The trial court concluded that due to the situation and location of the parcel of land, the size and area of the property, the physical structure and appurtenances on the property, and other factors, a physical partition of the property would not be feasible. ~~An examination of the subordinate~~ ~~findings of facts and the exhibits, however, demonstrates that the court~~ ~~erred in this respect.~~ *error in partition feasibility by lower court*

It is undisputed that the property in question consists of one 20.5 acre parcel, basically rectangular in shape, and one dwelling, located at the extreme western end of the property. Two roads, Dino Road and Lucien Court, abut the property and another, Birch Street, provides access through use of a right-of-way. Unlike cases where there are numerous fractional owners of the property to be partitioned, and the practicability of a physical division is therefore drastically reduced; ~~in this case there are~~ ~~only two competing ownership interests:~~ the plaintiffs' undivided 99/144 interest and the defendant's 45/144 interest. These facts, taken together, do not support the trial court's conclusion that a physical partition of the property would not be "feasible" in this case. Instead, the above facts demonstrate that the opposite is true: a partition in kind clearly would be practicable under the circumstances of this case.

§1

Although a partition in kind is physically practicable, it remains to be considered whether a partition in kind would also promote the best interests of the parties. ~~In order to resolve this issue, the consequences of~~ ~~a partition in kind must be compared with those of a partition by~~ sale.

§2

The trial court concluded that a partition in kind could not be had without great prejudice to the parties ~~since the continuation of the defendant's~~ ~~business would hinder or preclude the development of the plaintiffs'~~ ~~parcel for residential purposes,~~ which the ~~trial court concluded was the~~ ~~highest and best use of the property.~~ The court's concern over the possible adverse economic effect upon the plaintiffs' interest in the event of a partition in kind was based essentially on four findings: (1) approval by the city planning commission for subdivision of the parcel would be difficult to obtain if the defendant continued her garbage hauling business; (2) lots in a residential subdivision might not sell, or might sell at a lower price, if the defendant's business continued; (3) if the defendant were granted the one-acre parcel, on which her residence is situated and on which her business now operates, three of the lots proposed in the plaintiffs' plan to subdivide the property would have to be consolidated and would be lost; and (4) the proposed extension of one of the neighboring roads would have to be rerouted through one of the proposed building lots if a partition in kind were ordered. The trial court also found that the defendant's use of the portion of the property that she occupies is in violation of existing zoning regulations. The court presumably inferred from this finding that it is not likely that the defendant will be able to continue her rubbish hauling operations from this property in the future. The court also premised its forecast that the planning commission would reject the plaintiffs' subdivision plan for the remainder of the property on the finding that the defendant's use was invalid. These factors basically led the trial court to conclude that the interests of the parties would best be protected if the land were sold as a unified unit for residential subdivision development and the proceeds of such a sale were distributed to the parties.

... The defendant claims that the trial court erred in finding that the defendant's use of a portion of the property is in violation of the existing zoning regulations, and in refusing to find that such use is a valid nonconforming use. ... [T]he court's finding in this regard must be stricken as unsupported by sufficient competent evidence. We are left, then, with an unassailed finding that the defendant's family has operated a "garbage business" on the premises since the 1920s and that the city of Bristol has granted the defendant the appropriate permits and licenses each year to operate her business. There is no indication that this practice will not continue in the future.

Our resolution of this issue makes it clear that any inference that the defendant would probably be unable to continue her rubbish hauling activity on the property in the future is unfounded. We also conclude that the court erred in concluding that the city's planning commission would probably not approve a subdivision plan relating to the remainder of the property. Any such forecast must be carefully scrutinized as it is difficult to project what a public body will decide in any given matter. ... The court's finding indicates that only garbage trucks and dumpsters are stored on the property; that no garbage is brought there; and that the defendant's business operations involve "mostly containerized ... dumpsters, a contemporary development in technology which has substantially reduced the odors previously associated with the rubbish and garbage hauling industry." These facts do not support the court's speculation that the city's planning commission would not approve a subdivision permit for the undeveloped portion of the parties' property.

The court's remaining observations relating to the effect of the defendant's business on the probable fair market value of the proposed residential lots, the possible loss of building lots to accommodate the defendant's business[13] and the rerouting of a proposed subdivision road, which may have some validity, are not dispositive of the issue. It is the interests of all of the tenants in common that the court must consider; and not merely the economic gain of one tenant, or a group of tenants. The trial court failed to give due consideration to the fact that one of the tenants in common has been in actual and exclusive possession of a portion of the property for a substantial period of time; that the tenant has made her home on the property; and that she derives her livelihood from the operation of a business on this portion of the property, as her family before her has for many years. A partition by sale would force the defendant to surrender her home and, perhaps, would jeopardize her livelihood. It is under just such circumstances, which include the

---

[13] It should be noted in this regard that a partition in kind would result in a physical division of the land according to the parties' respective interests. The defendant would, therefore, not obtain any property in excess of her beneficial share of the parties' concurrent estates.

demonstrated practicability of a physical division of the property, that the wisdom of the law's preference for partition in kind is evident.

...Since the property in this case may practicably be physically divided, and since the interests of all owners will better be promoted if a partition in kind is ordered, we conclude that the trial court erred in ordering a partition by sale, and that, under the facts as found, the defendant is entitled to a partition of the property in kind.

2 Subdivision plot plan for the 20.5 acre parcel

Notes and Questions

1. **Owelty.** [8] Courts have the equitable power to order owelty payments when it is impractical to partition in kind according to exact shares, but when monetary payments can adjust for the variance in the value of the parcels from the interests held by the respective cotenants. *See* Dewrell v. Lawrence, 58 P.3d 223, 227 (Okla. Civ. App. 2002); Code of Ala. § 35-6-24 (2010); Cal. Civ. Proc. Code § 873.250 (West 2009).

2. **Denouement.** Thomas Merrill and Henry Smith did some digging for their property casebook, *Property: Principles and Policies.* Apparently, Vealencis was a difficult client and antagonized the trial judge, which meant that her victory on the law did not translate to victory in the real world. In *Delfino*, Vealencis was awarded three lots, including her homestead, a total of about one acre worth $72,000. (See lot 135-1 on far left of image.) She was also required to pay $26,000 in owelty to the Delfinos to compensate them for the harm her garbage operation imposed on the proposed subdivision.

   While Vealencis had a 5/16 interest in the land, her net benefit was only $46,000, or less than one-fourth of what she was due. Three years later, the Delfinos sold their roughly 19 acres to a developer for $725,000. The developer separated Vealencis' lot from the rest of the subdivision by a two-foot-wide strip of land (see lots 39 and 40). This deprived her of access to Dino Road and its sewer and water connections, as well as preventing her trucks from entering the subdivision (even though she'd already paid for diminishing the value of the homes in the subdivision). Vealencis' only access

---

[8] This charming term is followed in *Black's Legal Dictionary* by another winner: To quote Blackstone, "Owling, so called from its being usually carried on in the night, … is the offense of transporting sheep or wool out of this kingdom."

to the land was a 16.5 foot easement over lot 9C. She was required to use an artesian well and a septic tank. *See* Manel Baucells & Steven A. Lippman, *Justice Delayed Is Justice Denied: A Cooperative Game Theoretic Analysis to Hold-up in Coownership*, 22 CARDOZO L. REV. 1191 (2001). Vealencis died in 1990, still running the garbage business.

Why was she required to pay owelty up-front rather than waiting to see if the harm materialized and allowing the Delfinos to recover in an action for nuisance later? Is there anything the court could have done in its division to avoid the unfairness to Vealencis? And what does this result suggest about the appropriate choice of remedies—injunction or damages—in nuisance cases?

3. **Implementing partition in kind.** In a partition in kind, how should the court determine who gets what land? *See* Anderson v. Anderson, 560 N.W.2d 729 (Minn. Ct. App. 1997) (cotenants awarded parcel on which they had a residence); Barth v. Barth, 901 P.2d 232 (Okla. Ct. App. 1995) (considering cotenant's ownership of adjacent land). In Louisiana, partition in kind is not allowed unless parcels of equal value can be created, and parcels must be drawn by lot. See McNeal v. McNeal, 732 So. 2d 663 (La. Ct. App. 1999). Is this a good idea? What about "I cut, you choose" as a way of implementing partition in kind? There's a large literature in game theory, mathematics, and computer science on these problems, dealing with more than two parties, heterogenous resources, etc. Very little of this seems to have made its way into law. *But see* Note, *Cutting the Baby in Half*, 77 BROOK. L. REV. 263 (2011) (surveying some of the literature).

Some state laws also provide for allotment, in which the court allocates part of the property to a cotenant – which can include an owelty payment if the allocated portion is more than the cotenant's share – and then sells the remainder. E.g., 25 Del. Code §730; S.C. Code Ann. §15-61-50; Va. Code Ann. §8.01-83. Sometimes a cotenant must show an equitable claim to allotment in order to get it. Haw. Rev. Stat. §§668-7(5)-(6).

4. **Partition by sale as the default?** Consider the court's claims about the preference for partition in kind. Partition in kind will essentially always diminish the market value of the land compared to partition by sale. Do other, intangible interests nonetheless adequately justify a preference for partition in kind?

Ark Land Co. v. Harper, 599 S.E.2d 754 (W. Va. 2004), suggests that a rule favoring maximization of market value "would permit commercial entities to always 'evict' pre-existing co-owners, because a commercial entity's interest in property will invariably increase its value."

Though partition in kind is supposedly favored by the law on the books, governing legal practice is different, as the Uniform Law Commission has written:

> Despite the overwhelming statutory preference for partition in kind, courts in a large number of states typically resolve partition actions by ordering partition by sale which usually results in forcing property owners off their land without their consent. This occurs even in cases in which the property could easily have been divided in kind or an overwhelming majority of the cotenants had opposed partition by sale or even in some cases when the only remedy any cotenant petitioned the court to order was partition in kind and not partition by sale.

UNIFORM PARTITION OF HEIRS PROPERTY ACT, Prefatory Note. "Heirs' property," that is, property whose ownership is divided by intestate succession over several generations, has resulted in highly fractionated ownership of land in many African-American families. The ULC explains that "many of these owners [in possession] believe that their property ownership is secure because they pay property taxes, they live on the land, and they make productive use of the land. They also believe that their property may only be sold against their will if a majority or more of their cotenants agree, which gives some of these families with a large number of members with an interest in the property false confidence that their ownership is extremely secure." But their rights are, in fact, highly insecure. "Unfortunately, the first time that many of these owners are informed about the actual legal rules governing partition is after a partition action has been filed, and often after critical, early court rulings have been made against them."

When heirs' property became valuable for development, third parties would often acquire the interest of a distant relative who has a fractional share and petition for partition. Given the often hundreds of people who own interests in a piece of heirs' property, courts generally hold that partition in kind is impossible. The resulting sale can dispossess people who have lived on or used the land for decades; family members who would like to keep the land are rarely able to outbid developers, who nonetheless usually pay substantially below-market prices because of the forced nature of the sale. Ironically, once sale is ordered, courts will not overturn a sale price unless it "shocks the conscience," even though the rationale for ordering the sale was that it would provide the cotenants with more benefit than partition in kind. Sales have been confirmed even though the property sold for twenty percent or less of its market value. In many states, family members who oppose partition by sale can even be required to pay the petitioner's attorneys' fees. Thomas Mitchell, a law professor at the University of Wisconsin-Madison, says, "It would be like if you owned incredibly small shares of Microsoft, and you were given the right to go to your local state court and file a motion to liquidate Microsoft at a fire sale."

The problem is substantial. *See* Anna Stolley Persky, *In the Cross-Heirs*, ABA JOURNAL, May 2, 2009:

> According to the Land Loss Prevention Project, a Durham, N.C.-based organization that provides legal support to financially distressed farmers and landowners in the state, of the 15 million acres of land acquired by African-Americans after Emancipation, about 2 million remain owned by their descendants. Nationally, it's estimated that African-American land ownership has decreased from as much as 19 million acres in 1910 to 1.5 million acres in 1997, according to the Southern Coalition for Social Justice.

The problem also occurs in urban areas, where a family home may have been passed down through several generations. Barriers to transfers by will include poverty, lack of knowledge, or an unwillingness to cause family conflict by picking specific heirs. Heirs property created significant problems in New Orleans after Hurricane Katrina, when many people who thought they were owners were unable to show title to their homes.

The common law operated under a presumption that grants to multiple grantees created a joint tenancy—precisely the opposite of the modern presumption in favor of a tenancy in common. Should we return to a presumption in favor of joint tenancy, at least for family homes where children are the heirs by intestacy?

Or should small fractional interests disappear over time? Recall that traditionally, one cotenant's possession is not adverse to any other cotenant's possession, unless there is an ouster. Although cotenants are due their share of rents or other income arising from use of the property, mere failure to pay them does not start the adverse possession clock running. Would it make sense to change these rules? What are the risks from doing so? (There would be due process and takings issues if legislatures tried to extinguish fractional interests outright.[9])

The Uniform Partition of Heirs' Property Act, enacted in six states as of 2015, provides co-owners with a right of first refusal to buy the petitioning co-owner's share, and, if they do not exercise that right, attempts to create a more competitive bidding process. The expectation is that even co-owners who can't raise enough money to buy the entire parcel at fair market value, as at a traditional

---

[9] Due to previous legislation attempting to assimilate members of Indian tribes into (white) American society, combined with generations of inherited interests, reservation land has often become highly fractionated. Many allotments have several hundred owners. Fractional shares have been denominated in millions, billions, and even 54 trillion. For example, one tract of forty acres produced $1080 in annual income. It had 439 owners, one-third of whom received less than five cents in annual rent and two-thirds of whom received less than a dollar. The largest interest holder received $82.85 a year, while the smallest was entitled to one penny every 177 years. The administrative costs to the Bureau of Indian Affairs of managing this distribution were over $17,000 per year. Hodel v. Irving, 481 U.S. 704 (1987). Fractionation makes productive use of land almost impossible. Indian Land Consolidation Act Amendment, S. Rep. No. 98-632, at 82-83 (1984), reprinted in 1984 U.S.C.C.A.N. 5470. Allotment lands can only be leased or partitioned with the unanimous consent of all interest holders. The Indian Land Consolidation Act of 1983 attempted to solve these problems by mandating that extremely fractionated interests would escheat to the relevant tribe, without compensation to the fractional owners. The Supreme Court invalidated this law as an unconstitutional taking, *Hodel*, and likewise invalidated the attempted replacement, *Babbitt v. Youpee*, 519 U.S. 234 (1997).

The American Indian Probate Reform Act of 2004 tried again; the Department of the Interior runs a land consolidation program under which it buys back fractionated shares. Under the AIPRA, if Indian land would pass by intestate succession, the Department of the Interior can buy any interests in the land that are under 5%. This purchase can occur even if the heir objects, unless the heir is living on the land. Other heirs, co-owners, and the tribe on whose reservation the land is located can also buy the land, as long as they pay fair market value and have the consent of anyone holding more than a 5% interest.

partition sale, are more likely to be able to buy another cotenant's fractional share. Under the Act, courts can also consider the historical and cultural value of the land to the people living on it, not just the economic value of the land, in deciding whether to reject partition by sale. See, e.g., Chuck v. Gomes, 532 P.2d 657 (Haw. 1975) (Richardson, C.J., dissenting):

> [T]here are interests other than financial expediency which I recognize as essential to our Hawaiian way of life. Foremost is the individual's right to retain ancestral land in order to perpetuate the concept of the family homestead. Such right is derived from our proud cultural heritage. . . . [W]e must not lose sight of the cultural traditions which attach fundamental importance to keeping ancestral land in a particular family line.

5. **Contracting around partition rights.** Should cotenants be able to waive their right to partition? *See* Gore v. Beren, 867 P.2d 330 (Kan. 1994) (cotenants agreed to a right of first refusal if any cotenant wished to sell; this agreement impliedly waived the right to partition and didn't violate the Rule Against Perpetuities because it was personal to the parties and would necessarily end during the lifetime of one of the parties); *see also* Michalski v. Michalski, 142 A.2d 645 (N.J. Super. 1958) (otherwise valid restriction on right to partition may be unenforceable when circumstances have changed so much that enforcement would be unduly harsh); Reilly v. Sageser 467 P.2d 358 (Wash. Ct. App. 1970) (option to purchase from cotenant at cost of cotenant's investment in land and improvements was valid unless both parties agreed or one party substantially breached other elements of agreement); *cf.* Low v. Spellman, 629 A.2d 57 (Me. 1993) (invalidating right of first refusal given to grantors, heirs, and

assigns as in violation of the Rule Against Perpetuities; fixed price of $6500 also created unreasonable restraint on alienation).

6.   Partitioning a future interest. Can owners who own only a future interest seek partition of that interest? At common law, the answer was no because they lacked a present possessory interest, and some states still adhere to this rule. See, e.g., Trieber v. Citizens State Bank, 598 N.W.2d 96 (N.D. 1999). Many states, however, allow co-owners of vested future interests to seek partition of that interest. See, e.g., Ark. Code §18-60-401.

7.   **Partitioning personal property.**   Are there circumstances in which a physical partition of personal property would make sense? How would you divide up a photo album with hundreds of photographs? *Cf.* In re Estate of McDowell, 345 N.Y.S.2d 828 (Sur. Ct. 1973) (custody of rocking chair desired by both heirs should be divided in six-month increments, remainder to the survivor); Ronen Perry & Tal Zarsky, *Taking Turns*, 43 FLA. ST. U. L. REV. (2015). This solution raises a more general question: why don't we see more co-ownership of real property on the time-share model?

C.   Joint Tenancy

Joint tenancy (in some jurisdictions called a "joint tenancy with right of survivorship" and abbreviated "JTWROS") is a form of ownership that can be unilaterally severed and turned into a tenancy in common. Its distinctive feature is the right of survivorship: If a joint tenancy is not severed before a joint tenant's death, that joint tenant's interest disappears and the remaining tenant continues to own an undivided interest, allowing the survivor to avoid probate. Thus, joint tenancy is most widely used today as a substitute for a will.[10]

In modern times, tenancy in common is preferred to other kinds of co-ownership. A conveyance "to Alice and Beth" therefore creates a tenancy in common by default, though it's relatively standard to include "as tenants in common" to avoid all uncertainty. The creation and continuation of a joint tenancy is beset with traps, even though it may well be most co-owners' preferred form of ownership for residential property. Some states have statutes that appear to abolish the joint tenancy, but they will often find joint tenancies with a right of survivorship if the intent to create them is clear enough. See, e.g., McLeroy v. McLeroy, 40 S.W.2d 1027 (Tenn. 1931).

1.   Creating a Joint Tenancy

The traditional test for the creation and continuation of a joint tenancy depended upon the presence of the four "unities": (1) time – the joint tenants' interests were all acquired at the same time; (2) title – the interests were all acquired by the same document or by joint adverse possession; (3) interest – the tenants' shares must all be equal and undivided; and (4) possession – all joint tenants must have equal rights to possess the whole (in the absence of an agreement to the contrary[11]:

> Unless the unities existed at the tenancy's inception, or if they were
> broken at any subsequent point, the joint tenancy was

---

[10] Note that the federal government does not follow the fiction that nothing passes at death to the surviving joint tenant; the decedent's interest will be taxed as if it were transferred to the survivor, though if the joint tenants are married no tax will be due.

[11] At common law, joint tenants could not hold unequal shares, and attempting to create such a tenancy would create a tenancy in common. However, modern courts are increasingly willing to accept a clearly shown intent to hold unequal shares. See Moat v. Ducharme, 555 N.E.2d 897 (Mass. App. 1990) (unequal contributions); Jezo v. Jezo, 127 N.W.2d 246 (Wis. 1964) (evidence of contrary intent can override presumption of equal shares).

automatically severed, and the owners became tenants in common. This requirement meant, for example, that the owner of property could not create a joint tenancy in himself and others without first making use of a straw man. Because all joint tenants had to receive their interest in the property at the same time and by the same title, the owner had first to convey to a third party, who would in turn convey the property back to the grantor and the other tenants. They would then take in joint tenancy. Without this purely formal step, however, they would be only tenants in common.

R. H. Helmholz, *Realism and Formalism in the Severance of Joint Tenancies*, 77 NEB. L. REV. 1 (1998). Today (as was already largely true in the 1950s), the necessity for using a straw man to create a joint tenancy has been largely eliminated from American law, sometimes by judicial decision but more often by statutory enactment. We will examine this issue further below, when we discuss severance of a joint tenancy.

A conveyance "to Alice and Beth as joint tenants, and not as tenants in common," will create a joint tenancy in most states. *See* Kurpiel v. Kurpiel, 271 N.Y.S.2d 114 (N.Y. Sup. Ct. 1966) (joint tenancy created). Most states consider that this language confirms the grantor's intent – "joint" alone might have been misunderstood by a layperson who thinks that tenants in common are joint owners in a general sense, though some states accept "to Alice and Beth jointly" as sufficient to create a joint tenancy. *Compare* Downing v. Downing, 606 A.2d 208 (Md. 1992) ("to A and B as joint tenants" creates a joint tenancy where the state statute provides that a tenancy in common is created unless a written instrument "expressly provides that the property granted is to be held in joint tenancy"), *and* Germaine v. Delaine, 318 So. 2d 681 (Ala. 1975) ("jointly as tenants in common" created a joint tenancy where the deed indicated a clear intent for survivorship), *with* Taylor v. Taylor, 17 N.W.2d 745 (Mich. 1945) ("jointly," absent circumstantial evidence of intent to create the legal effect of a joint tenancy, does not suffice to create a joint tenancy);

Montgomery v. Clarkson, 585 S.W.2d 483 (Mo. 1979) ("jointly" is not "express declaration" of joint tenancy, as required by state statute); Overheiser v. Lackey, 100 N.E. 738 (N.Y. 1913) (where the layman who prepared a will used "jointly," the will created a tenancy in common), *and* Householter v. Householter, 164 P.2d 101 (Kan. 1945) ("jointly," used five times in a will prepared by a person who had served as a probate judge, created a joint tenancy).

In some states, precedents require more, usually specific invocation of a right of survivorship. *Compare* Germaine v. Delaine, 318 So. 2d 681 (Ala. 1975) (deed to A and B "jointly, as tenants in common and to the survivor thereof" created joint tenancy because of survivorship language), *with* Hoover v. Smith, 444 S.E.2d 546 (Va. 1994) ("to A and B as joint tenants, and not as tenants in common" was insufficient to create a joint tenancy because it was not explicit about the right of survivorship).

In other states, however, use of that same language will cause problems. *See, e.g.,* Hunter v. Hunter, 320 S.W.2d 529 (Mo. 1959) (will devising property to A and B "as joint tenants with the right of survivorship" created life estates with remainder to the survivor); Snover v. Snover, 502 N.W.2d 370 (Mich. Ct. App. 1993) ("to A and B as joint tenants with full rights of survivorship and not as tenants in common" created life estate in tenancy in common with remainder to survivor). Be sure you understand what the problem is: under what circumstances will it make a difference whether A and B have a joint tenancy, with right of survivorship, or instead have a tenancy in common in life estate, with the remainder to the survivor? Courts sometimes refer to the latter as an "indestructible" remainder, which is confusing language – the remainder can't be destroyed by the *other* cotenant, whereas a right of survivorship in a joint tenancy can be unilaterally destroyed.

It is vitally important to consult your state's statutes and precedent before drafting a conveyance to more than one owner. James v. Taylor, 969

S.W.2d 672 (Ark. App. Ct. 1998), is an example of how the law can lay traps for the well-intentioned but poorly advised. The issue in the case was whether a deed conveyed property from a mother to her three children as tenants in common or as joint tenants. The court of appeals reversed an initial ruling that the conveyance created a joint tenancy. The deed named the three children "jointly and severally, and unto their heirs, assigns and successors forever," and the mother retained a life estate. Two of the three children subsequently died, and then the mother died. Melba Taylor, the surviving child, sought a declaration that she was the sole owner, while the heirs of the other two children opposed her. Arkansas, like most states, provides that every shared interest in land "shall be in tenancy in common unless expressly declared in the grant or devise to be a joint tenancy." Ark. Code Ann. § 18-12-603 (1987).

The heirs argued that any ambiguity therefore pointed to a tenancy in common, whereas Taylor argued that her mother's intent to create a joint tenancy could be determined from the surrounding circumstances. The evidence of such intent was relatively strong: Taylor testified that her mother told her lawyer that she wanted the deed drafted so that, if one of her children died, the property would belong to the other two children, and so on; and that her mother was upset when she learned, just before her death, that there was a problem with the deed. In addition, after the first child died, the mother drafted a new will splitting her property between her two living children and giving nothing to the dead child's heirs, and the mother deleted the names of each dead child from bank accounts payable on death, leaving only Taylor's name.

The court of appeals nonetheless held that the policy of the statute, favoring tenancy in common unless a joint tenancy was expressly granted, overrode any inquiry into the mother's intent. While the words "joint tenancy" didn't need to be used, some intent to convey a survivorship estate needed to appear in the grant. The words "jointly and severally" were insufficient, contradictory, and therefore meaningless in the context of estates.

Assuming a court looked for extrinsic evidence of the drafter's intent in a case involving ambiguous language, what would constitute persuasive evidence of an intent to create a joint tenancy?

2.   Severance of a Joint Tenancy

Severance is any act that destroys one or more of the four unities required to maintain a joint tenancy. The legal consequence of severance is that the joint tenancy is converted to a tenancy in common. (For those rare joint tenancies involving three or more joint tenants, one joint tenant may sever the joint tenancy as to his interest, but the others remain joint tenants with each other.) The traditional rule for severance required either that all the tenants expressly agree to hold as tenants in common, or that one of the tenants convey to a third person in order to destroy the unities (particularly the unities of time and title), to turn a joint tenancy into a tenancy in common. In modern times, a conveyance from oneself as joint tenant to oneself as tenant in common is likely to succeed just as well as a conveyance by one tenant to a straw owner plus a reconveyance from the straw. *See* Hendrickson v. Minneapolis Fed. Sav. & Loan Ass'n, 161 N.W.2d 688 (Minn. 1968); Riddle v. Harmon, 162 Cal. Rptr. 530 (Cal. Ct. App. 1980); *see also* Countrywide Funding Corp. v. Palmer, 589 So. 2d 994 (Fla. Dist. Ct. App. 1991) (one joint tenant forged the other's signature in purported conveyance to himself; court held that his act severed the tenancy). *But see* Krause v. Crossley, 277 N.W.2d 242 (Neb. 1979) (rejecting this modern trend and requiring conveyance to a third party for an effective severance); L.B. 694, § 11, 1980 Neb. Laws 577 (codified as Neb. Rev. Stat. § 76-118(4) (Reissue 1996)) (reversing result in *Krause* and allowing self-conveyance to sever).

The largest problem in severance is one of surprise, which can occur whether or not a third party straw is required to partipate in the severance. As Helmholz explains:

> Since one joint tenant has always been able to sever the tenancy without the concurrence or even the knowledge of the other, the possibility of a severance that is unfair to the other has long existed. It can take several forms, as where the joint tenant who has contributed nothing to the purchase of the assets then severs unilaterally, thereby upsetting the normal expectations of the other joint tenant. Its most extreme form is the secret severance. If the tenant who severs secretly is the first to die, the heirs or successors produce the severing document and take half of the property. It accrues to them under the tenancy in common that was the result of the severance. If the severing tenant survives, however, the severing document is suppressed and the survivor takes the whole. The heirs or successors of the first to die get nothing. It is what the economists call "strategic behavior."

Helmholz, *supra*, at 25-26.

Why not impose a notice requirement for a deliberate severance? What about imposing a requirement that a severing instrument be timely recorded in the public land records? See Cal. Civ. Code § 683.2 (West 1998) (if a joint tenancy is recorded, severance is only effective against the non-severing tenant if the severance is recorded either before the severing tenant's death or, in limited circumstances, recorded within seven days after death; the severing tenant's right of survivorship is cut off even without recording); Minn. Stat. Ann. § 500.19--5 (West 1997) (requiring recording to make unilateral severance valid); N.Y. Real Prop. Law §240-c(2) (similar). Does a recording requirement solve the problem of surprise?

Joint tenants may also take acts that are more ambiguous with respect to their rights. Courts then have to decide what kinds of acts are sufficient to work a severance.

Harms v. Sprague
473 N.E.2d 930 (1984)

Thomas J. MORAN, Justice.

Plaintiff, William H. Harms, filed a complaint to quiet title and for declaratory judgment in the circuit court of Greene County. Plaintiff had taken title to certain real estate with his brother John R. Harms, as a joint tenant, with full right of survivorship. The plaintiff named, as a defendant, Charles D. Sprague, the executor of the estate of John Harms and the devisee of all the real and personal property of John Harms. Also named as defendants were Carl T. and Mary E. Simmons, alleged mortgagees of the property in question. Defendant Sprague filed a counterclaim against plaintiff, challenging plaintiff's claim of ownership of the entire tract of property and asking the court to recognize his (Sprague's) interest as a tenant in common, subject to a mortgage lien. At issue was the effect the granting of a mortgage by John Harms had on the joint tenancy. Also at issue was whether the mortgage survived the death of John Harms as a lien against the property.

The trial court held that the mortgage given by John Harms to defendants Carl and Mary Simmons severed the joint tenancy. Further, the court found that the mortgage survived the death of John Harms as a lien against the undivided one-half interest in the property which passed to Sprague by and through the will of the deceased. The appellate court reversed, finding that the mortgage given by one joint tenant of his interest in the property does not sever the joint tenancy. Accordingly, the appellate court held that plaintiff, as the surviving joint tenant, owned the property in its entirety, unencumbered by the mortgage lien....

Two issues are raised on appeal: (1) Is a joint tenancy severed when less than all of the joint tenants mortgage their interest in the property? and (2) Does such a mortgage survive the death of the mortgagor as a lien on the property?

A review of the stipulation of facts reveals the following. Plaintiff, William Harms, and his brother John Harms, took title to real estate located in Roodhouse, on June 26, 1973, as joint tenants. The warranty deed memorializing this transaction was recorded on June 29, 1973, in the office of the Greene County recorder of deeds.

Carl and Mary Simmons owned a lot and home in Roodhouse. Charles Sprague entered into an agreement with the Simmons whereby Sprague was to purchase their property for $25,000. Sprague tendered $18,000 in cash and signed a promissory note for the balance of $7,000. Because Sprague had no security for the $7,000, he asked his friend, John Harms, to co-sign the note and give a mortgage on his interest in the joint tenancy property. Harms agreed, and on June 12, 1981, John Harms and Charles Sprague, jointly and severally, executed a promissory note for $7,000 payable to Carl and Mary Simmons. The note states that the principal sum of $7,000 was to be paid from the proceeds of the sale of John Harms' interest in the joint tenancy property, but in any event no later than six months from the date the note was signed. The note reflects that five monthly interest payments had been made, with the last payment recorded November 6, 1981. In addition, John Harms executed a mortgage, in favor of the Simmonses, on his undivided one-half interest in the joint tenancy property, to secure payment of the note. William Harms was unaware of the mortgage given by his brother.

John Harms moved from his joint tenancy property to the Simmons property which had been purchased by Charles Sprague. On December 10, 1981, John Harms died. By the terms of John Harms' will, Charles

Sprague was the devisee of his entire estate. The mortgage given by John Harms to the Simmonses was recorded on December 29, 1981.

Prior to the appellate court decision in the instant case no court of this State had directly addressed the principal question we are confronted with herein-the effect of a mortgage, executed by less than all of the joint tenants, on the joint tenancy. Nevertheless, there are numerous cases which have considered the severance issue in relation to other circumstances surrounding a joint tenancy. All have necessarily focused on the four unities which are fundamental to both the creation and the perpetuation of the joint tenancy. These are the unities of interest, title, time, and possession. The voluntary or involuntary destruction of any of the unities by one of the joint tenants will sever the joint tenancy.

In a series of cases, this court has considered the effect that judgment liens upon the interest of one joint tenant have on the stability of the joint tenancy. In Peoples Trust & Savings Bank v. Haas (1927), 328 Ill. 468, 160 N.E. 85, the court found that a judgment lien secured against one joint tenant did not serve to extinguish the joint tenancy. As such, the surviving joint tenant "succeeded to the title in fee to the whole of the land by operation of law."

…Clearly, this court adheres to the rule that a lien on a joint tenant's interest in property will not effectuate a severance of the joint tenancy, absent the conveyance by a deed following the expiration of a redemption period. It follows, therefore, that if Illinois perceives a mortgage as merely a lien on the mortgagor's interest in property rather than a conveyance of title from mortgagor to mortgagee, the execution of a mortgage by a joint tenant, on his interest in the property, would not destroy the unity of title and sever the joint tenancy.

Early cases in Illinois, however, followed the title theory of mortgages. In 1900, this court recognized the common law precept that a mortgage was a conveyance of a legal estate vesting title to the property in the mortgagee. Consistent with this title theory of mortgages, therefore, there are many cases which state, in dicta, that a joint tenancy is severed by one of the joint tenants mortgaging his interest to a stranger. Yet even the early case of Lightcap v. Bradley, cited above, recognized that the title held by the mortgagee was for the limited purpose of protecting his interests. The court went on to say that "the mortgagor is the owner for every other purpose and against every other person. The title of the mortgagee is anomalous, and exists only between him and the mortgagor * * *." Lightcap v. Bradley (1900), 186 Ill. 510, 522-23, 58 N.E. 221.

Because our cases had early recognized the unique and narrow character of the title that passed to a mortgagee under the common law title theory, it was not a drastic departure when this court expressly characterized the execution of a mortgage as a mere lien …

[A] joint tenancy is not severed when one joint tenant executes a mortgage on his interest in the property, since the unity of title has been preserved. As the appellate court in the instant case correctly observed: "If giving a mortgage creates only a lien, then a mortgage should have the same effect on a joint tenancy as a lien created in other ways." Other jurisdictions following the lien theory of mortgages have reached the same result.

…An inherent feature of the estate of joint tenancy is the right of survivorship, which is the right of the last survivor to take the whole of the estate. Because we find that a mortgage given by one joint tenant of his interest in the property does not sever the joint tenancy, we hold that the plaintiff's right of survivorship became operative upon the death of his brother. As such plaintiff is now the sole owner of the estate, in its entirety.

Further, we find that the mortgage executed by John Harms does not survive as a lien on plaintiff's property. A surviving joint tenant succeeds to the share of the deceased joint tenant by virtue of the conveyance which created the joint tenancy, not as the successor of the deceased. The property right of the mortgaging joint tenant is extinguished at the moment of his death. While John Harms was alive, the mortgage existed as a lien on his interest in the joint tenancy. Upon his death, his interest ceased to exist and along with it the lien of the mortgage. Under the circumstances of this case, we would note that the mortgage given by John Harms to the Simmonses was only valid as between the original parties during the lifetime of John Harms since it was unrecorded. In addition, recording the mortgage subsequent to the death of John Harms was a nullity. As we stated above, John Harms' property rights in the joint tenancy were extinguished when he died. Thus, he no longer had a property interest upon which the mortgage lien could attach....

Notes and Questions

1. The result in Harms, in which the mortgage disappears if the joint tenant who granted it predeceases the other joint tenant, is the most common result in "lien theory" states, which represent the vast majority of states today. However, for the reasons discussed in Harms, the results in "title theory" states are mixed. Compare Downing v. Downing, 606 A.2d 208 (Md. 1992) (no automatic severance although Maryland is a "title" state), with Schaefer v. Peoples Heritage Savings Bank, 669 A.2d 185 (Me. 1996) (mortgage severs joint tenancy), and General Credit Co. v. Cleck, 609 A.2d 553 (Pa. Sup. Ct. 1992) (same); Taylor Mattis, Severance of Joint Tenancies by Mortgages: A Contextual Approach, 1977 S. Ill. U. L.J. 27.

    Suppose we adopted an intent-based standard to determine whether the joint tenancy was severed. How would we have determined John Harms' intent after his death?

2. Is the result in *Harms* fair? Suppose John had instead survived William. Would the mortgage burden half the interest in the property, or the whole interest? *See* People v. Nogarr, 330 P.2d 858 (Cal. Ct. App. 1958) (if the mortgaging joint tenant survives the nonmortgaging joint tenant, the lien attaches to the entire interest). Wouldn't the mortgagees get a windfall if the value of their secured interest suddenly jumped in value? On the other hand, isn't that just the flip side of the loss they suffer if William survives John? Should we create a hybrid that would protect the lender, and burden William's interest after John's death, even without severing?

   Suppose the mortgage had worked a severance. If John had paid the mortgage off before dying, should the severance be undone and the joint tenancy restored? What would the parties likely have expected?

3. Given the result in *Harms*, how will lenders behave when one co-owner seeks to take out a loan? Sophisticated lenders make mistakes, see Texas American Bank v. Morgan, 733 P.2d 864 (N.M. 1987), but mostly the lenders at risk are ordinary people, often relatives or friends of the borrower.
   What about a creditor who has a judgment against one joint tenant – what should she do to make sure she can get access to the property to satisfy the judgment? In practice, the creditor must act during the debtor's life to attach a lien to the property and foreclose on that lien. *See, e.g.*, Rembe v. Stewart, 387 N.W.2d 313 (Iowa 1986); Jamestown Terminal Elev., Inc. v. Knopp, 246 N.W.2d 612 (N.D. 1976) (judgment lien on joint tenancy property did not survive when debtor cotenant died before execution sale); Jackson v. Lacy, 97 N.E.2d 839 (Ill. 1951) (severance doesn't occur at foreclosure, but only on expiration of the redemption period after foreclosure sale); *see also* Harris v. Crowder, 322 S.E.2d 854

(W. Va. 1984) (a creditor may do what the debtor could do, so a creditor of one joint tenant could convert a joint tenancy into a tenancy in common, as long as the other cotenant's interest wouldn't be otherwise prejudiced; an example of prejudice would be the loss of a favorable interest rate on a mortgage due to the timing of the creditor's act).

4. According to Charles Sprague's lawyer, Charles and John were romantically involved. If the events underlying the case occurred today, they could have married before John's death. Would that have changed anything?

In Riccelli v. Forcinito, 595 A.2d 1322 (Pa. Super. Ct. 1991), discussed above, Sam Riccelli and Carmen Pirozek had a joint tenancy. Four years later, Sam Riccelli married Rita Riccelli. Carmen Pirozek lived in the Riccelli-Pirozek property until her death in 1984. Her son lived in the house until Sam Riccelli died in 1987; Rita Riccelli then sued to kick him out, claiming to be the sole owner because Sam had inherited the whole property by right of survivorship. Did the marriage sever the joint tenancy? It might seem that the marriage, which gave Rita at least a potential interest in the property, severed the unities of time, title, interest, and possession. However, the court held that marriage of one joint tenant did not sever the joint tenancy. What's the best argument against severance? Is it the same as the argument in *Harms* against allowing a mortgage given by only one joint tenant to sever the joint tenancy?

Compare the case of *Goldman v. Gelman*, 77 N.E.2d 200 (N.Y. 2000). Before a divorce decree became final, the wife gave her divorce attorney a mortgage on the marital home, which was owned by the entirety, in order to secure her debt to her attorney. The husband was awarded exclusive title to the whole marital home. New

York's highest court held that the divorce did not destroy the mortgage, because the wife's interest was valid until the final divorce decree, which turned the tenancy by the entirety into a tenancy in common. The mortgage still burdened the wife's interest, and survived when the wife's interest was transferred to the husband. Who ultimately has to pay the wife's divorce lawyer?

5. **Other acts that might work a severance**. Technical breaches of the four unities are unlikely to work a severance. For example, when one joint tenant is adjudged an incompetent and the legal title to the incompetent's property is assigned to a guardian, courts hold that no severance occurred. *See, e.g.,* Moses v. Butner (In re Estate and Guardianship of Wood), 14 Cal. Rptr. 147 (Cal. Ct. App. 1961). Cases are divided on whether the grant of a lease by one joint tenant works a severance. *Compare* Tenhet v. Boswell, 554 P.2d 330 (Cal. 1976) (lease by one joint tenant does not sever joint tenancy, though lease is terminated by death of leasing joint tenant), *with* Estate of Gulledge, 673 A.2d 1278 (D.C. 1996) (lease to third person severs joint tenancy); *see also* In re Estate of Johnson, 739 N.W.2d 493 (Iowa 2007) (adopting intent-based approach to severance). Some cases even suggest that a lease only works a temporary severance, and the joint tenancy is automatically reformed when the lease ends. Isn't that a ridiculous rule? Are the four unities doing any real work here?

The traditional rule was that, when property is held jointly by spouses, divorce did not sever the joint tenancy. Unlike entireties property, jointly held property need not be held by spouses, so the four unities remain intact even after divorce. Does this make sense? Some states now presume severance upon divorce. See e.g., Ohio Rev. Code Ann. § 5302.20(c)(5) (Anderson 1996). Others require courts to deal with the status of property as part of the divorce decree. *See, e.g.,* Johnson v. Johnson, 169 N.W.2d 595 (Minn. 1969). The majority rule is that divorce works a severance, though the cases are divided; Helmholz argues that the results turn not on the four unities but on the courts' best understanding of the parties' intent. In a divorce case, both parties are alive, so it may seem possible to determine that intent. As Helmholz points out, matters get dicey when a divorce or a sale is pending and one of the spouses dies:

> Most of these disputes arose where the parties were not thinking at all about what would happen if one of them died. Why would they? They assumed that the divorce would be completed or that the contract for sale would be fulfilled. In most situations that is exactly what did happen. But not all. Where the unexpected does happen and one party dies, litigation all too easily ensues. In it, the courts have been left with the task of discovering the intent of the parties from what are very often the slenderest of indications.

Helmholz, *supra*, at 25. Given that "intent" may be an unworkable standard, is a formalist approach looking only to the four unities preferable in that it at least provides courts with an answer?

Finally, where joint tenants have sought partition but the partition hasn't yet occurred, the almost universal rule is that there is no severance until a court has granted the partition, or at least until only the barest formalities remain to finalize it. *See, e.g.,* Heintz v. Hudkins, 824 S.W.2d 139 (Mo. Ct. App. 1992). Helmholz again:

> Although it may be said in favor of this rule that the parties might always have changed their mind before the final decree, that seems a poor justification in the face of their clearly expressed intent to sever and the untimely death of

one of them. The true reason for the rule must be a formal one: the rule is necessary in order to safeguard the integrity of the underlying action for partition. Partition cannot be effective before it is obtained. One cannot secure the results of a judicial action simply by asking for it.

Helmholz, *supra*, at 30.

6. **What shares exist after severance?** The general assumption is that joint tenants have equal shares after severance—after all, the unity of interest requires that all joint tenants have equal shares *before* severance. However, if the equities strongly favored unequal shares, courts might well bend the rules. *Compare* Cunningham v. Hastings, 556 N.E.2d 12 (Ind. Ct. App. 1990) (though one cotenant paid the purchase price, the creation of a joint tenancy entitles each party to an equal share of the proceeds on partition; equitable adjustments to cotenants' equal shares are allowed for tenancies in common, not joint tenancies), *with* Moat v. Ducharme, 555 N.E.2d 897 (Mass. App. Ct. 1990) (presumption of equal shares is rebuttable because partition must be equitable), *and* Jezo v. Jezo, 127 N.W.2d 246 (Wis. 1964) (presumption of equal shares is rebuttable).

7. **Joint tenants who kill.** The general rule is that a person who intentionally causes another's death loses any inheritance rights he otherwise would have had from his victim's estate. In *Estate of Castiglioni*, 47 Cal. Rptr. 2d 288 (Ct. App. 1995), the surviving spouse petitioned for half of the property she held in joint tenancy with her deceased husband, of whose murder she was subsequently convicted. California Probate Code Section 251 provides in part: "A joint tenant who feloniously and intentionally kills another joint tenant thereby effects a severance of the interest of the decedent so that the share of the decedent passes as the

decedent's property and the killer has no rights by survivorship." Thus, there was no question that she could not inherit the entire property through a right of survivorship; her husband's share went to her husband's heir, a daughter.

However, years before the murder, the husband put his separate property in joint tenancy with the wife. The question was therefore whether the husband's share was an undivided half of the former joint tenancy property, or whether equitable tracing rules should apply to increase that share. The court of appeals held the latter, and that it was error to give the killer half of the joint tenancy property. The court noted that, had the tenancy been severed by divorce rather than by murder, the widow/murderer wouldn't have received any of the property at issue, because under California's community property regime the husband would have been reimbursed by tracing his contributions to their joint property. Cal. Family Code § 2640(b). Thus, equitable principles dictated that she should not be allowed to benefit from her crime, and her share would be reduced by the amount necessary to reflect his contribution.

What should have happened if the couple had lived in a state without community property rules, the source of the court's equitable tracing principle? Suppose section 251 instead read: "If a joint tenant feloniously and intentionally kills another joint tenant, the share of the decedent passes as though the killer had predeceased the decedent." What would the result be in *Estate of Castiglioni* in that situation?

8. **Simultaneous death.** What happens when two joint tenants die in the same accident, or the order of their death can't be determined? The Uniform Simultaneous Death Act initially provided that, without sufficient evidence of the order of death,

half of the property should be distributed as if the first joint tenant had died first, and the other half as if the other joint tenant had died first. This rule led to some unpleasant litigation and "gruesome" attempts by heirs to prove that a specific joint tenant died first. The 1993 revision of the USDA states that, unless a governing instrument such as a will specifies otherwise, the half-and-half approach will be used in the absence of "clear and convincing" evidence that one joint tenant survived the other by 120 hours.

9. **Joint accounts with rights of survivorship.** "Joint accounts" are bank accounts generally held by couples, children and parents, or business partners. Each account holder has the ability to draw on the account. Many joint accounts come with a right of survivorship: If a joint account owner dies, the survivor(s) get all the money – creating another way around the delays involved in probating a will.

In many states, joint account-holders do not have the same undivided interest and rights to the use and enjoyment of the deposits that joint owners of real property do. That is, the donee/nondepositor isn't entitled to the funds unless she survives the donor/depositor. See Uniform Probate Code §6-211 (2008). On the donor/depositor's death, the majority rule is that the surviving joint tenant takes the balance in a joint account unless there is clear and convincing evidence that the depositor's intent was to create a "convenience account," that is, an account that was supposed to be used by the nondepositor – usually a younger relative – to take care of the depositor's business affairs. Some jurisdictions conclusively presume that the surviving joint tenant should receive the balance. See Wright v. Bloom, 635 N.E.2d 31 (Ohio 1994).

What should happen if Orlando deposits $10,000 in a joint bank account with Abbie, and Abbie then withdraws $5000 from the account while Orlando is alive, without his permission or later agreement? Orlando can force Abbie to return the money. Why not presume that Orlando intended a present gift to Abbie? By the same logic, her creditors can't reach all the money to satisfy their claims against her unless and until she survives the donor/depositor. N. William Hines, Personal Property Joint Tenancies: More Law, Fact and Fancy, 54 Minn. L. Rev. 509 (1970).

However, the presumption against a present gift can be overcome by clear and convincing evidence. In a minority of jurisdictions, joint account owners have equal shares in the account during their lifetimes, as in a joint tenancy in land.

Joint accounts with a right of survivorship can be used as a will substitute, but there are potential tax consequences, not to mention risks of dispute during the time the person who put the money in the account is alive, or disputes after death when alternate heirs argue that the account was never intended to benefit the survivor. If the depositor's intent is to give whatever money is in the account to the non-depositing joint account holder when the depositor dies but not before, many states allow accounts to be designated "payable on death," preventing the non-depositing account holder from withdrawing the money while the depositor is alive. In the alternative, a revocable inter vivos trust will also provide the desired results. As for an elderly parent who wants her child to use money for her care, a better solution would be a power of attorney, making her child into her agent with the power to act on her behalf. This power of attorney would end with the parent's death.

10. **Why not allow severance by will?** If a joint tenant can sever without constraint during her lifetime, why not by will? Courts will not recognize such a transfer. *See, e.g.,* Gladson v. Gladson, 800 S.W.2d 709 (Ark. 1990).   There is an easy formalist explanation: by definition, the joint tenant's interest ends at her death and ownership automatically passes to the survivor, so there is nothing for her to pass by will. But isn't this just playing with definitions? A number of cases have allowed severance by will when the joint owners make joint wills, indicating a clear intent to sever at death, on the theory that it's the agreement to make the joint will that severs the joint tenancy.

The best explanation for the "no severance by will" rule is that it is about the operation of the system of wills, and preserves the use of joint tenancy as a device to avoid probate, even if it frustrates the intent of the testator. In addition, a joint tenant who severs by will is playing a no-lose game at the other tenant's expense. If she dies first, her designated heir takes her share. If she survives the other tenant, she takes all. If she has to sever during her lifetime, the severance occurs, whether that ends up benefiting her or not. This rule may not matter much given the cavalier way states allow secret severances, but still, severance by will is so contrary to the sharing spirit of joint tenancies that the rule requiring joint wills makes sense.

Leasing Real Property

The law of concurrent ownership, discussed in the previous chapter, generally regulates relationships between intimates. Arrangements like the joint tenancy generally arise between individuals who know each other and remain locked in ongoing relationships. As a result, there's not much arms-length bargaining and relatively few disputes work their way into the court system.

The law of landlord-tenant is very different. It is the law of strangers— strangers who often have little in common and may never interact after the lease terminates. How the law responds to this difference is one of the central theoretical questions you will wrestle with in this chapter. More practically, in this section of the course you will learn about the types of leaseholds, tenant selection, transferring leases, ending leases, and the various rights and responsibilities of tenants and landlords during the course of the lease.

A.   The Dual Nature of the Lease

In its simplest form, the lease is a transfer in which the owner of real property conveys exclusive possession to a tenant (generally in exchange for rent). Most law students know through personal experience that the process of renting generally entails signing a lease contract. Like other contracts, a lease's terms can be negotiated and they explicitly govern many of the rights and responsibilities of the parties involved. So why then are leases discussed in the property course rather than contracts?

The short response is that a lease is a property-contract hybrid. While it is surely a contract, it's a contract for a very particular kind of property interest. The fuller answer, like so much in property, lies in the history of feudal land law. Under the traditional common law, a leasehold was understood primarily as a property interest, similar in nature to the estates covered in our chapter on Estates and Future Interests. A lord (often a baron) conveyed a possessory right to a tenant (usually a peasant) and retained for himself a future interest (typically a reversion). Importantly, once the landlord transferred the right to possession, he had few other obligations to the tenant.

This basic model survived until the 1960s, when many jurisdictions began to introduce general contract law principles (e.g. the implied duty of good faith and fair dealing) into the law of landlord-tenant. Importing contract theories into the lease has had two practical effects. First, parties to a lease now have the option to terminate in the case of *any* material breach; in the past tenants could only terminate if the landlord interfered with their possession. Second, modern tenants have far more protections from indifferent and unscrupulous landlords than their counterparts 50 years ago. Courts and legislatures have proven particularly eager to help residential tenants—whom they view as vulnerable—from predations of the free market.

B.   Creating the Leasehold

1.   A Lease or Something Else?

A lease is a transfer of the right of possession of specific property for a limited period of time. It's important to see that not all legal relationships that grant the use of an owner's property qualify as leaseholds. Take, for example, the case of Snow White and Seven Dwarfs. If the Dwarfs give Snow White sole possession of their cottage for 12 months in exchange for a monthly payment, they have almost certainly created a lease. If, however, the Dwarfs invite Snow White to sleep on their couch for a few nights while she evades the Queen, they probably have created something called a *license* (a revocable permission to use the property of another, which we'll study in greater detail later in the book) rather than a leasehold. This determination matters (as we'll soon see) because the law extends a number of protections to grantees who qualify as tenants. It affects, among other things, whether the grantee can exclude the owner from certain spaces, how the parties can terminate the interest, whether the grantee can invite outsiders onto the property, who has the obligation to perform maintenance, who is liable if the grantee suffers an injury on the property, and what remedies the parties have if a disagreement arises.

To determine whether parties have created a leasehold or some other legal interest, courts have traditionally focused on whether a grantor has turned over exclusive possession or a more limited set of use rights. Possession, however, remains a slippery concept, difficult to define. Consider the following post from an internet message board:

---

wobble2847   ▶ **Add your comment**

Two months ago we hired a nanny for our three children. In addition to his salary, we offered him lodging in a room in our house. His duties with the children begin very early in the morning and we thought it would be a convenient arrangement for everyone. He is great with our kids but it turns out that he's a terrible houseguest. There are some real hygiene and noise issues. Rather than fire him and disrupt his (great) relationship with the kids, I thought I'd tell him he has to move out immediately because we're going to remodel the room. Can I do that legally? Is he our tenant?

Does the nanny have a lease? Do we need any other information? Should courts look beyond mere facts of possession and consider the policy considerations of extending landlord-tenant protections to the parties in the case? What might those policy considerations entail? As you read through the materials, you may want to revisit this question.

2.   Types of Leasehold

As we have seen throughout this course, property interests come in a limited number of forms, many of which we have inherited directly from feudal England. This theme holds in landlord-tenant. The common law developed three types of leaseholds that our modern property system still recognizes: the term of years, the periodic tenancy, and the tenancy at will.

The Term of Years

The *term of years* is a leasehold measured by any fixed period of time. The most familiar term of years lease is the residential one-year lease. The actual term, however, may vary greatly. In 2001, the U.S. government signed a 99-year lease for an embassy in Singapore. Leases of hundreds or even thousands of years are not unheard of, either. *See* Monbar v. Monaghan, 18 Del. Ch. 395 (1932) (two thousand year lease). At the other end of the spectrum, vacation properties like beach condos and lake houses commonly rent for one-week periods.

Whatever the duration, a term of years automatically ends when the stated term expires. For example, imagine L leases Blackacre to T "from September 1, 2015 to August 31, 2016." Neither party is required to give the other notice of termination. The tenant must simply surrender possession to the landlord by midnight on August 31. The death of either contracting party does not affect a term of years lease, unless the landlord and tenant have agreed otherwise. If the tenant dies, the law requires her estate to carry out the lease.

The Periodic Tenancy

The *periodic tenancy* is a lease for some fixed duration that automatically renews for succeeding periods until either the landlord or tenant gives notice of termination. This automatic renewal is the chief practical difference between the periodic tenancy and the term of years. The most common type of periodic tenancy is the month-to-month lease. As the name suggests, a month-to-month lease lasts for a month and then continues for subsequent months, until either the landlord or tenant ends the lease. Periodic tenancies have no certain end date; some residential tenants with month-to-month leases stay in their apartments for decades.

Termination requires one party to give advance notice to the other. These notice requirements are now heavily regulated by statute in most jurisdictions. Under the common law (which is still the basis for many state regulations), for year-to-year periodic leases (or any periodic lease with a longer initial duration), parties must give notice at least six months before the period ends. For leases less than a year, the minimum notice equals the length of the lease period. Additionally, unless the parties make an agreement to the contrary, the lease must terminate on the final day of a period. Assume, for example, that T signs a month-to-month lease that begins May 1. On August 20, T gives notice of termination to her landlord. When will the lease end? T must give the landlord a minimum of one month notice. That pushes T's obligations under the lease to September 19. A periodic tenancy, however, must end on the last day of a period. Thus, T's lease will terminate on September 30 at midnight.

The death of either the landlord or tenant does not end a periodic tenancy. If, for example, the tenant dies before the lease terminates, the law vests the tenant's estate with the responsibility to fulfill the remaining obligations under the lease.

The Tenancy at Will

The *tenancy at will* has no fixed duration and endures so long as both of the parties desire. For example, if the landlord and tenant sign a document that reads, "Tenant will pay the Landlord $500 on the first of the month and the lease will endure as long as both of us wish" they have created a tenancy at will. Under the common law, either party could end such a lease at any moment. Today, most states have enacted statutes that establish minimum notice periods—30 days is common. Tenancies at will also terminate if the landlord sells the property, the tenant abandons the unit, or either party dies.[12]

Tenancies at will can arise as a result of the clear intention of the parties—the ease of termination is a valued feature in some negotiations. But note, the tenancy at will is also the catchall lease category. If a leasehold doesn't qualify as either a term of years or periodic tenancy, the law crams it into the tenancy at will box—even if that clearly violates the goals of the parties. This occasionally creates real hardship for individuals with sloppily drafted leases.

Effel v. Rosberg

360 S.W.3d 626 (Tex. App. 2012)

MORRIS, Justice.

This is an appeal from the trial court's judgment awarding Robert G. Rosberg possession of property in a forcible detainer action. Appellant Lena Effel brings seventeen issues generally contending the trial court . . . erred in concluding Rosberg was entitled to possession of the property. After examining the record on appeal and reviewing the applicable law,

---

[12] In jurisdictions that require 30-day notice periods before the termination of a tenancy at will, this is one of the key remaining differences between the month-to-month periodic lease and the tenancy at will.

we conclude appellant's arguments are without merit. We affirm the trial court's judgment.

I.

[On March 1, 2006, Robert G. Rosberg filed suit against Lena Effel's nephews, Henry Effel and Jack Effel. The parties settled the dispute out of court and signed a compromise settlement agreement. As part of the settlement, Rosberg received a piece of land owned by Henry and Jack Effel. The property contained the home where Lena Effel lived. The settlement agreement between the Effels and Rosberg stated that Lena Effel] "shall continue to occupy the property for the remainder of her natural life, or until such time as she voluntarily chooses to vacate the premises." The settlement agreement further stated that a lease agreement incorporating the terms of the settlement agreement would be prepared before the closing date of the purchase. . . .

The property in question was deeded to Rosberg with no reservation of a life estate. A lease for appellant was prepared by the Effels' attorney. The term of the lease was "for a term equal to the remainder of the Lessee's life, or until such time that she voluntarily vacates the premises." The lease also contained various covenants relating to payment of rent and charges for utilities as well as the use and maintenance of the grounds. The lease provided that if there was any default in the payment of rent or in the performance of any of the covenants, the lease could be terminated at the option of the lessor. The lease was signed by Rosberg as lessor and by Henry Effel on behalf of appellant under a power of attorney as lessee.

Three years later, on February 24, 2010, Rosberg, through his attorney, sent a letter to appellant both by regular mail and certified mail stating that he was terminating her lease effective immediately. The reason for the termination, according to the letter, was Rosberg's discovery that appellant had installed a wrought iron fence in the front yard of the property in violation of two covenants of the lease. The letter stated that appellant was required to leave and surrender the premises within ten days and, if she did not vacate the premises, Rosberg would commence eviction proceedings. Appellant did not vacate the property.

On April 29, 2010, Rosberg filed this forcible detainer action in the justice court. The justice court awarded possession of the property to Rosberg, and appellant appealed the decision to the county court at law. The county court held a trial de novo without a jury and, again, awarded the property to Rosberg. The court concluded the lease created a tenancy at will terminable at any time by either party. The court further concluded that Rosberg was authorized to terminate the lease, whether because it was terminable at will or because appellant violated the terms of the lease, and the lease was properly terminated on February 24, 2010. Appellant now appeals the county court's judgment.

II.

. . . In appellant's remaining issues, she challenges the findings of fact and conclusions of law made by the county court. In her tenth issue, appellant challenges the county court's first conclusion of law in which it stated "[t]he lease, which purported to be for the rest of Lena Effel's life, created only a tenancy at will terminable at any time by either party." Appellant argues that the lease must be read together with the settlement agreement and the court must give effect to the intent of the parties. Appellant was not a party to the settlement agreement, however. Appellant was a party only to the lease. It is the lease, and not the settlement agreement, that forms the basis of this forcible detainer action. Accordingly, we look solely to the lease to determine appellant's rights in this matter.

The lease states that appellant was a lessee of the property "for a term equal to the remainder of Lessee's life, or until such time as she voluntarily vacates the premises." It is the long-standing rule in Texas that a lease must be for a certain period of time or it will be considered a tenancy at will. *See Holcombe v. Lorino*, 124 Tex. 446, 79 S.W.2d 307, 310 (1935).

Courts that have applied this rule to leases that state they are for the term of the lessee's life have concluded that the uncertainty of the date of the lessee's death rendered the lease terminable at will by either party.

Appellant argues the current trend in court decisions is away from finding a lease such as hers to be terminable at will. Appellant relies on the 1982 decision of *Philpot v. Fields*, 633 S.W.2d 546 (Tex. App. 1982). In *Philpot*, the court stated that the trend in law was away from requiring a lease to be of a definite and certain duration. In reviewing the law since *Philpot*, however, we discern no such trend. *See Kajo Church Square, Inc. v. Walker*, 2003 WL 1848555, at *5 (Tex. App. 2003). The rule continues to be that a lease for an indefinite and uncertain length of time is an estate at will. *See Providence Land Servs., L.L.C. v. Jones*, 353 S.W.3d 538, 542 (Tex. App. 2011). In this case, not only was the term of the lease stated to be for the uncertain length of appellant's life, but her tenancy was also "until such time that she voluntarily vacates the premises." If a lease can be terminated at the will of the lessee, it may also be terminated at the will of the lessor. Because the lease at issue was terminable at will by either party, the trial court's first conclusion of law was correct. We resolve appellant's tenth issue against her.

In her fourth issue, appellant contends the trial court erred in concluding that Rosberg sent her a proper notice to vacate the premises under section 24.005 of the Texas Property Code. Section 24.005 states that a landlord must give a tenant at will at least three days' written notice to vacate before filing a forcible detainer suit unless the parties contracted for a longer or shorter notice period in a written lease or agreement. TEX. PROP. CODE ANN. § 24.005(b) (West Supp. 2011). The section also states that the notice must be delivered either in person or by mail at the premises in question. Id. § 24.005(f). If the notice is delivered by mail, it may be by regular mail, registered mail, or certified mail, return receipt requested, to the premises in question.

The undisputed evidence in this case shows that Rosberg, through his attorney, sent appellant a written notice to vacate the premises by both regular mail and certified mail on February 24, 2010. The notice stated that appellant had ten days to surrender the premises. Nothing in the lease provided for a longer notice period. Henry Effel testified at trial that appellant received the notice and read it. Rosberg did not bring this forcible detainer action until April 29, 2010. The evidence conclusively shows, therefore, that Rosberg's notice to vacate the property complied with section 24.005. . . .

Because Rosberg had the right to terminate appellant's tenancy at any time and properly notified her of the termination under section 24.005 of the Texas Property Code, the trial court did not err in awarding the property at issue to Rosberg. Consequently, it is unnecessary for us to address the remainder of appellant's issues.

We affirm the trial court's judgment.

Notes and Questions

1. **The parties' intent?** When Henry and Jack Effel drafted the settlement agreement transferring their property to Robert Rosberg, what where they trying to accomplish? Did the court carry out the intentions of the parties? Why?

2. **Other approaches.** In *Garner v. Gerrish*, 473 N.E.2d 223 (N.Y. 1984), the New York Court of Appeals faced a case with very similar facts. The tenant, Lou Gerrish, had a lease stating, "Lou Gerrish [sic] has the privilege of termination [sic] this agreement at a date of his own choice." The New York court found that the document created a new kind of leasehold—a lease for life. The *Garner* opinion attacked the argument in favor of the tenancy at will as being grounded in the "antiquated notion[s]" of medieval property law. Is there any good reason for the law to only

recognize three leasehold tenancies? What if, instead, the lease gave only the *landlord* the power to terminate, and required the tenant to stay and pay as long as the landlord desired?

3. **Working within the system.** Could the lease have been drafted in a way that would have let Lena Effel stay on the property for the duration of her life or until she chose to move, as long as she kept paying the rent?

4. **Institutional competence.** Are courts or legislatures better positioned to create new property forms?

5. **The background story.** Lena Effel lived in the house owned by her nephews for over 20 years. Before that, her twin brother (Henry and Jack's father) had lived in the home for many years. At the time the compromise settlement agreement was signed, Lena was 93 years old. At the time Rosberg sought to evict her, Lena was 97. Should any of those facts have influenced the judges in the case?

Lease Hypotheticals

A professionally drafted lease will almost always make clear what type of leasehold the parties have elected. When problems arise it's often because lessors and lessees have drafted legal documents without the help of a qualified lawyer. In the following examples try to figure out what kind of leasehold the parties have created. If it's a term of years, how long is the term? If it's a periodic tenancy, what is the period?

1. L and T sign an agreement that reads, "The term is one year, beginning September 1."
2. L and T sign a lease that reads, "This agreement lasts as long as the parties consent."

3. L and T sign an agreement that reads, "The lease will run from September 1 until the following August 31. One thousand dollars payable on the first of every month."

4. L and T enter a lease that reads in relevant part, "the rent is $48,000 per year, payable $4,000 on the first of each month."

5. L and T enter a lease that reads, "the rent is $1,000 per month."

6. L and T enter a lease that reads, "the rent is $1,000 per month and lasts until the tenant completes medical school."

7. L and T are negotiating on the phone over an apartment lease. At the end of the conversation L says, "Have we got a deal? Five years lease with rent at $10,000 a year?" T replies, "Great. I accept. It's a deal."

3.   The Problem of Holdovers

<u>The Tenancy at Sufferance</u>

Imagine that you own a small apartment building in a college town. At the end of the school year, one of your tenants refuses to move out. The law refers to such tenants as *holdovers*. As a landlord, what are your options in this situation? How does the legal system treat individuals who stay past the end of their leases? Can you kick them out? Are they obligated to pay you rent?

When a tenant stays in possession after the lease has expired, the law allows the landlord to make a one-time election. The landlord has the option to treat the holdover as a trespasser, bring an eviction proceeding, and sue for damages. Alternatively, the landlord may renew the holdover's lease for another term. This second option is typically referred to as a *tenancy at sufferance*. Some hornbooks list the tenancy at sufferance as a fourth type of common law leasehold. The tenancy at sufferance, however, is not based on any affirmative agreement between parties and is probably better understood as a remedy for wrongful occupancy. Also note that disputes sometimes pop-up over what election the landlord has made. For example, what if the landlord does nothing for two months but then initiates eviction?

In most jurisdictions, when a landlord chooses to hold the tenant to a new lease, it creates a periodic tenancy. States differ, however, on how to compute the length of the period and, thus, the amount of the damages. Some simply copy over the length of the original lease (with a maximum of one year). Others divine the repeating period by looking at how the rent was paid. Imagine, for example, your tenant had originally signed a lease reading, "This lease will run from January 1, 2014 to December 31, 2014. Rent is due on the first of each month." The tenancy created by the holdover would either be a year-to-year lease or a month-to-month lease depending on the jurisdiction.

Still other states take other approaches. Some, for example, specify that a holdover must pay double (or triple) rent for the holdover period.

Notes and Questions

1. **The landlord's options.** Under what circumstances should a landlord move to evict a tenant who holds over? Are there any scenarios where a landlord might want to keep a tenant who has already proven themselves untrustworthy by staying past the agreed-upon term?

2. **Drafting.** How can landlords draft leases to better protect themselves from the threat of holdovers?

3. **A holdover problem.** Seven years ago, Tommy Hillclimber leased a commercial building on a busy street from Lisa. The lease was for a five-year term with annual rent of $100,000. At the end of the term, Tommy retained possession of the building but continued to make rent payments. Lisa has cashed all of Tommy's

rent checks. Last week, Sprawl-Mart contacted Lisa and offered to rent the building for $200,000 a year. Lisa quickly sent notice to Tommy stating that the lease will terminate in 30 days. Does Tommy have to vacate?

Delivering Possession

Holdovers can also cause problems for other renters. Suppose that before the start of law school you agree to a one-year lease that begins on August 1. Although you've signed a binding lease agreement and have received a set of keys, when your van pulls into the driveway on move-in day, you find that the previous tenant hasn't left "your" apartment. If the lease doesn't include a contingency for such an event, what are your rights?

Hannan v. Dusch
153 S.E. 824 (Va. 1930)

PRENTIS, C.J.,

The declaration filed by the plaintiff, Hannan, against the defendant, Dusch, alleges that Dusch had on August 31, 1927, leased to the plaintiff certain real estate in the city of Norfolk, Virginia, therein described, for fifteen years, the term to begin January 1, 1928, at a specified rental; that it thereupon became and was the duty of the defendant to see to it that the premises leased by the defendant to the plaintiff should be open for entry by him on January 1, 1928, the beginning of the term, and to put said petitioner in possession of the premises on that date; that the petitioner was willing and ready to enter upon and take possession of the leased property, and so informed the defendant; yet the defendant failed and refused to put the plaintiff in possession or to keep the property open for him at that time or on any subsequent date; and that the defendant suffered to remain on said property a certain tenant or tenants who occupied a portion or portions thereof, and refused to take legal or other action to oust said tenants or to compel their removal from the property so occupied. Plaintiff alleged damages which he had suffered by reason of this alleged breach of the contract and deed, and sought to recover such damages in the action. There is no express covenant as to the delivery of the premises . . . .

The single question of law therefore presented in this case is whether a landlord, who without any express covenant as to delivery of possession leases property to a tenant, is required under the law to oust trespassers and wrongdoers so as to have it open for entry by the tenant at the beginning of the term — that is, whether without an express covenant there is nevertheless an implied covenant to deliver possession. . . .

It seems to be perfectly well settled that there is an implied covenant in such cases on the part of the landlord to assure to the tenant the legal right of possession — that is, that at the beginning of the term there shall be no legal obstacle to the tenant's right of possession. This is not the question presented. Nor need we discuss in this case the rights of the parties in case a tenant rightfully in possession under the title of his landlord is thereafter disturbed by some wrongdoer. In such case the tenant must protect himself from trespassers, and there is no obligation on the landlord to assure his quiet enjoyment of his term as against wrongdoers or intruders.

Of course, the landlord assures to the tenant quiet possession as against all who rightfully claim through or under the landlord.

The discussion then is limited to the precise legal duty of the landlord in the absence of an express covenant, in case a former tenant, who wrongfully holds over, illegally refuses to surrender possession to the new tenant. This is a question about which there is a hopeless conflict of the authorities. It is generally claimed that the weight of the authority favors the particular view contended for. There are, however, no scales upon which we can weigh the authorities. In numbers and respectability they may be quite equally balanced.

It is then a question about which no one should be dogmatic, but all should seek for that rule which is supported by the better reason. . . .

It is conceded by all that the two rules, one called the English rule, which implies a covenant requiring the lessor to put the lessee in possession, and that called the American rule, which recognizes the lessee's legal right to possession, but implies no such duty upon the lessor as against wrongdoers, are irreconcilable.

The English rule is that in the absence of stipulations to the contrary, there is in every lease an implied covenant on the part of the landlord that the premises shall be open to entry by the tenant at the time fixed by the lease for the beginning of his term. . . .

[A] case which supports the English rule is *Herpolsheimer v. Christopher*, 76 Neb. 352, 107 N.W. 382, 111 N.W. 359, 9 L.R.A. (N.S.) 1127, 14 Ann. Cas. 399, note. In that case the court gave these as its reasons for following the English rule:

> We think . . . that the English rule is most in consonance with good conscience, sound principle, and fair dealing. Can it be supposed that the plaintiff in this case would have entered into the lease if he had known at the time that he could not obtain possession on the 1st of March, but that he would be compelled to begin a lawsuit, await the law's delays, and follow the case through its devious turnings to an end before he could hope to obtain possession of the land he had leased? Most assuredly not. It is unreasonable to suppose that a man would knowingly contract for a lawsuit, or take the chance of one. Whether or not a tenant in possession intends to hold over or assert a right to future term may nearly always be known to the landlord, and is certainly much more apt to be within

his knowledge than within that of the prospective tenant. Moreover, since in an action to recover possession against a tenant holding over, the lessee would be compelled largely to rely upon the lessor's testimony in regard to the facts of the claim to hold over by the wrongdoer, it is more reasonable and proper to place the burden upon the person within whose knowledge the facts are most apt to lie. We are convinced, therefore, that the better reason lies with the courts following the English doctrine, and we therefore adopt it, and hold that, ordinarily, the lessor impliedly covenants with the lessee that the premises leased shall be open to entry by him at the time fixed in the lease as the beginning of the term. . . .

So let us not lose sight of the fact that under the English rule a covenant which might have been but was not made is nevertheless implied by the court, though it is manifest that each of the parties might have provided for that and for every other possible contingency relating to possession by having express covenants which would unquestionably have protected both.

Referring then to the American rule: Under that rule, in such cases, [ ]the landlord is not bound to put the tenant into actual possession, but is bound only to put him in legal possession, so that no obstacle in the form of superior right of possession will be interposed to prevent the tenant from obtaining actual possession of the demised premises. If the landlord gives the tenant a right of possession he has done all that he is required to do by the terms of an ordinary lease, and the tenant assumes the burden of enforcing such right of possession as against all persons wrongfully in possession, whether they be trespassers or former tenants wrongfully holding over.[ ] . . .

So that, under the American rule, where the new tenant fails to obtain possession of the premises only because a former tenant wrongfully holds over, his remedy is against such wrongdoer and not against the landlord — this because the landlord has not covenanted against the wrongful acts of another and should not be held responsible for such a tort unless he has expressly so contracted. This accords with the general rule as to other wrongdoers, whereas the English rule appears to create a specific exception against lessors. It does not occur to us now that there is any other instance in which one clearly without fault is held responsible for the independent tort of another in which he has neither participated nor concurred and whose misdoings he cannot control. . . .

For the reasons which have been so well stated by those who have enforced the American rule, our judgment is that there is no error in the judgment complained of.

Affirmed

Notes and Questions

1. **The basic law.** U.S. jurisdictions remain split over the landlord's duty to provide possession. A majority of jurisdictions (and the Uniform Residential Landlord and Tenant Act) now follow the English rule, but the American rule remains alive and well. As should be obvious, the biggest difference between the two approaches is the remedy available to the dispossessed tenant. Under the English view, the tenant may terminate the lease and sue the landlord for damages. The tenant can also choose to withhold payment from the landlord until the tenant is able to take possession. In contrast, under the American rule, the tenant must bring an eviction action directly against the holdover.

2. **Justifying the rules.** What policies support the English view? What polices support the American view? Would you find the remedies available under the American rule helpful?

3. **Conceptual Arguments.** The *Hannan* case does an excellent job discussing the policy rationales for and against the two rules. But what about the more conceptual arguments? If we view the lease as a conveyance of the legal right to possession, isn't the American rule "correct?" Once a landlord turns over possessory rights, aren't her obligations fulfilled?

4. **What do tenants know?** Do you think that tenants in American rule jurisdictions know that their landlord has no obligation provide them with actual possession? Should that matter?

5. **What rules are mandatory?** Imagine that you sit in a state legislature that wants to adopt the English Rule by statute. Should you make the new law a mandatory rule or a default position that parties can negotiate around?

6. **Your Lease?** Does the lease for the apartment you're currently renting make any provision for this problem?

4.   Tenant Selection

As we saw earlier in the textbook, the right to exclude remains a cornerstone of property ownership. Owners have expansive power to keep others off of their land and out of their homes. Generally speaking, this right extends to landlords, who have broad discretion to select tenants as they see fit. Landlords, for example, remain free to exclude smokers from their properties. They can also refuse to rent to a tenant who acts erratically, possesses a criminal record, or has a low credit score. Landlords, however, cannot violate state or federal anti-discrimination laws when they go through the leasing process.

The Civil Rights Act of 1866

One of the oldest laws that protects tenants against discrimination in the housing market is the Civil Rights Act of 1866. Passed in the aftermath of the Civil War, the Civil Rights Act of 1866 prohibits all discrimination based on race in the purchase or rental of real or personal property. *See Jones v. Alfred H. Mayer Co.*, 392 U.S. 409 (1968). Thus, landlords cannot deny an apartment unit to a potential tenant based on tenant's heritage or the color of their skin. There are no exceptions.

The Fair Housing Act of 1968

The Fair Housing Act of 1968 (and its many amendments) greatly expanded the number of individuals covered by anti-discrimination law. Broadly speaking, the Fair Housing Act (FHA) prohibits discrimination in the renting, selling, advertising, or financing of real estate on the basis of race, color, national origin, religion, sex, familial status, and disability. It is worth looking closely at some of its provisions. The Act begins with a statement of policy and a few (counter-intuitive) definitions:

§3601. Declaration of Policy
It is the policy of the United States to provide, within constitutional limitations, for fair housing throughout the United States.

§3602. Definitions
As used in this subchapter . . .
    (c) "Family" includes a single individual. .. .
    (h) "Handicap" means, with respect to a person—
        (1) a physical or mental impairment which substantially limits one or more of such person's major life activities,

(2) a record of having such an impairment, or

(3) being regarded as having such an impairment, but such term does not include current, illegal use of or addiction to a controlled substance (as defined in section 802 of title 21). . . .

(k) "Familial status" means one or more individuals (who have not attained the age of 18 years) being domiciled with—

(1) a parent or another person having legal custody of such individual or individuals; or

(2) the designee of such parent or other person having such custody, with the written permission of such parent or other person.

The protections afforded against discrimination on the basis of familial status shall apply to any person who is pregnant or is in the process of securing legal custody of any individual who has not attained the age of 18 years.

The definition of "familial status" surprises many students. Whom, exactly, does it protect? Unmarried people? Single mothers? Although more intuitive, the definition of handicap has generated a number of legal disputes. Alcohol, for example, is not a controlled substance under section 802 of title 21. Does that mean that a landlord cannot refuse to rent to a person who drinks heavily or sounds very drunk (and belligerent) over the phone?

The real meat of the Fair Housing act comes in §3604. The first subsection makes it unlawful to "refuse to sell or rent . . . or otherwise make unavailable" a "dwelling" to any person because of race, color, religion, sex, familial status, or national origin. *See* 42 U.S.C. §3604(a). Later sections provide similar protections for the handicapped. The Act then takes a number of additional steps designed to eliminate discrimination from the housing market. Under the terms of the law it is illegal to:

(1) discriminate in the terms or conditions of a sale or rental [§3604(b)];

(2) create or publish an advertisement or statement that express a preference or hostility toward individuals in any of the protected categories [§3604(c)];

(3) lie about or misrepresent the availability of housing [§3604(d)];

(4) refuse to permit handicapped tenants from making reasonable modifications of the existing premise at their own expense [§3604(f)(3)(A)];

(5) refuse to make reasonable accommodations in rules and policies to accommodate individuals with handicaps [§3604(f)(3)(B)];

(6) Harass or intimidate persons in their enjoyment of a dwelling [§3617].

Unlike the Civil Rights Act of 1866, the Fair Housing Act does contain a number of important exemptions. Section 3607(b), for example, allows housing designated for older persons to bar families with young children. Similarly, section 3607(a) allows religious organizations and private clubs to give preferences to their own members. The most controversial exemption, reproduced below, is the so-called Mrs. Murphy exemption:

(b) Nothing in section 3604 of this title (other than subsection (c)) shall apply to—

(1) any single-family house sold or rented by an owner: Provided, That such private individual owner does not own more than three such single-family houses at any one time: Provided further , That in the case of the sale of any such single-family house by a private individual owner not residing in such house at the time of such sale or who was not the most recent resident of such house prior to such sale, the exemption granted by this subsection shall apply only with respect to

one such sale within any twenty-four month period: Provided further , That such bona fide private individual owner does not own any interest in, nor is there owned or reserved on his behalf, under any express or voluntary agreement, title to or any right to all or a portion of the proceeds from the sale or rental of, more than three such single-family houses at any one time: Provided further , That after December 31, 1969, the sale or rental of any such single-family house shall be excepted from the application of this subchapter only if such house is sold or rented (A) without the use in any manner of the sales or rental facilities or the sales or rental services of any real estate broker, agent, or salesman, or of such facilities or services of any person in the business of selling or renting dwellings, or of any employee or agent of any such broker, agent, salesman, or person and (B) without the publication, posting or mailing, after notice, of any advertisement or written notice in violation of section 3604(c) of this title; but nothing in this proviso shall prohibit the use of attorneys, escrow agents, abstractors, title companies, and other such professional assistance as necessary to perfect or transfer the title, or

(2) rooms or units in dwellings containing living quarters occupied or intended to be occupied by no more than four families living independently of each other, if the owner actually maintains and occupies one of such living quarters as his residence.

What does this exemption allow? If the act is intended to root out pernicious discrimination, why include this provision?

It is crucial to note that the plain text of the Mrs. Murphy exemption states that it does not apply to 3604(c)—the subsection that prohibits discriminatory advertising. Thus, although certain categories of landlords are exempted from the statute's basic framework, they are still not allowed to post discriminatory advertisements.

State Anti-Discrimination Efforts

Some state legislatures have passed laws that afford far more protection from discrimination than the federal statutes provide. Minnesota, for example, protects against housing discrimination on the basis of sexual orientation, gender identity, marital status, and source of income. Other states in the Northeast and West Coast provide similar coverage, but these positions are in no way a majority. As the map below indicates, in most states nothing prevents a landlord from denying an apartment to an engaged heterosexual couple, based on the belief that cohabitation before marriage is sinful.

States Where You Can Be Denied Housing Because of Your Marital Status

Denial Allowed

Proving Discrimination

Two broad categories of cases may be brought under the FHA: disparate
treatment claims and disparate impact claims.

A sign erected by white homeowners trying to prevent black tenants from
moving into their Detroit neighborhood (1942).

Disparate treatment claims target intentional forms of discrimination,
including the refusal to rent based on one of the protected categories. A
plaintiff can show intent to discriminate with "smoking gun" style
evidence, such as statements by the landlord that he "would never rent to
an Irishman." Of course, modern landlords rarely make such forthright
admissions. As a result, courts in the United States have established a
burden-shifting approach that allows plaintiffs to prove intentional
discrimination with indirect circumstantial evidence. The initial burden is
on the plaintiff to make a *prima facie* case of discrimination. In a refusal to
rent case, the plaintiff must show that (1) that she is a member of a class
protected by the FHA; (2) that she applied for and was qualified to rent
the unit; (3) that she was rejected; and (4) the unit remained unrented.
Once the plaintiff has established sufficient evidence to state a *prima facie*
case, the burden shifts to the defendant landlord to proffer a legitimate

nondiscriminatory reason for the refusal to rent. If the defendant meets this requirement, the burden then shifts back to the tenant to prove that the reason offered is a pretext.

Discrimination is often ferreted out through the use of "testers." Advocacy groups, many of which are funded by the federal government, will send comparable white and black individuals to inquire about renting a vacant unit. If the landlord treats the testers differently (e.g., provides different levels of assistance, shows different units, provides different information about unit availability) this provides persuasive evidence of illegal discrimination.

Disparate impact claims allege that some seemingly neutral policy has a disproportionately harmful effect on members of a group protected by the FHA. These cases rely heavily on statistical evidence and employ a very similar burden-shifting methodology as the disparate treatment claims. Using statistics, plaintiffs need to show that a defendant's policy has actually caused some disparity.   The defendant then has the opportunity to escape liability if it can show show that its actions are necessary to achieve a valid goal. See *Texas Department of Housing & Community Affairs v. Inclusive Communities Project, Inc.*, 135 S. Ct. 2507 (2015).

Problems

1. William Neithamer, who is gay and HIV positive attempted to rent an apartment from Brenneman Properties. Neithamer did not reveal his HIV status, but admitted to the property manager that he had dismal credit because he had recently devoted all of his resources to taking care of a lover who had died of AIDS. Neithamer, however, offered to pre-pay one year's rent. Brenneman Properties rejected Neithamer's application and, in turn, Neithamer sued under the FHA. Does he have a case? *See*

Neithamer v. Brenneman Property Services, Inc., 81 F. Supp 2d 1 (D.D.C. 1999).

2. Over the phone, Landlord said to Plaintiff, "Do you have children? I don't want any little boys because they'll mess up the house and nobody would be here to watch them. Really, this house isn't good for kids because it's right next to a main road." Plaintiff sues. Landlord argues that her statements only show that she is concerned about the welfare of children. Is that a legitimate non-discriminatory reason to refuse to rent?

3. A local government has decided to knock down two high-rise public housing projects within its borders. The high-rises primarily house recent immigrants from Guatemala. A local advocacy group brings a lawsuit on their behalf, claiming that the government action has a disparate impact on a protected group. Is this a disparate treatment or disparate impact case? Can you think of a non-discriminatory reason why the government may have taken such an action?

4. The FHA requires landlords to make "reasonable accommodations" for individuals with handicaps. Which of the following requests by a tenant would qualify as a reasonable accommodation? (a) Asking a landlord with a first-come/first-served parking policy to create a reserved parking space for a tenant who has difficulty walking; (b) Requesting that a landlord waive parking fees for a disabled tenant's home health care aide; (c) Asking the landlord to make an exception to the building's "no pets" rule for a tenant with a service animal; (d) Requesting landlord to pay for a sign language interpreter for a deaf individual during the application process; (e) Asking the landlord to provide

oral reminders to pay the rent for a tenant with documented short-term memory loss.

An Exercise in Advertising

Imagine that you are a lawyer for a newspaper in a large metropolitan area. The local chapter of the ACLU has raised concerns that some advertisements in the classifieds section of your paper violate the Fair Housing Act.[13] Your boss has asked you to review the ads for any offending language. Which of the following would you feel comfortable printing?[14]

---

[13] Would any of these ads violate the Civil Rights Act of 1866?

[14] The government does provide some guidance to landlords worried about triggering FHA liability through their advertisements. There are, for example, published lists of "words to avoid" and "acceptable language." Although context is important, landlords can generally use these phrases: good neighborhood, secluded setting, single family home, quality construction, near public transportation, near places of worship, and assistance animals only.

Rectangular Snip

FOR RENT
Seeking tenant for 1 bed apt. $500/m. I only rent to black people.

FOR RENT
New apartment building. $650/m. Walking distance to synagogue. Great amenities.

FOR RENT
Great Deal! Apt. in exclusive Danbury area. Very selective. Contact ASAP. $700/m

FOR RENT
Perfect apt. for rent. Near park. $400/m. Absolutely no pets.

FOR RENT
Snazzy digs near downtown! Looking for muscular football players to rent rooms. 500/m

FOR RENT
Looking for tenants. Absolutely no lawyers. Only couples. Must show income 3x monthly rent.

FOR RENT
Seeking new tenants for 2 br. Pref for women – I'm female & want female tenants!

FOR RENT
Great place by University. $600/m. Kids ok, but must pay 2x security dep. Kids = trouble

What about this ad for a roommate on Craigslist? Is it objectionable to you? Does it violate the FHA? Does it matter that the poster is looking for a *roommate*? Would your answers change if the advertisement read, "Have a room available for an able-bodied white man with no children?"

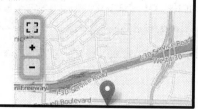

★ **$650 / 1010ft² - Have a room available for female Christian elderly woman none smoker** (I 30 & st frances)

Nice comfortable furnished room available access to patio, backyard, 1/2 bath & full bath available, wyfi available, cable TV available, This all for that special Christian elderly none smoking or drinking church going female.
Thank you
Serious inquiries only!!!

Fair Housing Council of San Fernando Valley v. Roommate.com, LLC
666 F.3d 1216 (9th Cir. 2012)

KOZINSKI, Chief Judge:

There's no place like home. In the privacy of your own home, you can take off your coat, kick off your shoes, let your guard down and be completely yourself. While we usually share our homes only with friends and family, sometimes we need to take in a stranger to help pay the rent. When that happens, can the government limit whom we choose? Specifically, do the anti-discrimination provisions of the Fair Housing Act ("FHA") extend to the selection of roommates?

Roommate.com, LLC ("Roommate") operates an internet-based business that helps roommates find each other. Roommate's website receives over 40,000 visits a day and roughly a million new postings for roommates are created each year. When users sign up, they must create a profile by answering a series of questions about their sex, sexual orientation and whether children will be living with them. An open-ended "Additional Comments" section lets users include information not prompted by the questionnaire. Users are asked to list their preferences for roommate characteristics, including sex, sexual orientation and familial status. Based on the profiles and preferences, Roommate matches users and provides them a list of housing-seekers or available rooms meeting their criteria. Users can also search available listings based on roommate characteristics, including sex, sexual orientation and familial status. The Fair Housing Councils of San Fernando Valley and San Diego ("FHCs") sued Roommate in federal court, alleging that the website's questions requiring disclosure of sex, sexual orientation and familial status, and its sorting, steering and matching of users based on those characteristics, violate the Fair Housing Act ("FHA"), 42 U.S.C. § 3601 et seq. . . .

ANALYSIS

If the FHA extends to shared living situations, it's quite clear that what Roommate does amounts to a violation. The pivotal question is whether the FHA applies to roommates.

I

The FHA prohibits discrimination on the basis of "race, color, religion, sex, familial status, or national origin" in the "sale or rental *of a dwelling.*" 42 U.S.C. § 3604(b) (emphasis added). The FHA also makes it illegal to:

> make, print, or publish, or cause to be made, printed, or published any notice, statement, or advertisement, with respect to the sale or rental *of a dwelling* that indicates any preference, limitation, or discrimination based on race, color, religion, sex, handicap, familial status, or national origin, or an intention to make any such preference, limitation, or discrimination.

Id. § 3604(c) (emphasis added). The reach of the statute turns on the meaning of "dwelling."

The FHA defines "dwelling" as "any building, structure, or portion thereof which is occupied as, or designed or intended for occupancy as, a residence by one or more families." Id. § 3602(b). A dwelling is thus a living unit designed or intended for occupancy by a family, meaning that it ordinarily has the elements generally associated with a family residence: sleeping spaces, bathroom and kitchen facilities, and common areas, such as living rooms, dens and hallways.

It would be difficult, though not impossible, to divide a single-family house or apartment into separate "dwellings" for purposes of the statute. Is a "dwelling" a bedroom plus a right to access common areas? What if roommates share a bedroom? Could a "dwelling" be a bottom bunk and half an armoire? It makes practical sense to interpret "dwelling" as an independent living unit and stop the FHA at the front door.

There's no indication that Congress intended to interfere with personal relationships inside the home. Congress wanted to address the problem of landlords discriminating in the sale and rental of housing, which deprived protected classes of housing opportunities. But a business transaction between a tenant and landlord is quite different from an arrangement between two people sharing the same living space. We seriously doubt Congress meant the FHA to apply to the latter. Consider, for example, the FHA's prohibition against sex discrimination. Could Congress, in the 1960s, really have meant that women must accept men as roommates? Telling women they may not lawfully exclude men from the list of acceptable roommates would be controversial today; it would have been scandalous in the 1960s.

While it's possible to read dwelling to mean sub-parts of a home or an apartment, doing so leads to awkward results. . . . Nonetheless, this interpretation is not wholly implausible and we would normally consider adopting it, given that the FHA is a remedial statute that we construe broadly. Therefore, we turn to constitutional concerns, which provide strong countervailing considerations.

II

The Supreme Court has recognized that "the freedom to enter into and carry on certain intimate or private relationships is a fundamental element of liberty protected by the Bill of Rights." *Bd. of Dirs. of Rotary Int'l v. Rotary Club of Duarte*, 481 U.S. 537 (1987). "[C]hoices to enter into and maintain certain intimate human relationships must be secured against undue intrusion by the State because of the role of such relationships in safeguarding the individual freedom that is central to our constitutional scheme." *Roberts v. U.S. Jaycees*, 468 U.S. 609, 617-18 (1984). Courts have extended the right of intimate association to marriage, child bearing, child rearing and cohabitation with relatives. *Id.* While the right protects only "highly personal relationships," *IDK, Inc. v. Clark Cnty.*, 836 F.2d 1185, 1193 (9th Cir. 1988) (quoting *Roberts*, 468 U.S. at 618), the right isn't restricted exclusively to family, *Bd. of Dirs. of Rotary Int'l*, 481 U.S. at 545. The right to association also implies a right not to associate. *Roberts*, 468 U.S. at 623.

To determine whether a particular relationship is protected by the right to intimate association we look to "size, purpose, selectivity, and whether others are excluded from critical aspects of the relationship." *Bd. of Dirs. of Rotary Int'l*, 481 U.S. at 546. The roommate relationship easily qualifies: People generally have very few roommates; they are selective in choosing roommates; and non-roommates are excluded from the critical aspects of the relationship, such as using the living spaces. Aside from immediate family or a romantic partner, it's hard to imagine a relationship more intimate than that between roommates, who share living rooms, dining rooms, kitchens, bathrooms, even bedrooms.

Because of a roommate's unfettered access to the home, choosing a roommate implicates significant privacy and safety considerations. The home is the center of our private lives. Roommates note our comings and goings, observe whom we bring back at night, hear what songs we sing in the shower, see us in various stages of undress and learn intimate details most of us prefer to keep private. . . .

Equally important, we are fully exposed to a roommate's belongings, activities, habits, proclivities and way of life. This could include matter we find offensive (pornography, religious materials, political propaganda); dangerous (tobacco, drugs, firearms); annoying (jazz, perfume, frequent overnight visitors, furry pets); habits that are incompatible with our lifestyle (early risers, messy cooks, bathroom hogs, clothing borrowers). When you invite others to share your living quarters, you risk becoming a suspect in whatever illegal activities they engage in.

Government regulation of an individual's ability to pick a roommate thus intrudes into the home, which "is entitled to special protection as the center of the private lives of our people." Minnesota v. Carter, 525 U.S. 83, 99 (1998) (Kennedy, J., concurring). . . . Holding that the FHA applies inside a home or apartment would allow the government to restrict our ability to choose roommates compatible with our lifestyles. This would be a serious invasion of privacy, autonomy and security.

For example, women will often look for female roommates because of modesty or security concerns. As roommates often share bathrooms and common areas, a girl may not want to walk around in her towel in front of a boy. She might also worry about unwanted sexual advances or becoming romantically involved with someone she must count on to pay the rent.

An orthodox Jew may want a roommate with similar beliefs and dietary restrictions, so he won't have to worry about finding honey-baked ham in the refrigerator next to the potato latkes. Non-Jewish roommates may not understand or faithfully follow all of the culinary rules, like the use of different silverware for dairy and meat products, or the prohibition against warming non-kosher food in a kosher microwave. . . .

It's a "well-established principle that statutes will be interpreted to avoid constitutional difficulties." Frisby v. Schultz, 487 U.S. 474, 483 (1988). "[W]here an otherwise acceptable construction of a statute would raise serious constitutional problems, the Court will construe the statute to avoid such problems unless such construction is plainly contrary to the intent of Congress." Pub. Citizen v. U.S. Dep't of Justice, 491 U.S. 440, 466

(1989). Because the FHA can reasonably be read either to include or exclude shared living arrangements, we can and must choose the construction that avoids raising constitutional concerns. . . . Reading "dwelling" to mean an independent housing unit is a fair interpretation of the text and consistent with congressional intent. Because the construction of "dwelling" to include shared living units raises substantial constitutional concerns, we adopt the narrower construction that excludes roommate selection from the reach of the FHA. . . .

As the underlying conduct is not unlawful, Roommate's facilitation of discriminatory roommate searches does not violate the FHA.

Notes and Questions

1. **What's a dwelling?** The FHA defines "dwelling" as "any building, structure, or portion thereof which is occupied as, or designed or intended for occupancy as, a residence by one or more families." Id. § 3602(b). Do you think the FHA applies to college dormitories? Is it illegal to reserve some dormitories for women or to have ethnic-themed dorms?

2. **A broader Craigslist problem.** It's not unusual to stumble across advertisements for apartments (as opposed to just roommate ads) on Craigslist that violate the FHA. If a local newspaper published similar ads they would be liable under the FHA for publishing discriminatory material. Why doesn't anyone sue Craigslist? The answer is that section 230(c) of the Communications Decency Act provides internet service providers and website owners with broad immunity from liability for content posted by third parties. Craigslist and other similar sites may voluntarily remove offending posts, but they are not required to do so.

C.   Exiting a Lease

Most leases expire either at the end of the agreed-upon term or when one party serves the other with notice that they've decided not to renew for another period. Sometimes, however, either a tenant or landlord seeks to get out of the lease before the negotiated term concludes. For example, a new job in a faraway state, a family emergency, or a business failure can all change a tenant's needs or ability to pay the rent. We turn now to the legal consequences of exiting a lease.

1.   Landlord Exit: Transfer

Landlords may sell their properties to third parties at any time. The law categorizes a landlord's interest in rented property as a reversion and, like most other property interests, the landlord's reversion is fully alienable. But what happens to a lease if a property is transferred? As a default rule, when a landlord sells his interest, the purchaser takes subject to any leases. If there are tenants with unexpired term-of-years leases, for example, the new landlord cannot evict them. Conversely, the tenants must continue to pay the agreed upon rent to the new owner. If the lease is a periodic tenancy (or tenancy at will), the new landlord may end the leasehold by providing the tenant with the required notice. Until then, the leases continue unabated.

Remember that these are default rules, alterable by contract. In fact, landlords often insert provisions into leases that give them the option to terminate rental agreements upon sale of the property.

2.   **Tenant Exit: Transfer**

Tenants have exit options, too. The default rule is that a tenant's interest in a term of years lease or periodic tenancy is also freely transferable. (Note, however, that a tenant cannot transfer a tenancy at will to another party.) The law recognizes two types of transfer: the *assignment* and the *sublease*. The vast majority of jurisdictions use an objective test to distinguish the two. In an assignment, the original tenant transfers all of the remaining interest under the lease to a new tenant. In a sublease, on the other hand, the original tenant transfers less than all of her remaining rights in the unexpired period—the original tenant either gets the unit back at the end of the sublease or reserves a right to cut the sublease short.

An example should illuminate the concepts. Imagine that the Witch leases her Gingerbread Cottage to Hansel for a period of one year—January 1 to December 31—in exchange for $100 a month. Four months into the lease, Hansel then transfers all of his remaining interest in the property to Gretel so that she now has exclusive possessory rights until the end of the term. This transfer is an assignment because Hansel has no further rights in the property. If Hansel had retained for himself the final two months of the lease or if he'd rented the cottage to Gretel for only the summer months, we would then categorize the agreement as a sublease.

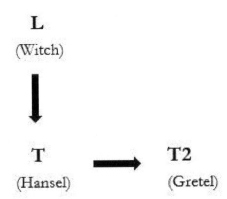

A minority of jurisdictions takes a less formalistic approach to the assignment/sublease division. In these states, the subjective intent of the parties, rather than the structure of the transaction, controls. Arkansas, for example, allows parties to designate their leases as subleases or assignment (and receive all the attendant rights and obligations under the chosen category) regardless of whether the new tenant takes the unit for the entire remaining term.

The distinction between subleases and assignments has a few significant legal consequences. Primarily, it affects who can benefit from the promises in the original lease and who is on the hook for the obligations. Think again about the Hansel and Gretel example described above. If Gretel, who took over the lease, stops making rent payments, whom can the landlord sue? The original tenant, Hansel? Gretel? Both? What if the original one-year lease contained a provision allowing the tenant to renew for a second year with the same terms? Can Gretel take advantage of that clause?

To enforce any promise, the law requires a certain type of legal relationship between the parties, known as *privity*. Donald Trump, for example, cannot successfully sue you if one of his Trump Tower tenants suddenly fails to pay rent—there's simply no connection between Trump and you. Trump could only sue you if a privity relationship exists: either *privity of contract* or *privity of estate.* Privity of contract is easy enough to understand. Parties are in privity of contract if they have entered into a valid contract with each other. In our example, the Witch and Hansel are in privity of contract because they signed the original lease agreement. The Witch gave Hansel the right to exclusive possession for one year and Hansel promised to pay rent every month. As a result of this legal relationship, the Witch has the option to sue Hansel if she doesn't receive rent. That remains true even if Hansel transfers his lease to someone else. That bears repeating: the original tenant's promise to pay the landlord stands until the original lease expires (or until the landlord releases the tenant from this obligation).

When Hansel and the Witch first sign the lease, they also stand in privity of estate with each other. This concept is yet another holdover from feudal times. Privity of estate makes concrete the medieval belief that an individual takes on a series of rights and obligations when they occupy land owned by another.[15] For our purposes, privity of estate arises when two parties have successive ownership claims in the same property. Hansel and the Witch have privity of estate because once Hansel's possessory interest concludes, his property rights flow immediately back to the Witch. Despite its archaic origin, the idea remains important in modern property law because individuals in privity of estate can sue each other directly for (some) violations of a rental agreement.[16]

Consider, again, what happens when Hansel transfers his rights in the gingerbread cottage to Gretel. Can the Witch successfully haul Gretel into

---

[15] The medieval mind thought of rent as something that came from the land itself: the tenant paid the land-*lord* out of the fruits of the land, sometimes metaphorically but sometimes literally, with crops harvested from the land being leased.

[16] We'll learn more about which promises "run with the land" in a later chapter about covenants. For now, it's enough to know that transferees can only enforce promises that concern the property or land.

court if she stops making payments? It should be obvious that Gretel has not made any direct agreement with the Witch (or made any promise to benefit her) so they are not in privity of contract. But what about privity of estate? This is where the distinction between assignments and subleases matters. If Hansel assigns his interest to Gretel, then Gretel and the Witch would be in privity of estate (and the Witch could sue Gretel for the missing rent). We know they have privity of estate because when Gretel's rights end under the assignment, the Witch would immediately be entitled to exclusive possession of the cottage—they have successive interests in the same piece of real estate. Conversely, if Hansel subleases his apartment to Gretel for the summer, a privity relationship would not arise between Gretel and the Witch. Instead, Gretel would have privity of estate with Hansel because at the conclusion of Gretel's interest, Hansel would have the right to exclusive possession. Thus, under the sublease, the Witch could not sue Gretel for rent.

Figuring out which parties stand in privity of estate can initially cause a lot of confusion. However, asking two quick questions can help define these relationships. The first step is to ask, "Have any tenants made an assignment of their rights?" If a tenant has assigned their rights they have no chance of possessing the property again and, thus, cannot stand in privity of estate with anyone (although they may still be in privity of contract with various parties). For all the remaining tenants ask, "Who receives the property when this tenant's possessory rights finally end?" Remember, parties with successive interests have privity of estate.

Although it may be redundant, a few diagrams may help clarify these relationships. Assume that L leases an apartment to T. Whenever a landlord initially leases to a tenant the two parties are in both privity of contract and privity of estate:

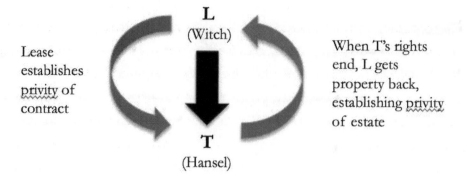

L and T are in privity of contract because they agreed on a lease contract. To figure out the privity of estate relationships, we first ask if anyone has assigned their interest. The answer here is "no." For all remaining tenants, we inquire "who gets control over the property when this tenant's possessory rights end?" In this hypothetical, who gets the leased premise when T's term concludes? The answer, of course, is the landlord. T and L are in privity of estate because the landlord gets the property back from the tenant at the end of the lease.

The relationships change if T assigns his rights to a new party, T2. The diagram of an assignment is below:

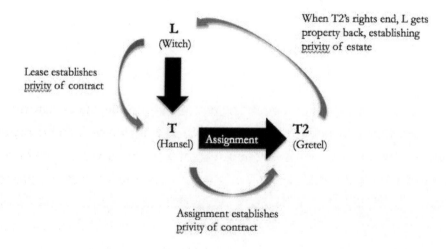

The contractual relationships are easy enough to map. As discussed earlier, when T assigns his interest, he remains in privity of contract with L—they signed a rental agreement that has not expired. T and T2 are also in privity of contract as a result of the assignment contract. But what about privity of estate? L and T are no longer in privity of estate because T has relinquished all of his property interests. Remember that parties who assign their rights stand in privity of estate with no one. For all other tenants we ask, "Who receives the property when this tenant's possessory rights finally end?" When T2's possessory rights conclude, who takes control of the property? The answer is the landlord. L and T2 now have a privity of estate relationship.

How do things change with a sublease?

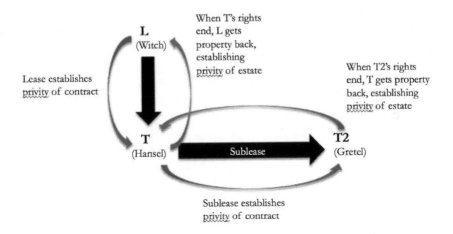

As before, T remains in privity of contract with L for the duration of the original lease. In this example, there are no assignments, so we begin by asking which parties have successive property interests. When the possessory rights of T2 end, T will then have control over the property. Thus T2 and T have a privity of estate relationship. Then, when T's rights over the property conclude, the possessory rights will flow back to the landlord, meaning that T and L also have privity of estate.

Before moving on, one final wrinkle merits attention. As discussed earlier, when the original tenant subleases or assigns his leasehold, the default rule is that the landlord and the new tenant are not in privity of contract. It is possible, however, to create a privity of contract relationship between the L and T2. Most often this is accomplished by including a clause in the takeover agreement between the original tenant and the new tenant that reads, "New Tenant assumes the obligation to perform all of the original tenant's duties under the original lease." If the new tenant takes on this responsibility, the landlord becomes a third-party beneficiary to the agreement and comes into privity of contract with the new tenant.

Problems

1. Landlord leases property to T1 from January 1, 2015 to December 31, 2015. On March 1, T1 sold T2 her remaining interest in the property. On October 1, T2 rented the property to T3 for two months. Describe the privity relationships between all of the parties. If T3 stops sending rent payments to Landlord, whom can the Landlord sue to recover the money?

2. Alger, a landlord, rents a commercial building to Brown for 5 years. Six months into the lease, Brown subleases his interest to Clancy for 3 years. Clancy then turns around and assigns his interest to Dahl. Describe the privity relationships between all of the parties. If Dahl stops sending rent checks to Alger, whom can Alger sue to recover the money.

3. Picasso, a landlord, rents an apartment to Renoir for one year. The lease contains a provision allowing the tenant to renew the leasehold for a second year on the same terms. Renoir assigns his interest in the lease to Seurat. Seurat then assigns his interest to Turner. What are the privity relationships between the parties? Can Turner exercise the renewal clause in the original lease? *See*

Castle v. Double Time, Inc., 737 P.2d 900 (Okla. 1987) (discussing renewal clauses).

4. Landlord leases a unit to T1 for ten years beginning in 2010. In 2012, T1 transfers all of his right to T2 "for a period of five" years. In 2013, T2 subleases to T3 for one year. What are the privity relationships and whom can the landlord sue if T3 stops paying rent?

5. L leases a commercial property to T1 for ten years beginning in 2010. In 2012, T1 assigns all of her interest to T2. A year later, T2 assigns all of her interest to T3. In 2014, T3 subleases to T4 for a term of four years. In the sublease contract, T4 agrees to assume "all of the covenants and promises" in the original lease between L and T1. In 2015, T4's business fails and she ceases making paying rent. What are the privity relationships? Whom can L sue to recover the unpaid rent money?

3.   Tenant Exit: Limiting the Right to Transfer

Under the traditional common law, leaseholds were freely transferable property interests. Modern courts continue to recognize the alienability of tenancies as a default position, but allow parties to contract around the basic rule. As a result, most leases (including yours, probably) now contain some restriction on a tenant's ability to assign or sublease her property interests. For example, one oft-used lease agreement, which can be downloaded for free from the Internet, includes the following provision: "The tenant will not assign this Lease, or sublet or grant any concession or license to use the Property or any part of the Property. Any assignment or subletting will be void and will, at the Landlord's option, terminate the Lease." In most states, courts uphold such bars on transfer as reasonable restraints on alienation. More controversial are clauses that allow sublease or assignment but only "with the consent of the landlord."

Julian v. Christopher
575 A.2d 735 (Md. 1990)

CHASANOW, Judge.
In 1961, this Court decided the case of *Jacobs v. Klawans*, 169 A.2d 677 (1961) and held that when a lease contained a "silent consent" clause prohibiting a tenant from subletting or assigning without the consent of the landlord, landlords had a right to withhold their consent to a subletting or assignment even though the withholding of consent was arbitrary and unreasonable. . . . We now have before us the issue of whether the common law rule applied in *Klawans* should be changed.

In the instant case, the tenants, Douglas Julian and William J. Gilleland, III, purchased a tavern and restaurant business, as well as rented the business premises from landlord, Guy D. Christopher. The lease stated in clause ten that the premises, consisting of both the tavern and an upstairs apartment, could not be assigned or sublet "without the prior written consent of the landlord." Sometime after taking occupancy, the tenants requested the landlord's written permission to sublease the upstairs apartment. The landlord made no inquiry about the proposed sublessee, but wrote to the tenants that he would not agree to a sublease unless the tenants paid additional rent in the amount of $150.00 per month. When the tenants permitted the sublessee to move in, the landlord filed an action in the District Court of Maryland in Baltimore City requesting repossession of the building because the tenants had sublet the premises without his permission.

At the district court trial, the tenants testified that they specifically inquired about clause ten, and were told by the landlord that the clause was merely included to prevent them from subletting or assigning to "someone who would tear the apartment up." The district court judge refused to consider this testimony. He stated in his oral opinion that he would "remain within the four corners of the lease, and construe the document strictly," at least as it pertained to clause ten. Both the District Court and, on appeal, the Circuit Court for Baltimore City found in favor of the landlord. The circuit judge noted: "If you don't have the words that consent will not be unreasonably withheld, then the landlord can withhold his consent for a good reason, a bad reason, or no reason at all in the context of a commercial lease, which is what we're dealing with." We granted certiorari to determine whether the *Klawans* holding should be modified in light of the changes that have occurred since that decision.

While we are concerned with the need for stability in the interpretation of leases, we recognize that since the *Klawans* case was decided in 1961, the foundations for that holding have been substantially eroded. The *Klawans* opinion cited Restatement of Property § 410 as authority for its holding. The current Restatement (Second) of Property § 15.2 rejects the *Klawans* doctrine and now takes the position that:

> A restraint on alienation without the consent of the landlord of the tenant's interest in the leased property is valid, but the landlord's consent to an alienation by the tenant cannot be withheld unreasonably, unless a freely negotiated provision in the lease gives the landlord an absolute right to withhold consent.

Another authority cited in *Klawans* in support of its holding was 2 R. Powell, Powell on Real Property. The most recent edition of that text now states:

> Thus, if a lease clause prohibited the tenant from transferring his or her interest without the landlord's consent, the landlord could withhold consent arbitrarily. This result was allowed because it was

believed that the objectives served by allowing the restraints outweighed the social evils implicit in them, inasmuch as the restraints gave the landlord control over choosing the person who was to be entrusted with the landlord's property and was obligated to perform the lease covenants. It is doubtful that this reasoning retains full validity today. Relationships between landlord and tenant have become more impersonal and housing space (and in many areas, commercial space as well) has become scarce. These changes have had an impact on courts and legislatures in varying degrees. Modern courts almost universally adopt the view that restrictions on the tenant's right to transfer are to be strictly construed. (Footnotes omitted.)

2 R. Powell, Powell on Real Property § 248[1] (1988).

Finally, in support of its decision in *Klawans*, this Court noted that, "although it, apparently, has not been passed upon in a great number of jurisdictions, the decisions of the courts that have determined the question are in very substantial accord." *Klawans*, 169 A.2d at 679. This is no longer true. Since *Klawans*, the trend has been in the opposite direction. "The modern trend is to impose a standard of reasonableness on the landlord in withholding consent to a sublease unless the lease expressly states otherwise." *Campbell v. Westdahl*, 715 P.2d 288, 292 (Ariz. Ct. App. 1985). . . .

Traditional property rules favor the free and unrestricted right to alienate interests in property. Therefore, absent some specific restriction in the lease, a lessee has the right to freely alienate the leasehold interest by assignment or sublease without obtaining the permission of the lessor. R. Schoshinski, *American Law of Landlord and Tenant* § 5:6 (1980); 1 *American Law of Property* § 3.56 (1952).

Contractual restrictions on the alienability of leasehold interests are permitted. R. Cunningham, W. Stoebuck, and D. Whitman, *The Law of*

Property § 12.40 (1984). Consequently, landlords often insert clauses that restrict the lessee's common law right to freely assign or sublease. *Id.* Probably the most often used clause is a "silent consent" clause similar to the provision in the instant case, which provides that the premises may not be assigned or sublet without the written consent of the lessor.

In a "silent consent" clause requiring a landlord's consent to assign or sublease, there is no standard governing the landlord's decision. Courts must insert a standard. The choice is usually between 1) requiring the landlord to act reasonably when withholding consent, or 2) permitting the landlord to act arbitrarily and capriciously in withholding consent.

Public policy requires that when a lease gives the landlord the right to withhold consent to a sublease or assignment, the landlord should act reasonably, and the courts ought not to imply a right to act arbitrarily or capriciously. If a landlord is allowed to arbitrarily refuse consent to an assignment or sublease, for what in effect is no reason at all, that would virtually nullify any right to assign or sublease.

Because most people act reasonably most of the time, tenants might expect that a landlord's consent to a sublease or assignment would be governed by standards of reasonableness. Most tenants probably would not understand that a clause stating "this lease may not be assigned or sublet without the landlord's written consent" means the same as a clause stating "the tenant shall have no right to assign or sublease." Some landlords may have chosen the former wording rather than the latter because it vaguely implies, but does not grant to the tenant, the right to assign or sublet.

There are two public policy reasons why the law enunciated in *Klawans* should now be changed. The first is the public policy against restraints on alienation. The second is the public policy which implies a covenant of good faith and fair dealing in every contract.

Because there is a public policy against restraints on alienation, if a lease is silent on the subject, a tenant may freely sublease or assign. Restraints on alienation are permitted in leases, but are looked upon with disfavor and are strictly construed. *Powell on Real Property, supra.* If a clause in a lease is susceptible of two interpretations, public policy favors the interpretation least restrictive of the right to alienate freely. Interpreting a "silent consent" clause so that it only prohibits subleases or assignments when a landlord's refusal to consent is reasonable, would be the interpretation imposing the least restraint on alienation and most in accord with public policy.

Since the *Klawans* decision, this Court has recognized that in a lease, as well as in other contracts, "there exists an implied covenant that each of the parties thereto will act in good faith and deal fairly with the others." *Food Fair v. Blumberg,* A.2d 166, 174 (1964). When the lease gives the landlord the right to exercise discretion, the discretion should be exercised in good faith, and in accordance with fair dealing; if the lease does not spell out any standard for withholding consent, then the implied covenant of good faith and fair dealing should imply a reasonableness standard.

We are cognizant of the value of the doctrine of *stare decisis,* and of the need for stability and certainty in the law. However, as we noted in *Harrison v. Mont. Co. Bd. of Educ.,* 456 A.2d 894, 903 (1983), a common law rule may be modified "where we find, in light of changed conditions or increased knowledge, that the rule has become unsound in the circumstances of modern life, a vestige of the past, no longer suitable to our people." The *Klawans* common law interpretation of the "silent consent" clause represents such a "vestige of the past," and should now be changed.

REASONABLENESS OF WITHHELD CONSENT

In the instant case, we need not expound at length on what constitutes a reasonable refusal to consent to an assignment or sublease. We should, however, point out that obvious examples of reasonable objections could include the financial irresponsibility or instability of the transferee, or the unsuitability or incompatibility of the intended use of the property by the transferee. We also need not expound at length on what would constitute an unreasonable refusal to consent to an assignment or sublease. If the reasons for withholding consent have nothing to do with the intended transferee or the transferee's use of the property, the motivation may be suspect. Where, as alleged in this case, the refusal to consent was solely for the purpose of securing a rent increase, such refusal would be unreasonable unless the new subtenant would necessitate additional expenditures by, or increased economic risk to, the landlord.

PROSPECTIVE EFFECT

The tenants ask us to retroactively overrule *Klawans,* and hold that in all leases with "silent consent" clauses, no matter when executed, consent to assign or sublease may not be unreasonably withheld by a landlord. We decline to do so. In the absence of evidence to the contrary, we should assume that parties executing leases when *Klawans* governed the interpretation of "silent consent" clauses were aware of *Klawans* and the implications drawn from the words they used. We should not, and do not, rewrite these contracts.

In appropriate cases, courts may "in the interest of justice" give their decisions only prospective effect. Contracts are drafted based on what the law is; to upset such transactions even for the purpose of improving the law could be grossly unfair. . . .

For leases with "silent consent" clauses which were entered into before the mandate in this case, *Klawans* is applicable, and we assume the parties were aware of the court decisions interpreting a "silent consent" clause as giving the landlord an unrestricted right to withhold consent.

For leases entered into after the mandate in this case, if the lease contains a "silent consent" clause providing that the tenant must obtain the landlord's consent in order to assign or sublease, such consent may not be unreasonably withheld. If the parties intend to preclude any transfer by assignment or sublease, they may do so by a freely negotiated provision in the lease. . . . For example, the clause might provide, "consent may be withheld in the sole and absolute subjective discretion of the lessor."

The final question is whether the tenants in the instant case, having argued successfully for a change in the law, should receive the benefit of the change. . . . [Even though our decision is to have only prospective effect] [t]he tenants in the instant case should get the benefit of the interpretation of the "silent consent" clause that they so persuasively argued for, unless this interpretation would be unfair to the landlord. We note that the tenants testified they were told that the clause was only to prevent subleasing to "someone who would tear the apartment up." Therefore, we will reverse the judgment of the Circuit Court with instructions to vacate the judgment of the District Court and remand for a new trial. At that trial, the landlord will have the burden of establishing that it would be unfair to interpret the "silent consent" clause in accordance with our decision that a landlord must act reasonably in withholding consent. He may establish that it would be unfair to do so by establishing that when executing the lease he was aware of and relied on the *Klawans* interpretation of the "silent consent" clause. . . .

Notes and Questions

1. **Landlords love restrictions.** Why are restrictions on transfer so common in both commercial and residential leases? You might want to refer back to the Sprawl-Mart example from earlier in the chapter, which makes clear why a landlord and tenant might disagree about who should get the benefit of the remaining term.

2. **Status of the *Julian* rule.** The approach taken in *Julian*, which reads a reasonableness requirement into the lease, is still a minority rule. Roughly 15 states have taken a position similar to Maryland's highest court, including California, Illinois, North Carolina, and Ohio. Although the *Julian*/minority approach has gained popularity in the last two decades (and is considered the "modern" rule), it's important to note that in most states a landlord may still arbitrarily refuse to consent to any sublease or assignment under a "silent consent" clause.

3. **Contracting around the rule?** Imagine a lease that includes the following provision: "The tenant shall not sublease or assign any part of their interest in the property without the Landlord's written permission. The Landlord reserves the absolute right to deny any request for any and all reasons at his sole and absolute discretion." Under the holding in *Julian*, would this clause be valid? *See* Restatement (Second) Property § 15.2 ("A restraint on alienation with the consent of the landlord of the tenant's interest in the leased property is valid, but the landlord's consent to an alienation by the tenant cannot be withheld unreasonably, unless a freely negotiated provision in the lease gives the landlord an absolute right to withhold consent.")

4. **Defining reasonableness.** What counts as a reasonable objection to a sublease or assignment request? Courts in Illinois have found that it's proper to consider: (1) the sublessee's credit history, (2) the sublessee's capital on hand, (3) whether the subleesee's business is compatible with landlord's other properties, (4) whether the sublessee's business will compete with those of the leassor or any other lessee, and, (5) the subleesee's expertise and business plan. See, for example, *Jack Frost Sales, Inc. v. Harris Trust & Savings Bank*, 433 N.E. 2d 941 (Ill. App. 3d 1982). In most

jurisdictions, tenants have the burden to show the sublessee or assignee meets the reasonable commercial standard.

5. **The Landlord's Stance.** Is the reasonableness rule fair to landlords? Imagine you're a landlord and your original tenant announces that they're moving out and proffers a subleasee for your approval. If you're not completely satisfied with the new tenant, should you object? If you say "no" and the tenant either leaves or sues you, how much will that enforcement action cost?

6. **Residential v. Commercial.** Courts have not imposed the rule articulated in *Julian* on residential tenants. Why not? Aren't commercial tenants better able to protect themselves and bargain than residential tenants? Consider the following statute from a jurisdiction where residential leases account for a huge proportion of extremely scarce housing stock: New York. As you read it, consider whether and to what extent the statute permits parties to residential leases to contract around its provisions, and whether it is more or less restrictive than the rule of *Julian*.

New York Real Property Law § 226-B

1. Unless a greater right to assign is conferred by the lease, a tenant renting a residence may not assign his lease without the written consent of the owner, which consent may be unconditionally withheld without cause provided that the owner shall release the tenant from the lease upon request of the tenant upon thirty days notice if the owner unreasonably withholds consent which release shall be the sole remedy of the tenant. If the owner reasonably withholds consent, there shall be no assignment and the tenant shall not be released from the lease.

2. (a) A tenant renting a residence pursuant to an existing lease in a dwelling having four or more residential units shall have the right to sublease his premises subject to the written consent of the landlord in advance of the subletting. Such consent shall not be unreasonably withheld.

(b) The tenant shall inform the landlord of his intent to sublease by mailing a notice of such intent by certified mail, return receipt requested. Such request shall be accompanied by the following information: (i) the term of the sublease, (ii) the name of the proposed sublessee, (iii) the business and permanent home address of the proposed sublessee, (iv) the tenant's reason for subletting, (v) the tenant's address for the term of the sublease, (vi) the written consent of any cotenant or guarantor of the lease, and (vii) a copy of the proposed sublease, to which a copy of the tenant's lease shall be attached if available, acknowledged by the tenant and proposed subtenant as being a true copy of such sublease.

(c) Within ten days after the mailing of such request, the landlord may ask the tenant for additional information as will enable the landlord to determine if rejection of such request shall be unreasonable. Any such request for additional information shall not be unduly burdensome. Within thirty days after the mailing of the request for consent, or of the additional information reasonably asked for by the landlord, whichever is later, the landlord shall send a notice to the tenant of his consent or, if he does not consent, his reasons therefor. Landlord's failure to send such a notice shall be deemed to be a consent to the proposed subletting. If the landlord consents, the premises may be sublet in accordance with the request, but the tenant thereunder, shall nevertheless remain liable for the performance of tenant's obligations under said lease. If the landlord reasonably withholds consent, there shall be no subletting and the tenant shall not be released from the lease. If the landlord unreasonably withholds consent, the tenant may sublet in accordance with the request and may recover the costs of the proceeding and attorneys fees if it is found that the owner acted in bad faith by withholding consent.

. . .

5. Any sublet or assignment which does not comply with the provisions of this section shall constitute a substantial breach of lease or tenancy.

6. Any provision of a lease or rental agreement purporting to waive a provision of this section is null and void.

Problems

1. Last year, X rented a storefront in a local strip mall and opened a successful coffee shop. The lease is for 10 years and includes the following provision: "No assignments or subleases without the landlord's consent. Landlord can only deny consent based on commercially reasonable objections." Recently X was offered her dream job on a coffee plantation in a faraway country. She now wishes to exit her lease. Must the Landlord consent to the following assignment proposals?

    a. Alfred plans to open a mattress store. He's a college dropout with no business experience but his rich father will co-sign the lease and guarantee all payments get made on time.

    b. Bob, an experienced therapist with good credit, wants to open a marriage counseling practice targeted at same-sex couples. The landlord, however, believes same-sex marriage is immoral and worries that the counseling center will hurt the business of a Christian bookstore in the strip mall.

  c. Cathy has a well-thought out plan to open a shooting range. The Landlord agrees to the assignment on the condition that Cathy increase the rent payment by $100/month. Cathy refuses.

4. Tenant Exit: Abandonment and the Duty to Mitigate

A tenant who needs to exit a lease early and cannot find another party to sublet must seek out other alternatives. For example, a tenant can always ask her landlord to terminate the lease before the term ends. The tenant generally agrees to turn over the property and pay a small fee and, in return, the landlord releases the tenant from all further obligations. This is called a *surrender.*

Alternatively, a tenant may simply pack her things, abandon the premise, and stop making rent payments. This often happens if a tenant cannot work out a surrender agreement or finds herself in desperate financial circumstances. What are the rights and obligations of the parties in this scenario? What happens if a tenant breaks a lease and leaves?

The Pierre Apartments today

Sommer v. Kridel
378 A.2d 767 (N.J. 1977)

PASHMAN, J.

We granted certification in these cases to consider whether a landlord seeking damages from a defaulting tenant is under a duty to mitigate damages by making reasonable efforts to re-let an apartment wrongfully vacated by the tenant. Separate parts of the Appellate Division held that, in accordance with their respective leases, the landlords in both cases could recover rents due under the leases regardless of whether they had attempted to re-let the vacated apartments. Although they were of different minds as to the fairness of this result, both parts agreed that it was dictated by *Joyce v. Bauman*, 174 A. 693 (1934) . . . . We now reverse and hold that a landlord does have an obligation to make a reasonable effort to mitigate damages in such a situation. We therefore overrule *Joyce v. Bauman* to the extent that it is inconsistent with our decision today.

I.

This case was tried on stipulated facts. On March 10, 1972 the defendant, James Kridel, entered into a lease with the plaintiff, Abraham Sommer, owner of the "Pierre Apartments" in Hackensack, to rent apartment 6-L in that building. The term of the lease was from May 1, 1972 until April 30, 1974, with a rent concession for the first six weeks, so that the first month's rent was not due until June 15, 1972.

One week after signing the agreement, Kridel paid Sommer $690. Half of that sum was used to satisfy the first month's rent. The remainder was paid under the lease provision requiring a security deposit of $345. Although defendant had expected to begin occupancy around May 1, his plans were changed. He wrote to Sommer on May 19, 1972, explaining:

> I was to be married on June 3, 1972. Unhappily the engagement was broken and the wedding plans cancelled. Both parents were to assume responsibility for the rent after our marriage. I was discharged from the U.S. Army in October 1971 and am now a student. I have no funds of my own, and am supported by my stepfather.
>
> In view of the above, I cannot take possession of the apartment and am surrendering all rights to it. Never having received a key, I cannot return same to you.
>
> I beg your understanding and compassion in releasing me from the lease, and will of course, in consideration thereof, forfeit the 2 month's rent already paid.
> Please notify me at your earliest convenience.

Plaintiff did not answer the letter.

Subsequently, a third party went to the apartment house and inquired about renting apartment 6-L. Although the parties agreed that she was ready, willing and able to rent the apartment, the person in charge told her that the apartment was not being shown since it was already rented to Kridel. In fact, the landlord did not re-enter the apartment or exhibit it to anyone until August 1, 1973. At that time it was rented to a new tenant for a term beginning on September 1, 1973. The new rental was for $345 per month with a six week concession similar to that granted Kridel.

Prior to re-letting the new premises, plaintiff sued Kridel in August 1972, demanding $7,590, the total amount due for the full two-year term of the lease. Following a mistrial, plaintiff filed an amended complaint asking for $5,865, the amount due between May 1, 1972 and September 1, 1973. The amended complaint included no reduction in the claim to reflect the six week concession provided for in the lease or the $690 payment made to plaintiff after signing the agreement. Defendant filed an amended answer to the complaint, alleging that plaintiff breached the contract, failed to mitigate damages and accepted defendant's surrender of the premises. He also counterclaimed to demand repayment of the $345 paid as a security deposit.

The trial judge ruled in favor of defendant. Despite his conclusion that the lease had been drawn to reflect "the 'settled law' of this state," he found that "justice and fair dealing" imposed upon the landlord the duty to attempt to re-let the premises and thereby mitigate damages. He also held that plaintiff's failure to make any response to defendant's unequivocal offer of surrender was tantamount to an acceptance, thereby terminating the tenancy and any obligation to pay rent. As a result, he dismissed both the complaint and the counterclaim. The Appellate Division reversed in a per curiam opinion, 153 N.J.Super. 1 (1976), and we granted certification. . . .

II

As the lower courts in both appeals found, the weight of authority in this State supports the rule that a landlord is under no duty to mitigate damages caused by a defaulting tenant. *See Joyce v. Bauman, supra* . . . . This rule has been followed in a majority of states . . . and has been tentatively adopted in the American Law Institute's Restatement of Property. . . .

Nevertheless, while there is still a split of authority over this question, the trend among recent cases appears to be in favor of a mitigation requirement. . . .

The majority rule is based on principles of property law which equate a lease with a transfer of a property interest in the owner's estate. Under this rationale the lease conveys to a tenant an interest in the property which forecloses any control by the landlord; thus, it would be anomalous to require the landlord to concern himself with the tenant's abandonment of his own property. *Wright v. Baumann*, 398 P.2d 119, 120-21 (Or. 1965).

For instance, in *Muller v. Beck*, supra, where essentially the same issue was posed, the court clearly treated the lease as governed by property, as opposed to contract, precepts. The court there observed that the "tenant had an estate for years, but it was an estate qualified by this right of the landlord to prevent its transfer," 110 A. at 832, and that "the tenant has an estate with which the landlord may not interfere." *Id.* at 832. Similarly, in *Heckel v. Griese, supra*, the court noted the absolute nature of the tenant's interest in the property while the lease was in effect, stating that "when the tenant vacated, . . . no one, in the circumstances, had any right to interfere with the defendant's possession of the premises." 171 A. 148, 149. Other cases simply cite the rule announced in *Muller v. Beck, supra*, without discussing the underlying rationale. *See Joyce v. Bauman, supra*, 174 A. 693 . . . .

Yet the distinction between a lease for ordinary residential purposes and an ordinary contract can no longer be considered viable. As Professor Powell observed, evolving "social factors have exerted increasing influence on the law of estates for years." 2 *Powell on Real Property* (1977 ed.), § 221(1) at 180-81. The result has been that:

[t]he complexities of city life, and the proliferated problems of modern society in general, have created new problems for lessors and lessees and these have been commonly handled by specific clauses in leases. This growth in the number and detail of specific lease covenants has reintroduced into the law of estates for years a predominantly contractual ingredient.

(*Id.* at 181). . . .

This Court has taken the lead in requiring that landlords provide housing services to tenants in accordance with implied duties which are hardly consistent with the property notions expressed in *Muller v. Beck, supra*, and *Heckel v. Griese, supra. See Braitman v. Overlook Terrace Corp.*, 346 A.2d 76 (1975) (liability for failure to repair defective apartment door lock); *Berzito v. Gambino*, 308 A.2d 17 (1973) (construing implied warranty of habitability and covenant to pay rent as mutually dependent); *Marini v. Ireland*, 265 A.2d 526 (1970) (implied covenant to repair); *Reste Realty Corp. v. Cooper*, 251 A.2d 268 (1969) (implied warranty of fitness of premises for leased purpose). In fact, in *Reste Realty Corp. v. Cooper, supra*, we specifically noted that the rule which we announced there did not comport with the historical notion of a lease as an estate for years. 251 A.2d 268. And in *Marini v. Ireland, supra*, we found that the "guidelines employed to construe contracts have been modernly applied to the construction of leases." 265 A.2d at 532.

Application of the contract rule requiring mitigation of damages to a residential lease may be justified as a matter of basic fairness.[4] Professor McCormick first commented upon the inequity under the majority rule when he predicted in 1925 that eventually:

the logic, inescapable according to the standards of a 'jurisprudence of conceptions' which permits the landlord to stand idly by the vacant, abandoned premises and treat them as the property of the tenant and recover full rent, [will] yield to the more realistic notions of social advantage which in other fields of the law have forbidden a recovery for damages which the plaintiff by reasonable efforts could have avoided. (McCormick, *The Rights of the Landlord Upon Abandonment of the Premises by the Tenant*, 23 Mich. L. Rev. 211, 221-22 (1925)).

Various courts have adopted this position.

The pre-existing rule cannot be predicated upon the possibility that a landlord may lose the opportunity to rent another empty apartment because he must first rent the apartment vacated by the defaulting tenant. Even where the breach occurs in a multi-dwelling building, each apartment may have unique qualities which make it attractive to certain individuals. Significantly, in *Sommer v. Kridel*, there was a specific request to rent the apartment vacated by the defendant; there is no reason to believe that absent this vacancy the landlord could have succeeded in renting a different apartment to this individual.

We therefore hold that antiquated real property concepts which served as the basis for the pre-existing rule, shall no longer be controlling where there is a claim for damages under a residential lease. Such claims must be governed by more modern notions of fairness and equity. A landlord has a duty to mitigate damages where he seeks to recover rents due from a defaulting tenant.

If the landlord has other vacant apartments besides the one which the tenant has abandoned, the landlord's duty to mitigate consists of making reasonable efforts to re-let the apartment. In such cases he must treat the apartment in question as if it was one of his vacant stock.

As part of his cause of action, the landlord shall be required to carry the burden of proving that he used reasonable diligence in attempting to re-let the premises. We note that there has been a divergence of opinion concerning the allocation of the burden of proof on this issue. *See* Annot., *supra*, s 12 at 577. While generally in contract actions the breaching party has the burden of proving that damages are capable of mitigation . . . here the landlord will be in a better position to demonstrate whether he exercised reasonable diligence in attempting to re-let the premises. . . .

III

The *Sommer v. Kridel* case presents a classic example of the unfairness which occurs when a landlord has no responsibility to minimize damages. Sommer waited 15 months and allowed $4658.50 in damages to accrue before attempting to re-let the apartment. Despite the availability of a tenant who was ready, willing and able to rent the apartment, the landlord needlessly increased the damages by turning her away. While a tenant will not necessarily be excused from his obligations under a lease simply by finding another person who is willing to rent the vacated premises, see, e. g., *Reget v. Dempsey-Tegler & Co.*, 216 N.E.2d 500 (Ill. App.1966) (new tenant insisted on leasing the premises under different terms); *Edmands v. Rust & Richardson Drug Co.*, 77 N.E. 713 (Mass. 1906) (landlord need not accept insolvent tenant), here there has been no showing that the new tenant would not have been suitable. We therefore find that plaintiff could have avoided the damages which eventually accrued, and that the defendant was relieved of his duty to continue paying rent. Ordinarily we would require the tenant to bear the cost of any reasonable expenses incurred by a landlord in attempting to re-let the premises . . . but no such expenses were incurred in this case. . . .

In assessing whether the landlord has satisfactorily carried his burden, the trial court shall consider, among other factors, whether the landlord, either personally or through an agency, offered or showed the apartment to any prospective tenants, or advertised it in local newspapers. Additionally, the tenant may attempt to rebut such evidence by showing that he proffered suitable tenants who were rejected. However, there is no standard formula for measuring whether the landlord has utilized satisfactory efforts in attempting to mitigate damages, and each case must be judged upon its own facts.

Compare . . . *Carpenter v. Wisniewski*, 215 N.E.2d 882 (Ind. App.1966) (duty satisfied where landlord advertised the premises through a newspaper, placed a sign in the window, and employed a realtor); *Re Garment Center Capitol, Inc.*, 93 F.2d 667, 115 A.L.R. 202 (2 Cir. 1938) (landlord's duty not breached where higher rental was asked since it was known that this was merely a basis for negotiations); *Foggia v. Dix*, 509 P.2d 412, 414 (Or. 1973) (in mitigating damages, landlord need not accept less than fair market value or "substantially alter his obligations as established in the pre-existing lease"); *with Anderson v. Andy Darling Pontiac, Inc.*, 43 N.W.2d 362 (Wis. 1950) (reasonable diligence not established where newspaper advertisement placed in one issue of local paper by a broker); . . . *Consolidated Sun Ray, Inc. v. Oppenstein*, 335 F.2d 801, 811 (8 Cir. 1964) (dictum) (demand for rent which is "far greater than the provisions of the lease called for" negates landlord's assertion that he acted in good faith in seeking a new tenant).

IV

The judgment in *Sommer v. Kridel* is reversed.

Notes and Questions

1. **The basic law.** Today almost all states impose a duty to mitigate on residential landlords. The rule also applies to commercial tenancies in many states. The Restatement (Second) of Property § 12.1(3), however, continues to cling to the common law notion that a landlord can wait until the end of the term and then sue the tenant for all of the unpaid rent. The authors of the Restatement believe the traditional rule discourages abandonment, limits vandalism, and better protects the expectations of landlords.

2. **Tenants still on the hook.** Importantly, the duty to mitigate does not relieve an abandoning tenant of all liability. Even if a new tenant rents the unit, the landlord can still recover damages for all of the costs of finding the replacement tenant and for any time that the unit remained empty. The landlord can also recoup any unpaid rent that accrued before the abandonment. Finally, if the rental market in the area has softened and landlord is forced to rent the unit at lower price, the tenant is responsible for the difference between the new rent and the original rent.

3. **Property v. Contract.** The lingering controversy over the duty to mitigate stems largely from the property/contract tension inherent in the nature of the lease. If a leasehold is primarily a property interest, then the landlord has few responsibilities to the tenant after ceding possession and control—the tenant is free to use the property or let it lay fallow. If, on the other hand, the lease is viewed through the lens of contract law, the parties clearly have a responsibility to mitigate damages. *But see* Edward Chase & E. Hunter Taylor, Jr., *Landlord and Tenant: A Study in Prooperty and Contract*, 30 VILL. L. REV. 571 (1985) (arguing the distinction is overstated).

4. **What's a good faith effort?** Ken rents an apartment to Sarah for one year. Three months into the lease, Sarah gets a new job in a different state and turns the apartment back over to Ken. Ken puts an 8x11 "for rent" sign in the window of the unit. Has he made a good faith effort to mitigate damages? Does it matter how he advertises the other units? What if Tim offers to rent Sarah's unit but Tim has bad credit: does Ken have to accept Tim?

5. **The Legend of Jim Kridel.** The woman Jim Kridel intended to marry came from a family with significant assets. When the engagement fell through, Kridel—who had no income of his own—could not afford the rent at the Pierre Apartments. The opinion mentions that Kridel notified Sommer of his predicament in writing, but does not reflect that Kridel and Sommer also had a heated discussion on the phone. During the telephone conversation, Kridel offered Sommer $750 of the pre-paid rent as compensation for breaking the lease (adjusted for inflation, that's roughly equivalent to $3000 today). Sommer, however, knew that Kridel's stepfather was a prominent (and presumably well-off) physician and demanded an additional $750. Kridel refused, and told Sommer, "If you don't like it, you can sue me, baby!" Sommer did just that. When the litigation began, Kridel was a first year law student at Rutgers. He initially represented himself but gradually picked up pro bono help from lawyers he met at summer jobs and partners in the firm where he worked after graduating. Kridel estimates that Sommer—a very wealthy landlord—spent over $500,000 on legal fees. Kridel also recalls that the law of New Jersey was firmly against his position that the lease should be governed by contract principles. On appeal, he relied primarily on a case from the state of Oregon, which opposing counsel disparaged as a place full of bumpkin fishermen and loggers. When Kridel won, he wrapped the opinion around an Oregon salmon and sent to Sommer's lawyers. Asked why he pursued the case with such vigor, he replied, "Sommer was wrong. The rule was unfair. And I was probably the only tenant in New Jersey who could afford to pour that much time and attention into a case like that." In the intervening years, Kridel has had a long and successful legal career in New Jersey and New York. He's currently best known for representing *Real Housewives of New Jersey* star Teresa Giudice in her bankruptcy proceeding.

5.   Tenant Exit: Eviction

If a tenant fails to pay rent or otherwise commits a material breach of the lease, the landlord can elect to terminate the leasehold and evict the tenant from the property. It is undoubtedly true that the eviction process and the subsequent scramble for a new place to live can be a traumatic, humiliating, and disruptive occurrence. Eviction displaces children from their schools, rends the social networks of the poor, and forces many families into shelters or onto the streets. Matthew Desmond, a sociologist at Harvard, has found that forced relocations are also shockingly common. In Milwaukee, the location of Desmond's research, 17 percent of the moves undertaken by renters over a two-year period were forced relocations. *See* Matthew Desmond et al., *Forced Relocation and Residential Instability Among Urban Renters*, 89 SOC. SCI. REV. 227 (2015). In response to the social cost of eviction, some American cities and many countries around the world make it difficult for landlords to remove tenants. Should more U.S. jurisdictions follow suit? Consider the following story:

> A patient political scientist ... might be able to place American cities on a left-to-right spectrum according to how long tenants whose eviction has become a cause manage to stay where they are. It may be, for instance that some city like Houston is on the far right of the spectrum. . . . Houston's most powerful citizens are known for a devotion to private property so intense that they see routine planning and zoning as acts of naked confiscation. . . . San Francisco might qualify for the left end of the spectrum. [I]ts best-known evictees [are] the tenants of the run-down three-story building called the International Hotel . . . . In the fall of 1968, about a hundred and fifty people who were living in the hotel . . . were told to be out of the building by January 1, 1969. The building was finally cleared—in what amounted to a military

operation requiring several hundred policemen—on August 4, 1977.

Calvin Trillin, *Some Thoughts on the International Hotel Controversy*, New Yorker, Dec. 19, 1977, at 116.

Notes and Questions

1. Would you rather be a tenant in a place like Houston—where evictions happen quickly—or in San Francisco—where they do not?

2. Imagine you're a landlord in a jurisdiction where it takes a long time to remove a tenant for non-payment of rent. How would that change your business strategy? Would you ever take a chance on a tenant with bad credit or a history of being evicted?

We turn now to the procedure of eviction. When a landlord believes that a tenant has committed a material breach of the lease, how exactly does she go about removing a lessee from the property?

Berg v. Wiley
264 N.W.2d 145 (Minn. 1978)

ROGOSHESKE, Justice.

Defendant landlord, Wiley Enterprises, Inc., and defendant Rodney A. Wiley (hereafter collectively referred to as Wiley) appeal from a judgment upon a jury verdict awarding plaintiff tenant, A Family Affair Restaurant, Inc., damages for wrongful eviction from its leased premises. The issues for review are whether the evidence was sufficient to support the jury's finding that the tenant did not abandon or surrender the premises and whether the trial court erred in finding Wiley's reentry forcible and wrongful as a matter of law. We hold that the jury's verdict is supported by sufficient evidence and that the trial court's determination of unlawful entry was correct as a matter of law, and affirm the judgment.

On November 11, 1970, Wiley, as lessor . . . executed a written lease agreement letting land and a building in Osseo, Minnesota, for use as a restaurant. The lease provided a 5-year term beginning December 1, 1970, and specified that the tenant agreed to bear all costs of repairs and remodeling, to "make no changes in the building structure" without prior written authorization from Wiley, and to "operate the restaurant in a lawful and prudent manner." Wiley also reserved the right "at (his) option (to) retake possession" of the premises "(s)hould the Lessee fail to meet the conditions of this Lease."[1] In early 1971, plaintiff Kathleen Berg took assignment of the lease from the prior lessee, and on May 1, 1971, she opened "A Family Affair Restaurant" on the premises. In January 1973, Berg incorporated the restaurant and assigned her interest in the lease to "A Family Affair Restaurant, Inc." As sole shareholder of the corporation, she alone continued to act for the tenant.

The present dispute has arisen out of Wiley's objection to Berg's continued remodeling of the restaurant without procuring written permission and her consequent operation of the restaurant in a state of disrepair with alleged health code violations. Strained relations between the parties came to a head in June and July 1973. In a letter dated June 29, 1973, Wiley's attorney charged Berg with having breached lease items 5 and 6 by making changes in the building structure without written authorization and by operating an unclean kitchen in violation of health regulations. The letter demanded that a list of eight remodeling items be completed within 2 weeks from the date of the letter, by Friday, July 13, 1973, or Wiley would retake possession of the premises under lease item 7. Also, a June 13 inspection of the restaurant by the Minnesota Department of Health had produced an order that certain listed changes be completed within specified time limits in order to comply with the health code. The major items on the inspector's list, similar to those listed by Wiley's attorney, were to be completed by July 15, 1973.

During the 2-week deadline set by both Wiley and the health department, Berg continued to operate the restaurant without closing to complete the required items of remodeling. The evidence is in dispute as to whether she intended to permanently close the restaurant and vacate the premises at the end of the 2 weeks or simply close for about 1 month in order to remodel to comply with the health code. At the close of business on Friday, July 13, 1973, the last day of the 2-week period, Berg dismissed her employees, closed the restaurant, and placed a sign in the window saying "Closed for Remodeling." Earlier that day, Berg testified, Wiley came to the premises in her absence and attempted to change the locks. When she returned and asserted her right to continue in possession, he complied with her request to leave the locks unchanged. Berg also testified that at about 9:30 p. m. that evening, while she and four of her friends were in the restaurant, she observed Wiley hanging from the awning peering into the window. Shortly thereafter, she heard Wiley pounding on the back door demanding admittance. Berg called the county sheriff to come and preserve order. Wiley testified that he observed Berg and a group of her friends in the restaurant removing paneling from a wall. Allegedly fearing destruction of his property, Wiley called the city police, who, with the sheriff, mediated an agreement between the parties to preserve the status quo until each could consult with legal counsel on Monday, July 16, 1973.

Wiley testified that his then attorney advised him to take possession of the premises and lock the tenant out. Accompanied by a police officer and a locksmith, Wiley entered the premises in Berg's absence and without her knowledge on Monday, July 16, 1973, and changed the locks. Later in the day, Berg found herself locked out. The lease term was not due to expire until December 1, 1975. The premises were re-let to another tenant on or about August 1, 1973. Berg brought this damage action against

Wiley . . . . [for] intentional infliction of emotional distress . . . and other tort damages based upon claims in wrongful eviction. . . . Wiley answered with an affirmative defense of abandonment and surrender and counterclaimed for damage to the premises. . . . With respect to the wrongful eviction claim, the trial court found as a matter of law that Wiley did in fact lock the tenant out, and that the lockout was wrongful.

The jury, by answers to the questions submitted, found no liability on Berg's claim for intentional infliction of emotional distress and no liability on Wiley's counterclaim for damages to the premises, but awarded Berg $31,000 for lost profits and $3,540 for loss of chattels resulting from the wrongful lockout. The jury also specifically found that Berg neither abandoned nor surrendered the premises. . . .

On this appeal, Wiley seeks an outright reversal of the damages award for wrongful eviction, claiming insufficient evidence to support the jury's finding of no abandonment or surrender and claiming error in the trial court's finding of wrongful eviction as a matter of law.

The first issue before us concerns the sufficiency of evidence to support the jury's finding that Berg had not abandoned or surrendered the leasehold before being locked out by Wiley. Viewing the evidence to support the jury's special verdict in the light most favorable to Berg, as we must, we hold it amply supports the jury's finding of no abandonment or surrender of the premises. While the evidence bearing upon Berg's intent was strongly contradictory, the jury could reasonably have concluded, based on Berg's testimony and supporting circumstantial evidence, that she intended to retain possession, closing temporarily to remodel. Thus, the lockout cannot be excused on ground that Berg abandoned or surrendered the leasehold.

The second and more difficult issue is whether Wiley's self-help repossession of the premises by locking out Berg was correctly held wrongful as a matter of law.

Minnesota has historically followed the common-law rule that a landlord may rightfully use self-help to retake leased premises from a tenant in possession without incurring liability for wrongful eviction provided two conditions are met: (1) The landlord is legally entitled to possession, such as where a tenant holds over after the lease term or where a tenant breaches a lease containing a reentry clause; and (2) the landlord's means of reentry are peaceable. *Mercil v. Broulette*, 69 N.W. 218 (1896). Under the common-law rule, a tenant who is evicted by his landlord may recover damages for wrongful eviction where the landlord either had no right to possession or where the means used to remove the tenant were forcible, or both. *See, e. g., Poppen v. Wadleigh*, 51 N.W.2d 75 (1952) . . . .

Wiley contends that Berg had breached the provisions of the lease, thereby entitling Wiley, under the terms of the lease, to retake possession, and that his repossession by changing the locks in Berg's absence was accomplished in a peaceful manner. In a memorandum accompanying the post-trial order, the trial court stated two grounds for finding the lockout wrongful as a matter of law: (1) It was not accomplished in a peaceable manner and therefore could not be justified under the common-law rule, and (2) any self-help reentry against a tenant in possession is wrongful under the growing modern doctrine that a landlord must always resort to the judicial process to enforce his statutory remedy against a tenant wrongfully in possession. Whether Berg had in fact breached the lease and whether Wiley was hence entitled to possession was not judicially determined. . . .

In applying the common-law rule, we have not before had occasion to decide what means of self-help used to dispossess a tenant in his absence will constitute a nonpeaceable entry, giving a right to damages without regard to who holds the legal right to possession. Wiley argues that only actual or threatened violence used against a tenant should give rise to damages where the landlord had the right to possession. We cannot agree.

It has long been the policy of our law to discourage landlords from taking the law into their own hands, and our decisions and statutory law have looked with disfavor upon any use of self-help to dispossess a tenant in circumstances which are likely to result in breaches of the peace. We gave early recognition to this policy in *Lobdell v. Keene*, 88 N.W. 426, 430 (1901), where we said:

> "The object and purpose of the legislature in the enactment of the forcible entry and unlawful detainer statute was to prevent those claiming a right of entry or possession of lands from redressing their own wrongs by entering into possession in a violent and forcible manner. All such acts tend to a breach of the peace, and encourage high-handed oppression. The law does not permit the owner of land, be his title ever so good, to be the judge of his own rights with respect to a possession adversely held, but puts him to his remedy under the statutes."

To facilitate a resort to judicial process, the legislature has provided a summary procedure in Minn. St. 566.02 to 566.17 whereby a landlord may recover possession of leased premises upon proper notice and showing in court in as little as 3 to 10 days. As we recognized in *Mutual Trust Life Ins. Co. v. Berg*, 246 N.W. 9, 10 (1932), "(t)he forcible entry and unlawful detainer statutes were intended to prevent parties from taking the law into their own hands when going into possession of lands and tenements . . . ." To further discourage self-help, our legislature has provided treble damages for forcible evictions, ss 557.08 and 557.09, and has provided additional criminal penalties for intentional and unlawful exclusion of a tenant. § 504.25. In *Sweeney v. Meyers, supra*, we allowed a business tenant not only damages for lost profits but also punitive damages against a landlord who, like Wiley, entered in the tenant's absence and locked the tenant out.

In the present case, as in Sweeney, the tenant was in possession, claiming a right to continue in possession adverse to the landlord's claim of breach of the lease, and had neither abandoned nor surrendered the premises. Wiley, well aware that Berg was asserting her right to possession, retook possession in her absence by picking the locks and locking her out. The record shows a history of vigorous dispute and keen animosity between the parties. Upon this record, we can only conclude that the singular reason why actual violence did not erupt at the moment of Wiley's changing of the locks was Berg's absence and her subsequent self-restraint and resort to judicial process. Upon these facts, we cannot find Wiley's means of reentry peaceable under the common-law rule. Our long-standing policy to discourage self-help which tends to cause a breach of the peace compels us to disapprove the means used to dispossess Berg. To approve this lockout, as urged by Wiley, merely because in Berg's absence no actual violence erupted while the locks were being changed, would be to encourage all future tenants, in order to protect their possession, to be vigilant and thereby set the stage for the very kind of public disturbance which it must be our policy to discourage. . . .

We recognize that the growing modern trend departs completely from the common-law rule to hold that self-help is never available to dispossess a tenant who is in possession and has not abandoned or voluntarily surrendered the premises. Annotation, 6 A.L.R.3d 177, 186; 76 Dickinson L.Rev. 215, 227. This growing rule is founded on the recognition that the potential for violent breach of peace inheres in any situation where a landlord attempts by his own means to remove a tenant who is claiming possession adversely to the landlord. Courts adopting the rule reason that there is no cause to sanction such potentially disruptive self-help where adequate and speedy means are provided for removing a tenant peacefully through judicial process. At least 16 states have adopted this modern rule, holding that judicial proceedings, including the summary procedures provided in those states' unlawful detainer statutes, are the exclusive remedy by which a landlord may remove a tenant claiming possession. . . .

While we would be compelled to disapprove the lockout of Berg in her absence under the common-law rule as stated, we approve the trial court's reasoning and adopt as preferable the modern view represented by the cited cases. To make clear our departure from the common-law rule for the benefit of future landlords and tenants, we hold that, subsequent to our decision in this case, the only lawful means to dispossess a tenant who has not abandoned nor voluntarily surrendered but who claims possession adversely to a landlord's claim of breach of a written lease is by resort to judicial process. We find that Minn.St. 566.02 to 566.17 provide the landlord with an adequate remedy for regaining possession in every such case. Where speedier action than provided in §§ 566.02 to 566.17 seems necessary because of threatened destruction of the property or other exigent circumstances, a temporary restraining order under Rule 65, Rules of Civil Procedure, and law enforcement protection are available to the landlord. Considered together, these statutory and judicial remedies provide a complete answer to the landlord. In our modern society, with the availability of prompt and sufficient legal remedies as described, there is no place and no need for self-help against a tenant in claimed lawful possession of leased premises.

Applying our holding to the facts of this case, we conclude, as did the trial court, that because Wiley failed to resort to judicial remedies against Berg's holding possession adversely to Wiley's claim of breach of the lease, his lockout of Berg was wrongful as a matter of law. The rule we adopt in this decision is fairly applied against Wiley, for it is clear that, applying the older common-law rule to the facts and circumstances peculiar to this case, we would be compelled to find the lockout nonpeaceable for the reasons previously stated. The jury found that the lockout caused Berg damage and, as between Berg and Wiley, equity dictates that Wiley, who himself performed the act causing the damage, must bear the loss.

Affirmed.

Notes and Questions

1. **Who did what wrong?** Kathleen Berg, the tenant, never missed a rent payment. Why, exactly, did Wiley think he was entitled to enter the property and exclude the tenant? Is Rodney Wiley at fault for this dispute? If you were his lawyer at the time, would you have given him different advice? If he was entitled to possession, how did he end up owing $34,500 to Berg?

2. **Tending to Cause a Breach of the Peace.** In case you aren't convinced that repossession carries an inherent risk of a breach of the peace, consider the story of Erskine G. Bryce. In the summer of 2001, Mr. Bryce—a 66-year-old city marshal in Brooklyn, New York—arrived at the second-story apartment of 53-year-old JoAnne Jones to remove her from possession pursuant to a duly issued court order for her eviction. At the time, Ms. Jones owed about $14,000 in back rent. She violently attacked the marshal, knocking him over a stairwell railing down to the ground floor below. Mr. Bryce's head hit a refrigerator on the way down. Ms. Jones grabbed an aluminum rod, ran down the stairs, and began beating Mr. Bryce with the rod. She then doused his body with paint thinner and set him on fire with a cigarette lighter. Almost as quickly as it had arisen, Ms. Jones's rage subsided, and she attempted to put out the flames she had ignited by running back and forth to her apartment to fetch basins of water—but it was too late. The medical examiner concluded that Mr. Bryce died from a combination of blunt force injuries and the flames that quickly consumed his upper body—in other words, that he had been beaten to within an inch of his life and then burned alive. C.J.

Chivers, *Tenant Held in Murder of Marshal,* N.Y. Times (Aug. 23, 2001).

3. Mr. Bryce had two decades of experience as a marshal and a reputation for dealing calmly and compassionately with those he evicted. He was a stranger to Ms. Jones until he arrived to evict her. But in the moment, the situation still exploded into horrific, deadly violence. How much more likely do we think such violence would be where a landlord—who has a personal stake in recovering possession, no particular professional experience in managing or defusing tense situations, no imprimatur of government authority, and a bitter history with the tenant—attempts to repossess?

4. **Do landlords love violence?** If the court here is correct that all self-help remedies contain the inherent potential for violence, why do landlords seem so eager to employ them? Why would a landlord ever resist going through the court process, which the Justice Rogosheske describes as "adequate and speedy"?

5. **Can landlords stand their ground?** Many states have so-called "stand your ground" laws. Stand your ground laws authorize individuals to use deadly force in self-defense when faced with a reasonable threat. There is no duty to retreat first. Why are legislatures concerned about violence in the landlord/tenant context but not in the self-defense setting?

6. **Costs.** Who does the demise of self-help hurt?

7. **Basic eviction procedure.** Every state has now enacted statutes—often referred to as forcible entry and detainer laws— that help landlords to promptly regain possession when a tenant

holds over or commits a material breach of the lease. In most jurisdictions, statutes mandate that landlords pursue relief through the court system and refrain from self-help remedies. While these eviction procedures vary between jurisdictions, there are some significant commonalities between most states' forced entry and detainer laws. In all jurisdictions, for example, a landlord who wishes to evict a tenant must first send the tenant proper written notice. The notice requirement generally obliges the landlord to accurately state the tenant's name and address, and reveal the nature of the alleged breach. Most states also require the landlord to give the tenant an opportunity (often 3 days, but sometimes as long as 14) to either cure the default or move out. These are often referred to as "Cure or Quit" notices. If the tenant corrects the problem, they must be allowed to stay. However, if the tenant stays in the unit and does not cure the default, the landlord can file a petition for eviction with the local housing court. Upon the landlord's request, the court will quickly set a trial date and a process server will deliver a summons and complaint to each tenant. Most tenants do not contest their evictions. If the tenant does not respond to the summons, the court will enter a judgment in favor of the landlord and the landlord will then hire a local sheriff to remove the tenant from the property. The entire process generally takes from 20 to 60 days.

8. **Defending against eviction.** Occasionally a tenant will mount a vigorous defense to an eviction notice. The most commonly raised defenses are (1) notice was faulty, (2) the tenant cured the default, (3) the landlord illegally retaliated against the tenant, and, (4) the tenant had a right to withhold rent because the unit failed to meet certain minimum standards required by law.

6.   Tenant Exit: Security Deposits

Most landlords require their tenants to pay a security deposit—a sum of money that the landlord can raid if the tenant defaults on the rent, leaves the unit untidy, or damages any property during the course of the tenancy. State law mandates that if the tenant has compiled with all terms of the lease and kept the unit in good order, the landlord must return the security deposit (generally within 30 or 60 days). If the tenant causes damage, the landlord has the right to use the security to restore the unit to its previous condition, but must provide the tenant with a list of damages and receipts for the repairs.

Although the law of security deposits is generally crystal-clear, a huge number of renters report that they have unfairly lost deposit money to their landlords. Why is this so? Game theorists argue that the structure of the landlord-tenant relationship makes disputes over security deposits almost unavoidable. The key insight is that while the tenancy is ongoing, landlords and tenants have incentives to get along and make compromises—the landlord wants the tenant to make timely rent payments and the tenant wants the landlord to respond quickly when problems arise. However, once the landlord and tenant decide to end their relationship, there are few checks to prevent bad behavior. If the landlord will never interact with the tenant again, why not fudge a little bit with security deposit? Additionally, the small amounts of money involved security deposit disputes mean that it's rarely worth hiring a lawyer or taking the time to sue the landlord in small claims court.

Notes and Questions

1. **Tenant self help?** If tenants recognize that landlords often cheat them out of their security deposits, why don't more tenants respond by refusing to pay the last month's rent? After all, eviction procedures almost always take longer than 30 days.

2. **America v. England.** To solve the security deposit dilemma, English law does not permit landlords to keep their tenants' deposits. Rather, they must place them with a government-approved holding agency. If a dispute arises over the money at the end of the lease, the parties are referred to an arbitrator who works for the organization that holds the money. The dispute resolution service does not charge either party but they are bound by its decision. Should jurisdictions in the U.S. move toward this model? Would it change your opinion to know that English landlords routinely fail to comply with these rules? Are there other solutions worth considering?

D. The Quest for Clean, Safe, and Affordable Premises

In feudal England, policy makers and government officials expressed little concern over the housing conditions of renters. The law was well-settled: Once a landlord turned over the right of possession, the tenant became responsible for maintenance of the leased property. If a tenant decided to live in squalor rather than complete basic repairs, that was the tenant's problem, not the landlord's worry. Although it may seem counterintuitive to modern readers (who rely on landlords to fix nearly everything), putting the burden on the tenant to maintain the property actually produced efficient results in the medieval world: landlords often lived long distances from their lessees, communication was slow, houses were simply constructed, and most tenants had the knowledge and skills to complete basic repairs.

The basic principle that tenants are responsible for their own living conditions remained unchallenged until the 1960s, when both academics and politicians expressed growing concern about the rental housing stock in central cities. Many worried that exploitative landlords were flouting safety regulations and taking advantage of tenants who had few housing choices as a result of their poverty and the rampant discrimination in the housing market. The problems in the poorest neighborhoods also had spillover effects in surrounding communities—disease, vermin, and fires do not respect municipal borders. In response to these problems, the law began to vest tenants with a new series of rights against their landlords. This subsection traces the evolution of these rights and explores the rise of legal tools to ensure minimum housing standards for all renters.

1.   The Covenant of Quiet Enjoyment

Traditional common law principles do not leave renters completely defenseless against unprincipled landlords. Every lease, whether residential or commercial, contains a *covenant of quiet enjoyment*. Often this promise is explicitly stated in the lease contract. Where it's not specifically mentioned, all courts will imply it into the agreement. The basic idea is that the landlord cannot interfere with the tenant's use of the property. Most courts state the legal test this way: A breach of the covenant of quiet enjoyment occurs when the landlord substantially interferes with the tenant's use or enjoyment of the premises.

Consider the following hypothetical:

> Little Bo Peep Detective Services rents the second floor of a four-floor building. A year into the five-year lease, the landlord suddenly begins a construction project designed to update the suites on the first floor. These renovations create loud noise and regular interruptions of electric service. The construction work has also made the parking lot inaccessible. Employees and customers

need to walk a quarter-mile to access the building from a nearby parking garage.

Do these problems amount to a violation of the covenant of quiet enjoyment? To determine whether the interference is "substantial" courts generally consider the purpose the premises are leased for, the foreseeability of the problem, the potential duration, and the degree of harm. In this example, if the construction project lasts for more than a few days, then Little Bo Peep can most likely bring a successful claim against its landlord under the covenant of quiet enjoyment. The problems here are not mere trifles—the noise, lack of electricity, and inadequate parking fundamentally affect the company's ability to use the property as they intended.

The difficult conceptual issue with the covenant of quiet enjoyment concerns the remedy. If the landlord breaks the covenant, what are the tenant's options? After a breach, the tenant can always choose to stay in the leased property, continue to pay rent, and sue the landlord for damages.

Additionally, certain violations of the covenant of quiet enjoyment allow the tenant to consider the lease terminated, leave, and stop paying rent. Recall from earlier in the chapter that the landlord's fundamental responsibility is to provide the tenant with possession (or, in some jurisdictions, the right to possession). From that principle, courts developed a rule that in cases where the landlord wrongfully evicts the tenant, all the tenant's obligations under the lease cease. Imagine:

> Landlord and tenant both sign a lease that reads, "Landlord agrees to provide Tenant with possession of 123 Meadowlark Lane for a period of 12 months beginning April 1. Tenant agrees to pay $100 per month." After 4 months, however, the Landlord retakes

possession of the property by forcing the tenant out and changing the locks.

Assuming the tenant hasn't committed a material breach, the landlord's actions constitute an obvious violation of the covenant of quiet enjoyment—the tenant can no longer use the property for any purpose. Thus, any eviction where the tenant is physically denied access to the unit ends the tenant's obligation to pay rent and allows the tenant to sue for damages incurred from being removed from possession (A tenant could also sue to regain the unit). The law is very clear on this point. Relatedly, if the landlord denies the tenant access to some portion of the rented space (say, an allotted parking space) that, too, constitutes a breach of the covenant of quiet enjoyment. The tenant subject to such a partial eviction has the option to terminate the lease and sue for damages.

But what if the landlord doesn't physically interfere with her tenant's occupancy? What if the landlord creates an environment that's so miserable that the tenant is forced to flee? Is this an "eviction" that would allow the tenant to consider the lease terminated or must the tenant stay and continue paying rent while he brings a damages lawsuit

Fidelity Mutual Life Insurance Co. v. Kaminsky
768 S.W.2d 818 (Tex. App. 1989)

MURPHY, Justice.

The issue in this landlord-tenant case is whether sufficient evidence supports the jury's findings that the landlord and appellant, Fidelity Mutual Life Insurance Company ["Fidelity"], constructively evicted the tenant, Robert P. Kaminsky, M.D., P.A. ["Dr. Kaminsky"] by breaching the express covenant of quiet enjoyment contained in the parties' lease. We affirm.

Dr. Kaminsky is a gynecologist whose practice includes performing elective abortions. In May 1983, he executed a lease contract for the rental of approximately 2,861 square feet in the Red Oak Atrium Building for a two year term which began on June 1, 1983. The terms of the lease required Dr. Kaminsky to use the rented space solely as "an office for the practice of medicine." Fidelity owns the building and hires local companies to manage it. At some time during the lease term, Shelter Commercial Properties ["Shelter"] replaced the Horne Company as managing agents. Fidelity has not disputed either management company's capacity to act as its agent.

The parties agree that: (1) they executed a valid lease agreement; (2) Paragraph 35 of the lease contains an express covenant of quiet enjoyment conditioned on Dr. Kaminsky's paying rent when due, as he did through November 1984; Dr. Kaminsky abandoned the leased premises on or about December 3, 1984 and refused to pay additional rent; anti-abortion protestors began picketing at the building in June of 1984 and repeated and increased their demonstrations outside and inside the building until Dr. Kaminsky abandoned the premises.

When Fidelity sued for the balance due under the lease contract following Dr. Kaminsky's abandonment of the premises, he claimed that Fidelity constructively evicted him by breaching Paragraph 35 of the lease. Fidelity apparently conceded during trial that sufficient proof of the constructive eviction of Dr. Kaminsky would relieve him of his contractual liability for any remaining rent payments. Accordingly, he assumed the burden of proof and the sole issue submitted to the jury was whether Fidelity breached Paragraph 35 of the lease, which reads as follows:

Quiet Enjoyment.

Lessee, on paying the said Rent, and any Additional Rental, shall and may peaceably and quietly have, hold and enjoy the Leased Premises for the said term.

A constructive eviction occurs when the tenant leaves the leased premises due to conduct by the landlord which materially interferes with the tenant's beneficial use of the premises. *See Downtown Realty, Inc. v. 509 Tremont Bldg.*, 748 S.W.2d 309, 313 (Tex.App.—Houston [14th Dist.] 1988, n.w.h.). Texas law relieves the tenant of contractual liability for any remaining rentals due under the lease if he can establish a constructive eviction by the landlord. . . .

In order to prevail on his claim that Fidelity constructively evicted him and thereby relieved him of his rent obligation, Dr. Kaminsky had to show the following: 1) Fidelity intended that he no longer enjoy the premises, which intent the trier of fact could infer from the circumstances; 2) Fidelity, or those acting for Fidelity or with its permission, committed a material act or omission which substantially interfered with use and enjoyment of the premises for their leased purpose, here an office for the practice of medicine; 3) Fidelity's act or omission permanently deprived Dr. Kaminsky of the use and enjoyment of the premises; and 4) Dr. Kaminsky abandoned the premises within a reasonable period of time after the act or omission. *E.g., Downtown Realty, Inc.*, 748 S.W.2d at 311 . . . .

[T]he jury found that Dr. Kaminsky had established each element of his constructive eviction defense. The trial court entered judgment that Fidelity take nothing on its suit for delinquent rent.

Fidelity raises four points of error. . . .

Fidelity's first point of error relies on *Angelo v. Deutser*, 30 S.W.2d 707 (Tex.Civ.App.—Beaumont 1930, no writ), *Thomas v. Brin*, 38 Tex.Civ.App. 180, 85 S.W. 842 (1905, no writ) and *Sedberry v. Verplanck*, 31 S.W. 242 (Tex.Civ.App.1895, no writ). These cases all state the general proposition that a tenant cannot complain that the landlord constructively evicted him and breached a covenant of quiet enjoyment, express or implied, when the eviction results from the actions of third parties acting without the landlord's authority or permission. Fidelity insists the evidence conclusively establishes: a) that it did nothing to encourage or sponsor the protestors and; b) that the protestors, rather than Fidelity or its agents, caused Dr. Kaminsky to abandon the premises. Fidelity concludes that reversible error resulted because the trial court refused to set aside the jury's answers to the special issues and enter judgment in Fidelity's favor and because the trial court denied its motion for a new trial. We disagree. . . .

The protests took place chiefly on Saturdays, the day Dr. Kaminsky generally scheduled abortions. During the protests, the singing and chanting demonstrators picketed in the building's parking lot and inner lobby and atrium area. They approached patients to speak to them, distributed literature, discouraged patients from entering the building and often accused Dr. Kaminsky of "killing babies." As the protests increased, the demonstrators often occupied the stairs leading to Dr. Kaminsky's office and prevented patients from entering the office by blocking the doorway. Occasionally they succeeded in gaining access to the office waiting room area.

Dr. Kaminsky complained to Fidelity through its managing agents and asked for help in keeping the protestors away, but became increasingly frustrated by a lack of response to his requests. The record shows that no security personnel were present on Saturdays to exclude protestors from the building, although the lease required Fidelity to provide security service on Saturdays. The record also shows that Fidelity's attorneys prepared a written statement to be handed to the protestors soon after Fidelity hired Shelter as its managing agent. The statement tracked TEX.PENAL CODE ANN. § 30.05 (Vernon Supp.1989) and generally served to inform trespassers that they risked criminal prosecution by failing to leave if asked to do so. Fidelity's attorneys instructed Shelter's representative to "have several of these letters printed up and be ready to distribute them and verbally demand that these people move on and off the property." The same representative conceded at trial that she did not distribute these notices. Yet when Dr. Kaminsky enlisted the aid of the Sheriff's office, officers refused to ask the protestors to leave without a directive from Fidelity or its agent. Indeed, an attorney had instructed the protestors to remain unless the landlord or its representative ordered them to leave. It appears that Fidelity's only response to the demonstrators was to state, through its agents, that it was aware of Dr. Kaminsky's problems.

Both action and lack of action can constitute "conduct" by the landlord which amounts to a constructive eviction. *E.g., Downtown Realty Inc.,* 748 S.W.2d at 311. In *Steinberg v. Medical Equip. Rental Serv., Inc.,* 505 S.W.2d 692 (Tex. Civ. App.—Dallas 1974, no writ) accordingly, the court upheld a jury's determination that the landlord's failure to act amounted to a constructive eviction and breach of the covenant of quiet enjoyment. 505 S.W.2d at 697. Like Dr. Kaminsky, the tenant in Steinberg abandoned the leased premises and refused to pay additional rent after repeatedly complaining to the landlord. The *Steinberg* tenant complained that Steinberg placed trash bins near the entrance to the business and allowed trucks to park and block customer's access to the tenant's medical equipment rental business. The tenant's repeated complaints to Steinberg yielded only a request "to be patient." Id. Fidelity responded to Dr. Kaminsky's complaints in a similar manner: although it acknowledged his problems with the protestors, Fidelity, like Steinberg, effectively did nothing to prevent the problems.

This case shows ample instances of Fidelity's failure to act in the fact of repeated requests for assistance despite its having expressly covenanted Dr. Kaminsky's quiet enjoyment of the premises. These instances provided a legally sufficient basis for the jury to conclude that Dr. Kaminsky abandoned the leased premises, not because of the trespassing protestors, but because of Fidelity's lack of response to his complaints about the protestors. Under the circumstances, while it is undisputed that Fidelity did not "encourage" the demonstrators, its conduct essentially allowed them to continue to trespass. The general rule of the *Angelo*, *Thomas* and *Sedberry* cases, that a landlord is not responsible for the actions of third parties, applies only when the landlord does not permit the third party to act. *See e.g., Angelo*, 30 S.W.2d at 710 ["the act or omission complained of must be that of the landlord and not merely of a third person *acting without his authority or permission*" (emphasis added)]. We see no distinction between Fidelity's lack of action here, which the record shows resulted in preventing patients' access to Dr. Kaminsky's medical office, and the *Steinberg* case where the landlord's inaction resulted in trucks' blocking customer access to the tenant's business. We overrule the first point of error. . . . .

In its [final] point of error, Fidelity maintains the evidence is factually insufficient to support the jury's finding that its conduct permanently deprived Dr. Kaminsky of use and enjoyment of the premises. Fidelity essentially questions the permanency of Dr. Kaminsky's being deprived of the use and enjoyment of the leased premises. To support its contentions, Fidelity points to testimony by Dr. Kaminsky in which he concedes that none of his patients were ever harmed and that protests and demonstrations continued despite his leaving the Red Oak Atrium building. Fidelity also disputes whether Dr. Kaminsky actually lost patients due to the protests.

The evidence shows that the protestors, whose entry into the building Fidelity failed to prohibit, often succeeded in blocking Dr. Kaminsky's patients' access to his medical office. Under the reasoning of the *Steinberg* case, omissions by a landlord which result in patients' lack of access to the office of a practicing physician would suffice to establish a permanent deprivation of the use and enjoyment of the premises for their leased purpose, here "an office for the *practice* of medicine." *Steinberg*, 505 S.W.2d at 697; *accord, Downtown Realty, Inc.*, 748 S.W.2d at 312 (noting jury's finding that a constructive eviction resulted from the commercial landlord's failure to repair a heating and air conditioning system in a rooming house).

Texas law has long recited the requirement, first stated in *Stillman*, 266 S.W.2d at 916, that the landlord commit a "material and permanent" act or omission in order for his tenant to claim a constructive eviction. However, as the *Steinberg* and *Downtown Realty, Inc.* cases illustrate, the extent to which a landlord's acts or omissions permanently and materially deprive a tenant of the use and enjoyment of the premises often involves a question of degree. Having reviewed all the evidence before the jury in this case, we cannot say that its finding that Fidelity's conduct permanently deprived Dr. Kaminsky of the use and enjoyment of his medical office space was so against the great weight and preponderance of the evidence as to be manifestly unjust. We overrule the fourth point of error.

We affirm the judgment of the trial court.

Notes and Questions

1. **Evolution of the doctrine.** As discussed above, English judges widely recognized that tenants could terminate the lease (and sue for damages) if the landlord physically denied them possession of the rented property. Eventually the basic concept was expanded to situations where the landlord commits some act that, while it falls short of an actual eviction, so severely affects the value of the tenancy that the tenant is forced to flee. This is known as *constructive eviction.*

2. **Basic constrictive eviction law.** To make a claim of constructive eviction a tenant must show that some act or omission by the landlord substantially interferes with the tenant's use and enjoyment of the property. The tenant also needs to notify the landlord about the problem, give the landlord an opportunity to

cure the defect, and then vacate the premise within a reasonable amount of time.

3. **Stay or go?** Why might a tenant contemplating bringing a constructive eviction claim worry about the requirement to vacate the premises? Is constructive eviction a more powerful remedy in a place like San Francisco, which has a very tight housing market, or Houston, which has more open units?

4. **Landlord's wrongful conduct.** To make use of the doctrine of quiet enjoyment, the tenant must show that the landlord committed some wrongful act. There's wide agreement that any affirmative step taken by the landlord that impedes the tenant's use of the property can meet the requirement of an "act." Examples would include burning toxic substances on the property, prolonged construction activities, or a substantial alteration of an essential feature of the leased premises. The trickier doctrinal question is whether a landlord's failure to act can ever qualify as the wrongful conduct. Traditionally, courts hesitated to impose liability on landlords for their omissions, but the law of most states now asserts that a "lack of action" can constitute the required act. For example, a landlord's failure to provide heat in the winter months is generally found to violate the covenant of quiet enjoyment. Some courts, nervous about unjustly expanding landlords' potential liability, deem omissions wrongful only when the landlord fails to fulfill some clear duty—either a duty bargained for in the lease or a statutory duty.

5. **Troublesome tenants.** Suppose your landlord rents the floor above your apartment to the members of a Led Zeppelin cover band. If the band practices every night between the hours of 3:00

am and 4:00 am, could you bring a successful constructive eviction claim against the landlord?

6. **Third parties.** What if the Led Zeppelin cover band played every night at a club across the street? If the noise from the bar kept you awake, could you sue your landlord for constructive eviction?

2.   The Implied Warranty of Habitability

Although the covenant of quiet enjoyment offers tenants some protections, the doctrine—without more—can leave renters exposed to dreadful living conditions. What if cockroaches invade a tenant's apartment? Or a sewer pipe in the basement begins to leak? What if a storm shatters the windows of the apartment? Or a wall of a building falls down? Unless the landlord somehow caused any of these disasters (or had a clearly articulated duty to fix them) a tenant cannot bring a successful case under the covenant of quiet enjoyment. In *Hughes v. Westchester Development Corp.*, 77 F.2d 550 (D.C. Cir. 1935), for example, vermin invaded the tenant's apartment, making it "impossible to use the kitchen and toilet facilities." Despite the infestation, the court found that the tenant remained responsible for the rent because the landlord was not to blame for the bugs' sudden appearance. Leases, the court ruled, contained no implied promise that the premise was fit for the purpose it was leased. If tenants desired more and better protection, they had the burden to bargain for such provisions in the lease.

All of this changed in the late 1960s and early 70s. The most lasting accomplishment of the tenants' rights movement was the widespread adoption of the *implied warranty of habitability*. In the United States, only Arkansas has failed to adopt the rule. In a nutshell, the implied warranty of habitability imposes a duty on landlords to provide residential tenants with a clean, safe, and habitable living space.

Hilder v. St. Peter
478 A.2d 202 (Vt. 1984)

BILLINGS, Chief Justice.

Defendants appeal from a judgment rendered by the Rutland Superior Court. The court ordered defendants to pay plaintiff damages in the amount of $4,945.00, which represented "reimbursement of all rent paid and additional compensatory damages" for the rental of a residential apartment over a fourteen month period in defendants' Rutland apartment building. Defendants filed a motion for reconsideration on the issue of the amount of damages awarded to the plaintiff, and plaintiff filed a cross-motion for reconsideration of the court's denial of an award of punitive damages. The court denied both motions. On appeal, defendants raise [two] issues for our consideration: first, whether the court correctly calculated the amount of damages awarded the plaintiff; secondly, whether the court's award to plaintiff of the entire amount of rent paid to defendants was proper since the plaintiff remained in possession of the apartment for the entire fourteen month period. . . .

The facts are uncontested. In October, 1974, plaintiff began occupying an apartment at defendants' 10–12 Church Street apartment building in Rutland with her three children and new-born grandson. Plaintiff orally agreed to pay defendant Stuart St. Peter $140 a month and a damage deposit of $50; plaintiff paid defendant the first month's rent and the damage deposit prior to moving in. Plaintiff has paid all rent due under her tenancy. Because the previous tenants had left behind garbage and items of personal belongings, defendant offered to refund plaintiff's damage deposit if she would clean the apartment herself prior to taking possession. Plaintiff did clean the apartment, but never received her deposit back because the defendant denied ever receiving it. Upon moving into the apartment, plaintiff discovered a broken kitchen window. Defendant promised to repair it, but after waiting a week and fearing that her two year old child might cut herself on the shards of glass, plaintiff repaired the window at her own expense. Although defendant promised to provide a front door key, he never did. For a period of time, whenever plaintiff left the apartment, a member of her family would remain behind for security reasons. Eventually, plaintiff purchased and installed a padlock, again at her own expense. After moving in, plaintiff discovered that the bathroom toilet was clogged with paper and feces and would flush only by dumping pails of water into it. Although plaintiff repeatedly complained about the toilet, and defendant promised to have it repaired, the toilet remained clogged and mechanically inoperable throughout the period of plaintiff's tenancy. In addition, the bathroom light and wall outlet were inoperable. Again, the defendant agreed to repair the fixtures, but never did. In order to have light in the bathroom, plaintiff attached a fixture to the wall and connected it to an extension cord that was plugged into an adjoining room. Plaintiff also discovered that water leaked from the water pipes of the upstairs apartment down the ceilings and walls of both her kitchen and back bedroom. Again, defendant promised to fix the leakage, but never did. As a result of this leakage, a large section of plaster fell from the back bedroom ceiling onto her bed and her grandson's crib. Other sections of plaster remained dangling from the ceiling. This condition was brought to the attention of the defendant, but he never corrected it. Fearing that the remaining plaster might fall when the room was occupied, plaintiff moved her and her grandson's bedroom furniture into the living room and ceased using the back bedroom. During the summer months an odor of raw sewage permeated plaintiff's apartment. The odor was so strong that the plaintiff was ashamed to have company in her apartment. Responding to plaintiff's complaints, Rutland City workers unearthed a broken sewage pipe in the basement of defendants' building. Raw sewage littered the floor of the basement, but defendant failed to clean it up. Plaintiff also discovered that the electric service for her furnace was attached to her breaker box, although defendant had agreed, at the commencement of plaintiff's tenancy, to furnish heat.

In its conclusions of law, the court held that the state of disrepair of plaintiff's apartment, which was known to the defendants, substantially reduced the value of the leasehold from the agreed rental value, thus constituting a breach of the implied warranty of habitability. The court based its award of damages on the breach of this warranty and on breach of an express contract. Defendant argues that the court misapplied the law of Vermont relating to habitability because the plaintiff never abandoned the demised premises and, therefore, it was error to award her the full amount of rent paid. Plaintiff counters that, while never expressly recognized by this Court, the trial court was correct in applying an implied warranty of habitability and that under this warranty, abandonment of the premises is not required. Plaintiff urges this Court to affirmatively adopt the implied warranty of habitability.

Historically, relations between landlords and tenants have been defined by the law of property. Under these traditional common law property concepts, a lease was viewed as a conveyance of real property. *See* Note, *Judicial Expansion of Tenants' Private Law Rights: Implied Warranties of Habitability and Safety in Residential Urban Leases*, 56 Cornell L.Q. 489, 489–90 (1971) (hereinafter cited as *Expansion of Tenants' Rights*). The relationship between landlord and tenant was controlled by the doctrine of caveat lessee; that is, the tenant took possession of the demised premises irrespective of their state of disrepair. Love, *Landlord's Liability for Defective Premises: Caveat Lessee, Negligence, or Strict Liability?*, 1975 Wis. L. Rev. 19, 27–28. The landlord's only covenant was to deliver possession to the tenant. The tenant's obligation to pay rent existed independently of the landlord's duty to deliver possession, so that as long as possession remained in the tenant, the tenant remained liable for payment of rent. The landlord was under no duty to render the premises habitable unless there was an express covenant to repair in the written lease. *Expansion of Tenants' Rights, supra*, at 490. The land, not the dwelling, was regarded as the essence of the conveyance.

An exception to the rule of caveat lessee was the doctrine of constructive eviction. *Lemle v. Breeden*, 462 P.2d 470, 473 (Haw. 1969). Here, if the landlord wrongfully interfered with the tenant's enjoyment of the demised premises, or failed to render a duty to the tenant as expressly required under the terms of the lease, the tenant could abandon the premises and cease paying rent. *Legier v. Deveneau*, 126 A. 392, 393 (Vt. 1924).

Beginning in the 1960's, American courts began recognizing that this approach to landlord and tenant relations, which had originated during the Middle Ages, had become an anachronism in twentieth century, urban society. Today's tenant enters into lease agreements, not to obtain arable land, but to obtain safe, sanitary and comfortable housing.

> [T]hey seek a well known package of goods and services—a package which includes not merely walls and ceilings, but also adequate heat, light and ventilation, serviceable plumbing facilities, secure windows and doors, proper sanitation, and proper maintenance.

Javins v. First National Realty Corp., 428 F.2d 1071, 1074 (D.C.Cir.), cert. denied, 400 U.S. 925, 91 S.Ct. 186, 27 L.Ed.2d 185 (1970).

Not only has the subject matter of today's lease changed, but the characteristics of today's tenant have similarly evolved. The tenant of the Middle Ages was a farmer, capable of making whatever repairs were necessary to his primitive dwelling. *Green v. Superior Court*, 517 P.2d 1168, 1172 (Cal. 1974). Additionally, "the common law courts assumed that an equal bargaining position existed between landlord and tenant. . . ." Note, *The Implied Warranty of Habitability: A Dream Deferred*, 48 UMKC L.REV. 237, 238 (1980) (hereinafter cited as *A Dream Deferred*).

In sharp contrast, today's residential tenant, most commonly a city dweller, is not experienced in performing maintenance work on urban, complex living units. *Green v. Superior Court, supra*, 517 P.2d at 1173. The landlord is more familiar with the dwelling unit and mechanical equipment attached to that unit, and is more financially able to "discover and cure" any faults and break-downs. *Id.* Confronted with a recognized shortage of safe, decent housing, see 24 V.S.A. § 4001(1), today's tenant is in an inferior bargaining position compared to that of the landlord. *Park West Management Corp. v. Mitchell*, 391 N.E.2d 1288, 1292 (N.Y. 1979). Tenants vying for this limited housing are "virtually powerless to compel the performance of essential services." *Id.*

In light of these changes in the relationship between tenants and landlords, it would be wrong for the law to continue to impose the doctrine of caveat lessee on residential leases.

> The modern view favors a new approach which recognizes that a lease is essentially a contract between the landlord and the tenant wherein the landlord promises to deliver and maintain the demised premises in habitable condition and the tenant promises to pay rent for such habitable premises. These promises constitute interdependent and mutual considerations. Thus, the tenant's obligation to pay rent is predicated on the landlord's obligation to deliver and maintain the premises in habitable condition.

Boston Housing Authority v. Hemingway, 293 N.E.2d 831, 842 (Mass. 1973).

Recognition of residential leases as contracts embodying the mutual covenants of habitability and payment of rent does not represent an abrupt change in Vermont law. Our case law has previously recognized that contract remedies are available for breaches of lease agreements. *Clarendon Mobile Home Sales, Inc. v. Fitzgerald*, 381 A.2d 1063, 1065 (Vt. 1977). . . . More significantly, our legislature, in establishing local housing authorities, 24 V.S.A. § 4003, has officially recognized the need for assuring the existence of adequate housing.

[S]ubstandard and decadent areas exist in certain portions of the state of Vermont and . . . there is not . . . an adequate supply of decent, safe and sanitary housing for persons of low income and/or elderly persons of low income, available for rents which such persons can afford to pay . . . this situation tends to cause an increase and spread of communicable and chronic disease . . . [and] constitutes a menace to the health, safety, welfare and comfort of the inhabitants of the state and is detrimental to property values in the localities in which it exists . . . .

24 V.S.A. § 4001(4). In addition, this Court has assumed the existence of an implied warranty of habitability in residential leases. *Birkenhead v. Coombs*, 465 A.2d 244, 246 (Vt. 1983).

Therefore, we now hold expressly that in the rental of any residential dwelling unit an implied warranty exists in the lease, whether oral or written, that the landlord will deliver over and maintain, throughout the period of the tenancy, premises that are safe, clean and fit for human habitation. This warranty of habitability is implied in tenancies for a specific period or at will. *Boston Housing Authority v. Hemingway, supra*, 293 N.E.2d at 843. Additionally, the implied warranty of habitability covers all latent and patent defects in the essential facilities of the residential unit. *Id.* Essential facilities are "facilities vital to the use of the premises for residential purposes. . . ." *Kline v. Burns*, 276 A.2d 248, 252 (N.H. 1971). This means that a tenant who enters into a lease agreement with knowledge of any defect in the essential facilities cannot be said to have assumed the risk, thereby losing the protection of the warranty. Nor can this implied warranty of habitability be waived by any written provision in the lease or by oral agreement.

In determining whether there has been a breach of the implied warranty of habitability, the courts may first look to any relevant local or municipal housing code; they may also make reference to the minimum housing code standards enunciated in 24 V.S.A. § 5003(c)(1)–5003(c)(5). A substantial violation of an applicable housing code shall constitute prima facie evidence that there has been a breach of the warranty of habitability. "[O]ne or two minor violations standing alone which do not affect" the health or safety of the tenant, shall be considered *de minimus* and not a breach of the warranty. *Javins v. First National Realty Corp., supra,* 428 F.2d at 1082 n. 63. . . . In addition, the landlord will not be liable for defects caused by the tenant. *Javins v. First National Realty Corp., supra,* 428 F.2d at 1082 n. 62.

However, these codes and standards merely provide a starting point in determining whether there has been a breach. Not all towns and municipalities have housing codes; where there are codes, the particular problem complained of may not be addressed. *Park West Management Corp. v. Mitchell, supra,* 391 N.E.2d at 1294. In determining whether there has been a breach of the implied warranty of habitability, courts should inquire whether the claimed defect has an impact on the safety or health of the tenant. *Id.*

In order to bring a cause of action for breach of the implied warranty of habitability, the tenant must first show that he or she notified the landlord "of the deficiency or defect not known to the landlord and [allowed] a reasonable time for its correction." *King v. Moorehead, supra,* 495 S.W.2d at 76.

Because we hold that the lease of a residential dwelling creates a contractual relationship between the landlord and tenant, the standard contract remedies of rescission, reformation and damages are available to the tenant when suing for breach of the implied warranty of habitability. *Lemle v. Breeden, supra,* 462 P.2d at 475. The measure of damages shall be the difference between the value of the dwelling as warranted and the value of the dwelling as it exists in its defective condition. *Birkenhead v. Coombs, supra,* 465 A.2d at 246. In determining the fair rental value of the dwelling as warranted, the court may look to the agreed upon rent as evidence on this issue. *Id.* "[I]n residential lease disputes involving a breach of the implied warranty of habitability, public policy militates against requiring expert testimony" concerning the value of the defect. *Id.* at 247. The tenant will be liable only for "the reasonable rental value [if any] of the property in its imperfect condition during his period of occupancy." *Berzito v. Gambino*, 308 A.2d 17, 22 (N.J. 1973).

We also find persuasive the reasoning of some commentators that damages should be allowed for a tenant's discomfort and annoyance arising from the landlord's breach of the implied warranty of habitability. *See* Moskovitz, *The Implied Warranty of Habitability: A New Doctrine Raising New Issues*, 62 CAL. L. REV. 1444, 1470–73 (1974) (hereinafter cited as *A New Doctrine*); *A Dream Deferred, supra,* at 250–51. Damages for annoyance and discomfort are reasonable in light of the fact that:

> the residential tenant who has suffered a breach of the warranty . . . cannot bathe as frequently as he would like or at all if there is inadequate hot water; he must worry about rodents harassing his children or spreading disease if the premises are infested; or he must avoid certain rooms or worry about catching a cold if there is inadequate weather protection or heat. Thus, discomfort and annoyance are the common injuries caused by each breach and hence the true nature of the general damages the tenant is claiming.

Moskovitz, *A New Doctrine, supra,* at 1470–71. Damages for discomfort and annoyance may be difficult to compute; however, "[t]he trier [of fact] is not to be deterred from this duty by the fact that the damages are not susceptible of reduction to an exact money standard." *Vermont Electric Supply Co. v. Andrus*, 315 A.2d 456, 459 (Vt. 1974).

Another remedy available to the tenant when there has been a breach of the implied warranty of habitability is to withhold the payment of future rent. *King v. Moorehead, supra*, 495 S.W.2d at 77. The burden and expense of bringing suit will then be on the landlord who can better afford to bring the action. In an action for ejectment for nonpayment of rent, 12 V.S.A. § 4773, "[t]he trier of fact, upon evaluating the seriousness of the breach and the ramification of the defect upon the health and safety of the tenant, will abate the rent at the landlord's expense in accordance with its findings." *A Dream Deferred, supra*, at 248. The tenant must show that: (1) the landlord had notice of the previously unknown defect and failed, within a reasonable time, to repair it; and (2) the defect, affecting habitability, existed during the time for which rent was withheld. *See A Dream Deferred, supra*, at 248–50. Whether a portion, all or none of the rent will be awarded to the landlord will depend on the findings relative to the extent and duration of the breach. *Javins v. First National Realty Corp., supra*, 428 F.2d at 1082–83. Of course, once the landlord corrects the defect, the tenant's obligation to pay rent becomes due again. *Id.* at 1083 n. 64.

Additionally, we hold that when the landlord is notified of the defect but fails to repair it within a reasonable amount of time, and the tenant subsequently repairs the defect, the tenant may deduct the expense of the repair from future rent. 11 Williston on Contracts § 1404 (3d ed. W. Jaeger 1968); *Marini v. Ireland*, 265 A.2d 526, 535 (N.J. 1970).

In addition to general damages, we hold that punitive damages may be available to a tenant in the appropriate case. Although punitive damages are generally not recoverable in actions for breach of contract, there are cases in which the breach is of such a willful and wanton or fraudulent nature as to make appropriate the award of exemplary damages. *Clarendon Mobile Home Sales, Inc. v. Fitzgerald, supra*, 381 A.2d at 1065. A willful and wanton or fraudulent breach may be shown "by conduct manifesting personal ill will, or carried out under circumstances of insult or oppression, or even by conduct manifesting . . . a reckless or wanton disregard of [one's] rights . . . ." *Sparrow v. Vermont Savings Bank*, 112 A. 205, 207 (Vt. 1921). When a landlord, after receiving notice of a defect, fails to repair the facility that is essential to the health and safety of his or her tenant, an award of punitive damages is proper. *111 East 88th Partners v. Simon*, 434 N.Y.S.2d 886, 889 (N.Y. Civ. Ct. 1980).

> The purpose of punitive damages . . . is to punish conduct which is morally culpable. . . . Such an award serves to deter a wrongdoer . . . from repetitions of the same or similar actions. And it tends to encourage prosecution of a claim by a victim who might not otherwise incur the expense or inconvenience of private action. . . . The public benefit and a display of ethical indignation are among the ends of the policy to grant punitive damages.

Davis v. Williams, 402 N.Y.S.2d 92, 94 (N.Y.Civ.Ct.1977).

In the instant case, the trial court's award of damages, based in part on a breach of the implied warranty of habitability, was not a misapplication of the law relative to habitability. Because of our holding in this case, the doctrine of constructive eviction, wherein the tenant must abandon in order to escape liability for rent, is no longer viable. When, as in the instant case, the tenant seeks, not to escape rent liability, but to receive compensatory damages in the amount of rent already paid, abandonment is similarly unnecessary. *Northern Terminals, Inc. v. Smith Grocery & Variety, Inc.*, *supra*, 418 A.2d at 26–27. Under our holding, when a landlord breaches the implied warranty of habitability, the tenant may withhold future rent, and may also seek damages in the amount of rent previously paid.

In its conclusions of law the trial court stated that the defendants' failure to make repairs was compensable by damages to the extent of reimbursement of all rent paid and additional compensatory damages. The court awarded plaintiff a total of $4,945.00; $3,445.00 represents the entire amount of rent plaintiff paid, plus the $50.00 deposit. . . .

Additionally, the court denied an award to plaintiff of punitive damages on the ground that the evidence failed to support a finding of willful and wanton or fraudulent conduct. *See Clarendon Mobile Home Sales, Inc. v. Fitzgerald, supra*, 381 A.2d at 1065. The facts in this case, which defendants do not contest, evince a pattern of intentional conduct on the part of defendants for which the term "slumlord" surely was coined. Defendants' conduct was culpable and demeaning to plaintiff and clearly expressive of a wanton disregard of plaintiff's rights. The trial court found that defendants were aware of defects in the essential facilities of plaintiff's apartment, promised plaintiff that repairs would be made, but never fulfilled those promises. The court also found that plaintiff continued, throughout her tenancy, to pay her rent, often in the face of verbal threats made by defendant Stuart St. Peter. These findings point to the "bad spirit and wrong intention" of the defendants, *Glidden v. Skinner*, 458 A.2d 1142, 1144 (Vt. 1983), and would support a finding of willful and wanton or fraudulent conduct, contrary to the conclusions of law and judgment of the trial judge. However, the plaintiff did not appeal the court's denial of punitive damages, and issues not appealed and briefed are waived. *R. Brown & Sons, Inc. v. International Harvester Corp.*, 453 A.2d 83, 84 (Vt. 1982).

Notes and Questions

1. **Residential v. commercial.** Unlike the covenant of quiet enjoyment, the implied warranty of habitability only applies to residential leases. Commercial tenants still largely operate under common-law legal rules. Commonly, commercial landlords and tenants do not rely on the default rules, but rather assign the duty of upkeep and repair with an express provision in the lease.

2. **What is habitability?** Do all defects in an apartment amount to violations? What is the standard of habitability as laid out in *Hilder?*

3. **Paternalism?** Is the implied warranty of habitability too paternalistic? Some economists argue that the poorest Americans

should have more freedom over how they spend their limited dollars. Isn't it possible that some individuals might want to occupy a really cheap (if slightly dangerous) dwelling so that they have more money to spend on healthy foods, transportation, and clothes? Would it matter if the evidence showed that such apartments were in fact cheaper than "habitable" apartments?

4. **Necessary?** Do you agree with the arguments made by the court in *Hilder* about the necessity of the implied warranty of habitability? Don't landlords already have excellent incentives to maintain their buildings?

5. **Arkansas and beyond.** As mentioned above, Arkansas is the one state that has not adopted the implied warranty of habitability—either by statute or judicial fiat. Is Arkansas a Mad Max-style hellscape for renters? Are tenants there worse (or worse off) than the tenants in other states? Some people think so. *Vice* magazine recently dubbed Arkansas, "The Worst Place to Rent in America." You can see the report on renting in Arkansas at: https://www.youtube.com/watch?v=9G2Pk2JZP-E. But does the implied warranty of habitability provide much practical protection? Do poor tenants know about it? Do they have the resources to push back against aggressive landlords who threaten lawsuits and other forms of retaliation? Professor David Super has suggested that the decision of tenants' rights movement to focus on habitability over affordability and overcrowding was a strategic mistake. *See* David A. Super, *The Rise and Fall of the Implied Warranty of Habitability*, 99 CAL. L. REV. 389-463 (2011). Is there a nirvana for renters anywhere?

6. **Procedure & remedies.** If a tenant believes his apartment does not meet the standard of habitability, he must first must notify the

landlord of the defects and give the landlord a reasonable amount of time to cure the problems. If the landlord either cannot or will not make repairs, the implied warranty of habitability offers the renter a menu of options. Each option presents a different combination of costs and risks to the tenant. If the landlord breaches, the tenant may:

a. *Leave, terminate contract.* The tenant may consider the lease terminated and move out.

b. *Stay and sue for damages.* As with the covenant of quiet enjoyment, a tenant may stay in the unit and pay rent, while suing the landlord for damages. There is significant disagreement among jurisdictions about how to calculate damages. In *Hilder*, the court uses the difference between the rental price of the dwelling if it met the standard of habitability and the value of the dwelling as it exists; the rent charged is not evidence of actual value, but rather evidence of the appropriate price if it met the standard of habitability. [Note that given the court's calculation, the value was apparently zero?] Other courts look at the difference between the amount of rent stated in the lease and the fair market value of the premises. What is the better approach? Should the rent charged be considered evidence of fair market value? If not, why not?

c. *Stay and charge the cost of repair.* A tenant has the option to fix the defect and then deduct the cost of repair from the rent.

d. *Stay and withhold rent.* In most jurisdictions, a tenant can withhold the entire rent for violations of the implied warranty of habitability (although, a cautious tenant should pay the rent into an escrow account). This is a very powerful remedy. First, it gives the landlord strong incentive to respond to valid complaints from tenants. Second, it puts the burden on the landlord (rather than the tenant) to initiate a lawsuit when contested issues arise. Finally, if the landlord does move to evict the tenant for non-payment, violations of the implied warranty of habitability can serve as a defense.

e. *Extreme violations.* Tenants have won punitive damages in cases where the landlord committed repeated or gruesome violations of the implied warranty.

Problem

1. The Mad Hatter and the Alice each decide to rent an apartment in Wonderland. The Mad Hatter walks into a large apartment and sees a hole in the roof, but he decides to rent the unit anyway. The apartment that Alice decides to lease has no obvious problems. The next day, however, some mold spots appear by one of the vents. The mold grows rapidly and Alice starts to have regular headaches and some trouble breathing. Additionally, an unknown troublemaker smashed Alice's air conditioning unit and it no longer works. Can either the Mad Hatter or Alice win a lawsuit against their landlord if their problems aren't fixed?

3.   Gentrification & Rent Control

Defined broadly, gentrification is the movement of wealthier people into a poor neighborhood, which results in a subsequent increase in rents and the ultimate displacement of longtime residents.   The stereotypic progression starts when artists and gay couples move into a run-down but centrally located neighborhood in the urban core. They fix up houses, open trendy cafes, and start galleries. The newcomers also demand better public services and police protection from the local government. As the number of amenities grows, home prices and rents begin to rise. Married couples without children start to flow into the area,

Photo courtesy of Flickr user Keith Hamm

followed quickly by bankers, lawyers, and families attracted the neighborhood's beautiful older homes and terrific location.   As rents continue to rise, many of the original residents—who are often poor and black—can no longer afford the neighborhood. They are forced to either move or pay an enormous percentage of their income toward rent.

One resident of a gentrifying neighborhood in Portland gives a personal account of the basic problem:

> Last week I heard a shuffle at my front door and saw that my building manager was slipping a notice under my door. I opened it only to read that my rent was being raised by 10%. . . . [In the last year], my rent has gone up a total of 14%. If it continues at this pace, I'll have to find another place to live because I'll be priced out of my very walkable, very centrally-located neighborhood.

[Gentrification is] an emotional tinderbox. People who are just going about their lives are having to face eviction, displacement, or just have to spend a lot more on housing if they want to stay where they are because of forces completely out of their control. In other words, you could be doing everything "right" in your life – being a responsible citizen, earning a viable income and doing your best – but it still isn't good enough. Not unlike the tragedy of having your house destroyed by a natural phenomenon like a hurricane or a flood, you could become a victim of the "greed phenomenon" where developers look with dollar signs in their eyes at the house you live in with the intention of razing it and building a hugely profitable and expensive condo building there instead.

For low-income individuals pushed out of their neighborhoods, the process of gentrification often produces traumatic effects. In addition to the financial costs of an unwanted move, gentrification often shatters valuable personal networks. People who have lived their entire lives within a small geographic area may suddenly find themselves separated from the friends and family who provide emotional support and economic resources that serve as a vital buffer against the ills of poverty.

Many activists have suggested that rent control laws are the best solution to problems spawned by gentrification. Rent control legislation comes in a variety of forms but most often puts caps on the amount of rent that a landlord can charge (first-generation controls) and/or requires that prices for rented properties do not increase by more than a certain percent each year (second-generation controls). Rent controls, activists argue, allow existing tenants to stay in their homes while continuing to devote the same percentage of their incomes to rent has they have in the past.

Economists have a very different perspective on fighting gentrification with rent control mechanisms. American legal economists are typically opposed to rent controls. Often heatedly so. To understand why, put yourself in the shoes of a landlord in a city that holds the price of rent below what the market will bear. How would you respond if you were forced to provide a service for less than the market price? First and foremost, you probably wouldn't build any new rental housing units. Why? Because you'd almost certainly make more money if you used your capital to build something that's not regulated by the government. Ultimately, the lack of proper incentive to build apartments lowers the supply of rental housing and thereby increases the price (for anyone who doesn't qualify for rent controls). Second, you might decide to skimp on the maintenance of your rent-controlled unit in order to recoup some of the lost profits. After all, will a tenant in a rent-controlled apartment really give up their unit if you don't respond to their request to fix the sink?

So goes the theory, at any rate—and it is a theory that has found expression in judicial opinions, particularly among those judges of the U.S. Court of Appeals for the Seventh Circuit who moonlight as academic legal economists of the so-called "Chicago School." *See* Chicago Board of Realtors, Inc. v. City of Chicago, 819 F.2d 732, 741-42 (7th Cir. 1987) (Opinion of Posner, J.). In apparent agreement with these theoretical arguments, very few American jurisdictions today maintain rent control policies—only New York, Los Angeles, and a few places in the Bay Area have significant rent control laws. State and local governments are much more likely to attack problems of affordable housing by either giving rent vouchers to the poor or building government-owned housing projects (are these better options?).

But perhaps the legal economists of a generation ago were mistaken—or at least insufficiently sensitive to the potential variety of rent control measures and the diversity of urban environments in which they can be deployed. While first-generation rent control measures have few academic defenders in the United States, there is some suggestion that the actual empirics of second-generation rent controls and other tenant protections may diverge from the dire theoretical predictions of the Chicago School. In particular, the effects of rent control on the supply, quality, and distribution of rental housing may depend significantly on the nature of the protective regulation imposed, the density of existing housing stock, availability of vacant land, the mix of other regulatory constraints on land use in general and housing in particular, and idiosyncrasies of the local economy—particularly the degree of competition among landlords. *See generally* Richard Arnott, *Time for Revisionism on Rent Control?*, 9 J. ECON. PERSPECT. 99 (1995); Bengt Turner & Stephen Malpezzi, *A review of empirical evidence on the costs and benefits of rent control*, 10 SWED. ECON. POLICY REV. 11 (2003). Outside of the United States, moreover, economists and politicians are less antagonistic toward rent control. Paris, for example, recently passed a law capping many rents. Germany, the Netherlands, and Sweden also have widespread limitations on how much rent landlords can charge.

Notes and Questions

1. **Europe v. America.** What do you think accounts for the different views on rent control between European policy makers and their American counterparts?

2. **Getting to Affordability.** If rent control isn't the answer, what steps should government take to ensure access to affordable housing? Should the government have any role at all in the housing market? Before the Great Depression the federal government played almost no part housing policy. How should government housing policy regarding affordable housing fit into the mix of economic regulations addressing problems of poverty and equity?

E.   Wrapping Up

The following rental agreement is modeled on an actual lease that a friend of the casebook authors was asked to sign. Do you see any potential problems for a tenant? Would you sign this lease?

Residential Rental Agreement and Contract

THIS AGREEMENT (hereinafter known as the "Lease" or the "Agreement") is made and entered into this 1st day of September 2015, between **Peter Rabbit** (hereinafter referred to as the "Tenant") and **Mr. McGregor** (hereinafter referred to as the "Landlord"). In exchange for valuable consideration, the landlord and tenant agree to the following:

1. Property. The landlord owns certain real property and improvements at **123 Vegetable Garden Way, Potterville, Beatrixia** (hereinafter referred to as the "Property" or the "Premise"). The Landlord wishes to lease the Premise to the Tenant upon the terms and conditions stated in this Lease. The Tenant wishes to lease the Premise from the Landlord upon the terms and conditions stated in this Lease.

2. Term. This agreement shall commence on September 1, 2015 and shall commence on August 31, 2018 at 11:59 PM. Upon any termination of the Agreement, the Tenant will pay off all outstanding bills, remove all personal property from the Premise, bring the leased premise back to the condition it was in upon move-in (excepting normal wear and tear), peacefully vacate the premise, return all keys to the Landlord, and give the Landlord a forwarding address.

3. Holdovers. If the Tenant holds over after the termination of the lease, a new tenancy from month-to-month shall be created. Under the new

month-to-month lease the Tenant shall be responsible for double the agreed upon rent.

4. Rent. The Tenant shall pay the landlord $1000 per month as rent for the entire term of the agreement. The rent shall be due on the 1st day of each calendar month. Weekends, holidays, and religious observances do not excuse the Tenant's obligation to make timely payments.

5. Delivery of Possession. The Landlord shall not be held liable for any failure to deliver possession of the Premise by the starting date of the agreed upon term.

6. Late Fees. A late fee of 5% shall be due if the rent is received after the 5th day of the month. A late of 10% shall be due if the rent is received after the 10th day of the month. Acceptance of a late fee does not affect or waive any other right or remedy the Landlord may exercise for Tenant's failure to timely pay rent.

7. Returned Checks. In the event that any payment by the Tenant is returned for insufficient funds or if the Tenant stops payment, the Tenant will pay $100 to the Landlord for each such event, in addition to the Late Fees described above.

8. Security Deposit. The Tenant shall deposit with the Landlord $1500 as a security deposit for this Agreement. All interest that accrues on such a security deposit shall belong to the Landlord alone. The Landlord may use the deposit money for any and all purposes allowed by law.

9. Utilities. It is the responsibility of the Tenant to obtain all utilities for the leased Property. Tenant's failure to make any payment for the utilities shall constitute a material breach of the agreement. The Landlord shall not be held liable for any failure to deliver any utility service or for any

damage caused by a problem with any utility service, whatever the cause of such problem. The Tenants do hereby waive any claim for damages that result from any problem with utility service.

10. Keys. The Tenant shall not install any new locks anywhere on the property or make any copies of the keys. The Tenant also shall refrain from providing any keys to any person not listed on this Agreement. When the lease terminates, the Tenant shall return all keys to the Landlord.

11. Pets. No pets of any kind, type, or breed shall be allowed on the property without the Landlord's express written consent. This consent, if given, will require an additional pet deposit.

12. Use of the Premise. The premise shall be used and occupied solely by the Tenant. Tenant shall not allow any other person to use or occupy the premise without first obtaining Landlord's written consent. No part of the Premise shall be used at any time during the term for any business, trade, or other commercial purpose. Additionally, the tenant agrees to comply with all local, state, and federal laws, regulations, and ordinances. No part of the property may be used in any way that aids or advances a criminal enterprise.

13. Assignments and Subletting. The Tenant shall not license, assign, or sublet the Property and/or this agreement without the written consent of the Landlord. An assignment, subletting or license without the Landlord's written consent shall be considered absolutely null and void and, at the Landlord's option, terminate this Agreement.

14. Alterations. The Tenant shall make no alterations to the Premise without written consent of the Landlord. If the Tenant makes any unauthorized improvement, modification, or change to the Property, the landlord has the option to charge the Tenant the cost of restoring the

Premise to its original condition. In the event that the Landlord approves an alteration made by the Tenant, such alternations shall become the property of the Landlord and remain on the Property.

15. Maintenance & Repair. Except for normal wear and tear, the Tenant shall maintain the Premise in the condition it was upon the starting date of the Agreement. Should any damages, malfunctions, breakages, or other problems occur during the course of the Lease, the Landlord shall have a reasonable amount of time to complete such repairs. During that time, the Tenant's rent shall remain due in full and on time despite any hardships such repairs or delays may cause. Tenant also has a contractual duty to (1) notify Landlord of any problems with the leased premise, (2) Deposit all trash, rubbish, refuse, and garbage in the trash cans provided by the city, (3) keep all windows, doors, and locks in good order, (4) inspect the fire alarms each and every month.

16. Noise. The Tenant and the Tenant's guests shall at all times keep the level of sound down to a level that does not annoy or interfere with other residents or neighbors.

17. Sale of the Property. The Landlord shall have the right to sell or transfer his ownership of the Property and this Agreement at any time and without restriction. Upon sale or transfer of the Landlord's interest, this agreement may be terminated by either the Landlord or the party who purchases the Landlord's interest. The Tenant agrees to release, waive, and hold harmless the Landlord and the Landlord's successor from all liabilty if such a transfer occurs.

18. Access. The Landlord and his agents shall have the right to enter the Property without notice to inspect the property, make repairs, or show the property to prospective tenants or purchasers.

19. Condition of the Premise. The Landlord makes no guarantees or warranties about the condition of the leased premise. The Tenant assumes all risk of injury or harm stemming from any accidents or criminal acts occurring on or around the Premise. The Tenant agrees to hold the Landlord harmless for all liability stemming any injury or harm to the Tenant, Tenant's property, or Tenant's guests. The Tenant further agrees to indemnify, defend, and hold harmless the Landlord from any and all claims over the condition of the premise. Should the Tenant damage the Premise, he shall indemnify the Landlord for all costs of repair or replacement within 30 days.

20. Natural Disaster. In the event of a natural disaster, fire, or other catastrophic event, the Landlord may choose not to repair the Premise, in which case the Lease shall terminate. The Landlord may also elect to fix the Premise, in which case the Tenant must continue to pay the full monthly rent so long as the repairs are completed within a reasonable time. In either case, any and all damages and injuries connected to acts of the Tenant, his guests, or property shall be the sole financial responsibility of the Tenant.

21. Eminent Domain. If a government or private entity takes the Premise or any part of the Premise by eminent domain, this Lease shall terminate. The new termination shall be the date of the final taking order. Any award or court judgment in favor of the Landlord in an eminent domain case or any settlement award stemming from an eminent domain proceeding shall belong to the Landlord in full. The Tenant shall have no claim over such awards.

22. Attorney's Fees. Tenant agrees to pay all reasonable attorney's fees, court costs, and other expenses if it becomes necessary for the Landlord to enforce any of the conditions of covenants of this Lease, including but not limited to eviction proceedings, collection of rents, and damage to the

Premise caused by the Tenant. The Tenant also agrees to indemnify the Landlord for all attorney's fees, court costs, and other expenses that the Landlord may incur while successfully defending a lawsuit brought by the Tenant.

22. Abandonment. If at any time during the term of this Lease the Tenant abandons the Premise, the Landlord may obtain possession of the Premise in any manner provided for by law. Any personal property left behind shall be considered abandoned. The Landlord may dispose of such personal property in any manner he deems fit and is released of all liability for doing so.

23. Severability. If any portion of this Lease shall be found unenforceable, invalid, or void under any law or public policy, that portion of the Lease shall be severed from the remainder of the Agreement. All remaining portions of the Agreement will remain in effect and enforceable.

24. Governing Law. This lease shall be governed and interpreted under the laws of the Commonwealth of Beatrixia.

25. Non-Waiver. No delay or non-enforcement of any term of this Agreement by the Landlord shall not be deemed a waiver. All terms and conditions of this Agreement shall remain fully enforceable should the Landlord seek to enforce any condition or covenant at a later date, even if the Landlord has intentionally or unintentionally neglected to do so in a previous instance.

26. Notices. Any notice required or permitted under this Agreement must be written on 8½ x 11 paper and sent by United Parcel Service (UPS). Notice shall be sent to the address of the Property for the Tenant or to **345 Bunny Pie Lane, Potterville, Beatrixia** for the Landlord.

27.   Spelling and Grammar.   Any mistakes in spelling, grammar, punctuation, or gender usage shall not be fatal to the Agreement. Rather, they shall be interpreted to carry out the intent of the parties.

28. Default. Tenant shall be in default of this Agreement if he fails to comply with any covenant, condition or term and/or fails to pay rent when due and/or causes damage to the Premise during the term which cumulatively equals or exceeds $100. Should the Tenant ever default, the Landlord may **with or without notice** either (1) terminate the Lease or (2) terminate the Tenant's right to possession of the Premise while leaving this Agreement operative. If the Landlord elects option (2), the Landlord will have the immediate right to possess the Premises and the Tenant shall lose all possessory rights and have the obligation to immediately vacate the Premise. However, the Tenant shall still have the duty to pay all rents, fees and expenses mandated under this Agreement and/or by the judicial system until either the agreed upon term concludes or the property is re-rented at a monthly rate not less than the amount owned under this Agreement with any negative balance owed by the Tenant.

_____   _____

Tenant Signature   Date

_____   _____

Landlord Signature   Date

Part III: Transfers

Land Transactions

In 1250, to transfer ownership of land, the grantor and grantee would physically go to the land. The grantor would physically (or perhaps metaphysically) put the grantee in possession by handing over a clod of dirt. The grantee would swear homage to the grantor, and the grantor would swear to defend the grantee's title. This was a public ceremony, performed in front of witnesses who could later be called on to recall what had happened if necessary. In contrast, written conveyances – called "charters" – were treated with skepticism; they were considered an inferior form of evidence because of the risk of forgery.

In the seven and a half centuries since, this attitude has completely flipped. Now, land transactions are paper transactions: the Statute of Frauds almost always requires a written conveyance – now called a "deed" – to transfer an interest in real property. Transfers by operation of law (primarily through adverse possession and intestacy) are very much the exception. In addition, land transactions are influenced by the common law's attitude that land is of distinctive importance, so that parties dealing with it need especial clarity about their rights, and by the fact that land transactions are often high-stakes, with hundreds of thousands, millions, or sometimes even billions of dollars at issue. This section focuses on the written instruments at the heart of land transactions. It considers when a deed is required, when a deed is effective, how deeds are interpreted, and what they promise about the property and the interest being conveyed.

Indiana Code

§ 32-21-1-1 – Requirement of written agreement; agreements or promises covered

(a) This section does not apply to a lease for a term of not more than three (3) years.

(b) A person may not bring any of the following actions unless the promise, contract, or agreement on which the action is based, or a memorandum or note describing the promise, contract, or agreement on which the action is based, is in writing and signed by the party against whom the action is brought or by the party's authorized agent: ...

(4) An action involving any contract for the sale of land.

§ 32-21-1-13 – Conveyance of land; written deed required

Except for a bona fide lease for a term not exceeding three (3) years, a conveyance of land or of any interest in land shall be made by a deed that is:

(1) written; and

(2) subscribed, sealed, and acknowledged by the grantor ... or by the grantor's attorney.

Questions

1. What is the difference between these two sections? Why are both necessary?

2. Consider the following sequence of text messages:

   A: still want apt 4C @ 321 sesame st?

   B: $450,000 ok?

   A: deal. :-) -A

   B: yay! kthx bai

   Can either of the parties treat this as an enforceable contract for the sale of land?

Harding v. Ja Laur
315 A.2d 132 (Md. Ct. Spec. App. 1974)

GILBERT, Judge: ...

The bill alleged that a deed had been obtained from the appellant through fraud practiced upon her by the agent of Ja Laur Corporation. The bill further averred that the paper upon which the appellant had affixed her signature was "falsely and fraudulently attached to the first page of a deed identified as the same deed" through which the appellee, Ja Laur Corporation, and its assigns, the other appellees, claim title. ...

There is no dispute that the appellant signed some type of paper. Her claim is not that her signature was forged in the normal sense, i.e., someone copied or wrote it, but rather that the forgery is the result of an alteration. Mrs. Harding alleges that at the time that she signed a blank paper she was told that her signature was necessary in order to straighten out a boundary line. She represents that she did not know that she was conveying away her interest in and to a certain 1517 acres of land in Montgomery County.

The parcel of land that was conveyed by the allegedly forged deed is contiguous to a large tract of real estate in which Ja Laur and others had "a substantial interest." It appears from the bill that Mrs. Harding's land provided the access from the larger tract to a public road, so that its value to the appellees is obvious. Mrs. Harding excuses herself for signing the "blank paper" by averring that she did so at the instigation of an attorney, an agent of Ja Laur, who had "been a friend of her deceased husband, and ... represented her deceased husband in prior business and legal matters, and that under [the] circumstances [she] did place her complete trust and reliance in the representations made to her ..." by the attorney. The "blank paper" was signed "on or about April 2, 1970." Mrs. Harding states that she did not learn of the fraud until the "summer of 1972." At that time an audit, by the Internal Revenue Service, of her deceased husband's business revealed the deed to Ja Laur, and its subsequent conveyance to the other appellees.

In *Smith v. State*, 256 A.2d 357, 360 (1970), we said that:

> Forgery has been defined as a false making or material alteration, with intent to defraud, of any writing which, if genuine, might apparently be of legal efficacy or the foundation of a legal liability. More succinctly, forgery is the fraudulent making of a false writing having apparent legal significance. It is thus clear that one of the essential elements of forgery is a writing in such form as to be apparently of some legal efficacy and hence capable of defrauding or deceiving.

Perkins, *Criminal Law* ch. 4, § 8 (2d ed. 1969) states, at 351:

> A material alteration may be in the form of (1) an addition to the writing, (2) a substitution of something different in the place of what originally appeared, or (3) the removal of part of the original. The removal may be by erasure or in some other manner, such as by cutting off a qualifying clause appearing after the signature.

A multitude of cases hold that forgery includes the alteration of or addition to any instrument in order to defraud. That a deed may be the subject of a forgery is beyond question.

The Bill of Complaint alleges that the signature of Mrs. Harding was obtained through fraud. More important, however, to the issue is whether or not the bill alleges forgery. In our view the charge that appellant's signature was written upon a paper, which paper was thereafter unbeknown to her made a part of a deed, if true, demonstrates that there has been a material alteration and hence a forgery. ...

We turn now to the discussion of whether *vel non* the demurrers of Macro Housing, Inc. and Montgomery County, the other appellees, should have been sustained. There was no allegation in the bill that their agent had perpetrated the fraud upon Mrs. Harding. If they are to be held in the case, it must be on the basis that they are not *bona fide* purchasers without notice. The title of a *bona fide* purchaser, without notice, is not vitiated even though a fraud was perpetrated by his vendor upon a prior title holder. A deed obtained through fraud, deceit or trickery is voidable as between the parties thereto, but not as to a *bona fide* purchaser. A forged deed, on the other hand, is void *ab initio*. ...

[T]he common law rule that a forger can pass no better title than he has is in full force and effect in this State. A forger, having no title can pass none to his vendee. Consequently, there can be no *bona fide* holder of title under a forged deed. A forged deed, unlike one procured by fraud, deceit or trickery is void from its inception. The distinction between a deed obtained by fraud and one that has been forged is readily apparent. In a fraudulent deed an innocent purchaser is protected because the fraud practiced upon the signatory to such a deed is brought into play, at least in part, by some act or omission on the part of the person upon whom the fraud is perpetrated. He has helped in some degree to set into motion the very fraud about which he later complains. A forged deed, on the other hand, does not necessarily involve any action on the part of the person against whom the forgery is committed. So that if a person has two deeds presented to him, and he thinks he is signing one but in actuality, because of fraud, deceit or trickery he signs the other, a bona fide purchaser, without notice, is protected. On the other hand, if a person is presented with a deed, and he signs that deed but the deed is thereafter altered e.g. through a change in the description or affixing the signature page to another deed, that is forgery and a subsequent purchaser takes no title.

In the instant case, the Bill of Complaint, for the reasons above stated, alleged a forgery of the deed by which Ja Laur took title from Mrs. Harding. This allegation, if true, renders that deed a nullity. Ja Laur could not have passed title to the other appellees, Macro Housing, Inc. and Montgomery County. Those two appellees would therefore have no title to the land of Mrs. Harding. ...

Questions

1. What is the point of the distinction between forging a deed (sometimes called "fraud in the factum") and tricking someone into signing it ("fraud in the inducement")? As between the fraudster and the victim, is there a significant difference? What about once third parties get involved?

2. Mrs. Harding signs a blank piece of paper, which Ja Laur then staples to a deed. Forgery? What if she signs the same piece of paper *after* it is stapled to the deed? Do the policy reasons for distinguishing forgery from fraud provide a convincing reason to treat these cases differently?

WEST HELFENSTEIN PARK

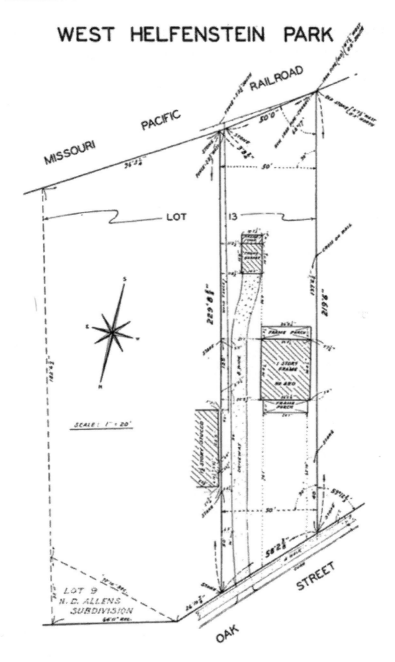

Walters v. Tucker
281 S.W.2d 843 (Sup. Ct. Mo. 1955)

This is an action to quiet title to certain real estate situate in the City of
Webster Groves, St. Louis County, Missouri. Plaintiff and defendants are

the owners of adjoining residential properties fronting northward on Oak Street. Plaintiff's property, known as 450 Oak Street, lies to the west of defendants' property, known as 446 Oak Street. The controversy arises over their division line. Plaintiff contends that her lot is 50 feet in width, east and west. Defendants contend that plaintiff's lot is only approximately 42 feet in width, east and west. The trial court, sitting without a jury, found the issues in favor of defendants and rendered judgment accordingly, from which plaintiff has appealed.

The common source of title is Fred F. Wolf and Rose E. Wolf, husband and wife, who in 1922 acquired the whole of Lot 13 of West Helfenstein Park, as shown by plat thereof recorded in St. Louis County. In 1924, Mr. and Mrs. Wolf conveyed to Charles Arthur Forse and wife the following described portion of said Lot 13:

> The West 50 feet of Lot 13 of West Helfenstein Park, a Subdivision in United States Survey 1953, Twp. 45, Range 8 East, St. Louis County, Missouri, ...

Plaintiff, through mesne conveyances carrying a description like that above, is the last grantee of and successor in title to the aforesaid portion of Lot 13. Defendants, through mesne conveyances, are the last grantees of and successors in title to the remaining portion of Lot 13.

At the time of the above conveyance in 1924, there was and is now situate on the tract described therein a one-story frame dwelling house (450 Oak Street), which was then and continuously since has been occupied as a dwelling by the successive owners of said tract, or their tenants. In 1925, Mr. and Mrs. Wolf built a 1 1/2-story stucco dwelling house on the portion of Lot 13 retained by them. This house (446 Oak Street) continuously since has been occupied as a dwelling by the successive owners of said portion of Lot 13, or their tenants.

Despite the apparent clarity of the description in plaintiff's deed, extrinsic evidence was heard for the purpose of enabling the trial court to interpret the true meaning of the description set forth therein. At the close of all the evidence the trial court found that the description did not clearly reveal whether the property conveyed 'was to be fifty feet along the front line facing Oak Street or fifty feet measured Eastwardly at right angles from the West line of the property ...'; that the 'difference in method of ascertaining fifty feet would result in a difference to the parties of a strip the length of the lot and approximately eight feet in width'; that an ambiguity existed which justified the hearing of extrinsic evidence; and that the 'West fifty feet should be measured on the front or street line facing Oak Street.' The judgment rendered in conformity with the above finding had the effect of fixing the east-west width of plaintiff's tract at about 42 feet.

Plaintiff contends that the description in the deed is clear, definite and unambiguous, both on its face and when applied to the land; that the trial court erred in hearing and considering extrinsic evidence; and that its finding and judgment changes the clearly expressed meaning of the description and describes and substitutes a different tract from that acquired by her under her deed. Defendants do not contend that the description, on its face, is ambiguous, but do contend that when applied to the land it is subject to 'dual interpretation'; that under the evidence the trial court did not err in finding it contained a latent ambiguity and that parol evidence was admissible to ascertain and determine its true meaning; and that the finding and judgment of the trial court properly construes and adjudges the true meaning of the description set forth in said deed.

[The plaintiff and defendants introduced dueling survey plats. The one included here is the plaintiff's. North is at the bottom. Note in particular the locations of the two houses and of the driveway. It may help to mark on the plat where the defendant's proposed line would fall.]

It is seen that Lot 13 extends generally north and south. It is bounded on the north by Oak Street (except that a small triangular lot from another subdivision cuts off its frontage thereon at the northeast corner). On the south it is bounded by the Missouri Pacific Railroad right of way. Both Oak Street and the railroad right of way extend in a general northeast-southwest direction, but at differing angles. ...

Both plats show a concrete driveway 8 feet in width extending from Oak Street to plaintiff's garage in the rear of her home, which, the testimony shows, was built by one of plaintiff's predecessors in title. The east line of plaintiff's tract, as measured by the Joyce (plaintiff's) survey, lies 6 or 7 feet east of the eastern edge of this driveway. Admittedly, the driveway is upon and an appurtenance of plaintiff's property. On the Elbring (defendants') plat, the east line of plaintiff's lot, as measured by Elbring, is shown to coincide with the east side of the driveway at Oak Street and to encroach upon it 1.25 feet for a distance of 30 or more feet as it extends between the houses. Thus, the area in dispute is essentially the area between the east edge of the driveway and the line fixed by the Joyce survey as the eastern line of plaintiff's tract. ...

The description under which plaintiff claims title, to wit: 'The West 50 feet of Lot 13 ...', is on its face clear and free of ambiguity. It purports to convey a strip of land 50 feet in width off the west side of Lot 13. So clear is the meaning of the above language that defendants do not challenge it and it has been difficult to find any case wherein the meaning of a similar description has been questioned.

The law is clear that when there is no inconsistency on the face of a deed and, on application of the description to the ground, no inconsistency appears, parol evidence is not admissible to show that the parties intended to convey either more or less or different ground from that described. But where there are conflicting calls in a deed, or the description may be made to apply to two or more parcels, and there is nothing in the deed to show which is meant, then parol evidence is admissible to show the true meaning of the words used.

No ambiguity or confusion arises when the description here in question is applied to Lot 13. The description, when applied to the ground, fits the land claimed by plaintiff and cannot be made to apply to any other tract. When the deed was made, Lot 13 was vacant land except for the frame dwelling at 450 Oak Street. The stucco house (446 Oak Street) was not built until the following year. Under no conceivable theory can the fact that defendants' predecessors in title (Mr. and Mrs. Wolf) thereafter built the stucco house within a few feet of the east line of the property described in the deed be construed as competent evidence of any ambiguity in the description. ...

Whether the above testimony and other testimony in the record constitute evidence of a mistake in the deed we do not here determine. Defendants have not sought reformation, and yet that is what the decree herein rendered undertakes to do. It seems apparent that the trial court considered the testimony and came to the conclusion that the parties to the deed did not intend a conveyance of the 'West 50 feet of Lot 13', but rather a tract fronting 50 feet on Oak Street. And, the decree, on the theory of interpreting an ambiguity, undertakes to change (reform) the description so as to describe a lot approximately 42 feet in width instead of a lot 50 feet in width, as originally described. That, we are convinced, the courts cannot do.

Questions

1. Why does the court apply such a strict integration rule?

2. The boundary line as enforced by the court comes within inches of the defendants' house. This does not seem like an ideal state of affairs. (Then again, the defendant's theory would have drawn the boundary line through the plaintiffs' driveway.) Are there any

doctrines that can clean up the messes that result when (by accident or otherwise) strict interpretation of deeds produces results at odds with natural features, structures, or uses of land?

3. The deed here used three different techniques to describe the land. Start at the end. "United States Survey 1953, Twp. 45, Range 8 East, St. Louis County, Missouri" is a reference to a government survey. Townships are standard 36-square-mile tracts established by federal government survey; "Twp. 45, Range 8 East" identifies a specific township in Missouri. Next, "of Lot 13 of West Helfenstein Park" is a reference to the *subdivision plat* filed by the developer who laid out the neighborhood; the plat is a survey map filed in the county recording office that shows the boundaries of individual parcels. Finally, "The West 50 feet" is a (crude attempt at) a *metes and bounds* description of the property in terms of its boundaries. Metes and bounds descriptions may refer to geospatial coordinates (e.g. latitude and longitude as measured by GPS), to natural landmarks ("Millers' Creek"), artificial markers ("the survey stake labelled G34"), and distances and directions ("300 feet along a course at 45°). How precise are these various means of description? Which of them strike you as most prone to error?

4. Note that the boundary lines as shown on the survey map are at an angle to the north-south axis. Does this affect how the court should interpret the deed?

Loughran v. Kummer
146 A. 534 (Pa. 1929)

KEPHART, J.

Appellee, a bachelor 67 years of age, conveyed, for $1, land in Pittsburgh to Mrs. Kummer, appellant, who was one of his tenants. A bill was filed to set aside this deed; the grounds laid were confidential relationship, undue influence, and impaired mentality. Inasmuch as the facts must again be considered, we will mention only such as raise the legal question on which the case was decided; we venture no opinion on the other facts.

The court below found from the evidence that a deed absolute on its face had been executed, acknowledged, and delivered to appellant by appellee, on condition that it should not be recorded until the latter's death; that undoubtedly in his mind this meant that the deed was not to take effect until after his death; and that he, demanding the return of the deed within a very few days after the delivery, thus revoked it and with that revocation revoked the gift. Appellant deceived appellee when she stated the deed had been destroyed. The excuse given was appellee was worried and she wanted to ease his mind by making him believe that it had been destroyed. …

The question we are asked to consider is whether a deed absolute on its face, acknowledged, executed, and delivered under circumstances as here indicated, vested such title in the grantee as could be revoked for the above reasons. It amounts in substance to this, that the grantor said the deed should not be recorded until after his death, and the grantee in accepting the deed took it on that condition. The evidence on which this finding was based was all oral, and the scrivener and defendant denied any such condition was imposed when the deed was delivered. All control over the deed was relinquished when it was handed appellant. The presumption must be that at that time it was the intention to pass title. 'The general principle of law is that the formal act of signing, sealing and delivering is the consummation of the deed, and it lies with the grantor to prove clearly that appearances are not consistent with truth. The presumption stands against him, and the burden is on him to destroy it by clear and positive proof that there was no delivery and that it was so understood at the time. … Where we have, as here, a deed, absolute and complete in itself, attacked as being in fact otherwise intended, … there is a further presumption that the title is in conformity with the deed, and it should not be dislodged except by clear, precise, convincing and satisfactory evidence to the contrary.' *Cragin's Estate,* 117 A. 445 (Pa. 1922).

The gift here was executed, and that defendant was not to record it was not of the slightest consequence when viewed as against these major actions, delivery and passing of title. It was merely a promise the keeping of which lay in good faith, the breach of which entailed no legal consequences. To have effected the grantor's purpose, the intervention of a third party was absolutely essential. There are circumstances where acknowledgment, together with physical possession of the deed in the grantee, does not conclusively establish an intention to deliver, and the presumption arising from signing, sealing, and acknowledging, accompanied by manual possession of the deed by the grantee, is not irrebuttable, but this presumption can be overcome only by evidence that no delivery was in fact intended and none made. Such evidence is not present in this case. Here the grantor by his own testimony intended the grantee to get the land. The only question was when it was to take effect.

Here is one of the instances in which the law fails to give effect to the honest intention of the parties, for the reason that they have not adopted the proper legal means of accomplishing their object. Therefore the legal effect of such delivery is not altered by the fact that both parties suppose the deed will not take effect until recorded, and that it may be revoked at any time before record, or by contemporaneous agreements looking to the reconveyance of the property to the grantor or to the third party upon the happening of certain contingent events or the nonperformance of certain conditions.

The reason for these rules is obvious. It is quite possible to prove in most deliveries that some parol injunction was attached to the formal delivery of the deed; if they are to be given the effect her[e] contended, there would be no safety in accepting a deed under most circumstances. It opens the door to the fabrication of evidence that would inevitably be appalling and go far toward violating the security of written instruments. We have so held in matters of less import than the conveyance of land. The rule must not be relaxed as to realty. Such conveyances are vastly more important, as they involve instruments of title and ownership which are used as a means of extending credit. Title to land ought not to be exposed to the peril of successful attack except where the right is clear and undoubted, and whatever may be our desire to recognize circumstances argued as unfortunate, we cannot go to the extent of overthrowing principles of law governing conveyances of real estate that have stood the test of ages.

In *Cragin's Estate*, supra, the deeds were in a tin box for more than 23 years in an envelope indorsed with the words: 'To be recorded upon Mrs. Cragin's death, if before me.' The deed was in grantee's possession, and it was urged the delivery was conditional. We said that indorsement may have been placed on the envelope for other reasons than to defer the transfer of title. In the present case it was evident appellee did not want his relatives to learn of the conveyance. Recording would be necessary to pass a title examiner's inspection, but nonrecording did not prevent the title from passing. It has been quite generally held that an oral understanding on the delivery of a deed that it should not be recorded will not affect the absolute character of the conveyance if free of other conditions. n agreement to deliver a deed in escrow to the person in whose favor it is made, and who is likewise a party to it, will not make the delivery conditional. If delivered under such an agreement, it will be deemed an absolute delivery and a consummation of the execution of the deed. ...

Questions

1. The old phrase is that a deed was effective when it was "signed, sealed, and delivered." But the seal is obsolete, so the principal elements are that it be a sufficient writing (discussed above), that

it be signed, and that it be delivered. Delivery of deeds has much in common with delivery in the law of gifts; it too can be a subtle question. In a famous passage of his landmark 17th-century treatise, *Institutes of the Lawes of England*, Edward Coke wrote, "As a deed may be delivered to a party without words, so may a deed be delivered by words without any act of delivery." That sounds paradoxical, but Coke continued, "as if the writing sealed lies upon the table, and the [grantor] says to the [grantee], 'Go and take up that writing, it is sufficient for you;' or 'it will serve your turn;' or 'Take it as my deed;' or the like words; either is a sufficient delivery." Is that better?

2. In *Wiggill v. Cheney*, 597 P.2d 1351 (Utah 1979), Lillian Cheney executed a deed to Flora Cheney and put it in a safety deposit box in the names of Lillian Cheney and Francis E. Wiggill. Lillian told Francis that his name was on the box, that on her death he would be granted access to the box, and that "in that box is an envelope addressed to all those concerned. All you have to do is give them that envelope and that's all." On her death, he gained access to the box, took the deed, and gave it to Flora. Delivery?

3. There are at least two ways to do delivery "right." One is to sign and hand over a deed at closing, when all of the necessary parties are in the same room and can execute all of the appropriate documents effectively simultaneously. Another is to use an escrow: a third party who receives custody of the signed deed along with instructions to deliver it to the grantee when appropriate events have taken place. What if the escrow agent disregards her instructions and hands over the deed early? Can a grantor who is concerned the transaction will fall through demand the deed back from the escrow agent?

4. *Loughran* is more complicated because the parties intended a conditional gift that would take effect at Loughran's death, rather than immediately. Grantors often try to put other kinds of conditions on transfers. In *Martinez v. Martinez*, 678 P.2d 1163 (N.M. 1984), Delfino and Eleanor Martinez gave their son Carlos and his wife Sennie a deed to a property in exchange for assuming a mortgage in it. Delfino and Eleanor instructed Carlos and Sennie to take the deed to the bank to be held in escrow until Carlos and Sennie had paid off the mortgage, but they recorded it first. Carlos and Sennie had marital difficulties and fell behind on the mortgage; eventually Delfino and Eleanor paid off the balance. Who owns the property?

5. The *Loughran* court says the parties "have not adopted the proper legal means of accomplishing their object." What does it mean? Is there anything they could have done differently that would avoided this mess?

New York Real Property Law

§ 258 – Short forms of deeds and mortgages.

The use of the following forms of instruments for the conveyance and mortgage of real property is lawful, but this section does not prevent or invalidate the use of other forms:

Statutory Form A (Individual)

DEED WITH FULL COVENANTS.

This indenture, made the ...... day of .... nineteen hundred and ......, between ....(insert residence) party of the first part, and .... (insert residence) party of the second part,

Witnesseth, that the party of the first part, in consideration of .... dollars, lawful money of the United States, paid by the party of the second part, does hereby grant and release unto the party of the second part, ... and assigns forever, all .... (description), together with the appurtenances and all the estate and rights of the party of the first part in and to said premises,

To have and to hold the premises herein granted unto the party of the second part, ... and assigns forever. And said .... covenants as follows:

First. That said .... is seized of said premises in fee simple, and has good right to convey the same;

Second. That the party of the second part shall quietly enjoy the said premises;

Third. That the said premises are free from incumbrances;

Fourth. That the party of the first part will execute or procure any further necessary assurance of the title to said premises;

Fifth. That said .... will forever warrant the title to said premises.

In witness whereof, the party of the first part has hereunto set his hand and seal the day and year first above written.

In presence of:

Statutory Form D. (Individual)

QUITCLAIM DEED.

This indenture, made the .... day of ...., nineteen hundred and ...., between ...., (insert residence), party of the first part, and ...., (insert residence), party of the second part:

Witnesseth, that the party of the first part, in consideration of .... dollars, lawful money of the United States, paid by the party of the second part, does hereby remise, release, and quitclaim unto the party of the second part, ... and assigns forever, all (description), together with the appurtenances and all the estate and rights of the party of the first part in and to said premises.

To have and to hold the premises herein granted unto the party of the second part, ... and assigns forever.

In witness whereof, the party of the first part has hereunto set his hand and seal the day and year first above written.

In presence of:

Questions

1. What is the difference between these two deed forms? Why would a grantee ever accept a quitclaim deed?

McMurray v. Housworth
638 S.E.2d 421 (Ga. Ct. App. 2006)

PHIPPS, Judge:

Michael and Deborah Housworth sold a 24-acre tract of land which the purchasers—Lance and Melanie McMurray, and James and Alberta McMurray— subdivided into two tracts. A lake created by a dam is situated on the property. The McMurrays brought this suit against the Housworths for breach of their general warranty of title upon discovering after purchasing the property that the owner and operator of the dam holds a floodwater detention easement that burdens the tract. The superior court awarded summary judgment to the Housworths on the ground that this easement is not such an encumbrance on the property as breaches the title warranty. We disagree and reverse.

Lance and Melanie McMurray purchased one of the twelve-acre parcels from the Housworths for $120,000 in 2004. On the same date, James and Alberta McMurray purchased the other parcel for the same price. The parcels were conveyed by warranty deeds that contained general warranties of title without any limitations applicable here. The McMurrays informed the Housworths that they were buying the property to build single-family residences on each parcel.

Apparently, however, the McMurrays failed to discover that recorded within the chain of title to their property in 1962 was a "floodwater retarding structure" easement which had been granted to the Oconee River Soil Conservation District. This easement is for construction, operation, and maintenance of a floodwater retarding structure or dam; for the flowage of waters in, over, upon, or through the dam; and for the permanent storage and temporary detention of any waters that are impounded, stored, or detained by the dam. It also reserved in the grantor and his successors the right to use the easement area for any purpose not inconsistent with full use and enjoyment of the grantee's rights and privileges, i.e., it is nonexclusive. After learning of the easement following their purchase of the property, the McMurrays demanded that the Housworths compensate them for the damages they would suffer as a result of the restrictions thereby placed on their usage.

Because the Housworths failed to comply with these demands, the McMurrays brought this suit against them seeking damages for breach of their warranties of title. ...

1. The McMurrays contend that the superior court erred in analogizing the floodwater detention easement to a public roadway easement or zoning regulation and in thereby concluding that a floodwater detention easement is not the type of easement that breaches a general warranty of title.

(a) Each of the deeds in this case contained a general warranty of title in which the grantors agreed to "defend the right and title to the above described property, unto [the grantees], their heirs, assigns, and successors in title, against the claims of all persons." Under OCGA § 44-5-62, "[a] general warranty of title against the claims of all persons includes covenants of a right to sell, of quiet enjoyment, and of freedom from encumbrances." "An incumbrance has been defined as 'Any right to, or interest in, land which may subsist in another to the diminution of its value, but consistent with the passing of the fee,' and this definition . . . encompasses an easement or right of way." OCGA § 44-5-63 provides that "[i]n a deed, a general warranty of title against the claims of all persons covers defects in the title even if they are known to the purchaser at the time he takes the deed."

(b) The rule in Georgia, as established in the early case of *Desvergers v. Willis*, 56 Ga. 515 (1876), is that the existence of a public road on land, of which the purchaser knew or should have known at the time of the purchase, is not such an encumbrance as would constitute a breach of a general warranty of title. The *Desvergers* rule is thus an exception to the general rule stated in OCGA § 44-5-63 that a general warranty of title by deed covers even defects known to the purchaser at the time he takes the deed.

Although the *Desvergers* rule is not uniform throughout the country, it is the majority rule. In adopting the rule, the court in *Desvergers* concluded that a contrary holding would produce a "crop of litigation" that would be "almost interminable." The reason, as later explained by the Supreme Court of Iowa in *Harrison v. The Des Moines & Ft. Dodge R. Co.*, was that the immense number of warranty deeds then in existence rarely contained exceptions as to public roadways because of the universal belief that roadway access was a benefit rather than a burden to land. Therefore, a determination that public roadway easements were warranty-breaching encumbrances would have created innumerable liabilities where none had been thought to exist.

Courts in other states have also based their adoption of the *Desvergers* rule on the broader ground that where easements are open, notorious, and presumably known to the purchaser at the time of the purchase, that knowledge will exclude the easement from operation of a title warranty. These courts have reasoned that where the encumbrance involves an open and obvious physical condition of the property, the purchaser is presumed to have seen it and fixed his price with reference to it. In view, however, of the Georgia rule that knowledge of a title defect will not exclude it from operation of a general warranty of title, creation of an exception for easements for public roadways or other purposes must be based on other grounds. And courts in other states have ultimately concluded that public roadway easements should not be regarded as encumbrances on the additional ground that "public highways are not depreciative, but, on the contrary, they are highly appreciative, of the value of the lands on which they constitute an easement, and are a means without which such lands are not available for use, nor sought after in the markets."

For a number of reasons, we do not find the floodwater detention easement in this case analogous to a public roadway easement. (1) We do not anticipate that we would open the litigation floodgates, so to speak, by holding that a floodwater detention easement breaches a general title warranty. (2) Moreover, a floodwater detention easement does not benefit the land to which it is subject. Although the property is benefitted by the lake or other body of water that creates the need for the easement (to the extent that the one enhances the value or enjoyment of the other), the easement burdens the property by permitting the impoundment of water on it to prevent flooding or increased water runoff on other property located downstream. (3) The McMurrays brought this action for damages because of the easement, not the lake. And even though the lake is certainly open and obvious, the same cannot necessarily be said of the easement. Although the superior court found that the dam is visible on the McMurrays' property, the McMurrays correctly point out that there is no evidence of record to support this finding. As argued by the McMurrays, not every lake is created by a dam or burdened by a floodwater detention easement. (4) And although the McMurrays' constructive notice of the easement by reason of its recordation within their chains of title would provide a compelling reason for exempting the easement from operation of the warranty deed, OCGA § 44-5-63 provides otherwise. (5) The recording of the easement certainly renders it binding on the McMurrays insofar as concerns the rights of the easement holder; but the question here is whether the existence of the easement gives rise to a claim against the grantor for breach of the warranty against encumbrances. For these reasons, the superior court erred in concluding that the floodwater detention easement should be excepted from the rule of OCGA § 44-5-63 in view of the exception for public roadways.

(c) The McMurrays also contend that the superior court erred in equating floodwater detention easements with zoning regulations, which have been held not to breach a general warranty of title. Because the floodwater detention easement does not function in the same manner as a zoning regulation in all respects, we agree with this contention.

The floodwater detention easement does more than impose zoning-type restrictions on development activities on the property. It also grants the county soil and water conservation district rights for the storage and detention of impounded waters on the property. And it grants the district a right of ingress and egress upon the property. Easement rights such as these constitute an interest in property that must be acquired either by agreement of the property owner or by condemnation. And although the easement does impose limitations on the McMurrays' use of their property that duplicate restrictions imposed under zoning-type regulations applicable to the property, the two do not appear to be coextensive. ...

Where an encumbrance is a servitude or easement which can not be removed at the option of either the grantor or grantee, damages will be awarded for the injury proximately caused by the existence and continuance of the encumbrance, the measure of which is deemed to be the difference between the value of the land as it would be without the easement and its value as it is with the easement.

Notes and Questions

1. Even the general warranty given by the Housworths is subject to significant exceptions, including one for public roadways and one for zoning regulations. What is the point of these exceptions? Did the court correctly interpret those underlying policies as not covering the floodwater detention easement?

2. The exception for zoning regulations can be tricky. Suppose that the property is a vacant lot and that local zoning laws restrict houses to 15 feet in height? Is this an encumbrance? What if the property contains a house 30 feet high? Would it make a difference in either case if the restriction came from a private neighborhood covenant rather than a public zoning law?

3. What should the Housworths (or rather, their attorney) have done? Presumably, the Oconee River Soil Conservation District is not interested in terminating its easement. Are the Housworths stuck with an unsaleable tract of land?

Engelhart v. Kramer
570 N.W.2d 550 (S.D. 1997)

GILBERTSON, Justice.

A $34,800 judgment was rendered against Crystal Kay Kramer based on violation of SDCL ch 43-4 and for failure to properly disclose a defect in the home she sold to Karen Engelhart. The case was tried without a jury before the Second Judicial Circuit Court. Kramer appeals the award claiming that Engelhart did not show that Kramer failed to meet the required standard in completing the seller's property disclosure statement.[1] We affirm.

FACTS AND PROCEDURE

In May of 1991, Crystal Kay Kramer purchased a home in Sioux Falls, South Dakota for $35,000. Over the next few years Kramer made several improvements. Four days prior to putting the home on the market, in September, 1993, Kramer enlisted the support of friends and family and began an extensive cleaning of the basement. There were several large cracks in the basement's cement walls and pieces of various sizes had fallen off. They removed old sheet rock and put up wood paneling over the basement walls. The basement project was memorialized by Kramer with several photographs depicting the before, during and after condition of the walls.

During this period Karen Engelhart was searching for a home commensurate with her income level. Engelhart was a first-time home buyer and was assisted by Dorothy Ecker, a real estate agent. Engelhart viewed Kramer's home, became interested, and then decided to purchase it.

Kramer was represented by Shirley Ullom, a Century 21 Advantage, Inc. real estate agent. Kramer completed the detailed "property condition disclosure statement" form required by SDCL 43-4-44. Part two of the form required the seller to disclose certain structural information. Specifically, question 2 asked "Have you experienced water penetration in the basement ... within the past two years?" Kramer replied, "Small amt of H20 penetration in NW + NE corners [when it] rains." (emphasis added). In answering question 3 "[a]re there any cracked walls or floors?"

---

[1] Kramer also argues that the trial court erred in finding Kramer's actions constituted fraud and deceit. In light of our disposition of the case on the disclosure requirement issue, the fraud and deceit issue need not be addressed.

Kramer responded "basement floor, some spots in basement walls, East bedroom walls." Under § 5, Miscellaneous Information, Kramer was required to disclose any additional problems that were not previously mentioned. Kramer offered, *"basement cement walls have some crumbling, behind paneling, basement floor cracked [and] uneven in spots."* (emphasis added).

The trial court found that Engelhart relied upon, among other things, Kramer's disclosure statement with regard to the condition of the basement walls and that Engelhart believed "some spots" and "some crumbling" to mean the problems were minimal. Kramer allegedly offered to remove the paneling to expose the basement walls but the trial court concluded that the offer was "a gambit, or a bluff ... without any real intention of performing" and that the typical buyer in Engelhart's position would be "reluctant to remove paneling from someone else's house." Kramer admitted taking photographs before installing the paneling and that showing the photos to a potential purchaser would have been easier than removing it. Kramer could not explain why she did not offer the photos.

Engelhart purchased the property in October 1994. In March of 1995, she discovered water seepage through the south wall of the basement. The paneling was removed and water was discovered running through cracks in the south wall. Also noted were several other large cracks, including a large horizontal crack running around the basement. Engelhart hired a structural engineer, Chester Quick (Quick) to diagnose the problem. Quick issued a report in which he found the basement walls "very badly cracked" and testified that the cement had "leeched out" which allowed dirt and water to pass into the basement.[2]

---

[2] Quick testified that the wall was "a mixture of sand, cement [which holds the mixture together], and usually some rock, and over time with excess water and cracks the cement 'leeches out' of the mixture and you wind up with nothing but sand and rock."

Further, Quick noted that the concrete was showing "considerable disintegration especially at the south wall" which was not repairable. He concluded that the foundation had to be replaced and that "As bad as [the walls] are cracked they could collapse at any time." When asked whether the disclosure statement adequately described the condition of the basement Quick testified that, although accurate in part, "some crumbling" did not adequately describe the damage that existed behind the paneling.

Engelhart brought suit against Kramer based upon misrepresentations made in the disclosure statement. The trial court ruled in favor of Engelhart on failure to comply with South Dakota's Disclosure Statutes and fraud. Kramer appeals the $34,800 award entered against her. ...

LEGAL ANALYSIS AND DECISION

Whether Kramer failed to complete the disclosure statement in good faith as required by SDCL Ch 43-A?

In 1993 the South Dakota legislature enacted specific requirements for disclosures in certain real estate transfers. SDCL §§ 43-4-38 to -44. SDCL 43-4-38 provides:

> The seller of residential real property shall furnish to a buyer a completed copy of the disclosure statement before the buyer makes a written offer. If after delivering the disclosure statement to the buyer or the buyer's agent and prior to the date of closing for the property or the date of possession of the property, whichever comes first, the seller becomes aware of any change of material fact which would affect the disclosure statement, the seller shall furnish a written amendment disclosing the change of material fact.

SDCL 43-4-41 requires that "The seller shall perform each act and make each disclosure in good faith." SDCL 43-4-40 absolves sellers of liability for defects in certain circumstances by providing:

> Except as provided in § 43-4-42, a seller is not liable for a defect or other condition in the residential real property being transferred if the seller *truthfully completes* the disclosure statement.

(Emphasis added). The disclosure form mandated by SDCL 43-4-44 establishes that beyond the above obligations, there is no warranty passing from the seller to the buyer:

> THIS STATEMENT IS A DISCLOSURE OF THE CONDITION OF THE ABOVE DESCRIBED PROPERTY.... IT IS NOT A WARRANTY OF ANY KIND BY THE SELLER OR ANY AGENT REPRESENTING ANY PARTY IN THIS TRANSACTION AND IS NOT A SUBSTITUTE FOR ANY INSPECTIONS OR WARRANTIES THE PARTIES MAY WISH TO OBTAIN.

(Capitals in original).

Kramer relies on SDCL 43-4-40 and contends that even if her description of the basement was inadequate or under Kramer's phraseology, an innocent misrepresentation, that it was truthful nonetheless and therefore no liability should attach. It is important to note that in SDCL 43-4-40, the terms "truthfully" and "complete" do not operate independently to the exclusion of the other. A plain reading of the terms together evince a more exacting standard than truth alone.

Until today, this Court has not addressed the scope of the disclosure statutes at issue. Of central concern to our resolution is what is required by the term "good faith," in the absence of a definition in SDCL 43-4-41, and whether the disclosure of "some crumbling" violates that standard? We recognize that the concept of "good faith" may, at times, seem as elusive as the "reasonableness" that is spoken of in the law of torts. However, there exists several sources from which meaning can be found.

Statutory guidance can be found at SDCL 2-14-2(13) which states that "good faith" is:

> an honest intention to abstain from taking any unconscientious advantage of another, even through the forms or technicalities of law, together with an absence of all information or belief of facts which would render the transaction unconscientious;

Black's Law Dictionary 693 (6th ed 1990) offers the following:

> Good faith is an intangible and abstract quality with no technical meaning or statutory definition, and it encompasses, among other things, an honest belief, the absence of malice and the absence of design to defraud or to seek an unconscionable advantage.... In common usage this term is ordinarily used to describe that state of mind denoting honesty of purpose, freedom of intention to defraud, and, generally speaking, means being faithful to one's duty or obligation.

Case law decided under different contexts has provided additional meaning to the term "good faith" to include "honesty in fact," *Garrett v. BankWest, Inc.*, 459 N.W.2d 833, 841 (S.D.1990) (contractual context; meaning of good faith "varies with the context and emphasizes faithfulness to an agreed common purpose and consistency with the justified expectations of the other party"), and an "honest belief in the suitability of the actions taken." *B.W. v. Meade Co.*, 534 N.W.2d 595, 598 (S.D.1995), (in the context of reporting and investigating child abuse). In the case now before us the trial court properly relied upon the definition found in SDCL 2-14-2(13).

Kramer contends that since she described the condition of the basement walls as having "some spots" and "some crumbling," she fulfilled her duty of good faith by truthfully completing the Disclosure Statement. Kramer argues that to hold otherwise would, in effect, result in a strict liability standard on sellers of real estate. We disagree.

SDCL 43-4-42 provides:

> A transfer that is subject to §§ 43-4-37 to 43-4-44, inclusive, is not invalidated solely because a person fails to comply with §§ 43-4-37 to 43-4-44, inclusive. However, a person *who intentionally or who negligently* violates §§ 43-4-37 to 43-4-44, inclusive, is liable to the buyer for the amount of the actual damages and repairs suffered by the buyer as a result of the violation or failure. A court may also award the buyer costs and attorney fees. Nothing in this section shall preclude or restrict any other rights or remedies of the buyer.

(Emphasis added).

Kramer relies on *Amyot v. Luchini*, 932 P.2d 244 (Alaska 1997), for the proposition that a disclosure statement can be truthful yet not "perfect" and that "innocent misrepresentations" do not violate good faith. However, it must be noted that Kramer's representation of the issue to this Court incorrectly assumes that the misrepresentation of the basement walls was found merely innocent by the trial court. To the contrary, the trial court specifically found that the Kramer's paneling of the walls four days before putting the house on the market was not "solely for aesthetic purposes" and was completed deliberately[3] in an attempt to hide their true

---

[3] The trial court relied on Kramer's deposition and trial testimony in that when she purchased the house "[t]he walls were crumbling with cracks in places," that the residue she had discovered on the basement floor was "Part of the basement wall ... whatever makes up the wall was there in a pile" and further that Kramer admitted in her disclosure statement that no water ever came in on the south wall.

condition. Kramer's colorful attempt to characterize her description of the basement as an innocent misrepresentation is inaccurate.

In 1993, Alaska enacted residential real property disclosure statement statutes (substantially similar to that of South Dakota enacted the same year). Alaska Stat. §§ 34.70.010 to 34.70.090 (Michie 1996).[4] The *Amyot* court stated:

> Prior to the enactment of [the mandatory disclosure statutes], sellers of real property were not required to make any representations about the property. However, sellers were strictly liable for those representations they made. (Citation omitted.) Under the disclosure statute a seller is now required to make representations about a wide range of the property's features and characteristics. We conclude that the legislature intended to offset the seller's increased disclosure responsibilities by the lower liability standard for misrepresentations.

Amyot, 932 P.2d at 246.

We agree with the *Amyot* court and hold that strict liability is not the requisite standard under South Dakota's disclosure statutes. A plain reading of SDCL 43-4-42 tells us that liability will not attach unless an intentional or negligent violation occurs. The legal maxim *"expressio unius est exlusio alterius"* means "the expression of one thing is the exclusion of another." Black's Law Dictionary 581 (6th ed.1990). The maxim is a general rule of statutory construction. Applying the general rule to SDCL

---

[4] The Alaska disclosure statutes did not define "good faith" but held that "good faith" envisioned an "honest and reasonable belief." *Id.* at 247. *Amyot* is distinguishable from the present facts in that the court held an "innocent misrepresentation" did not violate the good faith standard. South Dakota does not attach liability in this context unless the seller's conduct amounts to an "intentional or negligent" violation the disclosure statutes. SDCL 43-4-42.

43-4-42, we find the language "intentionally or ... negligently" is exclusive and negates strict liability.

It is fair to presume that sellers know the character of the property they convey. At present, when Kramer became aware of Engelhart's concern over the basement she could have simply shown the pictures of its true condition. Her failure to do so was unreasonable and amounts to negligence. SDCL 43-4-42. It must be noted that Kramer admitted taking the photographs before installing the paneling and that showing the photos would have been easier than removing it. Kramer could not explain why she did not offer the photos.

We hold that with the adoption of South Dakota's detailed disclosure statutes the doctrine of caveat emptor has been abandoned in favor of full and complete disclosure of defects of which the seller is aware. We are not inferring, as Kramer suggests, that a seller must possess the expertise of a structural engineer to pass good faith muster. Nor are we suggesting that a seller will be liable for defects of which she is unaware. Those claims are clearly disposed of in the closing section of the mandated disclosure form of SDCL 43-4-44:

> The Seller hereby certifies that the information contained herein is true and correct to the best of the Seller's information, knowledge and belief as of the date of the Seller's signature below.... THE SELLER AND THE BUYER MAY WISH TO OBTAIN PROFESSIONAL ADVICE AND INSPECTIONS OF THE PROPERTY TO OBTAIN A TRUE REPORT AS TO THE CONDITION OF THE PROPERTY AND TO PROVIDE FOR APPROPRIATE PROVISIONS IN ANY CONTRACT OF SALE AS NEGOTIATED BETWEEN THE SELLER AND THE BUYER WITH RESPECT TO SUCH PROFESSIONAL ADVICE AND INSPECTIONS.

(Capitals in original). It is clear that, as per SDCL § 43-4-41 and 43-4-44, a seller's "good faith" is determined under a reasonable person standard. Affirmed.

Questions

1. In *Lucero v. Van Wie*, 598 NW 2d 893 (S.D. 1999), the seller failed to provide the statutorily required disclosure statement, but the contract of sale contained the following clause:

    > The buyer acknowledges that she has examined the premises and the same are in satisfactory condition and they accept the property in the "as-is" condition … .

    This time, the South Dakota Supreme Court held that the buyer could not recover for undisclosed defects in the property; she "entered into an enforceable contract and purchased the property 'as is,' the result of which was to waive disclosure requirements." After *Lucero*, what do you expect happened to real estate sales contracts in South Dakota? What do you expect the South Dakota courts will do in cases where the sales contract contains an "as-is" clause but the buyer alleges that the seller affirmatively lied about the condition of the property – e.g., "No, the roof has never leaked."

2. In addition to the distinction between unknown defects and defects known to the seller, some courts draw a distinction between latent and apparent defects. Only hidden defects – e.g., rotting support beams in the walls – need to be disclosed, while readily visible defects, or ones that a reasonable inspection could discover – e.g., nonworking plumbing on the second floor – need not. The theory, at least, is that the buyer depends on the seller to tell her about conditions she could not reasonably discover herself. But isn't there a connection between defects the buyer doesn't

know about and defects the seller doesn't know about, either? Cases like *Engelhart* are one thing, where the Seller literally plasters (or at least panels) over the problem. But who should bear the loss if a previously unknown sinkhole surprises everyone by swallowing up the back porch the day after closing? Consider, in this regard, a seller who doesn't know whether her home's attic walls contain asbestos insulation, and a buyer whose offer to buy the house is contingent on drilling into the walls to confirm that they do not contain asbestos. If you represented the seller, would you advise your client to accept this contingency?

3. What kinds of conditions must be disclosed? A leaky roof? A leaky faucet? The presence of lead paint on the walls? The fact that a previous inhabitant of the home was gruesomely murdered by a family member? That the homeowner regularly gave "ghost tours" on which she pretended to tourists that the house was haunted? The fact that a registered sex offender lives on the block? The fact that there is a municipal garbage dump half a mile away?

4. In many states, new-home builders are required to give a non-waivable warranty of habitability that substantially parallels the warranty of habitability required of landlords. What might account for the decision to hold sellers of new houses to a higher standard than sellers of existing houses? When should the statute of limitations on breach of warranty claims start running? Should subsequent purchasers be able to sue the original builder for breach of the warranty if the defects become apparent only after a resale?

Brush Grocery Kart, Inc. v. Sure Fine Market, Inc.
47 P.3d 680 (Colo. 2002)

JUSTICE COATS delivered the opinion of the court: ...

In October 1992 Brush Grocery Kart, Inc. and Sure Fine Market, Inc. entered into a five-year "Lease with Renewal Provisions and Option to Purchase" for real property, including a building to be operated by Brush as a grocery store. Under the contract's purchase option provision, any time during the last six months of the lease, Brush could elect to purchase the property at a price equal to the average of the appraisals of an expert designated by each party.

Shortly before expiration of the lease, Brush notified Sure Fine of its desire to purchase the property and begin the process of determining a sale price. Although each party offered an appraisal, the parties were unable to agree on a final price by the time the lease expired. Brush then vacated the premises, returned all keys to Sure Fine, and advised Sure Fine that it would discontinue its casualty insurance covering the property during the lease. Brush also filed suit, alleging that Sure Fine failed to negotiate the price term in good faith and asking for the appointment of a special master to determine the purchase price. Sure Fine agreed to the appointment of a special master and counterclaimed, alleging that Brush negotiated the price term in bad faith and was therefore the breaching party.

During litigation over the price term, the property was substantially damaged during a hail storm. With neither party carrying casualty insurance, each asserted that the other was liable for the damage. The issue was added to the litigation at a stipulated amount of $60,000. ... The court then found that under the doctrine of equitable conversion, Brush was the equitable owner of the property and bore the risk of loss. It therefore declined to abate the purchase price or award damages to Brush for the loss.

Brush appealed the loss allocation, and the court of appeals affirmed on similar grounds. ...

In the absence of statutory authority, the rights, powers, duties, and liabilities arising out of a contract for the sale of land have frequently been derived by reference to the theory of equitable conversion. This theory or doctrine, which has been described as a legal fiction, is based on equitable principles that permit the vendee to be considered the equitable owner of the land and debtor for the purchase money and the vendor to be regarded as a secured creditor. The changes in rights and liabilities that occur upon the making of the contract result from the equitable right to specific performance. Even with regard to third parties, the theory has been relied on to determine, for example, the devolution, upon death, of the rights and liabilities of each party with respect to the land, and to ascertain the powers of creditors of each party to reach the land in payment of their claims.

The assignment of the risk of casualty loss in the executory period of contracts for the sale of real property varies greatly throughout the jurisdictions of this country. What appears to yet be a slim majority of states places the risk of loss on the vendee from the moment of contracting, on the rationale that once an equitable conversion takes place, the vendee must be treated as owner for all purposes. Once the vendee becomes the equitable owner, he therefore becomes responsible for the condition of the property, despite not having a present right of occupancy or control. In sharp contrast, a handful of other states reject the allocation of casualty loss risk as a consequence of the theory of equitable conversion and follow the equally rigid "Massachusetts Rule," under which the seller continues to bear the risk until actual transfer of the title, absent an express agreement to the contrary. A substantial and growing number of jurisdictions, however, base the legal consequences of no-fault casualty loss on the right to possession of the property at the time the loss occurs. This view has found expression in the Uniform Vendor and

Purchaser Risk Act, and while a number of states have adopted some variation of the Uniform Act, others have arrived at a similar position through the interpretations of their courts. ...

In *Wiley v. Lininger*, 204 P.2d 1083, [(1949)] where fire destroyed improvements on land occupied by the vendee during the multi-year executory period of an installment land contract, we held, according to the generally accepted rule, that neither the buyer nor the seller, each of whom had an insurable interest in the property, had an obligation to insure the property for the benefit of the other. We also adopted a rule, which we characterized as "the majority rule," that "the vendee under a contract for the sale of land, being regarded as the equitable owner, assumes the risk of destruction of or injury to the property *where he is in possession*, and the destruction or loss is not proximately caused by the negligence of the vendor." *Id.* (emphasis added). The vendee in possession was therefore not relieved of his obligation to continue making payments according to the terms of the contract, despite material loss by fire to some of the improvements on the property. ... Those jurisdictions that indiscriminately include the risk of casualty loss among the incidents or "attributes" of equitable ownership do so largely in reliance on ancient authority or by considering it necessary for consistent application of the theory of equitable conversion. Under virtually any accepted understanding of the theory, however, equitable conversion is not viewed as entitling the purchaser to every significant right of ownership, and particularly not the right of possession. As a matter of both logic and equity, the obligation to maintain property in its physical condition follows the right to have actual possession and control rather than a legal right to force conveyance of the property through specific performance at some future date. See 17 SAMUEL WILLISTON, A TREATISE ON THE LAW OF CONTRACTS § 50:46, at 457-58 (Richard A. Lord ed., 4th ed. 1990) ("[I]t is wiser to have the party in possession of the property care for it at his peril, rather than at the peril of another.").

The equitable conversion theory is literally stood on its head by imposing on a vendee, solely because of his right to specific performance, the risk that the vendor will be unable to specifically perform when the time comes because of an accidental casualty loss. It is counterintuitive, at the very least, that merely contracting for the sale of real property should not only relieve the vendor of his responsibility to maintain the property until execution but also impose a duty on the vendee to perform despite the intervention of a material, no-fault casualty loss preventing him from ever receiving the benefit of his bargain. Such an extension of the theory of equitable conversion to casualty loss has never been recognized by this jurisdiction, and it is neither necessary nor justified solely for the sake of consistency.

By contrast, there is substantial justification, both as a matter of law and policy, for not relieving a vendee who is entitled to possession before transfer of title, like the vendee in *Wiley*, of his duty to pay the full contract price, notwithstanding an accidental loss. In addition to having control over the property and being entitled to the benefits of its use, an equitable owner who also has the right of possession has already acquired virtually all of the rights of ownership and almost invariably will have already paid at least some portion of the contract price to exercise those rights. By expressly including in the contract for sale the right of possession, which otherwise generally accompanies transfer of title, the vendor has for all practical purposes already transferred the property as promised, and the parties have in effect expressed their joint intention that the vendee pay the purchase price as promised. ...

In the absence of a right of possession, a vendee of real property that suffers a material casualty loss during the executory period of the contract, through no fault of his own, must be permitted to rescind and recover any payments he had already made. ...

Here, Brush was clearly not in possession of the property as the equitable owner. Even if the doctrine of equitable conversion applies to the option contract between Brush and Sure Fine and could be said to have converted Brush's interest to an equitable ownership of the property at the time Brush exercised its option to purchase, neither party considered the contract for sale to entitle Brush to possession. Brush was, in fact, not in possession of the property, and the record indicates that Sure Fine considered itself to hold the right of use and occupancy and gave notice that it would consider Brush a holdover tenant if it continued to occupy the premises other than by continuing to lease the property. The casualty loss was ascertainable and in fact stipulated by the parties, and neither party challenged the district court's enforcement of the contract except with regard to its allocation of the casualty loss. Both the court of appeals and the district court therefore erred in finding that the doctrine of equitable conversion required Brush to bear the loss caused by hail damage.

Questions

1. Why is the risk of loss during the executory period even a thing? Why would the parties leave time between signing a contract of sale and closing? Why not just hand over a deed on the spot?

2. If the grocery store had been damaged by hail during the five-year lease preceding the sale, who would have borne the risk of loss? Would it matter whether Brush had taken possession of the property? Who bears the risk of loss if Brush owns a grocery store subject to Sure Fine's mortgage? Does it matter whether Colorado follows the title or lien theory of mortgages?

Foreclosures and the Mortgage Crisis

Introduction: What is a Mortgage?

A mortgage is an interest in land. It is not a possessory interest: the owner of a mortgage has no right to use the property, the way the owner of the fee or an easement owner would. Instead, mortgages exist to secure loans. A secured loan is backed, or secured, by a specific asset such as a house or a car, which the lender can seize in case of default. An unsecured loan is not secured by any specific asset – for example, credit card debt and student loans are unsecured. The borrower owes the money, and the lender can go after the borrower's unsecured assets in case of default, but if those assets are too small, the unsecured lender is out of luck. Secured loans are generally considered less risky than unsecured loans, for obvious reasons, and should bear lower interest rates (absent some foolery on the part of the lender or government intervention into the market, both of which do happen).

Most mortgages are residential mortgages. Usually, homebuyers in the U.S. can't afford to pay the entire purchase price of a house at the time they buy it. Instead, they take out a loan – a mortgage – to pay the bulk of the purchase price. They will sign a promissory note (the note) that creates personal liability for the borrowers if they fail to pay, and also sets out the terms of the mortgage such as the repayment period and the interest rate. They will also sign a mortgage, a written instrument that grants the lender an interest in their newly purchased land. Usually, this transaction occurs at the time the buyers buy the land, though mortgages can also be refinanced or taken out on already-owned property.

The homebuyers are the *mortgagors*. The lender is the *mortgagee*. Over time, the buyers pay off the loan. As they pay off the loan, they build "equity"

312

in their homes. Equity is the difference between what a home is worth and what the homeowners owe on their mortgage.[17] As a result of deliberate policy choices, the model residential mortgage in the U.S. is for no more than 80% of the value of the house at time of purchase; has a fixed interest rate; and amortizes over a period of years, usually twenty or thirty. Amortization means that the payments are the same throughout the period of the mortgage: at the beginning, most of the payments go to interest on the loan, while over time more and more of the payments go to reduce the loan principal.

The mortgagors can transfer the land at will. However, any transfer will not free the land from the mortgage (nor will a transfer free them from their contractual promise to pay the debt); the mortgage *runs with the land.* Thus, a sensible transferee will not be willing to pay full value for the land – the fair market value of the land is reduced by the amount of the mortgage. A transferee can either take "subject to the mortgage," which means that the original mortgagors still owe the debt and the transferee is at risk if they don't pay, or "assuming the mortgage," which means that the new owner agrees to pay the mortgage directly. When the purchaser assumes the mortgage, the seller still has a duty to pay the mortgage if the buyer doesn't, but the seller can pursue the buyer for reimbursement if that happens. However, this all risks some big messes; to avoid problems associated with transfers, many mortgages have "due on sale" clauses, which means that the full amount of the mortgage comes due ("accelerates") when the mortgagor sells the property. One important feature of a due on sale clause is that it enables lenders to reprice loans: if the interest rate has risen since the initial mortgage loan, the buyer can't

---

[17] This terminology has a historical basis in the "equity of redemption," which was a means by which early chancellors protected early mortgagors from abuses by lenders. Over time, the equitable procedures created by courts gave way to legislation establishing rules for how foreclosures could occur.

just assume the existing loan and receive a lower interest rate than would otherwise be available to him.

Suppose Joan Watson wants to sell her house to Sherlock Holmes. She still owes $400,000 on her house; Holmes will be buying it for $500,000. But she doesn't have $400,000 in the bank to pay off her mortgage, which has a due on sale clause. How can she accomplish the sale? The answer is that a series of transactions take place together. The day of the sale, Holmes will give Watson a check for $500,000 (most of which will likely come from Holmes' own new mortgage on the property). Watson will then pay her lender $400,000 and keep $100,000. As you can see, there will be some time at which both Holmes and Watson are relying on the value of the underlying property – Holmes to get his mortgage and Watson to pay hers off. For this reason, real estate transactions regularly involve the use of multiple third parties, including escrow agents, to facilitate and guarantee the sale.

If the mortgagors default on the mortgage by failing to pay the appropriate amounts at the appropriate times, the mortgagee can foreclose. Foreclosure can be time-consuming and expensive, so in some circumstances the mortgagee may accept a "deed in lieu of foreclosure," by which the mortgagor surrenders the property to the mortgagee and the mortgagee accepts the deed. However, deeds in lieu of foreclosure are relatively rare; most of the time, if a default is not cured and the loan is not modified, the result will be a foreclosure.

Either by a private sale (nonjudicial foreclosure) or under judicial supervision (judicial foreclosure), the mortgagee can have the property sold and apply the proceeds of the sale to the amount due on the note. The foreclosure is so called because it forecloses the mortgagee's ability to get the property back by paying off the mortgage debt; after the foreclosure, it is too late to become current.[18]

In a number of states, it is possible to avoid judicial foreclosure – which takes more time and money than nonjudicial foreclosure – through the use of a "deed of trust," which is recognized in most jurisdictions. Under a deed of trust, the borrower conveys title to the property to a person to hold in trust to secure the debt. If the borrower defaults, the trustee has the power of sale without needing to go to court. However, almost all states that allow this procedure do impose some procedural safeguards, such as notice and public sale. Other than the ability to avoid judicial foreclosure, you can expect a deed of trust to be treated like a mortgage.

In addition, there are two different types of secured loans: recourse and nonrecourse loans. For a nonrecourse loan, the only way the lender can get its money back in case of default is by seizing the asset, and if there's not enough money to satisfy the debt from the asset, too bad for the lender. The lender has no "recourse" against any of the borrower's other assets. A recourse loan is different: in case of default, the lender can seize and sell the asset, and if there's not enough money to satisfy the debt, the lender is now an unsecured creditor for the remaining balance (the deficiency) and can go after any of the borrower's other assets, such as her bank account. Foreclosure wipes out the lender's interest in the land, which means that the land can then be resold free of the lender's interest. However, with a recourse loan, foreclosure will not wipe out the borrower's debt, if it is greater than the foreclosure sale amount.

---

[18] At common law, the equity of redemption allowed the mortgagor to redeem the property from the mortgagee. This equity of redemption was extinguished by foreclosure sale. In about half of the states, there is also a statutory right to redeem the property from the *purchaser* at a foreclosure sale for a certain period of time. This right is rarely used, because most people would already have paid, if they could, before the sale.

Obviously, lenders ordinarily prefer recourse loans, but will grant nonrecourse loans in various circumstances.[19] Many businesses can get nonrecourse loans based on their assets. Some states bar deficiency judgments for residential mortgages, which makes them nonrecourse loans. Other states bar deficiency judgments unless there is a judicial foreclosure, with its greater expense and greater procedural protections for the borrower. Still others limit the amount of any deficiency judgment to the difference between the principal balance and the property's fair market value at the time of foreclosure – this limit recognizes that foreclosed properties often sell for below market value for a variety of reasons, including buyers' uncertainty about the true condition of the property and the limited number of potential buyers who bid at foreclosure sales. (Historically, the mortgagee is often the only bidder at a foreclosure sale. Why would this be true?)

Even states that allow deficiency judgments generally recognize an exception: if the sale price shocks the conscience, then a deficiency judgment may not be allowed. More generally, even in the absence of a potential deficiency judgment, the foreclosing entity has a limited duty of good faith to the mortgagor in seeking an acceptable price at the sale. However, mere inadequacy of price will not invalidate a sale in the absence of fraud, unfairness, or procedural problems that deterred bidding. As a result, very low sale prices are sometimes accepted by courts. *Compare* Moeller v. Lien, 30 Cal. Rptr. 2d 777 (Ct. App. 1994) (sale at 25% of market value was acceptable where sale was to bona fide purchaser and there was no irregularity in the sale procedure), *with* Murphy v. Fin. Dev. Corp., 495 A.2d 1245 (N.H. 1985) (finding that mortgagee violated duty

---

[19] In fact, the basic idea of a corporation is a way of limiting a lender's recourse: before the corporate form, if a business owner went bust, creditors could go after the owner's personal assets until they were gone. The corporation allows shareholders/owners to limit their liability to the extent of the corporation's assets. If a person owned shares of Lehman Brothers, its creditors could make her shares worthless, but they couldn't make her pay Lehman Brothers' debts.

to mortgagor when (1) sale was rescheduled and poorly advertised, (2) sale price was so low that it wiped out substantial equity for homeowners, and (3) mortgagee quickly resold property at substantially higher price).

One final introductory point: it is possible to take out a second and even a third mortgage. The first mortgage has "priority" over the second mortgage: it will be paid first at foreclosure. Only if there is money remaining after the first mortgage is paid off will the holder of the second mortgage be paid. As a result of the greater risk involved in second mortgages, they generally bear higher interest rates than first mortgages.

Problem

Betty Finn buys a house for $450,000. She puts down $90,000 and takes out a mortgage for $250,000 from Heather Chandler, and a second mortgage for $110,000 from Veronica Sawyer. When Betty defaults, the house is sold for $500,000 at foreclosure. Assuming the amounts due on the mortgages haven't changed at all, how should the proceeds be distributed? What would the answer be if the house brought $350,000 at foreclosure?

A.   Crystals and Mud in Property Law

We have skimped on the history of mortgage law, which is a long struggle between creditors and debtors. Mostly, legislatures and courts act to protect debtors, who are usually seen as the more vulnerable parties, from sharp dealing by creditors. As rules stretch to be more equitable and less hard-edged, pressure grows to create *new* clear rules, which then grow their own exceptions and qualifications.

Carol Rose describes the legal seesawing in the following excerpt, which has important lessons for property law generally:

Carol M. Rose, *Crystals And Mud In Property Law*
40 STAN. L. REV. 577 (1988) (excerpts reprinted by permission)

Property law, and especially the common law of property, has always been heavily laden with hard-edged doctrines that tell everyone exactly where they stand. Default on paying your loan installments? Too bad, you lose the thing you bought and your past payments as well. Forget to record your deed? Sorry, the next buyer can purchase free of your claim, and you are out on the street. Sell that house with the leak in the basement? Lucky you, you can unload the place without having to tell the buyer about such things at all.

In a sense, hard-edged rules like these – rules that I call 'crystals' – are what property is all about. If, as Jeremy Bentham said long ago, property is 'nothing but a basis of expectation,' then crystal rules are the very stuff of property: their great advantage, or so it is commonly thought, is that they signal to all of us, in a clear and distinct language, precisely what our obligations are and how we may take care of our interests. Thus, I should inspect the property, record my deed, and make my payments if I don't want to lose my home to unexpected physical, legal, or financial impairments. I know where I stand and so does everyone else, and we can all strike bargains with each other if we want to stand somewhere else.

Economic thinkers have been telling us for at least two centuries that the more important a given kind of thing becomes for us, the more likely we are to have these hard-edged rules to manage it. We draw these ever-sharper lines around our entitlements so that we know who has what, and so that we can trade instead of getting into the confusions and disputes that would only escalate as the goods in question became scarcer and more highly valued.

At the root of these economic analyses lies the perception that it costs something to establish clear entitlements to things, and we won't bother to undertake the task of removing goods from an ownerless 'commons' unless it is worth it to us to do so. What makes it worth it? Increasing scarcity of the resource, and the attendant conflicts over it. To use the example given by Harold Demsetz, one of the most notable of the modern economists telling this story, when the European demand for fur hats increased demand for (and scarcity of) fur-bearing animals among Indian hunters, the Indians developed a system of property entitlements to the animal habitat. Economic historians of the American West tell a similar story about the development of property rights in various minerals and natural resources. Easy-going, anything-goes patterns of appropriation at the outset came under pressure as competition for resources increased, and were finally superseded by much more sharply defined systems of entitlement. In effect, as our competition for a resource raises the costs of conflict about it, those conflict costs begin to outweigh the costs of taking it out of the commons and establishing clear property entitlements. We establish a system of clear entitlements so that we can barter and trade for what we want instead of fighting.

The trouble with this 'scarcity story' is that things don't seem to work this way, or at least not all the time. Sometimes we seem to substitute fuzzy, ambiguous rules of decision for what seem to be perfectly clear, open and shut, demarcations of entitlements. I call this occurrence the substitution of 'mud' rules for 'crystal' ones.

Thus, … over time, the straightforward common law crystalline rules have been muddied repeatedly by exceptions and equitable second-guessing, to the point that the various claimants under real estate contracts, mortgages, or recorded deeds don't know quite what their rights and obligations really are. And the same pattern has occurred in other areas too. …

Quite aside from the wealth transfer that may accompany a change in the rules, then, the change may sharply alter the *clarity* of the relationship between the parties. But a move to the uncertainty of mud seems disruptive to the very practice of a private property/contractual exchange society. Thus, it is hardly surprising that we individually and collectively attempt to clear up the mud with new crystal rules – as when private parties contract out of ambiguous warranties, or when legislatures pass new versions of crystalline record systems – only to be overruled later, when courts once again reinstate mud in a different form....

Early common law mortgages were very crystalline indeed. They had the look of pawnshop transactions and were at least sometimes structured as conveyances: I borrow money from you, and at the same time I convey my land to you as security for my loan. If all goes well, I pay back my debt on the agreed 'law day,' and you reconvey my land back to me. But if all does not go well and I cannot pay on the appointed day, then, no matter how heartrending my excuse, I lose my land to you and, presumably, any of the previous payments I might have made. As the fifteenth century commentator Littleton airily explained, the name 'mortgage' derived from the rule that, if the debtor 'doth not pay, then the land which he puts in pledge ... is gone from him for ever, and so dead.'

This system had the advantage of great clarity, but it sometimes must have seemed very hard on mortgage debtors to the advantage of scoundrelly creditors. Littleton's advice about the importance of specifying the precise place and time for repayment, for example, conjures up images of a wily creditor hiding in the woods on the repayment day to frustrate repayment; presumably, the unfound creditor could keep the property. But by the seventeenth century, the intervention of courts of equity had changed things. By the eighteenth and nineteenth centuries, the equity courts were regularly giving debtors as many as three or four 'enlargements' of the time in which they might pay and redeem the property before the final 'foreclosure,' even when the excuse was lame. One judge explained that an equity court might well grant more time even after the 'final' order of 'foreclosure absolute,' depending on the particular circumstances.

The muddiness of this emerging judicial remedy argued against its attractiveness. Chief Justice Hale complained in 1672 that, '[b]y the growth of Equity on Equity, the Heart of the Common Law is eaten out, and legal Settlements are destroyed; . . . as far as the Line is given, Man will go; and if an hundred Years are given, Man will go so far, and we know not whither we shall go.' Instead of a precise and clear allocation of entitlements between the parties, the 'equity of redemption' and its unpredictable foreclosure opened up vexing questions and uncertainties: How much time should the debtor have for repayment before the equitable arguments shifted to favor the creditor? What sort of excuses did the debtor need? Did it matter that the property, instead of dropping in the lap of the creditor, was sold at a foreclosure sale?

But as the courts moved towards muddiness, private parties attempted to bargain their way out of these costly uncertainties and to reinstate a crystalline pattern whereby lenders could get the property immediately upon default without the costs of foreclosure. How about a separate deal with the borrower, for example, whereby he agrees to convey an equitable interest to the lender in case of default? Nothing doing, said the courts, including the United States Supreme Court, which in 1878 stated flatly that a mortgagor could not initially bargain away his 'equity of redemption.' Well, then, how about an arrangement whereby it looks as if the lender already owns the land, and the 'borrower' only gets title if he lives up to his agreement to pay for it by a certain time? This seemed more promising: In the 1890s California courts thought it perfectly correct to hold the buyer to his word in such an arrangement, and to give him neither an extension nor a refund of past payments. By the 1960s, however, they were changing their minds about these 'installment land contracts.' After all, these deals really had exactly the same effect as the old-style mortgages – the defaulting buyer could lose everything if he missed a payment, even the very last payment. Human vice and error seemed to put the crystal rule in jeopardy: In a series of cases culminating with a default by a 'willful but repentant' little old lady who had stopped paying when she mistakenly thought that she was being cheated, the California Supreme Court decided to treat these land contracts as mortgages in disguise. It gave the borrower 'relief from forfeiture' – a time to reinstate the installment contract or get back her past payments.

With mortgages first and mortgage substitutes later, we see a back-and-forth pattern: crisp definition of entitlements, made fuzzy by accretions of judicial decisions, crisped up again by the parties' contractual arrangements, and once again made fuzzy by the courts. Here we see private parties apparently following the 'scarcity story' in their private law arrangements: when things matter, the parties define their respective entitlements with ever sharper precision. Yet the courts seem at times unwilling to follow this story or to permit these crystalline definitions, most particularly when the rules hurt one party very badly. The cycle thus alternates between crystal and mud.

Notes and Questions

1. Bear in mind that crystals don't just help lenders, and mud doesn't just help borrowers. It all depends on the particulars of the situation. In fact, as you read the materials, consider whether insistence on hard-edged rules might aid *borrowers* under today's circumstances, and whether this would be justified.

2. Carol Rose later describes the situations in which courts muddy crystalline rules as cases involving "ninnies, hard-luck cases, and the occasional scoundrels who take advantage of them." As you read through the rest of this chapter, consider whether that is a fair characterization of the parties to the various disputes we will be studying.

B.   The Rise of Mortgage Securitization

Adam J. Levitin, *The Paper Chase: Securitization, Foreclosure,*
and the Uncertainty of Mortgage Title
63 DUKE L.J. 637 (2013) (excerpts reprinted by permission)

... II. THE SHIFT IN MORTGAGE FINANCING TO SECURITIZATION

Securitization is a relatively recent development in residential mortgage lending. Residential mortgages began to be securitized in 1970, but securitization remained a relatively small part of American housing finance prior to the 1980s. In 1979 only 10 percent of outstanding mortgages by dollar amount were securitized. Instead, mortgage lending was primarily a local affair ... so mortgage loans were rarely transferred.

... By 1983, 20 percent of outstanding mortgages by dollar amount were securitized, and a decade later fully half of outstanding mortgages by dollar amount were securitized. Today nearly two-thirds of mortgage dollars outstanding are securitized.

A firm can raise funds on potentially more advantageous terms if it can borrow solely against its assets, not its assets and liabilities. Securitization enabled such borrowing. To do so, a firm sells assets to a legally separate, specially created entity. The legally separate entity pays for the assets by issuing debt. Because the entity is designed to have almost no other liabilities, the debt it issues will be priced simply on the quality of the transferred assets, without any concern about competing claims to those assets. Therefore, ensuring that the assets are transferred and are free of competing claims is central to securitization.

Although residential-mortgage securitization transactions are complex and vary somewhat depending on the type of entity undertaking the securitization, there is still a core standard transaction. First, a financial institution (the "sponsor" or "seller") assembles a pool of mortgage loans either made ("originated") by an affiliate of the financial institution or purchased from unaffiliated third-party originators. Second, the pool of loans is sold by the sponsor to a special-purpose subsidiary (the "depositor") that has no other assets or liabilities and is little more than a legal entity with a mailbox. This is done to segregate the loans from the sponsor's assets and liabilities. Third, the depositor sells the loans to a passive, specially created, single-purpose vehicle (SPV), typically a trust in the case of residential-mortgage securitization. The trustee will then typically convey the mortgage notes and security instruments to a document custodian for safekeeping. The SPV issues certificated debt securities to raise the funds to pay for the loans. As these debt securities are backed by the cash flow from the mortgages, they are called mortgage-backed securities (MBS). ...

Notes and Questions

1. You may not feel that you fully understand securitization. It will get clearer with time. Perhaps the most important thing to understand is that the entity that claims to own, and tries to enforce, the mortgage debt in case of default is usually not the entity that originated the loan. It's common to discuss "banks" and "lenders" without paying much attention to the details of the actual mortgage transactions, and the problem is worsened because the entities involved are often related and even bear highly similar names. But lawyers often need more precision.

2. Among other things, non-originator owners can claim that equitable defenses – such as fraudulent inducement, which was unconscionably common in the run-up to the mortgage crisis – are unavailable to homeowners/mortgagors under the "holder in due course" doctrine. The holder in due course doctrine is similar to

the rule, discussed in *O'Keeffe v. Snyder*, that a good faith purchaser who buys property from a fraudster acquires good title, even though the fraudster did not have good title. With a mortgage, that means that a homeowner who was deceived into taking a predatory loan, as discussed in the next section, is still bound to pay back the loan according to its terms as long as the mortgage was transferred to a holder in due course. *See, e.g.,* Kurt Eggert, *Held Up in Due Course: Predatory Lending, Securitization, and the Holder-in-Due-Course Doctrine*, 35 CREIGHTON L. REV. 502 (2002). Recently, some reforms have attempted to limit the holder in due course doctrine, at least with respect to loans with specific bad features.

3. Another important thing to understand about securitization is that it involves the creation of new property rights from old. Investors in mortgage-backed securities do not own individual mortgages. Rather, they own the right to benefit from the stream of payments from mortgagors to the trusts that hold the mortgages. This right has been turned into a separate property right through the magic of securitization. But the *value* of this right is still, as investors discovered to their sorrow, dependent on the value of the underlying assets.

C. Predatory Lending

Along with the actors in the mortgage securitization chain described by Levitin, many mortgage loans, particularly subprime loans, were made with the assistance of a mortgage broker, who matched borrowers with lenders. As you will see, the broker's incentives did not line up with those of his or her borrower-clients.

Reading notes: Focus on the elements that made these loans bad loans. The discrimination is important, but so is how it was carried out. If you don't understand a loan provision, consider whether an average borrower would – and then look it up!

McGlawn v. Pennsylvania Human Relations Commission
891 A.2d 757 (Commonwealth Ct. Penn. 2006)

This case involves an issue of first impression: whether the Pennsylvania Human Relations Act (Act) extends to a mortgage broker's predatory lending activities known as "reverse redlining."[2] We affirm the Commission's holding that the Act prohibits reverse redlining. However, we vacate part of the Commission's award of actual damages and remand for further proceedings.

Respondent McGlawn and McGlawn, Inc. (Broker) a state-licensed mortgage broker, and Respondent Reginald McGlawn (Reginald McGlawn) petition for review of the decision of the Pennsylvania Human Relations Commission (Commission). The decision held Respondents violated Sections 5(h)(4)(loan provision)[3] and 5(h)(8)(i)(real estate transaction provision) [20] of the Act by discriminating against

---

[2] In United Cos. Corp. v. Sargeant, 20 F.Supp.2d 192 (D.Mass.1998), the United States District Court defined "redlining" as[:]

> "the practice of denying the extension of credit to specific geographic areas due to the income, race or ethnicity of its residents. The term was derived from the actual practice of drawing a red line around certain areas in which credit would be denied. Reverse redlining is the practice of extending credit on unfair terms to those same communities."

[3] Section 5(h)(4) of the Act, 43 P.S. § 955(h)(4), makes it unlawful to

> "[d]iscriminate against any person in the terms or conditions of any loan of money, whether or not secured by a mortgage or otherwise for the acquisition, construction, rehabilitation, repair or maintenance of housing accommodation or commercial property because of ... race...."

[20] Section 5(h)(8)(i) of the Act, 43 P.S. § 955(h)(8)(i), makes it an unlawful to[:]

"[d]iscriminate in real estate related transactions, as described by and subject to the following: (i)[i]t shall be unlawful for any person or other entity whose business includes engaging in real estate-related transactions to discriminate against any person in making available such a transaction or in the terms [or] conditions of such a transaction because of race...."

Complainants and other similar situated persons (collectively, Complainants), in mortgage loan transactions, because of their race and the racial composition of their neighborhoods. The Commission's final order directed Respondents to (1) cease and desist from discriminating against African Americans because of their race; (2) pay Complainants actual damages;[6] (3) pay Complainants damages for embarrassment and humiliation;[7] and (4) pay a civil penalty of $25,000.00. Further, the Commission's order directed Broker to (5) provide employee training to its employees designed to educate them in their responsibility to treat clients in a non-discriminatory manner consistent with the provisions of the Act; and to (6) develop and implement a record-keeping system designed to accurately record information about Broker's charges in all mortgage transactions.[8] The order also required Respondents to report the means of compliance and directed the Commission to contact the Department of Banking so that it may take such licensing action as it deemed appropriate.

I. BACKGROUND
A.

Broker, a corporation which brokers mortgage loans, refinancing and insurance for its customers, was founded in 1985 by its chief officers,

---

[6] The Commission awarded Complainants actual damages in these amounts: Taylor, $45,770.68; Poindexter, $24,447.80; Brunson, $63,996.34; Jackson, $74,875.74; Slaughter, $29,685.46; Jacobs, $47,549.62; Hawkins, $41,952.72; Miles, $101,562.81; Watts, $116,298.87; and Norwood, $154,209.11.

[7] The Commission awarded Complainants damages for embarrassment and humiliation in the following amounts: Taylor, $25,000.00; Poindexter, $15,000.00; Brunson, $15,000.00; Jackson, $20,000.00; Slaughter, $20,000.00; Jacobs, $20,000.00; Hawkins, $20,000.00; Miles, $10,000.00; Watts, $20,000.00; and Norwood, $20,000.00.

[8] In particular, Broker must accurately record the following data for each transaction: (a) the dollar amount and percentage of the broker's fee charged; (b) any other fees paid; (c) the amount and type of the loan; and (d) the employee involved in the transaction. Broker shall submit this information to the Commission on a bi-annual basis for three years.

Reginald McGlawn, and his brother, Anthony McGlawn. Reginald McGlawn is Broker's mortgage loan specialist, and Anthony McGlawn is Broker's insurance specialist. Broker also employs other McGlawn family members.

Broker specializes in arranging sub-prime mortgage loans for its customers. The prime lending market provides credit to those considered good credit risks. The sub-prime lending market provides credit to people the financial industry considers enhanced credit risks. These people generally have a flawed credit history or a debt-to-income ratio outside the range the financial industry considers acceptable for prime credit. As discussed hereafter, sub-prime interest rates are usually two to three percentage points higher than prime rates.

In 1998-2000, Broker arranged sub-prime mortgage loans for Complainants, who own real property in Philadelphia County. Broker is an African American-owned company. Complainants are African Americans who reside in predominantly African American neighborhoods.

In April 2001, Complainant Lucrecia Taylor (Taylor) filed a verified complaint with the Commission alleging Broker unlawfully discriminated against her in the terms and conditions of a real estate-related transaction and loan of money because of her race and the racial composition of her neighborhood, African American. Specifically, Taylor alleged Broker targeted her, as an African American, for a mortgage loan transaction containing predatory and unfair terms in violation of the Act's loan and real estate transaction provisions. Significantly, Taylor stated her allegations were made not only on her own behalf, but on behalf of all other similarly situated persons affected by Broker's discriminatory practices. After the pleadings were closed, the Commission notified Taylor and Broker that probable cause existed to credit Taylor's allegations.

In August 2002, Complainant Lynn Poindexter (Poindexter) filed a like complaint against Broker on behalf of herself and all other similarly situated persons. The Commission subsequently found probable cause existed to credit Poindexter's allegations. The Commission consolidated the two cases....

The Commission was thereafter able to identify other individuals affected by Broker's alleged discriminatory practices....

B.

In its decision, the Commission found Broker engaged in predatory brokering activities regarding all Complainants. Those actions resulted in unfair and predatory mortgage loans. It also found Broker engaged in an aggressive marketing plan targeting African Americans and African American neighborhoods in the Philadelphia area. Nearly all of Complainants contacted Broker in response to radio, television and newspaper advertisements.

Broker's predatory practices, the Commission noted, included arranging loans containing onerous terms such as high interest rates, pre-payment penalties, balloon payments and mandatory arbitration clauses. In addition, Broker charged Complainants high broker fees, undisclosed fees, yield spread premiums and various other additional closing costs. Broker's predatory practices also included falsification of information on loan documents, failure to disclose information regarding terms of the loan, and high pressure sales tactics.

... The seminal case prohibiting reverse redlining is _Hargraves v. Capital City Mortgage Corp._, 140 F.Supp.2d 7 (D.D.C.2000). There, the United States District Court adopted a two-pronged test for discrimination under the FHA [Fair Housing Act] based on reverse redlining. First, the plaintiffs must establish the defendant's lending practices and loan terms were predatory and unfair. *Hargraves*. Second, the plaintiffs must establish that defendant intentionally targeted them because of their race or that the defendant's lending practices had a disparate impact on the basis of race.

Citing *Hargraves* and the opinions of Complainants' experts, the Commission concluded Complainants established a prima facie reverse redlining claim against Broker under the *Hargraves* test. The Commission rejected Broker's arguments that (1) it did not discriminate because it did not arrange loans for non-African Americans on more preferable terms, (2) it had a legitimate business necessity for its actions, (3) it is not responsible for the terms and conditions of the loans or the disclosure of information relating to the loans, and (4) all mortgage brokers are predators.

As a result, the Commission held Respondents violated the loan provisions and the real estate transaction provisions of the Act by unlawfully discriminating against Complainants in the terms and conditions of real estate-related transactions.... .

III. SUBSTANTIAL EVIDENCE

Respondents ... assert the Commission's conclusion Broker engaged in reverse redlining is not supported by substantial evidence.[14] In particular, Respondents maintain the evidence does not show Broker engaged in predatory lending practices or targeted African Americans.

"It is well settled that the party asserting discrimination bears the burden of proving a prima facie case of discrimination." "Once a prima facie case is established, a rebuttable presumption of discrimination arises." "The

---

[14] "Substantial evidence is such relevant evidence as a reasonable mind might accept as adequate to support a conclusion." "Further, substantial evidence supporting a finding of racial discrimination may be circumstantial and based on inferences."

burden then shifts to the defendant to show some legitimate, nondiscriminatory reason for its action." . . .

A. Predatory Lending

Respondents first argue Broker did not engage in predatory or unfair lending practices because it did not approve Complainants' loans or lend them the money. Therefore, they were not responsible either for the terms and conditions of Complainants' loans or for the disclosure of information related to the loans. Those responsibilities belong to the lending institutions that set the terms and approved the loans.

The Commission accepted the testimony of Complainants' expert witnesses. Michelle Lewis, President and Chief Executive Officer of Northwest Counseling Service, Inc. (Complainants' first expert), stated that a mortgage broker is significantly involved in making the loan. The broker is the middleman who creates the loan opportunity. The broker's customer relies on the broker's expertise in lending matters and has an expectation that the broker will be able to obtain the best available deal.

The Commission also relied on Ira Goldstein, Director of Public Policy and Program Assessment for the Reinvestment Fund (Complainants' second expert), who testified that, in brokered transactions, the broker's customer--the borrower, never actually meets the lender. As a result, in the borrower's mind, the broker is the lender. Complainants' second expert also testified that in loan transactions where a yield spread premium[17] is used, the broker plays a significant role in establishing the interest rate of the loan.

---

[17] In Taylor v. Flagstar Bank, FSB, 181 F.R.D. 509 (M.D.Ala.1998), the United States District Court defined "yield spread premiums" as:

> payments made by a mortgage lender to a mortgage broker on an "above par" loan brought to the lender by the broker. To be "above par" is to be above the going rate, to be above the lowest rate that a lender will offer without

As additional support for its determination, the Commission cited Reginald McGlawn's testimony. He testified, "[W]hen people come to us, I provide loans." Reginald McGlawn also testified he chooses which lender receives the borrower's loan application. He also stated he sets the broker fee and gives the borrower the option of using a yield spread premium, which has the effect of increasing the interest rate.

1.

There is substantial evidence to support the Commission's determination that Respondents engaged in brokering activities that resulted in predatory and unfair loans.

... Broker's activities were a substantial part of the loan transactions at issue. In particular, Broker selected which lender received Complainants' loan applications. Broker was the sole negotiator for Complainants with the ultimate lender. Also, Broker influenced the ultimate interest rates in loans involving yield spread premiums. Further, Broker received substantial sums directly from loan proceeds, such as broker fees and insurance premiums. As the Commission properly concluded, these items are considered terms of a loan transaction....

2.

We next review the Commission's determination that Respondents' practices were predatory and unfair. ...

In finding Broker arranged predatory and unfair loans for Complainants, the Commission applied the *Hargraves* definition of "predatory lending practices." The *Hargraves* Court stated predatory lending practices are indicated by loans with unreasonably high interest rates and loans based

---

charging "discount points." In crude terms, therefore, the yield spread premium is (allegedly) simply a payment made by the lender to the broker in return for the broker having brought the lender a high interest loan.

on the value of the asset securing the loan rather than the borrower's capacity to repay it. The Court also recognized predatory lending practices include "loan servicing procedures in which excessive fees are charged."

The Commission also noted the New Jersey Superior Court's decision in *Assocs. Home Equity Servs., Inc. v. Troup*, 343 N.J.Super. 254, 778 A.2d 529 (2001). The *Troup* Court explained the term "predatory lenders" refers to those lenders who target certain populations for credit on unfair or onerous terms. Characteristically, predatory loans do not fit the borrower either because the borrower's needs are not met or because the terms are so onerous there is a strong likelihood the borrower will be unable to repay the loan.

In determining what lending practices are predatory and unfair, the Commission also accepted as credible Complainants' experts opinions as to what constitutes a predatory loan. Complainants' first expert testified there are a number of loan features which are characteristic of a predatory loan. They include high interest rates, paying off a low interest mortgage with a high interest mortgage, payment of points, yield spread premiums, high broker fees, undisclosed fees, balloon payments, pre-payment penalties, arbitration clauses and fraud. A predatory and unfair loan may include any combination of these characteristics.

Complainants' second expert testified that, even assuming a borrower is an enhanced credit risk, the difference in interest rates between a sub-prime and prime market loan is usually no greater than three percentage points. Anything higher than a three-point difference is indicative of a predatory loan. This expert also testified predatory loan practices include, among other things: flipping (successive refinancing of the same loan); hiding critical terms, establishing loan terms the borrower cannot meet; packing (including unnecessary products such as insurance policies); charging improper fees for items outside the settlement sheet; creation of false documents; and failing to advise borrowers of their rescission rights.

The Commission examined the terms of Complainants' loans and their experiences with Respondents in light of the foregoing. We briefly review the Commission's findings regarding Complainants Taylor and Poindexter.

Taylor. Taylor contacted Broker in October 2000 in order to obtain a refinancing loan of $10,000.00 to make some emergency home repairs (leaky roof, doors and windows, plumbing repair). In 2000, she owed $7,300.00 on her home. Her home mortgage had a 3% interest rate with a monthly payment of $110.90. Taylor's sole income source was social security disability.

Broker arranged a 30-year mortgage loan for Taylor with Delta Funding Corporation (Delta) in the amount of $20,500.00 with a 13.09% interest rate. Taylor was not given an opportunity to review any of the documents before signing them. Taylor was told to sign the documents.

The Commission found Taylor's loan transaction had several predatory characteristics. Taylor's was charged $4,276.60 in total settlement costs, or approximately 20% of the loan.[20] Two days after Taylor signed the loan documents, her uncle reviewed them and advised her to cancel the loan. Taylor called Aaron McGlawn, a Broker employee, and stated she did not want the loan. He did not advise Taylor she could legally rescind the loan within a three-day period; rather, he told Taylor she could cancel the loan if she had the money to pay the people Broker already paid.

---

[20] Taylor was charged $440.00 for a broker fee and $410.00 for a yield spread premium. Taylor testified she was unaware her loan contained a yield spread premium or that it would raise her interest rate. Her loan also included a $370.31 charge for a homeowner's insurance policy even though she was covered by another policy. Taylor was unaware of this charge and stated her house was already insured. Taylor's settlement sheet also reflected charges for debts she did not owe at the time of closing, including a $83.81 water bill and two ambulance bills ($477.50 and $250.00). Though Broker told Taylor this money would be returned to her, she never received it.

The settlement sheet indicates Taylor received $8,902.07. At closing, Reginald McGlawn informed Taylor she owed an additional $1,200.00 fee because of where she lived. Anthony McGlawn cashed the check and gave Taylor the money. He then asked Taylor for the $1,200.00 fee. Taylor paid the fee out of the cash; but she was not given a receipt. This fee was not reflected on the settlement sheet.

Complainants' second expert reviewed Taylor's loan transaction. He noted several predatory characteristics. First, Taylor's 13.09% interest rate was substantially above the three-point spread between sub-prime and prime loans. The Commission noted Broker arranged a loan for Taylor at twice the amount she requested and increased her interest rate from 3% to 13.09%. Such loans are considered to be deceptive and detrimental.[21] In addition, Taylor's loan included an additional undisclosed $1,200.00 broker fee.

The Commission found Broker engaged in predatory brokering activities on Taylor's behalf. These Broker actions resulted in a predatory and unfair refinancing loan. This finding is supported by substantial evidence.

Poindexter. Poindexter testified by deposition that she acquired her home as a gift from her grandfather and owned it free and clear. She described the neighborhood as being African American.

In response to a radio advertisement, Poindexter contacted Broker to obtain a small loan to pay off her bills; she did not want a mortgage. She eventually met with Reginald McGlawn. Poindexter told him she was going to college and working part time at a grocery store.

---

[21] In addition to the higher interest rate, the Commission found Broker's charges for the homeowners' policy and broker fees to be predatory and unfair. It also found Broker's refusal to either inform Taylor of her rescission rights or permit her to cancel her loan within the three-day rescission period was a predatory practice intended to process the loan transaction despite Taylor's desire to cancel it.

During their conversations, Reginald McGlawn informed Poindexter she did not make enough money but that he would "take care of things." Broker subsequently submitted documentation to Gelt Financial Corporation indicating Poindexter had a second job as a receptionist with Ivory Towers, Contractors, Inc. Poindexter stated she did not prepare these documents, was never employed by Ivory Towers and was unaware of these documents.

Poindexter's settlement sheet indicates her loan was approved for $22,400.00. It listed a broker fee of $2,240.00 (10% of the loan amount) and a $423.87 charge for a homeowner's insurance policy. Poindexter's loan also contained a balloon payment of $20,193.79 and a pre-payment penalty. At the time she signed the documents, Poindexter was unaware of either the balloon payment or the pre-payment penalty. Prior to settlement, Poindexter never discussed the interest rate with Respondents. She did not have time to review the loan documents before signing them.

The Commission found Broker engaged in predatory brokering activities regarding Poindexter, which resulted in a predatory and unfair loan. This finding is supported by substantial evidence.

Similarly situated persons. The Commission also found Broker engaged in predatory brokering practices on behalf of the eight similarly situated persons (Brunson, Jackson, Slaughter, Jacobs, Hawkins, Miles, Watts and Norwood), which resulted in unfair and predatory loans. The Commission noted the terms of these individuals' mortgage loans, as well as their factual circumstances, were "disturbingly similar" to those of Taylor and Poindexter. These findings are also supported by substantial evidence.

In view of the foregoing, we conclude Complainants proved Respondents engaged in predatory and unfair lending practices. Respondents' actions resulted in onerous loans containing terms of a predatory nature designed to benefit Broker, not Complainants. Therefore, Complainants met the first requirement for proving a reverse redlining claim.

B. *Intentional Discrimination*

The second element of a reverse redlining claim is a showing that the defendant either intentionally targeted on the basis of race or that there was a disparate impact on the basis of race. Here, the Commission determined Broker intentionally targeted African Americans and African American neighborhoods. The Commission also found ample evidence of disparate impact.

... In reverse redlining cases, evidence of the defendant's advertising efforts in African American communities is sufficient to show intentional targeting on the basis of race.

The Commission reviewed Broker's advertisements. On its website, Broker states "[i]t is one of the first African American owned and operated Mortgage and Insurance Financial Services in Philadelphia and the surrounding area." Broker's website also states "[o]ur primary focus is to assist financially challenged customers in purchasing and or refinancing their existing mortgage, as well as providing various types of insurance."

In addition, Anthony McGlawn, Broker's co-founder and insurance specialist, testified Broker engaged in extensive advertising on radio and television, in the newspapers and in the yellow pages. Several of these sources are oriented toward African American audiences and readers. Reginald McGlawn also testified the majority of Broker's customers are African Americans.

... Complainants also testified the decision to contact Broker was influenced by the fact that it was an African American company. For example, both Taylor and Poindexter testified this fact played a role in their decisions to use Broker's services.

The record also indicates Broker's business activities have a disparate impact on African American neighborhoods. This can be established by statistical evidence. *Hargraves.* The Commission accepted the testimony of Radcliffe Davis, a Commission investigator (Investigator). In response to Taylor and Poindexter's complaints, Investigator visited Broker's office and reviewed 100 customer loan applications for things such as refinancing, debt consolidation and home improvement. Of those 100 applications, 66 identified the race of the applicant. Of those 66 applicants, 65 were African American.

In addition, Complainants' second expert testified he prepared a document mapping the 11 properties involved in this matter. Nine of these properties were in areas that have at least a 90% African American population. The other two areas have a 50-75% African American population.

Considering the foregoing, the Commission's conclusion regarding intentional discrimination is supported by substantial evidence and is in accord with applicable law. *Hargraves.* Complainants also established by statistical evidence that Broker's business activities had a disparate impact on African Americans and African American neighborhoods.

In sum, Complainants met their burden of establishing a prima facie reverse redlining claim against Broker.

C. Rebuttal

"Once a prima facie case is established, a rebuttable presumption of discrimination arises." "The burden then shifts to the defendant to show some legitimate, nondiscriminatory reason for its action." In predatory lending cases, the financial institution may avoid liability by showing its lending practices were legitimate.

Respondents contend Complainants did not prove Broker's business activities were discriminatory because they did not establish Broker made loans to non-African Americans on more preferable terms. This argument was rejected in *Hargraves*. Citing *Contract Buyers League v. F & F Investment, 300 F.Supp. 210 (N.D.Ill.1969)*, the *Hargaves* Court recognized that injustice cannot be permitted merely because it is visited exclusively upon African Americans. We adopt this reasoning now.

Respondents also argue that any mortgage broker which arranges sub-prime loans could be considered a predator. We disagree. The interest rates of Complainants' loans are far in excess of the three-point difference usually separating prime and sub-prime loans. In addition, Broker's high broker fees, undisclosed fees and padded closing costs benefited Broker, not Complainants. These types of loans do not serve the borrower's wants or needs. *See In re Barker* (broker's motivation for arranging this type of loan was not to serve borrower's interest, "but to serve its own interest of obtaining a handsome broker's fee.") 251 B.R. at 260. "Such self-dealing constitutes a flagrant violation of the Broker's fiduciary duties to the [borrower]."

Respondents further argue Broker had no legal obligation to ensure Complainants could repay their loans.

Whether or not a broker must ensure a client's ability to repay a loan, a broker cannot ignore circumstances suggesting an inability to repay. Indeed, one of the clearest indicators of a predatory and unfair loan is one which exceeds the borrower's needs and repayment capacity.

On several occasions, Broker arranged loans in excess of the amounts Complainants sought. Moreover, Broker discouraged several Complainants from canceling their loans within the three-day rescission period. Broker also submitted falsified documents with Complainants' loan applications indicating Complainants possessed greater income or assets than they really did. Broker's disregard of Complainants' ability to repay their loans strongly supports the Commission's decision to reject the legitimate practice defense.

Respondents also assert they did not target African Americans or African American neighborhoods. Rather, Respondents claim Complainants, who are poor credit risks, came to Broker after being turned down by other brokers.

... [N]early all Complainants contacted Broker in response to one of its radio, television or newspaper advertisements targeting individuals with poor credit. Further, Broker concentrated its advertising efforts in the African American media. The Commission did not err in concluding Broker intentionally targeted African Americans for sub-prime mortgage loans. *Hargraves.*

Accordingly, no error is evident in the Commission's rejection of the Respondents' legitimate practice defense.

[The court upheld damages constituting the amounts paid to the broker out of the loan proceeds for items that only benefited the broker, such as the disclosed and undisclosed broker fees and yield spread premiums. It remanded for further calculation of the damages constituting the difference between the total amount of interest Complainants would be paying as a result of the predatory loans and the total amount of interest they would have paid with a loan at the prevailing mortgage interest rate "realistically available" to them given their credit ratings.]

... Here, Complainants' testified regarding the emotional distress suffered as a result of their dealings with Broker. Taylor testified she no longer trusts anyone and does not socialize anymore. She further stated she frequently cries and suffers from anxiety-related sleep and appetite disturbances. All of these difficulties resulted from her dealing with Broker. The Commission awarded her $25,000.00.

Poindexter also testified she suffers from depression as a result of her dealings with Broker. Her self-esteem was shattered and she relives the experience with every payment. Poindexter further stated she suffers from headaches and sleeplessness. She feels like she was stabbed in the back by people she trusted. The Commission awarded Poindexter $15,000.00.

So low

The Commission reviewed each of the similarly situated Complainants' testimony regarding the emotional and physical distress they suffered as a result of their experiences with Broker and awarded each of them damages for humiliation and embarrassment.

Given the direct evidence of emotional distress as well as the circumstances of fraud, deceit, and betrayal of trust, we conclude the awards for embarrassment and humiliation were within the Commission's statutory authority. . . .

Notes and Questions

1. Some commentary on unaffordable mortgages asks "why would borrowers take out loans that were doomed to foreclosure?" Does the opinion offer any insights into this question? See Oren Bar-Gill, The Law, Economics and Psychology of Subprime Mortgage Contracts, 94 Cornell L. Rev. 1073 (2009); see also Jeff Sovern, Preventing Future Economic Crises Through Consumer Protection Law or How the Truth in Lending Act Failed the Subprime Borrowers, 71 Ohio St. L.J. 763 (2010) (arguing that the explanation of key terms, even in non-predatory loans, was simply insufficient for ordinary borrowers to understand). Here's another question: "why would *lenders* give out loans that were doomed to foreclosure?" As it turns out, given the collapse of the housing market, most foreclosures do not return enough to the lender to pay back the initial loan.

2. Resistance to helping homeowners at risk of foreclosure often focuses on the problem of "moral hazard" – if people weren't forced either to pay back the loans on the terms on which those loans were granted or to lose their homes, some argued, that would encourage irresponsible borrowing. More broadly: when we seek to hold one party responsible for harm, we often make another party less responsible. As a result of the subprime mortgage collapse, many banks failed or were bailed out by the federal government. However, homeowners generally were not bailed out.

3. For some larger context, consider this excerpt from Ta-Nehisi Coates' _The Case for Reparations_, Atlantic, May 2014:

> In 2010, Jacob S. Rugh, then a doctoral candidate at Princeton, and the sociologist Douglas S. Massey published a study of the recent foreclosure crisis. Among its drivers, they found an old foe: segregation. Black home buyers – even after controlling for factors like creditworthiness – were still more likely than white home buyers to be steered toward subprime loans. Decades of racist housing policies by the American government, along with decades of racist housing practices by American businesses, had conspired to concentrate African Americans in the same neighborhoods. ... [T]hese neighborhoods were filled with people who had been cut off from mainstream financial institutions. When subprime lenders went looking for prey, they found black people waiting like ducks in a pen.

> "High levels of segregation create a natural market for subprime lending," Rugh and Massey write, "and cause riskier mortgages, and thus foreclosures, to accumulate disproportionately in racially segregated cities' minority neighborhoods."

Plunder in the past made plunder in the present efficient. The banks of America understood this. In 2005, Wells Fargo promoted a series of Wealth Building Strategies seminars. Dubbing itself "the nation's leading originator of home loans to ethnic minority customers," the bank enrolled black public figures in an ostensible effort to educate blacks on building "generational wealth." But the "wealth building" seminars were a front for wealth theft. In 2010, the Justice Department filed a discrimination suit against Wells Fargo alleging that the bank had shunted blacks into predatory loans regardless of their creditworthiness. This was not magic or coincidence or misfortune. It was racism reifying itself. According to The New York Times, affidavits found loan officers referring to their black customers as "mud people" and to their subprime products as "ghetto loans."

"We just went right after them," Beth Jacobson, a former Wells Fargo loan officer, told The Times. "Wells Fargo mortgage had an emerging-markets unit that specifically targeted black churches because it figured church leaders had a lot of influence and could convince congregants to take out subprime loans."

In 2011, Bank of America agreed to pay $355 million to settle charges of discrimination against its Countrywide unit. The following year, Wells Fargo settled its discrimination suit for more than $175 million. But the damage had been done. In 2009, half the properties in Baltimore whose owners had been granted loans by Wells Fargo between 2005 and 2008 were vacant; 71 percent of these properties were in predominantly black neighborhoods.

4. African-American and other minority borrowers were disproportionately steered to expensive subprime loans even though they qualified for cheaper conventional loans – high-income African American borrowers were six times as likely to get subprime loans as white borrowers with similar incomes. However, it is not the case, as is sometimes asserted, that unwise loans to African-Americans driven by federal mandates for equality in lending were responsible for the crash. In fact, institutions subject to federal fair lending rules made loans which were less likely to default than loans from institutions that were not subject to such rules. David Min, Faulty Conclusions Based on Shoddy Foundations (Feb. 2011) National Consumer Law Center, Why Responsible Mortgage Lending Is a Fair Housing Issue   (Feb.   2012) (https://www.nclc.org/images/pdf/credit_discrimination/fair-housing-brief.pdf).

5. In recent years, legislatures and regulators have attempted to regulate mortgage lending to stamp out the worst origination abuses, such as the yield spread premium. Much regulation focuses on the concept of "suitability": loans that the borrowers are likely to be able to repay, rather than loans based merely on the market value of the house. Loans based on the value of property alone, without sufficient attention to borrower characteristics, encouraged lenders to believe that they could profit even in case of a default, or sometimes that they could profit even more from default than from payment. In 2014, the Consumer Financial Protection Bureau (CFPB) issued rules on high-cost loans and homeownership counseling, implementing the Home Ownership and Equity Protections Act and subsequent additions. (http://www.consumerfinance.gov/regulations/high-cost-mortgage-and-homeownership-counseling-amendments-to-

regulation-z-and-homeownership-counseling-amendments-to-regulation-x/) Under these rules, loans considered "high cost" are subject to a number of limitations; high cost loans are those that specify high interest rates, high fees rolled into the mortgage amount (as in *McGlawn*), or prepayment penalties that last more than 36 months or exceed more than 2% of the prepaid amount. Under the new rules, for high-cost loans, balloon payments are generally banned, with limited exceptions. Creditors are prohibited from charging prepayment penalties and financing points and fees. Late fees are restricted to four percent of the payment that is past due, and certain other fees are limited or banned. Before a lender gives a high-cost mortgage, they must confirm with a federally approved counselor that the borrower has received counseling on the advisability of the mortgage.

6. Whether or not borrowers are seeking high-cost loans, lenders are now subject to a rule requiring them to assess a borrower's ability to repay, though that rule does not cover home equity lines of credit, timeshare plans, reverse mortgages, or temporary loans. The lender must not use a "teaser" or introductory interest rate to calculate the borrower's ability to repay; for adjustable-rate mortgages, it must consider ability to repay under the highest possible rate allowed by the mortgage. Certain so-called "plain vanilla" mortgages – fixed-rate, fully amortized (with no balloon payments) loans for no longer than 30 years – are presumptively acceptable under the regulations. In addition, lenders have to make counseling information available to all borrowers. Although loan information remains complex, the CFPB has tested different versions of mandatory disclosures, trying to find the <u>most understandable ways</u> of communicating the costs and risks of mortgages to non-lawyers. See <u>CFPB Finalizes "Know Before You Owe" Mortgage Forms</u>, Nov. 20, 2013. Take a look at the

forms.   (http://www.consumerfinance.gov/newsroom/cfpb-finalizes-know-before-you-owe-mortgage-forms/) Now that you have read this far, can you understand them?

D.   The Mortgage Crisis

Predatory lending was a significant contributor to the housing crash of 2007-2008. Many people, whether or not they accept this proposition, believe that poor people were taking out the mortgages at issue. However, middle and high income borrowers took on more mortgage debt than poor people, and also contributed most significantly to the increase in defaults after 2007.   Manuel Adelino, Antoinette Schoar, & Felipe Severino, Loan Originations and Defaults in the Mortgage Crisis: Further Evidence (NBER Working Paper July 2015).

When home prices started to drop and defaults to accumulate, the mortgage-backed securities that had previously seemed so attractive to investors began to spread the damage widely, as payments dried up. The economic impact was multiplied by a variety of sophisticated financial instruments that, in the end, amounted to little more than bets that U.S. housing prices would never drop. When they did drop, the world economy did as well.

From 1942 to 2005, about 4% of mortgages were delinquent at any given time, and about 1% were in foreclosure. At the peak of the crisis in 2010, up to 15% of mortgages were delinquent, and 4.6% were in foreclosure. Foreclosures Public Data Summary Jan 2015. As of late 2014, less than 8% of mortgages were delinquent and more than 3% were in the foreclosure process, or about one million homes. The good news is that most of the still-troubled loans were originated before 2007, and new foreclosures are now less one-half of one percent of all mortgages. Still, between 2007 and 2015, about six million homes were sold at foreclosure sales. This foreclosure crisis has already outlasted the foreclosure crisis of the Great Depression.

Even homeowners who kept up with their payments often found themselves "underwater": owing more than their homes were worth. Nearly one-third of mortgaged homes were underwater in 2012, though the number dropped to 15.4% in early 2015. Homes with lower value were more likely to be underwater, contributing to income inequality. Michelle Jamrisko, *This Is the Housing Chart That Keeps One Economist Up at Night*, BloombergBusiness, Jun. 12, 2015. Unsurprisingly, underwater homeowners are substantially more likely to default on their mortgages than homeowners with equity, no matter the size of their monthly payments or their interest rates. Moreover, underwater homeowners who don't default find it very difficult to sell their homes, and are therefore constrained in where they can take jobs. This is a problem because job mobility historically has been a major contributor to improved economic prospects in the U.S.

Even when "strategic default" might be in a homeowner's best interest — where the homeowner is deeply underwater and lives in a non-recourse state, and alternative housing is readily available — Americans remain relatively unlikely to default if they have any alternatives. Most borrowers will run up credit card bills, drain retirement savings, and put off medical care to avoid default for as long as possible. Tess Wilkinson-Ryan, *Breaching the Mortgage Contract: The Behavioral Economics of Strategic Default*, 64 VAND. L. REV. 1547 (2011) (reporting that even though defaulting on a mortgage may be in an individual's financial self-interest, feelings of moral obligation may prevent or delay default). Under what circumstances might you counsel a client to engage in a strategic default? Default will have consequences for the defaulter's credit score and therefore possibly her ability to get other housing or even a job, depending on her location and her field of work. But then again, draining her retirement account, possibly only to postpone and not avoid foreclosure, will have negative repercussions as well.

E.   Foreclosure Abuses

One ongoing problem is that the complicated structure of post-securitization mortgage lending left responsibility for problems diffuse, and even put incentives in precisely the wrong places. Because the trusts that own the mortgages and package them into mortgage-backed securities are passive legal vehicles with no employees or activities of their own, they contracted with mortgage servicers, often divisions of the same banks that initially sponsored the mortgage originators. The basic job is straightforward: servicers collect payments from homeowners and pass them along to the trust that represents the investors. Servicers are also responsible for handling foreclosures. In exchange, servicers typically get a small percentage of the value of the outstanding loans each year in fees. For a $200,000 loan to a borrower with good credit, a servicer might collect about $50 per month, with income decreasing as the balance of the loan drops. Servicers also make money from the "float" – interest earned during the short time the servicer holds the loan payment.

It is standard for servicers to be contractually required to keep paying the trust every month, even when there's a default, until there's a foreclosure. This would seem a strong incentive to do everything possible to help homeowners avoid a default, which is usually what investors want. The holder of a mortgage loses an average $60,000 on a foreclosure, according to figures announced by the federal government.

But the systems weren't set up that way. Among other things, servicers hired very few people with the ability to work with borrowers to find an affordable repayment; they were largely set up to take in money and pass it on. When the crisis hit, they were overwhelmed with troubled loans. Further, at the beginning of the foreclosure crisis, servicers often took the position that they were contractually prohibited from negotiating with borrowers by their agreements with the trusts, which allegedly did not allow them to reduce mortgagors' nominal obligations without the consent of the trust. (Recall that the trusts are not functioning companies with humans making day-to-day decisions, so the servicers' position meant that *no one* could agree to a renegotiation.)

Separately, servicers had incentives that conflicted with borrowers' and investors' interests. Servicers can charge fees for late payments, title searches, property upkeep, inspections, appraisals and legal fees that can total hundreds of dollars each month and can all be charged against a homeowner's account. Servicers have first dibs on recouping those fees when a foreclosed home is sold, meaning they usually collect unless the home is essentially worthless. Moreover, when homeowners tried to catch up or make partial payments as they sought a renegotiated loan, servicers applied their payments first to the servicers' own fees rather than to the underlying loan. These fees can be lucrative. In 2010, major servicer Ocwen reported $32.8 million in revenue from late fees alone, representing 9 percent of its total revenue. Professor Levitin, who has done extensive work on the legal and business structures resulting from securitization, concluded that a loan kept in default for a year or two could prove more profitable to a servicer than a typical healthy, performing loan.

The following case involves a trustee rather than a typical servicer, but otherwise it provides a sense of the problems that can arise when participants in the mortgage transaction are indifferent to the welfare of mortgagors.

Klem v. Washington Mutual Bank
176 Wash.2d 771, 295 P.3d 1179 (Wash. 2013).

¶ 1 Dorothy Halstien, an aging woman suffering from dementia, owned a home worth somewhere between $235,000 and $320,000. At about the time she developed dementia, she owed approximately $75,000 to Washington Mutual Bank (WaMu), secured by a deed of trust on her home. Because of the cost of her care, her guardian did not have the funds to pay her mortgage, and Quality Loan Services (Quality), acting as the trustee of the deed of trust, foreclosed on her home. On the first day it could, Quality sold her home for $83,087.67, one dollar more than she owed, including fees and costs. A notary, employed by Quality, had falsely notarized the notice of sale by predating the notary acknowledgment. This falsification permitted the sale to take place earlier than it could have had the notice of sale been dated when it was actually signed.

¶ 2 Before the foreclosure sale, Halstien's court appointed guardian secured a signed purchase and sale agreement from a buyer willing to pay $235,000 for the house. Unfortunately, there was not enough time before the scheduled foreclosure sale to close the sale with that buyer. In Washington, the trustee has the discretion to postpone foreclosure sales. This trustee declined to consider exercising that discretion, and instead deferred the decision to the lender, WaMu. Despite numerous requests by the guardian, WaMu did not postpone the sale. A jury found that the trustee was negligent; that the trustee's acts or practices violated the Consumer Protection Act (CPA), chapter 19.86 RCW; and that the trustee breached its contractual obligations. The Court of Appeals reversed all but the negligence claim. We reverse the Court of Appeals in part and restore the award based upon the CPA. We award the guardian reasonable attorney fees and remand to the trial court to order appropriate injunctive relief.

FACTS

¶ 3 The issues presented require a detailed discussion of the facts. In 1996, Halstien bought a house on Whidbey Island for $147,500. In 2004, she borrowed $73,000 from WaMu, secured by a deed of trust on her home. That loan was the only debt secured by the property, which otherwise

Halstien owned free and clear. Unfortunately, by 2006, when Halstien was 74 years old, she developed dementia. At the time, Halstien's daughter and her daughter's boyfriend were living at the home with her.

¶ 4 Washington State's Adult Protective Services became concerned that Halstien was a vulnerable adult being neglected at home. After an investigation, protective services petitioned the court for the appointment of a professional guardian to protect Halstien. The court granted the petition and Dianne Klem, executive director of Puget Sound Guardians, was appointed Halstien's guardian in January 2007. Klem soon placed Halstien in the dementia unit of a skilled nursing facility in Snohomish County.

¶ 5 Halstien's care cost between $3,000 and $6,000 a month. At the time, Halstien received about $1,444 a month in income from Social Security and a Teamsters' pension. The State of Washington paid the balance of her care and is a creditor of her estate.

¶ 6 Halstien's only significant asset was her Whidbey Island home, which at the time was assessed by the county at $257,804. WaMu also had an appraisal indicating the home was worth $320,000, nearly four times the value of the outstanding debt. Klem testified that if she had been able to sell the home, she could have improved Halstien's quality of life considerably by providing additional services the State did not pay for.

¶ 7 Selling the home was neither quick nor easy. Even after Halstien was placed in a skilled care facility, her daughter still lived in the home (without paying rent) and both the daughter and her brother strongly opposed any sale. The record suggests Halstien's children expected to inherit the home and, Klem testified, getting the daughter and her family to leave "was quite a battle." Ultimately, Puget Sound Guardians prevailed, but before it could sell the home, it had to obtain court permission (complicated, apparently, by the considerable notice that had to be given to various state agencies and to family members, and because some of those entitled to notice were difficult to find), remove abandoned animals and vehicles, and clean up the property.

¶ 8 During this process Halstien became delinquent on her mortgage. Quality, identifying itself as "the agent for Washington Mutual," posted a notice of default on Halstien's home on or around October 25, 2007. The notice demanded $1,372.20 to bring the note current. The record establishes that the guardianship did not have available funds to satisfy the demand.

¶ 9 A notice of trustee sale was executed shortly afterward by Seth Ott for Quality. The notice was dated and, according to the notary jurat of "R. Tassle," notarized on November 26, 2007. However, the notice of sale was not actually signed that day. The sale was set for February 29, 2008.

¶ 10 This notice of sale was one of apparently many foreclosure documents that were falsely notarized by Quality and its employees around that time. There was considerable evidence that falsifying notarizations was a common practice, and one that Quality employees had been trained to do. While Quality employees steadfastly refused to speculate under oath how or why this practice existed, the evidence suggests that documents were falsely dated and notarized to expedite foreclosures and thereby keep their clients, the lenders, beneficiaries, and other participants in the secondary market for mortgage debt happy with their work. Ott acknowledged on the stand that if the notice of sale had been correctly dated, the sale would not have taken place until at least one week later.

¶ 11 On January 10, 2008, Puget Sound Guardians asset manager David Greenfield called Ott in his capacity as trustee. Greenfield explained that Halstien was in a guardianship and that the guardianship intended to sell the property. Greenfield initially understood, incorrectly, that the trustee would postpone the sale if Puget Sound Guardians presented WaMu with a signed purchase and sale agreement by February 19, 2008. Puget Sound Guardians sought, and on January 31, 2008, received, court permission to hire a real estate agent to help sell the house.

¶ 12 Unknown to Greenfield, Quality, as trustee, had an agreement with WaMu that it would not delay a trustee's sale except upon WaMu's express direction. This agreement was articulated in a confidential "attorney expectation document" that was given to the jury. This confidential document outlines how foreclosures were to be done and billed. It specifically states, "Your office is not authorized to postpone a sale without authorization from Fidelity or Washington Mutual." This agreement is, at least, in tension with Quality's fiduciary duty to both sides and its duty to act impartially. Cox v. Helenius, 103 Wash.2d 383, 389, 693 P.2d 683 (1985) (citing GEORGE E. OSBORNE, GRANT S. NELSON & DALE A. WHITMAN, REAL ESTATE FINANCE LAW § 7.21 (1979) ("[A] trustee of a deed of trust is a fiduciary for both the mortgagee and mortgagor and must act impartially between them.")).[3]

¶ 13 Regardless of what Washington law expected or required of trustees, David Owen, Quality's chief operations officer in San Diego, testified that Quality did what WaMu told it to do during foreclosures. Owen testified that there were two situations where Quality would postpone a sale without bank permission: if there was a bankruptcy or if the debt had been paid. Owen could not remember any time Quality had postponed a sale without the bank's permission.

¶ 14 By February 19, 2008, Puget Sound Guardians had a signed purchase and sale agreement, with the closing date set for on or about March 28, 2008. This was almost a month after the scheduled foreclosure sale, but

---

[3] Since then, the legislature has amended the deed of trust act to provide that the trustee owes a duty of good faith to both sides. LAWS OF 2008, ch. 153, § 1; RCW 61.24.010(4) (effective June 12, 2008).

well within the 120 day window a trustee has to hold the trustee's sale under RCW 61.24.040(6). Quality referred the guardians to the bank "to find out the process for making this happen." Klem testified Quality "told us on two occasions that they unequivocally could not assist us in that area, that only the bank could make the decision."

¶ 15 Puget Sound Guardians contacted WaMu, which instructed them to send copies of the guardianship documents and a completed purchase and sale agreement. Over the next few days, WaMu instructed the guardians to send the same documents to WaMu offices in Seattle, Washington, southern California, and Miami, Florida. Klem testified that Puget Sound Guardians called WaMu on "[m]any occasions," and that if the bank ever made a decision, it did not share what it was. The guardian also faxed a copy of the purchase and sale agreement to various WaMu offices on February 19, 21, 26, 27, and 28. In all, the guardian contacted Quality or WaMu over 20 times in the effort to get the sale postponed. Simply put, Quality deferred to WaMu and WaMu was unresponsive.

¶ 16 Accordingly, the trustee's sale was not delayed and took place on February 29, 2008. Quality, as trustee, sold the Halstien home to Randy and Gail Preston for $83,087.67, one dollar more than the amounts outstanding on the loan, plus fees and costs.[4] The Prestons resold the house for $235,000 shortly afterward.

¶ 17 Klem later testified it was "shocking when we found out that [the home] had actually been sold for $83,000.... Because we trusted that they would sell it for the value of the home." In previous cases where a ward's home had gone into foreclosure, Klem testified, either the trustee had postponed the sale to allow Puget Sound Guardians to sell the property or had sold the property for a reasonable price. Klem testified that if they

---

[4] [note 4] As of trial, Quality had not delivered that one dollar to the Halstien estate.

had just one more week, it was "very possible" that they could have closed the sale earlier.

¶ 18 In April 2008, represented by the Northwest Justice Project, Puget Sound Guardians sued Quality for damages on a variety of theories, including negligence, breach of contract, and violation of the CPA. Later, with permission of the court, Quality's California sister corporation was added as a defendant. Halstien died that December.

¶ 19 Quality defended itself vigorously on a variety of theories. Initially successfully, Quality argued that any cause of action based on the trustee's duties was barred by the fact Klem had not sought an injunction to enjoin the sale. The record suggests that it would have been impossible for the guardianship to get a presale injunction due to the time frame, the need for court approval, and the lack of assets in the guardianship estate. While Judge Monica Benton dismissed some claims based on the failure of the estate to seek an injunction, she specifically found that the negligence, breach of contract, and CPA claims could go forward.

¶ 20 The case proceeded to a jury trial. The heart of the plaintiff's case was the theory that Quality's acts and practices of deferring to the lender and falsifying dates on notarized documents were unfair and deceptive and that the trustee was negligent in failing to delay the sale. David Leen, an expert on Washington's deed of trust act, chapter 61.24 RCW, testified that it was common for trustees to postpone the sale to allow the debtors to pay off the default. He testified that under the facts of this case, the trustee "would absolutely have to continue the sale."

¶ 21 By contrast, Ott, representing Quality as trustee in this case, testified that he did not take into account whether the house was worth more than the debt when conducting foreclosures. When asked why, Ott responded, "My job was to process the foreclosure ... according to the state statutes." When pressed, Ott explained that he counted the days, prepared the forms, saw they were filed, and nothing more. He acknowledged that, prior to 2009, he would sometimes incorrectly date documents. He testified that he had been trained to do that. He also testified that Quality, as trustee, would not delay trustee sales without the lender's permission. And he testified that he had never actually read Washington's deed of trust statutes.[5]

¶ 22 The jury found for the plaintiff on three claims: negligence, CPA, and breach of contract. ... The jury determined that the damages on all three claims were the same: $151,912.33 (the difference between the foreclosure sale price and $235,000)....

¶ 24 Quality brought a blunderbuss of challenges to the trial court's decisions. ... The Court of Appeals concluded ... that the evidence was insufficient to uphold the breach of contract and CPA claims. ...

ANALYSIS

...

I. CPA CLAIMS

¶ 26 To prevail on a CPA action, the plaintiff must prove an "(1) unfair or deceptive act or practice; (2) occurring in trade or commerce; (3) public interest impact; (4) injury to plaintiff in his or her business or property; (5) causation." Hangman Ridge Training Stables, Inc. v. Safeco Title Ins. Co., 105 Wash.2d 778, 780, 719 P.2d 531 (1986). The plaintiff argues that both Quality's historical practice of predating notarized foreclosure documents and Quality's practice of deferring to the lender on whether to postpone most sales, satisfies the first element of the CPA. Deciding whether the first element is satisfied requires us to examine the role of the trustee in nonjudicial foreclosure actions. A deed of trust is a form of a mortgage, an age-old mechanism for securing a loan. 18 William B.

---

[5] This inspired a juror's question, "If you never read the statute, how did you know you were following it, following Washington law?" Ott responded that he relied on his training. ...

Stoebuck & John W. Weaver, Washington Practice: Real Estate: Transactions § 17.1, at 253, § 20.1, at 403 (2d ed. 2004). In Washington, it is a statutorily blessed "three-party transaction in which land is conveyed by a borrower, the 'grantor,' to a 'trustee,' who holds title in trust for a lender, the 'beneficiary,' as security for credit or a loan the lender has given the borrower." If the deed of trust contains the power of sale, the trustee may usually foreclose the deed of trust and sell the property without judicial supervision. Id. at 260–61; RCW 61.24.020; RCW 61.12. 090; RCW 7.28.230(1)....

A. Unfair or Deceptive Acts or Practices

¶ 28 The legislature has specifically stated that certain violations of the deed of trust act are unfair or deceptive acts or practices for purposes of the CPA. [The Supreme Court found that this list was not exclusive; other violations could be unfair or deceptive as determined by a common-law, evolutionary process: "'It is impossible to frame definitions which embrace all unfair practices. There is no limit to human inventiveness in this field. Even if all known unfair practices were specifically defined and prohibited, it would be at once necessary to begin over again'" (citation omitted).] ...

B. Failure To Exercise Independent Discretion To Postpone Sale

¶ 35 Until the 1965 deed of trust act, there was no provision in Washington law for a nonjudicial foreclosure. In 1965, the legislature authorized nonjudicial foreclosure for the first time, subject to strict statutory requirements. Because of the very nature of nonjudicial foreclosures, Washington courts have not shied away from protecting the rights of the parties. ...

¶ 36 The power to sell another person's property, often the family home itself, is a tremendous power to vest in anyone's hands. Our legislature has allowed that power to be placed in the hands of a private trustee, rather than a state officer, but common law and equity requires that trustee to be evenhanded to both sides and to strictly follow the law. This court has frequently emphasized that the deed of trust act "must be construed in favor of borrowers because of the relative ease with which lenders can forfeit borrowers' interests and the lack of judicial oversight in conducting nonjudicial foreclosure sales." We have invalidated trustee sales that do not comply with the act.

¶ 37 As a pragmatic matter, it is the lenders, servicers, and their affiliates who appoint trustees. Trustees have considerable financial incentive to keep those appointing them happy and very little financial incentive to show the homeowners the same solicitude. However, despite these pragmatic considerations and incentives

> under our statutory system, a trustee is not merely an agent for the lender or the lender's successors. Trustees have obligations to all of the parties to the deed, including the homeowner. RCW 61.24.010(4) ("The trustee or successor trustee has a duty of good faith to the borrower, beneficiary, and grantor."); Cox v. Helenius, 103 Wash.2d 383, 389, 693 P.2d 683 (1985) ("[A] trustee of a deed of trust is a fiduciary for both the mortgagee and mortgagor and must act impartially between them.") (citing George E. Osborne, Grant S. Nelson & Dale A. Whitman, Real Estate Finance LAW § 7.21 (1979)).

In a judicial foreclosure action, an impartial judge of the superior court acts as the trustee and the debtor has a one year redemption period. In a nonjudicial foreclosure, the trustee undertakes the role of the judge as an impartial third party who owes a duty to both parties to ensure that the rights of both the beneficiary and the debtor are protected. Cox, 103

Wash.2d at 389, 693 P.2d 683. While the legislature has established a mechanism for nonjudicial sales, neither due process nor equity will countenance a system that permits the theft of a person's property by a lender or its beneficiary under the guise of a statutory nonjudicial foreclosure.[10] An independent trustee who owes a duty to act in good faith to exercise a fiduciary duty to act impartially to fairly respect the interests of both the lender and the debtor is a minimum to satisfy the statute, the constitution, and equity, at the risk of having the sale voided, title quieted in the original homeowner, and subjecting itself and the beneficiary to a CPA claim.[11]

---

[10] Washington courts have a long tradition of guarding property from being wrongfully appropriated through judicial process. When "a jury ... returned a verdict which displeased [Territorial Judge J.E. Wyche] in a suit over 160 acres of land" he threatened to set aside their verdict and remarked, "'While I am judge it takes thirteen men to steal a ranch.'"

[11] We have not had occasion to fully analyze whether the nonjudicial foreclosure act, ch. 61.24 RCW, on its face or as applied, violates article I, section 3 of our state constitution's command that "[n]o person shall be deprived of life, liberty, or property, without due process of law." While article I, section 3 was mentioned in passing in Kennebec, Inc. v. Bank of the West, 88 Wash.2d 718, 565 P.2d 812 (1977), where we joined other courts in concluding that the Fourteenth Amendment does not bar nonjudicial foreclosures, no independent state constitutional analysis was, or has since been done. Certainly, there are other similar "self help" statutes for creditors that are subject to constitutional limitations despite the State's limited involvement. See, e.g., Culbertson v. Leland, 528 F.2d 426 (9th Cir.1975) (innkeeper's use of Arizona's innkeeper's lien statute to seize guest's property was under color of law and subject to a civil rights claim). "Misuse of power, possessed by virtue of state law and made possible only because the wrongdoer is clothed with the authority of state law, is action taken 'under color of state law.'" Id. at 428 (quoting United States v. Classic, 313 U.S. 299, 325–26, 61 S.Ct. 1031, 85 L.Ed. 1368 (1941)); accord Smith v. Brookshire Bros., Inc., 519 F.2d 93, 95 (5th Cir.1975) (exercise of statute that allowed merchant to detain suspected shoplifters subject to civil rights claim); Adams v. Joseph F. Sanson Inv. Co., 376 F.Supp. 61, 69 (D.C.Nev.1974) (finding Nevada's landlord lien act violated due process because it allowed landlord to seize tenant property without notice); Collins v. Viceroy Hotel Corp., 338 F.Supp. 390, 398 (N.D. Ill. 1972) (finding Illinois innkeepers' lien laws, which allowed an innkeeper to seize guest's property without notice, violated due process); Hall v. Garson, 430 F.2d 430, 440 (5th Cir. 1970) (exercise of a statute giving a landlord a lien over the tenant's property gave rise to a civil rights claim against private party).

¶ 38 The trustee argues that we "should not hold that it is unfair and deceptive either to honor a beneficiary's instructions not to postpone a sale without seeking its authorization, or to advise a grantor to contact her lender." We note that Quality contends that it did not have a practice of deferring to the lender but merely followed its "legally-mandated respect for its Beneficiary's instructions" and asserts that "[s]imply put, no competent Trustee would fail to respect its Beneficiary's instructions not to postpone a sale without first seeking the Beneficiary's permission." We disagree. The record supports the conclusion that Quality abdicated its duty to act impartially toward both sides.

¶ 39 Again, the trustee in a nonjudicial foreclosure action has been vested with incredible power. Concomitant with that power is an obligation to both sides to do more than merely follow an unread statute and the beneficiary's directions. If the trustee acts only at the direction of the beneficiary, then the trustee is a mere agent of the beneficiary and a deed of trust no longer embodies a three party transaction. If the trustee were truly a mere agent of the beneficiary there would be, in effect, only two parties with the beneficiary having tremendous power and no incentive to protect the statutory and constitutional property rights of the borrower.

¶ 40 We hold that the practice of a trustee in a nonjudicial foreclosure deferring to the lender on whether to postpone a foreclosure sale and thereby failing to exercise its independent discretion as an impartial third party with duties to both parties is an unfair or deceptive act or practice and satisfies the first element of the CPA. Quality failed to act in good faith to exercise its fiduciary duty to both sides and merely honored an agency relationship with one.

C. Predating notarizations

¶ 41 Klem submitted evidence that Quality had a practice of having a notary predate notices of sale. This is often a part of the practice known as "robo-signing." Specifically, in this case, it appears that at least from 2004–2007, Quality notaries regularly falsified the date on which documents were signed.

¶ 42 Quality suggests these falsely notarized documents are immaterial because the owner received the minimum notice required by law. This no-harm, no-foul argument again reveals a misunderstanding of Washington law and the purpose and importance of the notary's acknowledgment under the law. A signed notarization is the ultimate assurance upon which the whole world is entitled to rely that the proper person signed a document on the stated day and place. Local, interstate, and international transactions involving individuals, banks, and corporations proceed smoothly because all may rely upon the sanctity of the notary's seal. This court does not take lightly the importance of a notary's obligation to verify the signor's identity and the date of signing by having the signature performed in the notary's presence. Werner v. Werner, 84 Wash.2d 360, 526 P.2d 370 (1974). As amicus Washington State Bar Association notes, "The proper functioning of the legal system depends on the honesty of notaries who are entrusted to verify the signing of legally significant documents." While the legislature has not yet declared that it is a per se unfair or deceptive act for the purposes of the CPA, it is a crime in both Washington and California for a notary to falsely notarize a document. … A notary jurat is a public trust and allowing them to be deployed to validate false information strikes at the bedrock of our system. …

… ¶ 44 We hold that the act of false dating by a notary employee of the trustee in a nonjudicial foreclosure is an unfair or deceptive act or practice and satisfies the first three elements under the Washington CPA.

¶ 45 The trustee argues as a matter of law that the falsely notarized documents did not cause harm. The trustee is wrong; a false notarization is a crime and undermines the integrity of our institutions upon which all must rely upon the faithful fulfillment of the notary's oath. There remains, however, the factual issue of whether the false notarization was a cause of plaintiff's damages. That is, of course, a question for the jury. We note that the plaintiff submitted evidence that the purpose of predated notarizations was to expedite the date of sale to please the beneficiary. Given the evidence that if the documents had been properly dated, the earliest the sale could have taken place was one week later. [sic] The plaintiff also submitted evidence that with one more week, it was "very possible" Puget Sound Guardians could have closed the sale. This additional time would also have provided the guardian more time to persuade WaMu to postpone the sale. But given the trustee's failure to fulfill its fiduciary duty to postpone the sale, there is sufficient evidence to support the jury's CPA violation verdict, and we need not reach whether this deceptive act was a cause of plaintiff's damages....

Notes and Questions

1. What, if anything, is the relevance of the sale price of the home to the court's decision? Why would the bank bid a dollar more than what was owed on the loan?

2. *Klem* involves a variant on what is known as "robo-signing" – the creation of documents with important legal effects on foreclosure, without sufficient personal knowledge or even understanding by the person signing the document.

    Jay Patterson, a forensic accountant who has examined hundreds of mortgage loans in bankruptcy or foreclosure, concluded that "95 percent of these loans contain some kind of mistake," from an unnecessary $15 late fee to thousands of dollars in fees and charges stemming from a single mistake that snowballed into a wrongful foreclosure. Most of these cases resulted in defaults, but when they were litigated, the facts could be telling. For example, one bankruptcy case, *In re Stewart*, involved a home in Jefferson Parish,

New Orleans. Wells Fargo was the servicer. The debtor fell behind in her payments, and on September 12, 2005, Wells Fargo agents generated two opinions on the value of the home. Opinions require at least minimal inspection of the property. Stewart was charged $125 for each opinion. However, on September 12, 2005, Jefferson Parish was under an evacuation order due to the devastation then being wrought by Hurricane Katrina. These were only two of the numerous fees the bankruptcy judge found had been wrongly charged to Stewart.

What ought to be done to rein in servicer misbehavior of this sort?

F.   Chain of Title Problems

Klem features a foreclosure sale that did nothing to preserve the equity of the homeowner, as well as backdated documents that changed the time of sale. But documentation problems go much, much deeper than that evidenced in *Klem* – perhaps to the foundation of land title in the U.S.

U.S. Bank National Association, trustee vs. Antonio Ibanez
458 Mass. 637 (2011)

After foreclosing on two properties and purchasing the properties back at the foreclosure sales, U.S. Bank National Association (U.S.Bank), as trustee for the Structured Asset Securities Corporation Mortgage Pass-Through Certificates, Series 2006-Z; and Wells Fargo Bank, N.A. (Wells Fargo), as trustee for ABFC 2005-OPT 1 Trust, ABFC Asset Backed Certificates, Series 2005-OPT 1 (plaintiffs) filed separate complaints in the Land Court asking a judge to declare that they held clear title to the properties in fee simple. We agree with the judge that the plaintiffs, who were not the original mortgagees, failed to make the required showing that they were the holders of the mortgages at the time of foreclosure. As a result, they did not demonstrate that the foreclosure sales were valid to convey title to the subject properties, and their requests for a declaration of clear title were properly denied.

Procedural history. On July 5, 2007, U.S. Bank, as trustee, foreclosed on the mortgage of Antonio Ibanez, and purchased the Ibanez property at the foreclosure sale. On the same day, Wells Fargo, as trustee, foreclosed on the mortgage of Mark and Tammy LaRace, and purchased the LaRace property at that foreclosure sale.

In September and October of 2008, U.S. Bank and Wells Fargo brought separate actions in the Land Court under G.L. c. 240, § 6, which authorizes actions "to quiet or establish the title to land situated in the commonwealth or to remove a cloud from the title thereto." The two complaints sought identical relief: (1) a judgment that the right, title, and interest of the mortgagor (Ibanez or the LaRaces) in the property was extinguished by the foreclosure; (2) a declaration that there was no cloud on title arising from publication of the notice of sale in the Boston Globe; and (3) a declaration that title was vested in the plaintiff trustee in fee simple. U.S. Bank and Wells Fargo each asserted in its complaint that it had become the holder of the respective mortgage through an assignment made after the foreclosure sale.

In both cases, the mortgagors--Ibanez and the LaRaces--did not initially answer the complaints, and the plaintiffs moved for entry of default judgment... .

On March 26, 2009, judgment was entered against the plaintiffs. The judge ruled that the foreclosure sales were invalid because, in violation of G.L. c. 244, § 14, the notices of the foreclosure sales named U.S. Bank (in the Ibanez foreclosure) and Wells Fargo (in the LaRace foreclosure) as the mortgage holders where they had not yet been assigned the mortgages. The judge found, based on each plaintiff's assertions in its complaint, that the plaintiffs acquired the mortgages by assignment only after the foreclosure sales and thus had no interest in the mortgages being foreclosed at the time of the publication of the notices of sale or at the time of the foreclosure sales.[8]

The plaintiffs then moved to vacate the judgments. At a hearing on the motions on April 17, 2009, the plaintiffs conceded that each complaint alleged a postnotice, postforeclosure sale assignment of the mortgage at issue, but they now represented to the judge that documents might exist that could show a prenotice, preforeclosure sale assignment of the mortgages. The judge granted the plaintiffs leave to produce such documents, provided they were produced in the form they existed in at the time the foreclosure sale was noticed and conducted. In response, the plaintiffs submitted hundreds of pages of documents to the judge, which they claimed established that the mortgages had been assigned to them before the foreclosures. Many of these documents related to the creation of the securitized mortgage pools in which the Ibanez and LaRace mortgages were purportedly included.

The judge denied the plaintiffs' motions to vacate judgment on October 14, 2009, concluding that the newly submitted documents did not alter the conclusion that the plaintiffs were not the holders of the respective mortgages at the time of foreclosure. We granted the parties' applications for direct appellate review.

---

[8] In the third case, LaSalle Bank National Association, trustee for the certificate holders of Bear Stearns Asset Backed Securities I, LLC Asset-Backed Certificates, Series 2007-HE2 vs. Freddy Rosario, the judge concluded that the mortgage foreclosure "was not rendered invalid by its failure to record the assignment reflecting its status as holder of the mortgage prior to the foreclosure since it was, in fact, the holder by assignment at the time of the foreclosure, it truthfully claimed that status in the notice, and it could have produced proof of that status (the unrecorded assignment) if asked."

Factual background. We discuss each mortgage separately, describing when appropriate what the plaintiffs allege to have happened and what the documents in the record demonstrate.

The Ibanez mortgage. On December 1, 2005, Antonio Ibanez took out a $103,500 loan for the purchase of property at 20 Crosby Street in Springfield, secured by a mortgage to the lender, Rose Mortgage, Inc. (Rose Mortgage). The mortgage was recorded the following day. Several days later, Rose Mortgage executed an assignment of this mortgage in blank, that is, an assignment that did not specify the name of the assignee.[11] The blank space in the assignment was at some point stamped with the name of Option One Mortgage Corporation (Option One) as the assignee, and that assignment was recorded on June 7, 2006. Before the recording, on January 23, 2006, Option One executed an assignment of the Ibanez mortgage in blank.

According to U.S. Bank, Option One assigned the Ibanez mortgage to Lehman Brothers Bank, FSB, which assigned it to Lehman Brothers Holdings Inc., which then assigned it to the Structured Asset Securities Corporation,[12] which then assigned the mortgage, pooled with approximately 1,220 other mortgage loans, to U.S. Bank, as trustee for the Structured Asset Securities Corporation Mortgage Pass-Through Certificates, Series 2006-Z. With this last assignment, the Ibanez and other loans were pooled into a trust and converted into mortgage-backed securities that can be bought and sold by investors--a process known as securitization.

---

[11] This signed and notarized document states: "FOR VALUE RECEIVED, the undersigned hereby grants, assigns and transfers to _____ all beneficial interest under that certain Mortgage dated December 1, 2005 executed by Antonio Ibanez...."

[12]   The Structured Asset Securities Corporation is a wholly owned direct subsidiary of Lehman Commercial Paper Inc., which is in turn a wholly owned, direct subsidiary of Lehman Brothers Holdings Inc.

For ease of reference, the chain of entities through which the Ibanez mortgage allegedly passed before the foreclosure sale is:

Rose Mortgage, Inc. (originator)
↓
Option One Mortgage Corporation (record holder)
↓
Lehman Brothers Bank, FSB
↓
Lehman Brothers Holdings Inc. (seller)
↓
Structured Asset Securities Corporation (depositor)
↓
U.S. Bank National Association, as trustee for the Structured Asset Securities Corporation Mortgage Pass-Through Certificates, Series 2006-Z

According to U.S. Bank, the assignment of the Ibanez mortgage to U.S. Bank occurred pursuant to a December 1, 2006, trust agreement, which is not in the record. What is in the record is the private placement memorandum (PPM), dated December 26, 2006, a 273-page, unsigned offer of mortgage-backed securities to potential investors. The PPM describes the mortgage pools and the entities involved, and summarizes the provisions of the trust agreement, including the representation that mortgages "will be" assigned into the trust. According to the PPM, "[e]ach transfer of a Mortgage Loan from the Seller [Lehman Brothers Holdings Inc.] to the Depositor [Structured Asset Securities Corporation] and from the Depositor to the Trustee [U.S. Bank] will be intended to be a sale of that Mortgage Loan and will be reflected as such in the Sale and Assignment Agreement and the Trust Agreement, respectively." The PPM also specifies that "[e]ach Mortgage Loan will be identified in a schedule appearing as an exhibit to the Trust Agreement." However, U.S. Bank did not provide the judge with any mortgage schedule identifying the Ibanez loan as among the mortgages that were assigned in the trust agreement.

On April 17, 2007, U.S. Bank filed a complaint to foreclose on the Ibanez mortgage in the Land Court under the Servicemembers Civil Relief Act (Servicemembers Act), which restricts foreclosures against active duty members of the uniformed services.[13] In the complaint, U.S. Bank represented that it was the "owner (or assignee) and holder" of the mortgage given by Ibanez for the property. A judgment issued on behalf of U.S. Bank on June 26, 2007, declaring that the mortgagor was not entitled to protection from foreclosure under the Servicemembers Act. In June, 2007, U.S. Bank also caused to be published in the Boston Globe the notice of the foreclosure sale required by G.L. c. 244, § 14. The notice identified U.S. Bank as the "present holder" of the mortgage.

At the foreclosure sale on July 5, 2007, the Ibanez property was purchased by U.S. Bank, as trustee for the securitization trust, for $94,350, a value significantly less than the outstanding debt and the estimated market value of the property. The foreclosure deed (from U.S. Bank, trustee, as the purported holder of the mortgage, to U.S. Bank, trustee, as the purchaser) and the statutory foreclosure affidavit were recorded on May 23, 2008. On September 2, 2008, more than one year after the sale, and more than five months after recording of the sale, American Home Mortgage Servicing, Inc., "as successor-in-interest" to Option One, which was until then the record holder of the Ibanez mortgage, executed a written assignment of that mortgage to U.S. Bank, as trustee for the securitization trust. This assignment was recorded on September 11, 2008.

---

[13] As implemented in Massachusetts, a mortgage holder is required to go to court to obtain a judgment declaring that the mortgagor is not a beneficiary of the Servicemembers Act before proceeding to foreclosure. St.1943, c. 57, as amended through St.1998, c. 142.

The LaRace mortgage. On May 19, 2005, Mark and Tammy LaRace gave a mortgage for the property at 6 Brookburn Street in Springfield to Option One as security for a $103,200 loan; the mortgage was recorded that same day. On May 26, 2005, Option One executed an assignment of this mortgage in blank.

According to Wells Fargo, Option One later assigned the LaRace mortgage to Bank of America in a July 28, 2005, flow sale and servicing agreement. Bank of America then assigned it to Asset Backed Funding Corporation (ABFC) in an October 1, 2005, mortgage loan purchase agreement. Finally, ABFC pooled the mortgage with others and assigned it to Wells Fargo, as trustee for the ABFC 2005-OPT 1 Trust, ABFC Asset-Backed Certificates, Series 2005-OPT 1, pursuant to a pooling and servicing agreement (PSA).

For ease of reference, the chain of entities through which the LaRace mortgage allegedly passed before the foreclosure sale is:

Option One Mortgage Corporation (originator and record holder)
↓
Bank of America
↓
Asset Backed Funding Corporation (depositor)
↓
Wells Fargo, as trustee for the ABFC 2005-OPT 1, ABFC Asset-Backed Certificates, Series 2005-OPT 1

Wells Fargo did not provide the judge with a copy of the flow sale and servicing agreement, so there is no document in the record reflecting an assignment of the LaRace mortgage by Option One to Bank of America. The plaintiff did produce an unexecuted copy of the mortgage loan purchase agreement, which was an exhibit to the PSA. The mortgage loan purchase agreement provides that Bank of America, as seller, "does hereby agree to and does hereby sell, assign, set over, and otherwise convey to the Purchaser [ABFC], without recourse, on the Closing Date … all of its right, title and interest in and to each Mortgage Loan." The agreement makes reference to a schedule listing the assigned mortgage loans, but this schedule is not in the record, so there was no document before the judge showing that the LaRace mortgage was among the mortgage loans assigned to the ABFC.

Wells Fargo did provide the judge with a copy of the PSA, which is an agreement between the ABFC (as depositor), Option One (as servicer), and Wells Fargo (as trustee), but this copy was downloaded from the Securities and Exchange Commission website and was not signed. The PSA provides that the depositor "does hereby transfer, assign, set over and otherwise convey to the Trustee, on behalf of the Trust … all the right, title and interest of the Depositor … in and to … each Mortgage Loan identified on the Mortgage Loan Schedules," and "does hereby deliver" to the trustee the original mortgage note, an original mortgage assignment "in form and substance acceptable for recording," and other documents pertaining to each mortgage.

The copy of the PSA provided to the judge did not contain the loan schedules referenced in the agreement. Instead, Wells Fargo submitted a schedule that it represented identified the loans assigned in the PSA, which did not include property addresses, names of mortgagors, or any number that corresponds to the loan number or servicing number on the LaRace mortgage. Wells Fargo contends that a loan with the LaRace property's zip code and city is the LaRace mortgage loan because the payment history and loan amount matches the LaRace loan.

On April 27, 2007, Wells Fargo filed a complaint under the Servicemembers Act in the Land Court to foreclose on the LaRace mortgage. The complaint represented Wells Fargo as the "owner (or assignee) and holder" of the mortgage given by the LaRaces for the property. A judgment issued on behalf of Wells Fargo on July 3, 2007, indicating that the LaRaces were not beneficiaries of the Servicemembers Act and that foreclosure could proceed in accordance with the terms of the power of sale. In June, 2007, Wells Fargo caused to be published in the Boston Globe the statutory notice of sale, identifying itself as the "present holder" of the mortgage.

At the foreclosure sale on July 5, 2007, Wells Fargo, as trustee, purchased the LaRace property for $120,397.03, a value significantly below its estimated market value. Wells Fargo did not execute a statutory foreclosure affidavit or foreclosure deed until May 7, 2008. That same day, Option One, which was still the record holder of the LaRace mortgage, executed an assignment of the mortgage to Wells Fargo as trustee; the assignment was recorded on May 12, 2008. Although executed ten months after the foreclosure sale, the assignment declared an effective date of April 18, 2007, a date that preceded the publication of the notice of sale and the foreclosure sale.

Discussion. The plaintiffs brought actions under G.L. c. 240, § 6, seeking declarations that the defendant mortgagors' titles had been extinguished and that the plaintiffs were the fee simple owners of the foreclosed properties. As such, the plaintiffs bore the burden of establishing their entitlement to the relief sought. To meet this burden, they were required "not merely to demonstrate better title ... than the defendants possess, but ... to prove sufficient title to succeed in [the] action." There is no question that the relief the plaintiffs sought required them to establish the validity of the foreclosure sales on which their claim to clear title rested.

Massachusetts does not require a mortgage holder to obtain judicial authorization to foreclose on a mortgaged property. With the exception of the limited judicial procedure aimed at certifying that the mortgagor is not a beneficiary of the Servicemembers Act, a mortgage holder can foreclose on a property, as the plaintiffs did here, by exercise of the statutory power of sale, if such a power is granted by the mortgage itself.

Where a mortgage grants a mortgage holder the power of sale, as did both the Ibanez and LaRace mortgages, it includes by reference the power of sale set out in G.L. c. 183, § 21, and further regulated by G.L. c. 244, §§ 11-17C. Under G.L. c. 183, § 21, after a mortgagor defaults in the performance of the underlying note, the mortgage holder may sell the property at a public auction and convey the property to the purchaser in fee simple, "and such sale shall forever bar the mortgagor and all persons claiming under him from all right and interest in the mortgaged premises, whether at law or in equity." Even where there is a dispute as to whether the mortgagor was in default or whether the party claiming to be the mortgage holder is the true mortgage holder, the foreclosure goes forward unless the mortgagor files an action and obtains a court order enjoining the foreclosure.

Recognizing the substantial power that the statutory scheme affords to a mortgage holder to foreclose without immediate judicial oversight, we adhere to the familiar rule that "one who sells under a power [of sale] must follow strictly its terms. If he fails to do so there is no valid execution of the power, and the sale is wholly void."

. . .

One of the terms of the power of sale that must be strictly adhered to is the restriction on who is entitled to foreclose. The "statutory power of sale" can be exercised by "the mortgagee or his executors, administrators, successors or assigns." Under G.L. c. 244, § 14, "[t]he mortgagee or person having his estate in the land mortgaged, or a person authorized by the power of sale, or the attorney duly authorized by a writing under seal, or the legal guardian or conservator of such mortgagee or person acting in the name of such mortgagee or person" is empowered to exercise the statutory power of sale. Any effort to foreclose by a party lacking "jurisdiction and authority" to carry out a foreclosure under these statutes is void. See Davenport v. HSBC Bank USA, 275 Mich.App. 344, 347-348 (2007) (attempt to foreclose by party that had not yet been assigned mortgage results in "structural defect that goes to the very heart of defendant's ability to foreclose by advertisement," and renders foreclosure sale void).

A related statutory requirement that must be strictly adhered to in a foreclosure by power of sale is the notice requirement articulated in G.L. c. 244, § 14. That statute provides that "no sale under such power shall be effectual to foreclose a mortgage, unless, previous to such sale," advance notice of the foreclosure sale has been provided to the mortgagee, to other interested parties, and by publication in a newspaper published in the town where the mortgaged land lies or of general circulation in that town. "The manner in which the notice of the proposed sale shall be given is one of the important terms of the power, and a strict compliance with it is essential to the valid exercise of the power." See Chace v. Morse, supra ("where a certain notice is prescribed, a sale without any notice, or upon a notice lacking the essential requirements of the written power, would be void as a proceeding for foreclosure"). Because only a present holder of the mortgage is authorized to foreclose on the mortgaged property, and because the mortgagor is entitled to know who is foreclosing and selling the property, the failure to identify the holder of the mortgage in the notice of sale may render the notice defective and the foreclosure sale void. See Roche v. Farnsworth, supra (mortgage sale void where notice of sale identified original mortgagee but not mortgage holder at time of notice and sale).

For the plaintiffs to obtain the judicial declaration of clear title that they seek, they had to prove their authority to foreclose under the power of sale and show their compliance with the requirements on which this authority rests. Here, the plaintiffs were not the original mortgagees to whom the power of sale was granted; rather, they claimed the authority to foreclose as the eventual assignees of the original mortgagees. Under the plain language of G.L. c. 183, § 21, and G.L. c. 244, § 14, the plaintiffs had the authority to exercise the power of sale contained in the Ibanez and LaRace mortgages only if they were the assignees of the mortgages at the time of the notice of sale and the subsequent foreclosure sale. See In re Schwartz, 366 B.R. 265, 269 (Bankr.D.Mass.2007) ("Acquiring the mortgage after the entry and foreclosure sale does not satisfy the Massachusetts statute"). See also Jeff-Ray Corp. v. Jacobson, 566 So.2d 885, 886 (Fla.Dist.Ct.App.1990) (per curiam) (foreclosure action could not be based on assignment of mortgage dated four months after commencement of foreclosure proceeding).

The plaintiffs claim that the securitization documents they submitted establish valid assignments that made them the holders of the Ibanez and LaRace mortgages before the notice of sale and the foreclosure sale. We turn, then, to the documentation submitted by the plaintiffs to determine whether it met the requirements of a valid assignment.

Like a sale of land itself, the assignment of a mortgage is a conveyance of an interest in land that requires a writing signed by the grantor. In a "title theory state" like Massachusetts, a mortgage is a transfer of legal title in a property to secure a debt. Therefore, when a person borrows money to purchase a home and gives the lender a mortgage, the homeowner-mortgagor retains only equitable title in the home; the legal title is held by the mortgagee. See Vee Jay Realty Trust Co. v. DiCroce, 360 Mass. 751, 753 (1972), quoting Dolliver v. St. Joseph Fire & Marine Ins. Co., 128 Mass. 315, 316 (1880) (although "as to all the world except the mortgagee, a mortgagor is the owner of the mortgaged lands," mortgagee has legal title to property). Where, as here, mortgage loans are pooled together in a trust and converted into mortgage-backed securities, the underlying promissory notes serve as financial instruments generating a potential income stream for investors, but the mortgages securing these notes are still legal title to someone's home or farm and must be treated as such.

Focusing first on the Ibanez mortgage, U.S. Bank argues that it was assigned the mortgage under the trust agreement described in the PPM, but it did not submit a copy of this trust agreement to the judge. The PPM, however, described the trust agreement as an agreement to be executed in the future, so it only furnished evidence of an intent to assign mortgages to U.S. Bank, not proof of their actual assignment. Even if there were an executed trust agreement with language of present assignment, U.S. Bank did not produce the schedule of loans and mortgages that was an exhibit to that agreement, so it failed to show that the Ibanez mortgage was among the mortgages to be assigned by that agreement. Finally, even if there were an executed trust agreement with the required schedule, U.S. Bank failed to furnish any evidence that the entity assigning the mortgage--Structured Asset Securities Corporation--ever held the mortgage to be assigned. The last assignment of the mortgage on record was from Rose Mortgage to Option One; nothing was submitted to the judge indicating that Option One ever assigned the mortgage to anyone before the foreclosure sale. Thus, based on the documents submitted to the judge, Option One, not U.S. Bank, was the mortgage holder at the time of the foreclosure, and U.S. Bank did not have the authority to foreclose the mortgage.

Turning to the LaRace mortgage, Wells Fargo claims that, before it issued the foreclosure notice, it was assigned the LaRace mortgage under the PSA. The PSA, in contrast with U.S. Bank's PPM, uses the language of a present assignment ("does hereby ... assign" and "does hereby deliver") rather than an intent to assign in the future. But the mortgage loan schedule Wells Fargo submitted failed to identify with adequate specificity the LaRace mortgage as one of the mortgages assigned in the PSA. Moreover, Wells Fargo provided the judge with no document that reflected that the ABFC (depositor) held the LaRace mortgage that it was purportedly assigning in the PSA. As with the Ibanez loan, the record holder of the LaRace loan was Option One, and nothing was submitted to the judge which demonstrated that the LaRace loan was ever assigned by Option One to another entity before the publication of the notice and the sale.

Where a plaintiff files a complaint asking for a declaration of clear title after a mortgage foreclosure, a judge is entitled to ask for proof that the foreclosing entity was the mortgage holder at the time of the notice of sale and foreclosure, or was one of the parties authorized to foreclose under G.L. c. 183, § 21, and G.L. c. 244, § 14. A plaintiff that cannot make this modest showing cannot justly proclaim that it was unfairly denied a declaration of clear title.

We do not suggest that an assignment must be in recordable form at the time of the notice of sale or the subsequent foreclosure sale, although recording is likely the better practice. Where a pool of mortgages is assigned to a securitized trust, the executed agreement that assigns the pool of mortgages, with a schedule of the pooled mortgage loans that clearly and specifically identifies the mortgage at issue as among those assigned, may suffice to establish the trustee as the mortgage holder. However, there must be proof that the assignment was made by a party that itself held the mortgage. A foreclosing entity may provide a complete chain of assignments linking it to the record holder of the mortgage, or a single assignment from the record holder of the mortgage. The key in either case is that the foreclosing entity must hold the mortgage at the time of the notice and sale in order accurately to identify itself as the present holder in the notice and in order to have the authority to foreclose under the power of sale (or the foreclosing entity must be one of the parties authorized to foreclose under G.L. c. 183, § 21, and G.L. c. 244, § 14).

The judge did not err in concluding that the securitization documents submitted by the plaintiffs failed to demonstrate that they were the holders of the Ibanez and LaRace mortgages, respectively, at the time of the publication of the notices and the sales. The judge, therefore, did not err in rendering judgments against the plaintiffs and in denying the plaintiffs' motions to vacate the judgments.

We now turn briefly to three other arguments raised by the plaintiffs on appeal. First, the plaintiffs initially contended that the assignments in blank executed by Option One, identifying the assignor but not the assignee, not only "evidence[ ] and confirm[ ] the assignments that occurred by virtue of the securitization agreements," but "are effective assignments in their own right." But in their reply briefs they conceded that the assignments in blank did not constitute a lawful assignment of the mortgages. Their concession is appropriate. We have long held that a conveyance of real property, such as a mortgage, that does not name the assignee conveys nothing and is void; we do not regard an assignment of land in blank as giving legal title in land to the bearer of the assignment.

Second, the plaintiffs contend that, because they held the mortgage note, they had a sufficient financial interest in the mortgage to allow them to foreclose. In Massachusetts, where a note has been assigned but there is no written assignment of the mortgage underlying the note, the assignment of the note does not carry with it the assignment of the mortgage. Rather, the holder of the mortgage holds the mortgage in trust for the purchaser of the note, who has an equitable right to obtain an assignment of the mortgage, which may be accomplished by filing an action in court and obtaining an equitable order of assignment. [Barnes v. Boardman, 149 Mass. 106, 114, 21 N.E. 308 (1889)] ("In some jurisdictions it is held that the mere transfer of the debt, without any assignment or even mention of the mortgage, carries the mortgage with it, so as to enable the assignee to assert his title in an action at law.... This doctrine has not prevailed in Massachusetts, and the tendency of the decisions here has been, that in such cases the mortgagee would hold the legal title in trust for the purchaser of the debt, and that the latter might obtain a conveyance by a bill in equity"). In the absence of a valid written assignment of a mortgage or a court order of assignment, the mortgage holder remains unchanged. This common-law principle was later incorporated in the statute enacted in 1912 establishing the statutory power of sale, which grants such a power to "the mortgagee or his executors, administrators, successors or assigns," but not to a party that is the equitable beneficiary of a mortgage held by another.

Third, the plaintiffs ... argue that the use of postsale assignments was customary in the industry, and point to Title Standard No. 58(3) issued by the Real Estate Bar Association for Massachusetts, which declares: "A title is not defective by reason of ... [t]he recording of an Assignment of Mortgage executed either prior, or subsequent, to foreclosure where said Mortgage has been foreclosed, of record, by the Assignee." To the extent that the plaintiffs rely on this title standard for the proposition that an entity that does not hold a mortgage may foreclose on a property, and then cure the cloud on title by a later assignment of a mortgage, their reliance is misplaced because this proposition is contrary to G.L. c. 183, § 21, and G.L. c. 244, § 14. If the plaintiffs did not have their assignments to the Ibanez and LaRace mortgages at the time of the publication of the notices and the sales, they lacked authority to foreclose under G.L. c. 183, § 21, and G.L. c. 244, § 14, and their published claims to be the present holders of the mortgages were false. Nor may a postforeclosure assignment be treated as a preforeclosure assignment simply by declaring an "effective date" that precedes the notice of sale and foreclosure, as did Option One's assignment of the LaRace mortgage to Wells Fargo. Because an assignment of a mortgage is a transfer of legal title, it becomes effective with respect to the power of sale only on the transfer; it cannot become effective before the transfer.

However, we do not disagree with Title Standard No. 58(3) that, where an assignment is confirmatory of an earlier, valid assignment made prior to the publication of notice and execution of the sale, that confirmatory assignment may be executed and recorded after the foreclosure, and doing so will not make the title defective. A valid assignment of a mortgage gives the holder of that mortgage the statutory power to sell after a default regardless whether the assignment has been recorded. Where the earlier assignment is not in recordable form or bears some defect, a written assignment executed after foreclosure that confirms the earlier assignment may be properly recorded. A confirmatory assignment, however, cannot confirm an assignment that was not validly made earlier or backdate an assignment being made for the first time. Where there is no prior valid assignment, a subsequent assignment by the mortgage holder to the note holder is not a confirmatory assignment because there is no earlier written assignment to confirm. In this case, based on the record before the judge, the plaintiffs failed to prove that they obtained valid written assignments of the Ibanez and LaRace mortgages before their foreclosures, so the postforeclosure assignments were not confirmatory of earlier valid assignments.

Finally, we reject the plaintiffs' request that our ruling be prospective in its application. A prospective ruling is only appropriate, in limited circumstances, when we make a significant change in the common law. We have not done so here. The legal principles and requirements we set forth are well established in our case law and our statutes. All that has changed is the plaintiffs' apparent failure to abide by those principles and requirements in the rush to sell mortgage-backed securities.

Conclusion. For the reasons stated, we agree with the judge that the plaintiffs did not demonstrate that they were the holders of the Ibanez and LaRace mortgages at the time that they foreclosed these properties, and therefore failed to demonstrate that they acquired fee simple title to these properties by purchasing them at the foreclosure sale.

Judgments affirmed.

CORDY, J. (concurring, with whom Botsford, J., joins).

I concur fully in the opinion of the court, and write separately only to underscore that what is surprising about these cases is not the statement of principles articulated by the court regarding title law and the law of foreclosure in Massachusetts, but rather the utter carelessness with which the plaintiff banks documented the titles to their assets. There is no dispute that the mortgagors of the properties in question had defaulted on their obligations, and that the mortgaged properties were subject to foreclosure. Before commencing such an action, however, the holder of an assigned mortgage needs to take care to ensure that his legal paperwork is in order. Although there was no apparent actual unfairness here to the mortgagors, that is not the point. Foreclosure is a powerful act with significant consequences, and Massachusetts law has always required that it proceed strictly in accord with the statutes that govern it. As the opinion of the court notes, such strict compliance is necessary because Massachusetts is both a title theory State and allows for extrajudicial foreclosure.

The type of sophisticated transactions leading up to the accumulation of the notes and mortgages in question in these cases and their securitization, and, ultimately the sale of mortgaged-backed securities, are not barred nor even burdened by the requirements of Massachusetts law. The plaintiff banks, who brought these cases to clear the titles that they acquired at their own foreclosure sales, have simply failed to prove that the underlying assignments of the mortgages that they allege (and would have) entitled them to foreclose ever existed in any legally cognizable form before they exercised the power of sale that accompanies those assignments. The court's opinion clearly states that such assignments do not need to be in recordable form or recorded before the foreclosure, but they do have to have been effectuated....

Notes and Questions

1. In a "title" theory state like Massachusetts, the mortgagee in theory has legal title to the property, though the mortgagee holds it in trust for the mortgagor, who has equitable title. The alternative "lien" theory holds that legal title remains in the mortgagor, and the mortgage is merely a lien on the property. Does the difference between title theory and lien theory make any difference in this case? (Because of the mortgagor's equitable title in title theory states, the general modern answer is that there is no difference in the governing legal principles, but the reasoning may vary from state to state.) What about the fact that the foreclosure was done through a nonjudicial power of sale — should that make a difference?

2. One of the reasons the court gives for its judgment is that, in Massachusetts, assignment in blank isn't allowed for an interest in land. Why might the legislature make such a rule? This is not the rule in all states, but amazingly the originators didn't pay much attention to state by state variations.

3. Who owns the houses at issue, after the opinion? What steps should the banks take now? What is the effect of Massachusetts' recording statute on a scenario in which a third party buys the property at the foreclosure sale and records?

4. Consider the following excerpt from Paul McMorrow, *A new act in foreclosure circus*, January 14, 2011, Boston Globe:

According to the real estate tracker the Warren Group, there have been more than 44,000 residential foreclosures recorded in Massachusetts since 2006. In the majority of those cases, the foreclosing bank turned around and re-sold the seized property. So there are now tens of thousands of Massachusetts residents living in homes that, until relatively recently, belonged to somebody else.

... I took a random sample of 30 foreclosure deeds from Chelsea (one of the cities hit hardest by foreclosures) since the beginning of 2006. Of those 30 foreclosure cases, 10 had paperwork on file with the Registry of Deeds that raised the sort of chain-of-custody concerns at the heart of the Ibanez decision. In one case, no mortgage was on file with the registry. Another showed no paperwork assigning the note to a mortgage servicer. In other cases, mortgage originators didn't sign off on documents transferring the notes into mortgage pools, or transfer paperwork was filed after a foreclosure occurred. All of the properties have since been re-sold.

That's not to say any of those foreclosures will or should be overturned in court. But it is an indication of how pervasive sloppy record-keeping was, and how many foreclosures could be challenged on technical grounds based on the recent SJC decision. And it presents a series of terrible questions to anyone who bought a foreclosed house from a big bank. Among them: Is my mortgage valid? Will I be able to refinance or sell my home? Do I even really own my house?

How would you go about answering McMorrow's questions for a client?

5. Consider also Abigail Field, *Lawyers' Carelessness Was Key to the Mortgage Mess*, DailyFinance, Feb. 1, 2011:

> The *Ibanez* case highlighted a basic, non-due-diligence problem too -- one that, according to bankruptcy and legal-aid attorneys I speak with, is occurring across the country. The banks' lawyers can't produce complete sets of securitization contracts even after being given the specific opportunity to do so. In various cases, the banks have submitted unsigned drafts. They've submitted signed copies of some contracts, but not even drafts of others. And they've submitted contracts without their exhibits, like a list of the mortgages being securitized.
>
> Every corporate deal I was ever involved with resulted in "closing sets," a series of binders containing every contract with each exhibit. ... [A] key part of the value lawyers add is keeping the documents in good order and accessible to their clients when needed.
>
> So, the issue of partial deal documents that came to light in *Ibanez* and continues to crop up elsewhere means one of three things:
>
> 1. Securitization deals were so carelessly done that, despite all the proper documents being created, closing sets don't exist.
> 2. Securitization deals were so carelessly done that not all the proper documents were created (such as lists of the mortgages involved) and so closing sets don't exist.
>
> 3. All the documents and closing sets are fine, and the big banks have grown so incompetent they can't give their

foreclosure attorneys deal documents that they do have or could get from their securitization counsel.

I'm not sure which of these is worst.

What *should* the banks' lawyers have done with the documents they had available to use in the foreclosure process?

6. Review the alleged chain of title for the Ibanez/US Bancorp mortgage. US Bancorp took the mortgage from a now-bankrupt subsidiary of the now-bankrupt firm Lehman Brothers. Getting an assignment from Lehman may be difficult or even impossible. Among other things, because Lehman is bankrupt, it may not transfer assets out of its estate to particular creditors without going through extensive proceedings that are designed to be fair to all the creditors. Regardless, an assignment from Lehman would be insufficient: there is still the undocumented Option One-Lehman transfer. It might be simplest for US Bancorp to go straight to Option One and ask for an assignment. But US Bancorp didn't buy the mortgage from Option One. There is no contractual relationship between those two entities and thus no duty on Option One to do everything necessary to ensure that US Bancorp has good title. Even if US Bancorp asks Option One for an assignment, Option One likely regarded the mortgage as sold to Lehman many years back and may not have appropriate records. Furthermore, Option One may consider any attempt to assign a mortgage that was already sold to Lehman to be legally risky; it will certainly want US Bancorp to indemnify it and likely to pay extra for the privilege of getting the assignment. This problem is not confined to loans that passed through Lehman (though there were a great many that did) – many companies involved in the mortgage bubble have entered bankruptcy or changed ownership, making documentation of the assignments all but impossible.

7. Given that the mortgages were concededly in default, is there any reason to insist on the formalities in cases like this? After all, the one thing we know is that the homeowners weren't paying what they owed. *See, e.g.,* Editorial, *The Politics of Foreclosure*, WALL ST. J., Oct. 9, 2010. *But see* Miller v. Homecomings Financial, LLC, 881 F. Supp. 2d 825, 832 (S.D.Tex. 2012) ("Banks are neither private attorneys general nor bounty hunters, armed with a roving commission to seek out defaulting homeowners and take away their homes in satisfaction of some other bank's deed of trust."); David A. Dana, *Why Mortgage "Formalities" Matter*, 24 LOY. CONSUMER L. REV. 505 (2012) (given the importance of the home, and of the rule of law, formalities matter, and may also deter future careless lending).

8. Sometimes the sloppiness in record-keeping led to truly astonishing errors. In a random audit on WaMu Mortgage Pass-Through Certificates, Mortgage Loan Trusts, one loan was found in 6 different trusts, another loan was found in five trusts' original SEC loan level data, 39 were listed in 3 trusts, and 503 were listed in two separate trusts. The most extreme example, a New York condo, appeared in 6 different trusts from May through November 2006. Gary Victor Dubin, <u>Securitized Distrust</u>, Mar. 15, 2012 (https://deadlyclear.wordpress.com/2012/03/15/securitized-distrust/).

9. Occasionally, evidence of these careless procedures appears in official title records. Recall that, in order to move the mortgage from its originator to its ultimate holder, an assignment was required – usually more than one, with a chain going from the originator, to the sponsor who lent the originator money to make

the loan, to the depositor that funded the sponsor, to the trust that ultimately held the mortgages as assets underlying the mortgage-backed securities it issued. Who exactly is the assignee in this record from Nassau County, New York?

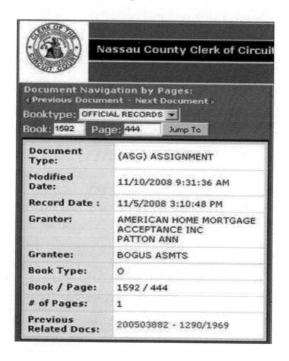

Note on Subsequent Purchasers

Bevilacqua v. Rodriguez, 460 Mass. 762, 955 N.E.2d 884 (2011), dealt with property owners with defective title resulting from *Ibanez*-style foreclosure problems earlier in the chain. In other words, the mortgagee (or, realistically, its representative/putative representative) had foreclosed in a manner held unlawful by *Ibanez*, then had sold the house again to a new buyer. The Massachusetts high court held that the new buyers could not clear title under the Massachusetts "try title" procedure, which is a way that an owner can quiet title and establish which of competing claims is valid. However, the court ruled, that procedure is only available to people who can plausibly claim to be owners. In *Bevilacqua*, the chain of title had been broken by the unsuccessful foreclosure before the purchase, and so the new buyer couldn't bring a plausible claim. This is not a terribly surprising result: if someone records a deed to the Brooklyn Bridge, then brings a try title claim to confirm her ownership, title to the bridge is not conveyed magically even if the true owner fails to show up.

The *Bevilacqua* court left open the possibility that owners/lenders could try to put the chain of title back together and conduct a new, valid foreclosure, though this will certainly prove complicated in practice, as the notes above suggest. Another possibility is to track down the old preforeclosure owner (who is still the owner because of the *Ibanez* problem) and obtain a quitclaim deed from her. If you represented an old owner in this situation, what would you counsel? What if you represented a new buyer?

Is it fair to strip the new buyer of title, when the buyer is unlikely to have any responsibility (or even much understanding of) the shoddy recording practices that caused the problem? How else should we resolve the problem? Bevilacqua/his title insurer will have a claim against the seller, but we still need to know who gets the house – you should be able to see similarities from our discussion of stolen property.

G. MERS and Other Title Workarounds

**Adam J. Levitin, *The Paper Chase: Securitization, Foreclosure,
and the Uncertainty of Mortgage Title***
63 DUKE L.J. 637 (2013) (excerpts reprinted by permission)

SECURITIZATION-ERA MORTGAGE TITLE SYSTEMS

…MERS [Mortgage Electronic Registration Systems, Inc.] is a private, contractual superstructure that is grafted onto the public land-recordation system. Financial institutions that are members of MERS register the loans they service (but do not necessarily own) with the MERS System electronic database. Each loan receives a unique identifier known as a MERS Identification Number (MIN). The MIN is sometimes stamped on the note or sometimes simply recorded in the lender's own records. MERS is then inserted in the local land records as the mortgagee, instead of the actual lender. Sometimes this involves an assignment of the mortgage from the lender to MERS, but the more prevalent arrangement has MERS recorded as the original mortgagee, thereby obviating any recordation of assignments. MERS serves as the mortgagee of record, but only as a nominee for the actual lender and supposedly for its successors and assigns. The language included in MERS mortgages is that MERS is acting "solely as nominee for Lender and Lender's successors and assigns." MERS claims no beneficial interest whatsoever in the loan.

MERS's goal is to immobilize mortgage title through a common-agency structure by acting as nominee for the lender and those subsequent transferees of the lender that are members of MERS. Although legal title remains in MERS's name, subsequent transfers are supposed to be tracked in MERS's database.

Thus, MERS aims to achieve the priority and enforcement benefits of public recordation while tracking beneficial ownership title in its own database. MERS's operation has two important implications. First, instead of paying county recordation and transfer fees, financial institutions pay only for MERS membership and MERS transaction fees. MERS thus offers potential cost savings in the securitization process through the avoidance of local recording fees. Second, MERS's electronic database, not the county land records, represents the main evidentiary source for determining who is currently the real party in interest on a mortgage.

In theory, MERS's database tracks two distinct characteristics: the identity of the party with the rights to service the mortgage (often an agent for the trustee for the trust created for the ultimate beneficial owners of the mortgage loan) and the legal title to mortgages (for example, the trustee for the trust created for the ultimate beneficial owners of the mortgage). MERS's publicly available records do not track chain of title. It is impossible for outsiders to determine if transfers were made in the MERS system and when. Instead, MERS publicly tracks only the current servicer and sometimes the current beneficial owner of a loan.

A major problem with MERS as a title system is that it is not accurate and reliable in terms of what it reports. MERS's members are nominally required to report transfers of mortgage servicing rights to MERS, but MERS does not actually compel reporting of servicing-rights transfers, and there is little incentive to be punctual with reporting. Indeed, the lack of record validation combined with voluntary reporting has led a federal judge to describe MERS as "the Wikipedia of land registration systems." Not surprisingly, the information in the MERS database is often inaccurate or incomplete.

MERS does not even formally require any reporting of legal title to the mortgages, much less of transfers of legal title; any information about legal title is supplied through strictly voluntary reporting. ...

MERS's database functions as a do-it-yourself private mortgage recordation system. Historically, MERS itself has had only around fifty employees who perform corporate and technology support functions. Employees of MERS's members carry out most of the tasks done in MERS's name, including the making of entries in the MERS database. These employees of MERS's members are listed as assistant secretaries or vice presidents of MERS, but they have no actual employment relationship with MERS. There are over twenty thousand of these "corporate signing officers." Accordingly, a transfer of either servicing or legal title in the MERS system involves nothing more than an employee of a MERS member entering the transfer in the MERS database.

A transfer within the MERS system involves voluntary self-reporting and nothing more and therefore fails to incentivize timely, accurate reporting. There are no formalities to a transfer in the MERS system. As a result, MERS may not in fact know who its principal is within the common-agency arrangement at any given point in time because MERS is relying on reporting from its members.

Notes and Questions

1. Along with the "Wikipedia" characterization of MERS as freely editable, a Reuters investigation used a different metaphor: "MERS has served in effect as an instant teller machine for mortgage assignments. Servicers simply have their own employees sign the needed documents as MERS officials." At least one bank has sued another bank for allegedly assigning the first bank's mortgages to itself using MERS.

2. According to Donald J. Kochan, public recording serves a number of important purposes:

   > Recording creates a network of information supporting a network of transactions. Property recording systems offer information to a number of constituencies, including: (1) owners, acting as sellers or as borrowers; (2) lenders, including mortgage providers; (3) other providers of capital; (4) buyers; (5) leaseholders; (6) title insurance companies; (7) governmental entities, such as police, regulators, and taxing authorities; and (8) other parties who may need to interact with the property at some time and know who the law deems to have ownership of the property. Recording allows all of these market and legal participants to connect. It is imperative that we recognize the variety of market players that use and benefit from the

recording statutes and from the existence of reliable, verifiable records of ownership.

It is not just the owner and the most immediate lender that care about proper recording. Those who wish to invest in, contract with, lease from, or provide capital to property owners demand the existence of a recording system so that they can identify the ownership interests associated with the property, including determining whether and to what extent that property is encumbered by a mortgage. So, too, do prospective buyers of property require a verifiable repository of title information to guide their purchasing decisions. These other players must be able to discover the limits on title with a level of clarity. Similarly, those who wish to provide loans secured by property or to make other capital investments in property need assurances that the owner owns the property that he says he owns and that the system reflects all competitive claims to or liens on title.

... At the very least, fragmentation of interests by securitization makes ownership interests in real property harder to identify, necessitating the existence of an accurate and complete means for tracking and recording these interests. ... [Securitization] is an important financial mechanism for the efficient provision of capital and should not be sacrificed in an effort to resolve the mortgage crisis or to prevent future crises. In fact, it is difficult to see the provision of loans in today's financial system without some reliance on securitization.

To make securitization effective, the loan-granting institution typically assigns its rights in both the note and the mortgage, sometimes to different parties. Due to transfers to the secondary market, securitization, and multiple assignments of notes and mortgages, it can become difficult to trace all of the steps along the way. This flurry of activity – and the number and variety of participants involved – can lead to problems in the chain of title and identifying who ultimately and currently holds the enforceable note and mortgage interests against the property owner. These problems are especially evident when the formalities of transfer, such as required endorsements of notes, are not satisfied and when the transfers are not recorded in some central repository.

Donald J. Kochan, Certainty of Title: Perspectives after the Mortgage Foreclosure Crisis on the Essential Role of Effective Recording Systems, 66 Ark. L. Rev. 267 (2013). Could MERS fulfill the functions of recording in such a system? What would need to change?

3. Many laws require notice to be given to anyone with a properly recorded interest in property. If MERS is listed as the "nominee" of the lender, does it have such an interest? Suppose the mortgagor failed to pay county property taxes and her home was subject to a tax sale. The county sent notice to the mortgagee for whom MERS was listed as nominee, but that entity had long ago sold the mortgage and subsequently went out of business, so it didn't respond. If the county had sent notice to MERS, it's at least possible that MERS would have informed the current owner of the mortgage, which would have participated in the tax sale to protect its interest. Instead, because no representative of the mortgagee showed up at the tax sale, the property was sold to a new owner free of the mortgage. Did MERS suffer a redressable injury? *See* Mortgage Elec. Regis. Sys., Inc. v. Ditto, No. E2012-

02292-SC-R11-CV (Tenn. Dec. 11, 2015) (MERS had none of the rights or duties of an owner; the fact that it wasn't entitled to notice might cause harm to its business model, but that wasn't enough to provide it a right to notice).

4. Why were large institutions so cavalier about record-keeping? Fannie Mae is a government-backed, now government-run institution that bought many mortgages. A 2006 internal Fannie Mae investigation explained:

> Fannie Mae's position is that it does not need to appear in the land records in order to have the benefit of the security provided by the mortgage…. [T]he transfer of an obligation secured by a security interest also transfers the security interest. Thus, the transfer of the promissory note, which is the obligation, also transfers the mortgage, which is the security interest. Once the note is sold to Fannie Mae, the mortgage also transfers, despite the fact that the servicer, lender, or MERS' name appears in the land records. Borrowers thus cannot determine the chain of owners from public records….
>
> Fannie Mae believes that lost note affidavits are the servicer's responsibility and can not be effectively reviewed under the current system. Fannie Mae has delegated the execution of lost note affidavits to servicers. It does not believe that it is in a position to make a subjective call as to whether a servicer has lost a note…. Fannie Mae views such an investigation as unnecessary because document custodians are responsible for retaining mortgage documents and must bear an expense if they are unable to locate mortgage documents. For these reasons, Fannie Mae

believes that *servicers are not likely to state that the notes are lost, stolen or missing if they in fact are not.* (emphasis added)

Can you spot the problem here? One entity, Lender Processing Services, at one point had a price list for "recreating" mortgage-related documents. A lost note affidavit was $12.95, as was a note allonge (a document that is supposed to be stapled to the original note documenting a transfer); an intervening assignment to fill a gap in the record chain of title was $35, and "recreating" an entire file was $95.

An important point to remember here is that recording usually only matters when there's a bona fide purchaser contesting ownership. As long as the originator didn't sell the mortgage twice, an unrecorded interest is still valid against the mortgagor, assuming the claimant can prove that it owns the interest. That may be a faulty assumption, but Fannie Mae figured that risk was low.

5. The toxic brew of carelessness, unprecedented volume of foreclosures, and disregard for the rights of borrowers has finally begun to attract judicial attention. A bankruptcy judge recently identified

> a general willingness and practice on Wells Fargo's part to create documentary evidence, after-the-fact, when enforcing its claims, **WHICH IS EXTRAORDINARY.** Moreover, [the Wells Fargo employee's] testimony does not stop at describing manufactured mortgage assignments. ... [T]he "assignment team" included people tasked with endorsing notes [from other entities to Wells Fargo]... Frankly, it does not appear that [the Wells Fargo employee] understood the difference between preparing legitimate assignments and indorsements *by* Wells Fargo and

improper assignments and indorsements *to* Wells Fargo. (emphasis in original)

In re Carrsow-Franklin, No. 10-20010 (S.D.N.Y. Bkcy. Jan. 29, 2015). What responsibility do lawyers have to train employees in charge of tasks with such legal relevance?

H.   An Additional Puzzle Piece: The Mortgage and the Note

As previously discussed, what we conventionally call a "mortgage" actually has two parts. The "note" is the borrower's promise to repay the debt: the note is governed by contract law, or more specifically commercial law. The note specifies the terms of the debt, including late fees and how interest is calculated. It can be replaced by a "Lost Note Affidavit," but that's supposed to be for special circumstances. The "mortgage" is the interest in land associated with the loan. It is a lien, governed by real estate law. The mortgage is the thing that should be filed and recorded. The mortgage is what gives the lender the right to take the collateral (the house) if the note isn't paid by the borrower.

Why split things up in this way? It seems to offer more opportunities for things to go wrong. Is there a reason not to put the two documents together and require the "mortgage" to contain all the terms of the debt? What happens if the ownership of the two legal interests, and custody of the two documents, becomes separated? The standard rule is that "[t]he note is the cow and the mortgage the tail. The cow can survive without a tail, but the tail cannot survive without the cow." Best Fertilizers of Ariz., Inc. v. Burns, 571 P.2d 675, 676 (Ariz. Ct. App. 1977), rev'd on other grounds, 570 P.2d 179 (Ariz. 1977) (quoting Professor Chester Smith). That is, the note is the real debt; a mortgage with no associated note is worthless. However, a note with no associated mortgage is just an unsecured loan.

Because of this, the law does not favor separation of the note and the mortgage, and works very hard to impute a relationship between them that makes the mortgage enforceable. The Restatement (Third) of Property (Mortgages) states that "in general a mortgage is unenforceable if it is held by one who has no right to enforce the secured obligation." As a result, if the mortgagee transfers the mortgage to A and the note to B, neither can foreclose *unless* A can foreclose on B's behalf. Thus, the Restatement concludes,

> The [necessary] trust or agency relationship may arise from the terms of the assignment, from a separate agreement, or from other circumstances. Courts should be vigorous in seeking to find such a relationship, since the result is otherwise likely to be a windfall for the mortgagor and the frustration of B's expectation of security.

See also Eaton v. Federal National Mortgage Association, 462 Mass. 569 (2012) (mortgage foreclosure may only be carried out by one who holds the mortgage and also either holds the note or acts on behalf of the note holder).

Most of our discussion, and most of the litigation over chain of title, has focused on problems with the mortgages, not the notes. It seems undeniable, however, that there are similar if not worse issues with the notes (and MERS never purported to track notes). Some have argued that transfers of the notes are governed by the Uniform Commercial Code's provisions for negotiable instruments, not by state foreclosure statutes. See, e.g., Dale A. Whitman & Drew Milner, *Foreclosing on Nothing: The Curious Problem of the Deed of Trust Foreclosure Without Entitlement to Enforce the Note*, 66 ARK. L. REV. 21 (2013). A number of states seem to agree that the mortgagor has nothing to complain about if she's in default, and that she lacks standing to challenge ownership of the note. If the wrong claimant takes the property, the right claimant can sue.

The contrary position relies on relativity of title: peaceable possessors have legitimate rights until someone proves better title. Just because a possessor doesn't have a right to be on the property doesn't mean that she can be ejected by someone with no better claim. See Tapscott v. Lessee of Cobbs, 11 Gratt. 172, 52 Va. 172 (1854); see also Yvanova v. New Century Mortgage Corp., No. S218973 (Cal. Feb. 18, 2016) (borrower has standing to sue for wrongful foreclosure when the foreclosing party allegedly didn't own the note and deed of trust; "[t]he borrower owes money not to the world at large but to a particular person or institution, and only the person or institution entitled to payment may enforce the debt by foreclosing on the security").

I.   What Now?

Despite all these flaws in the system, shouldn't the borrowers just have paid? After all, if they hadn't defaulted, they wouldn't have entered into the resulting hellscape.

Even if you excuse the victims of fraud from this claim — and there were many — it is important to remember that the mortgage contract is not just an agreement that the home may be sold upon a default on the loan. It's an agreement that if the homeowner defaults on the loan, the mortgagee may sell the property following the required legal procedure. A mortgage loan involves a bundle of rights, including procedural rights. These rights have a price: for example, loans in judicial foreclosure states have historically been more expensive than loans in nonjudicial foreclosure states. When the lender (or someone claiming rights as successor of the lender) ignores the rights, it's getting something it hasn't paid for.

Entirely separately, we might want people to be able to renegotiate their deals when renegotiation makes everyone better off — but with the system the way it is, that's proven extremely difficult. Procedural protections provide both time and negotiating leverage.

For an eye-opening account by one young lawyer of the messy process of seeking a loan modification for a borrower, see Wajahat Ali, <u>Could It Be That the Best Chance To Save a Young Family from Foreclosure Is a 28-Year-Old Pakistani American Playright-Slash-Attorney Who Learned Bankruptcy Law on the Internet?</u>, McSweeney's (Jan. 2010) (http://www.mcsweeneys.net/articles/could-it-be-that-the-best-chance-to-save-a-young-family-from-foreclosure-is-a-28-year-old-pakistani-american-playright-slash-attorney-who-learned-bankruptcy-law-on-the-internet). Essentially, Ali could never get the same answer twice from the servicer; it repeatedly denied receiving documents supporting his clients' request for modification; it denied modifications based on completely mistaken premises; and it didn't even tell him or his clients when it finally did grant a modification, leaving them expecting foreclosure. It took multiple threats to file bankruptcy, which would have automatically stayed a foreclosure, to induce the servicer to respond.

Federal bank regulators signed settlements in March 2011 with 14 loan servicers, who promised further internal investigations, remediation for some who were harmed, and a halt to the filing of false documents. The servicers claimed to have ended this behavior in late 2010. Reuters examined a large number of foreclosure filings and concluded that, to the contrary, robo-signing was ongoing. In February 2012 the servicers promised to stop again. There's very little indication that they've stopped. However, the major servicing companies did enter into a $25 billion settlement with federal and many state officials that was supposed to compensate homeowners for servicing errors and require better behavior going forward. In response, property professor Mark Edwards wrote:

> Let's say I hire an armed gang to expel you from your house. My gang removes all of your belongings, changes the locks, and warns you that you'd better not try to come back. I then sell your house to someone else. You might have called the police, but the armed gang I hired actually *are* the police. You might have gone to court

to stop me, but the court is on my side, because I deliberately mislead the courts. Now let's say I did the same thing thousands and thousands of times to other people as well. And you can prove it. I'd be in pretty big trouble, wouldn't I? ....

[The settlement provides for] $1500 to $2000 per home.... $1500-2000 is less than the legal expenses banks incur when a foreclosure is challenged. It's less than title insurance on homes worth over $200K.

Why would regulators agree to a settlement of this magnitude? What were the alternatives?

Mortgage crisis-related disputes continue. For example, in March 2015, the Department of Justice's U.S. Trustee Program (USTP), which oversees bankruptcy estates, entered into a national settlement agreement with JPMorgan Chase Bank N.A. requiring Chase to pay more than $50 million to over 25,000 homeowners who are or were in bankruptcy. Among other things, Chase acknowledged that it filed more than 50,000 payment change notices that were improperly signed, under penalty of perjury, by persons who had not reviewed the accuracy of the notices.

In 2013, the Consumer Finance Protection Bureau issued national rules on mortgage servicing standards. Except for smaller servicers, mortgage servicers must make good-faith efforts to contact borrowers by the 36th day of delinquency and tell them about loss mitigation options, such as short sales and loan modifications. By day 45, servicers must send written notice of these options and the name of a contact person. Servicers may only begin foreclosures if a homeowner is over 120 days delinquent, and a borrower's pending loss mitigation application precludes the initiation of a foreclosure. If the foreclosure has been initiated when a borrower submits a loss mitigation application, the servicer may not move for final judgment or sale as long as the application is complete 37 days before the sale. Servicers may not "double-track" – pursue mitigation measures with a borrower while also continuing the foreclosure process. If the servicer denies the borrower's application, it must give specific reasons and afford a right of appeal. Mortgage Servicing Rules Under the Real Estate Settlement Procedures Act (Regulation X), 78 Fed. Reg. 10696 (codified at 12 C.F.R. §1024) (2013).

As a result of changes in foreclosure procedures and servicer behavior, the average time between the beginning of a foreclosure and its end has increased substantially. In 2007, a foreclosure in New York took less than 300 days, while it took 1089 days by the end of 2012. California, which more commonly uses the speedier nonjudicial foreclosure process, experienced a more than doubled time of 347 days. RealtyTrak, 2013 Short   Sale   Trends   (2013) (http://www.slideshare.net/fullscreen/RealtyTrac/2013-short-sale-trends/1).

What are the possible benefits of delay for homeowners? What about the possible risks? In some cases, servicers initiate foreclosures but do not complete them, leading to so-called "zombie foreclosures." Completing the foreclosure would make the mortgagee the legal owner of the property, subject to property taxes and to the duty to avoid creating a nuisance condition on the property. In markets with many empty houses, the mortgagee may well wish to avoid this outcome, because it won't be able to sell the house quickly or otherwise recoup its maintenance costs. In addition, when people believe that they will soon be kicked out, they tend not to maintain the property, and some even deliberately inflict damage. However, the mortgagors are often unaware of their continuing legal duties, and abandon the property in the belief that the foreclosure will occur, exposing themselves to unforeseen liability and their communities to further deterioration of the tax base and the physical condition of homes. Is there anything law could do to mitigate the problem of such "zombie foreclosures"?

Various programs have attempted to help homeowners at risk of foreclosure, with generally modest results. The federal government set up the <u>Home Affordable Modification Program</u> (HAMP), which was supposed to keep four million homeowners in their homes by reducing interest rates and extending repayment times, though not by forgiving principal. Six years later, under 900,000 homeowners were participating in modifications. Servicers rejected four million applications, or 72% of requests. The main culprits were the fact that the program was voluntary, and that the servicers were allowed to run the process on their own. In 38% of cases, the servicers claimed that the borrowers failed to supply all the paperwork or to make the first modified payment. Office of the Special Inspector General for the Troubled Asset Relief Program (SIGTARP), <u>Quarterly Report to Congress</u> (July 29, 2015). Not all of that paperwork was actually absent. In 2014, SIGTARP found that the employees of one servicer piled so many unopened Federal Express packages from homeowners containing their HAMP supporting documents into one room that eventually the floor buckled. SIGTARP also found that this servicer denied homeowners from HAMP en masse, without reviewing their applications at all.

Incompetence plays a large role, but that incompetence also may redound to the benefit of servicers: in one case, for example, a servicer delayed responding to a HAMP modification request four times over nearly two years, adding $40,000 in interest, fees, and costs to the amount the borrower allegedly owed. The servicer first mistakenly denied a modification because it inexplicably decided that the borrower didn't live at the residence. Then it mistakenly denied a modification as unaffordable because it inexplicably used the wrong figures to calculate the borrower's income despite extensive documentation of the correct figures. Then it mistakenly denied a modification because the borrower allegedly had too much money in the bank to qualify; this money was in fact the amount the borrower had set aside in escrow to pay the mortgage, as directed by the court-appointed referree. The servicer also maintained that the borrower hadn't submitted complete documentation for his modification application, though when the referree directed a representative of the servicer to appear at a hearing, the representative (who had just testified to her personal knowledge of this incompleteness) was able to pull up the full application on her laptop. Finally, the servicer denied a modification as unaffordable, without further explanation of how it calculated affordability. *See* US Bank N.A. v Sarmiento, 121 A.D.3d 187 (N.Y. App. Div. 2014). The court found that the servicer's lack of good faith disqualified it from claiming the additional amount owed. As the lawyer for the borrower, how would you have dealt with two years of delay by the servicer?

In the absence of further federal legislation, states may have more options in dealing with foreclosure abuses, because foreclosure procedure is a state-law matter. See CENTER FOR RESPONSIBLE LENDING AND CONSUMERS UNION, CLOSING THE GAPS: WHAT STATES SHOULD DO TO PROTECT HOMEOWNERS FROM FORECLOSURE (May 2013). The most effective programs seem to be those that require mandatory mediation between the mortgagee and the homeowner before a foreclosure can proceed. The most effective of those require the mortgagee to send a representative with (1) authority to negotiate a modification and (2) proof of the chain of title to the mortgage. Why do you think that voluntary programs, under which homeowners are entitled to mediation but must affirmatively request it, are less effective than mandatory programs? What effects will requiring proof of the chain of title have on the parties' negotiations? If you were an attorney for a servicer, what would you ask for from homeowners in return for a modification that left them with the ability to stay in their homes?

Massachusetts law now prohibits a creditor from publishing notice of an intended foreclosure sale for many residential mortgages unless the creditor "has first taken reasonable steps and made a good faith effort to avoid foreclosure." Mass. Gen. L. ch. 244 §35B. The creditor must calculate the relative benefits of foreclosure and modification, and must offer the borrower a modified mortgage loan with an affordable payment (if the net present value of such a loan exceeds the anticipated recovery from foreclosure) or notify the borrower that he is not eligible for a modification and provide the borrower with copies of the creditor's net present value and affordable payment analyses. One might think that no law would be required to require creditors to maximize their profits from a loan, but creditors didn't want to engage in individualized determinations. Is the Massachusetts model a good one?

In New York, the courts implemented a requirement that lawyers filing for foreclosure had to certify that they had taken "reasonable" measures to verify the accuracy of documents submitted to the court, under penalty of sanctions. The month before this requirement went into place, roughly 100-200 foreclosures were filed each day. The next month, no more than 5 foreclosures were filed on any given day, with the exception of one day in which 22 foreclosures were filed. Amazingly, this requirement replaced a previous order requiring attorneys for foreclosing entities to certify that *to the best of their knowledge* there weren't any false statements of fact or law in their documents.

New York's system also includes pre-foreclosure conferences; although they are voluntary, they are encouraged, and the courts presently get 80% of foreclosure defendants to show up for a pre-foreclosure conference session. Thus, there is a real risk that someone will challenge the foreclosure documents if they're not in order. In order to make such programs work, it is important to convince homeowners that there is some hope – many have engaged in futile attempts to get a modification before. If they aren't encouraged, many of them believe that the judicial procedure is just another runaround. Is the New York model a good one?

J.   Concluding Thoughts

The history of mortgages includes many episodes in which financial and legal innovations hurt borrowers by undercutting the various protections they traditionally could depend on, such as clarity in knowing who they were dealing with in a loan transaction. In the most recent iteration of the cycle, the same financial and legal innovations created systematic trouble on the lender side. This too is a property story: the securitized pools (a new kind of property distinct from the property rights in the underlying mortgages) helped create the moral hazard that led brokers to make bad loans and stick the mortgage-backed security buyers with toxic junk. The investors in the securities were unwilling or unable, or sometimes both, to examine individual loans and instead invested on the theory that *enough* loans in the pool would pay off to justify the investment, so they didn't pay enough attention to the quality of the individual underlying loans. Is it possible to split property up in so many ways that the new rights become dangerous instead of productive?

Finally: Frederic Bastiat wrote, "When plunder becomes a way of life for a group of men living together in society, they create for themselves in the course of time a legal system that authorizes it and a moral code that glorifies it." Does his claim help explain MERS? What about *Johnson v. M'Intosh*?

Part IV: Use

Easements

A.   What is an easement?

Easements are interests in land. Unlike fee simple ownership, they are nonpossessory. Rather, they allow the easement holder to use or control someone else's land. Suppose Anna owns Blackacre, and Brad owns Whiteacre, which borders Blackacre. Anna would like to cross Whiteacre to reach Blackacre. She could ask Brad for permission to cross, but even if he says yes, permission can be revoked. Brad might also convey Whiteacre to a less welcoming owner. Anna may therefore wish to acquire a property interest that gives her an *irrevocable* right to cross over Whiteacre. If Brad conveys her this interest (by sale or grant), Anna now owns an **easement of access**, which is a right to enter and cross through someone's land on the way to someplace else.

Terminology. Easements come in multiple flavors. The first distinction is between affirmative and negative easements. An **affirmative easement** lets the owner do something on (or affecting) the land of another, known as the **servient estate** (or **servient tenement**). The right is the **benefit** of the easement, and the obligation on the servient estate is its **burden**.

As noted above, a common affirmative easement is an **easement of access** (also known as an **easement of way**), which requires the owner of the servient estate to allow the easement holder to travel on the land to reach another location. In the example above, Anna has an affirmative easement to cross Whiteacre, the servient estate, to access Blackacre.[21] A

---

[21] If the easement holder is allowed to take something from the land (suppose Anna has the right to harvest wheat from Whiteacre while in transit to Blackacre), the right is called a **profit a prendre** or **profit**. Profits were traditionally classified as distinct from easements, though their legal treatment is typically similar. *See, e.g.*, Figliuzzi v. Carcajou Shooting Club of Lake Koshkonong, 516 N.W.2d 410, 414 (Wis. 1994) ("[W]e can find no distinction between

negative easement prohibits the owner of the servient estate from engaging in some action on the land. For example, if Anna has a solar panel on her property, she might acquire a solar easement from Brad that would prohibit the construction of any structures on Whiteacre that might block the sun from Anna's panel on Blackacre.

Another distinction is between **easements appurtenant** and **easements in gross**. An easement appurtenant benefits another piece of land, the **dominant estate**. The owner of the dominant estate exercises the rights of the easement. If ownership of the dominant estate changes, the new owner exercises the powers of the easement; the prior owner retains no interest. So if Anna's easement to cross Whiteacre to reach Blackacre is an easement appurtenant, Blackacre is the dominant estate. If she conveys Blackacre to Charlie, Charlie becomes the owner of the easement.

In an easement in gross, the easement benefits a specific person, who exercises the rights of the easement rights regardless of land ownership. If Anna's easement to cross Whiteacre to reach Blackacre is an easement in gross, she keeps her easement even if she conveys Blackacre. In general, the presumption is in favor of an easement appurtenant over an easement in gross. Why do you think that is?

Easements are part of the larger law of **servitudes**, which include real covenants and equitable servitudes. A servitude is a legal device that creates a right or obligation that **runs with the land**. A right runs with the land when it is enjoyed not only by its initial owner but also by all successors to that owner's benefited property interest. A burden runs with the land when it binds not only its initial obligor but also all successors to that obligor's burdened property interest. A servitude can be, among other things, an easement, profit, or covenant. These interests overlap, and the

---

easements and profits relevant to recording the property interest[.]"). The *Restatement* characterizes the profit as a kind of easement. § 1.2.

Restatement (Third) of Property (Servitudes) (2000) seeks to unify them.[22] As a matter of history, however, easement law developed as a distinct set of doctrines, and this chapter gives them separate treatment.[23]

B.   Creating Easements

1.   Express easements

Because easements are interests in land, express easements are subject to the Statute of Frauds. Failures to comply with the statute may still be enforced in cases of reasonable detrimental reliance. *See, e.g., Restatement* (Third) of Property (Servitudes) § 2.9.

Third parties. Easements are often created as part of the transfer of land (e.g., selling a property, but retaining the right to use its parking lot). Traditionally, grantors could reserve an easement in the conveyed land for themselves, but could not create an easement for the benefit of a third party. This rule led to extra transactions. Where the traditional rule applied, if A wanted to convey to B while creating an easement for C, A could convey to C who would then convey to B, while reserving an easement.

---

[22] A covenant is a servitude if either its benefit or its burden runs with the land; otherwise it is merely a contract enforceable only as between the original contracting parties (or perhaps a gratuitous promise enforceable by nobody at all). When a covenant is a servitude, it may equivalently be described as either a "servitude" or "a covenant running with the land." We will discuss covenants in a later chapter.

[23] Moreover, the Third Restatement is somewhat notorious for the extent to which it seeks not only to "restate" the common law, but to push it in a particular direction. While the Third Restatement does tend to provide the modern approach to most servitudes issues, it has a tendency to advocate against traditional, formalist rules that are often still good law in many American jurisdictions. We will not thoroughly explore these distinctions here; you should however be aware of the importance of thoroughly investigating the applicable law in your jurisdiction if you ever encounter servitudes in practice.

The modern trend discards this restriction. *See, e.g.*, Minton v. Long, 19 S.W.3d 231, 238 (Tenn. Ct. App. 1999). The California Supreme Court explained:

> The rule derives from the common law notions of reservations from a grant and was based on feudal considerations. A reservation allows a grantor's whole interest in the property to pass to the grantee, but revests a newly created interest in the grantor. While a reservation could theoretically vest an interest in a third party, the early common law courts vigorously rejected this possibility, apparently because they mistrusted and wished to limit conveyance by deed as a substitute for livery by seisin. Insofar as this mistrust was the foundation of the rule, it is clearly an inapposite feudal shackle today. Consequently, several commentators have attacked the rule as groundless and have called for its abolition.
>
> California early adhered to this common law rule. In considering our continued adherence to it, we must realize that our courts no longer feel constricted by feudal forms of conveyancing. Rather, our primary objective in construing a conveyance is to try to give effect to the intent of the grantor. In general, therefore, grants are to be interested in the same way as other contracts and not according to rigid feudal standards. The common law rule conflicts with the modern approach to construing deeds because it can frustrate the grantor's intent. Moreover, it produces an inequitable result because the original grantee has presumably paid a reduced price for title to the encumbered property.

Willard v. First Church of Christ, Scientist, 7 Cal. 3d 473, 476-77 (1972) (citations omitted). The modern *Restatement* likewise dispenses with the traditional approach, allowing the direct creation of easements on behalf of third parties. *Restatement* § 2.6. Some jurisdictions nonetheless retain the bar, citing reliance interests and the prospect that such easements create instability in title records. Estate of Thomson v. Wade, 509 N.E.2d 309, 310 (N.Y. 1987) ("The overriding considerations of the public policy favoring certainty in title to real property, both to protect bona fide purchasers and to avoid conflicts of ownership, which may engender needless litigation, persuade us to decline to depart from our settled rule." (internal citation and quotation omitted)). There is an argument that the extra transactions required by the traditional rule promote better title indexing. The *Restatement* observes:

> To avoid the prohibition, two conveyances must be used: the first conveys the easement to the intended beneficiary; the second conveys the servient estate to the intended transferee. The only virtue of the rule is that it tends to ensure that a recorded easement will be properly indexed in the land-records system, but there are so many exceptions to the rule, where it is still in force, that it does not fill that function very well.

Restatement (Third) of Property (Servitudes) § 2.6 cmt. a (2000). In light of *Hartig v. Stratman*, from our chapter on Recording Acts, are you persuaded that the benefits of a separate transaction for recording purposes outweigh the costs?

2.   Implied Easements

Easements may come into being without explicit agreements. They may arise from equitable enforcement of implied agreements or references to maps or boundary references in conveyances. *Restatement (Third) of Property (Servitudes)* § 2.13. In this section, we focus on two forms of implied easements: An **easement implied by existing use** and an **easement by necessity**. Both such easements commonly arise as a byproduct of land transactions.

a. Easement implied by existing use

An easement implied by existing use may arise when a parcel of land is divided and amenities once enjoyed by the whole parcel are now split up, such that in order to enjoy the amenity (a utility line, or a driveway, for example), one of the divided lots requires access to the other. Imagine, for example, a home connected to a city sewer line via a privately owned drainpipe, on a parcel that is later divided by carving out a portion of the lot between the original house and the sewer line connection:

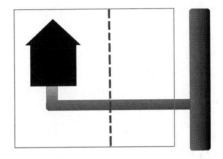

In such a situation, courts will frequently find an easement implied by prior existing use, allowing the owner of the house to continue using the drainpipe even though it is now under someone else's land. *See, e.g.,* Van Sandt v. Royster, 83 P.2d 698 (Kan. 1938). There are, however, some limits to the circumstances that will justify the implication of such an easement:

> [T]he easement implied from a preexisting use, [is] also characterized as a quasi-easement. Such an easement arises where, during the unity of title, an apparently permanent and obvious servitude is imposed on one part of an estate in favor of another part. The servitude must be in use at the time of severance and necessary for the reasonable enjoyment of the severed part. A grant of a right to continue such use arises by implication of law. An implied easement from a preexisting use is established by proof

of three elements: (1) common ownership of the claimed dominant and servient parcels and a subsequent conveyance or transfer separating that ownership; (2) before severance, the common owner used part of the united parcel for the benefit of another part, and this use was apparent and obvious, continuous, and permanent; and (3) the claimed easement is necessary and beneficial to the enjoyment of the parcel conveyed or retained by the grantor or transferrer.

Dudley v. Neteler, 924 N.E.2d 1023, 1027-28 (Ill. App. 2009) (internal citations and quotations omitted). The following notes consider each of these elements.

Notes and Questions

1. **Common Ownership.** Are easements implied by prior existing use fair to owners of subdivided land? Why shouldn't we require purchasers of subdivided lots to "get it in writing"—that is, to bargain for easements to obvious and necessary amenities when accepting a parcel carved out from a larger plot of land? For that matter, why don't we require the original owner to bargain for the right to continue to use land that they are purporting to sell? Who do we think is in a better position to identify the need for such an easement, the prior owner of the undivided parcel, or the purchaser of the carved-out portion of that parcel? Should the answer matter in determining whether to imply an easement or not?

   The common law did draw distinctions between implied *reservation* of an easement (to the owner of the original undivided lot) and implied *grant* of an easement (to the first purchaser of the separated parcel). The latter required a lesser showing of necessity than the former, which would only be recognized upon a showing of *strict* necessity. The theory was that the deed that first severed the parcels from one another should be construed against its grantor, who was in a better position to know of the need for an easement to property she already owned, and to write such an easement into the deed she was delivering. Indeed, a minority of jurisdictions still follow this rule.

The modern Restatement, in contrast, makes no distinction as to whether the easement is sought by the grantor or the grantee, providing simply that the use will continue if the parties had reasonable grounds to so expect. Factors tending to show that expectation are that: "(1) the prior use was not merely temporary or casual, and (2) continuance of the prior use was reasonably necessary to enjoyment of the parcel, estate, or interest previously benefited by the use, and (3) existence of the prior use was apparent or known to the parties, or (4) the prior use was for underground utilities serving either parcel." *Restatement (Third) of Property (Servitudes)* § 2.12 (2000). The commentary allows for the possibility that the balance of hardships and grantor knowledge might justify a court's refusing to imply a servitude in favor of the grantor when it would have for the grantee. *Id.* cmt. a. But the general approach is to accept and accommodate the fact that grantors do not always protect themselves as well as they perhaps should. *Id.* ("Although grantors might be expected to know that they should expressly reserve any use rights they intend to retain after severance, experience has shown that too often they do not.").

2. **Reasonable necessity**. Reasonable necessity is something less than absolute necessity. *See, e.g.,* Rinderer v. Keeven, 412 N.E.2d 1015, 1026 (Ill. App. 1980) ("It is well established that one who claims an easement by implication need not show absolute necessity in order to prevail; it is sufficient that such an easement be reasonable, highly convenient and beneficial to the dominant estate." (internal quotation and citation omitted)). Does this leave

courts with too much discretion to impose easements? A minority of jurisdictions make a formal distinction between implied easements in favor of grantees and grantors, requiring strict necessity in the case of the latter. *Restatement* § 2.12. *But see* Tortoise Island Communities, Inc. v. Moorings Ass'n, Inc., 489 So. 2d 22, 22 (Fla. 1986) (concluding that an absolute necessity is required in all cases).

3. **What is apparent?** Should home purchasers be expected to investigate the state of utility lines upon making a purchase? The *Restatement (Third) of Property (Servitudes)* reports that most cases to consider the question imply the easement when underground utilities are at issue. § 2.12 (Reporter's Note) (such easements "will be implied without regard to their visibility or the parties' knowledge of their existence if the utilities serve either parcel"). Are such uses plausibly apparent? Or is this simply a case of the law implying terms that the parties likely would have bargained for had they thought to consider the matter?

b. Easements by necessity

An **easement by necessity** (or sometimes **way by necessity**) arises when land becomes landlocked or incapable of reasonable use absent an easement. For example, if A owns a rectangular parcel bordered on the north, east, and west by privately owned land and on the south by a public street, and conveys to B a strip of her land on the northern boundary, B will acquire an easement by necessity across the southern portion of the parcel retained by A:

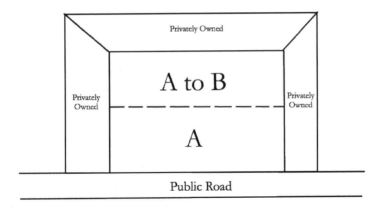

Thomas v. Primus
84 A.3d 916 (Conn. App. 2014)

MIHALAKOS, J.

The plaintiffs, William Thomas, Craig B. Thomas and Andrea Thomas Jabs, appeal from the trial court's declaratory judgment granting an easement by necessity and implication in favor of the defendant, Bruno Primus. On appeal, the plaintiffs claim that the court erred in finding an easement by necessity.[1] The plaintiffs also claim that the defendant's claim for an easement should have been barred by the defense of laches. We affirm the judgment of the trial court.

The following facts, as found by the court, are relevant to this appeal. The plaintiffs own property located at 460 Camp Street in Plainville. The defendant owns one and one-quarter acres of undeveloped land abutting the eastern boundary of the plaintiffs' property. The dispute at issue here concerns the northernmost portion of the plaintiffs' property, a twenty-five feet wide by three hundred feet long strip of land known as the

---

[1] The plaintiffs also claim that the court erred in finding an easement by implication. Because we conclude that the court properly found an easement by necessity, we need not consider this claim.

"passway," which stretches from the public road on the western boundary of the plaintiffs' property to the defendant's property to the east.

Both the plaintiffs' and the defendant's properties originally were part of a single lot owned by Martha Thomas, the grandmother of the plaintiffs. In 1959, Martha Thomas conveyed the one and one-quarter acres of landlocked property, currently owned by the defendant, to Arthur Primus, the defendant's brother. At the conveyance, which the defendant attended, Martha Thomas and Arthur Primus agreed that access to the landlocked property would be through the passway, which until that time had been used by Martha Thomas to access the eastern portions of her property. In 1969, the defendant took possession of the land. In 2002, the plaintiffs took possession of the western portion of Martha Thomas' property, including the passway.

In 2008, the plaintiffs decided to sell their property. When the defendant learned of their intention, he sent a letter to the plaintiffs asserting his right to use the passway to access his land. In 2009, the plaintiffs signed a contract to sell their property, but the prospective purchasers cancelled the contract when they learned of the defendant's claimed right to use the passway. The plaintiffs then brought the action to quiet title that is the subject of this appeal, seeking, among other things, a declaratory judgment that the defendant had no legal interest in the property. The defendant brought a counterclaim asking the court to establish his right to use the passway uninterrupted by the plaintiffs.... In response to the defendant's counterclaim, the plaintiffs asserted the special defense of laches.

A trial was held on June 5 and 6, 2012. On August 31, 2012, the court issued its decision, finding in favor of the defendant on the plaintiffs' complaint and on his counterclaim, and concluding that the defendant had an easement by necessity and an easement by implication over the passway. Specifically, the court found an easement by necessity was created when Martha Thomas conveyed a landlocked parcel to Arthur Primus, as it was absolutely necessary in order to access the property....

I

On appeal, the plaintiffs claim that the court erred in finding an easement by necessity because (1) the defendant's predecessor in title had the right to buy reasonable alternative access to the street, (2) the defendant failed to present full title searches of all adjoining properties, and (3) Martha Thomas and Arthur Primus did not intend for an easement to exist. . . .

Originating in the common law, easements by necessity are premised on the conception that "the law will not presume, that it was the intention of the parties, that one should convey land to the other, in such manner that the grantee could derive no benefit from the conveyance...." *Collins v. Prentice,* 15 Conn. 39, 44 (1842). An easement by necessity is "imposed where a conveyance by the grantor leaves the grantee with a parcel inaccessible save over the lands of the grantor...." *Hollywyle Assn., Inc. v. Hollister,* 164 Conn. 389, 398, 324 A.2d 247 (1973). The party seeking an easement by necessity has the burden of showing that the easement is reasonably necessary for the use and enjoyment of the party's property.

A

First, the plaintiffs claim that an easement by necessity does not exist because the defendant's predecessor in title had the right to buy reasonable alternative access to the street. We disagree.

In considering whether an easement by necessity exists, "the law may be satisfied with less than the absolute need of the party claiming the right of way. The necessity need only be a reasonable one." *Hollywyle Assn., Inc. v. Hollister,* supra, 164 Conn. at 399, 324 A.2d 247.

In this case, the plaintiffs presented evidence at trial that, at the time he purchased the property from Martha Thomas in 1959, Arthur Primus maintained bonds for deed that allowed him to purchase access to Camp Street through a different piece of property for $900. Although he did not exercise this right, the plaintiffs contend that the fact that Arthur Primus held this option establishes that the defendant's use of the passway is not reasonably necessary.

The plaintiffs correctly note that the ability of a party to create alternative access through his or her own property at a reasonable cost can preclude the finding of reasonable necessity required to establish an easement by necessity. Nonetheless, we are aware of nothing in our case law that suggests that a party is required to purchase *additional* property in order to create alternative access, even at a reasonable price.[2]

Furthermore, easements by necessity need not be created at the time of conveyance. See *D'Addario v. Truskoski*, 57 Conn.App. 236, 247, 749 A.2d 38 (2000) (recognizing easement by necessity created by state taking and natural disaster). Even if we were to assume, arguendo, that Arthur Primus' bonds for deed made use of the passway unnecessary at the time he owned the property, those bonds for deed expired in 1962, several years before the defendant owned the property, and provide no reasonable alternative access today. Thus, we see no reason to disturb the court's finding that use of the passway is currently necessary for the use and enjoyment of the defendant's property....

C

---

[2] The plaintiffs' sole authority in support of their position; Griffeth v. Eid, 573 N.W.2d 829 (N.D.1998); is distinguishable from the case before us. In that case, the North Dakota Supreme Court upheld a trial court's ruling that a party seeking an easement by necessity had not met his burden of establishing reasonable necessity because potential alternate access existed, including the possibility of purchasing an easement over another abutting property, and the party had not provided evidence that he had pursued these options and found them unavailing. In this case, there is no evidence in the record that the defendant had the opportunity to purchase alternate access.

Finally, the plaintiffs argue that an easement by necessity does not exist because Martha Thomas and Arthur Primus did not intend for the easement to exist. We disagree.

The seminal case in this state on easements by necessity recognized that "the law will not presume, that it was the intention of the parties, that one should convey land to the other, in such manner that the grantee could derive no benefit from the conveyance.... The law, under such circumstances, will give effect to the grant according to the presumed intent of the parties." *Collins v. Prentice,* supra, 15 Conn. at 44, 15 Conn. 39. This rationale does not, as the plaintiffs suggest, establish intent as an element of an easement by necessity. Instead, "[t]he presumption as to the intent of the parties is a fiction of law ... and merely disguises the public policy that no land should be left inaccessible or incapable of being put to profitable use." (Citation omitted.) *Hollywyle Assn., Inc. v. Hollister,* supra, 164 Conn. at 400, 324 A.2d 247. Thus, absent an explicit agreement by the grantor and grantee that an easement does *not* exist, a court need not consider intent in establishing an easement by necessity. See *O'Brien v. Coburn,* 46 Conn.App. 620, 633, 700 A.2d 81 (holding that "the intention of the parties [was] irrelevant" in case establishing easement by necessity), cert. denied, 243 Conn. 938, 702 A.2d 644 (1997).

In this case, the court found that the defendant's property was landlocked and that access over the pass-way was reasonably necessary for the use and enjoyment of the defendant's property. Therefore, the court found an easement by necessity to exist over the pass-way. This conclusion was supported by the record and there is no legal deficiency in the court's analysis. . . .

Notes

1. As *Thomas* indicates, there are two traditional rationales for easements by necessity. The first considers it an implied term of a conveyance, assuming that the parties would not intend for land

to be conveyed without a means for access. The second simply treats the issue as one of public policy favoring land use. *See* Restatement (Third) of Property (Servitudes) § 2.15 cmt. a (2000).

2. *Thomas*'s implication to the contrary aside, the traditional view is that the necessity giving rise to an easement by necessity must exist at the time the property is severed. Restatement (Third) of Property (Servitudes) § 2.15 (2000) ("Servitudes by necessity arise only on severance of rights held in a unity of ownership."); Roy v. Euro-Holland Vastgoed, B. V., 404 So. 2d 410, 412 (Fla. Dist. Ct. App. 1981) ("[I]n order for the owner of a dominant tenement to be entitled to a way of necessity over the servient tenement both properties must at one time have been owned by the same party .... In addition, the common source of title must have created the situation causing the dominant tenement to become landlocked. A further requirement is that at the time the common source of title created the problem the servient tenement must have had access to a public road.").

3. Easements by necessity are typically about access, but other kinds of uses may be necessary to the reasonable enjoyment of property. For example, suppose O conveys mineral rights to Blackacre to A. A would have both an easement of access to Blackacre and the right to engage in the mining necessary to reach the minerals. Likewise, an express easement of way may require rights to maintain and improve the easement. Access for utilities may also give rise to an easement by necessity, creating litigation over which utilities are "necessary":

> When questioned by defendants as to why he could not use a cellular phone on his property, plaintiff testified he ran a home business and a cellular phone was not adequate to

> handle his business needs; for example, a computer cannot access the Internet over a cellular phone. Plaintiff also testified solar power and gas generators were unable to produce enough electricity to make his home habitable.

Smith v. Heissinger, 745 N.E.2d 666, 672 (Ill. App. 2001) (affirming finding of necessity of easement for underground utilities).

Courts often describe the degree of necessity required to find an easement by necessity as being "strict." *See, e.g.*, Ashby v. Maechling, 229 P.3d 1210, 1214 (Mont. 2010) "Two essential elements of an easement by necessity are unity of ownership and strict necessity."). It is certainly higher than that needed for an easement implied by existing use. That said, considerable precedent indicates that the necessity need not be absolute. *See, e.g.*, Cale v. Wanamaker, 121 N.J. Super. 142, 148, 296 A.2d 329, 333 (Ch. Div. 1972) ("Although some courts have held that access to a piece of property by navigable waters negates the 'necessity' required for a way of necessity, the trend since the 1920's has been toward a more liberal attitude in allowing easements despite access by water, reflecting a recognition that most people today think in terms of 'driving' rather than 'rowing' to work or home.").

4. Several states provide owners of landlocked property a statutory right to obtain access through neighboring land by means of a **private condemnation** action. Some courts have held that the availability of private condemnation actions negate the necessity prong of a common law easement by necessity claim. *See, e.g.*, Ferguson Ranch, Inc. v. Murray, 811 P.2d 287, 290 (Wyo. 1991) ("[A] civil action for a common law way of necessity is not available because of the existence of W.S. 24–9–101."). Private condemnation actions may also extend to contexts beyond those

covered by the common law easement by necessity. *See, e.g.*, Cal. Civ. Code § 1001 (utilities).

3.   Prescriptive Easements

Easements may also arise from prescription. An easement by prescription is acquired in a manner similar to adverse possession, as it is a non-permissive use that ultimately ripens into a property interest. Recall the five elements of adverse possession: Entry and possession that is (1) actual, (2) exclusive, (3) hostile or under claim of right, (4) open and notorious, and (5) continuous for the statutory limitations period. Which (if any) of these elements might have to be modified where the right being acquired is not a right of possession, but a right of use?

Felgenhauer v. Soni
17 Cal.Rptr.3d 135 (Cal. App. 2004).

GILBERT, P.J.

Here we hold that to establish a claim of right to a prescriptive easement, the claimant need not believe he or she is legally entitled to use of the easement. Jerry and Kim Felgenhauer brought this action to quiet title to prescriptive easements over neighboring property owned by Ken and Jennifer Soni. A jury made special findings that established a prescriptive easement for deliveries. We affirm.

FACTS

In November of 1971, the Felgenhauers purchased a parcel of property consisting of the front portion of two contiguous lots on Spring Street in Paso Robles. The parcel is improved with a restaurant that faces Spring Street. The back portion of the lots is a parking lot that was owned by a bank. The parking lot is between a public alley and the back of the Felgenhauers' restaurant.

From the time the Felgenhauers opened their restaurant in 1974, deliveries were made through the alley by crossing over the parking lot to the restaurant's back door. The Felgenhauers never asked permission of the bank to have deliveries made over its parking lot. The Felgenhauers operated the restaurant until the spring of 1978. Thereafter, until 1982, the Felgenhauers leased their property to various businesses.

The Felgenhauers reopened their restaurant in June of 1982. Deliveries resumed over the bank's parking lot to the restaurant's back door. In November of 1984, the Felgenhauers sold their restaurant business, but not the real property, to James and Ann Enloe. The Enloes leased the property from the Felgenhauers. Deliveries continued over the bank's parking lot.

James Enloe testified he did not believe he had the right to use the bank's property and never claimed the right. Enloe said that during his tenancy, he saw the bank manager in the parking lot. The manager told him the bank planned to construct a fence to define the boundary between the bank's property and the Felgenhauers' property. Enloe asked the manager to put in a gate so that he could continue to receive deliveries and have access to a trash dumpster. The manager agreed. Enloe "guess[ed]" the fence and gate were constructed about three years into his term. He said, "[Three years] could be right, but it's a guess." In argument to the jury, the Sonis' counsel said the fence and gate were constructed in January of 1988.

The Enloes sold the restaurant to Brett Butterfield in 1993. Butterfield sold it to William DaCossee in March of 1998. DaCossee was still operating the restaurant at the time of trial. During all this time, deliveries continued across the bank's parking lot.

The Sonis purchased the bank property, including the parking lot in dispute in 1998. In 1999, the Sonis told the Felgenhauers' tenant,

DaCossee, that they were planning to cut off access to the restaurant from their parking lot.

The jury found the prescriptive period was from June of 1982 to January of 1988.

DISCUSSION
I

The Sonis contend there is no substantial evidence to support a prescriptive easement for deliveries across their property. They claim the uncontroverted evidence is that the use of their property was not under "a claim of right."…

At common law, a prescriptive easement was based on the fiction that a person who openly and continuously used the land of another without the owner's consent, had a lost grant. California courts have rejected the fiction of the lost grant. Instead, the courts have adopted language from adverse possession in stating the elements of a prescriptive easement. The two are like twins, but not identical. Those elements are open and notorious use that is hostile and adverse, continuous and uninterrupted for the five-year statutory period under a claim of right. Unfortunately, the language used to state the elements of a prescriptive easement or adverse possession invites misinterpretation. This is a case in point.

The Sonis argue the uncontroverted evidence is that the use of their property was not under a claim of right. They rely on the testimony of James Enloe that he never claimed he had a right to use the bank property for any purpose.

Claim of right does not require a belief or claim that the use is legally justified. It simply means that the property was used without permission of the owner of the land. As the American Law of Property states in the context of adverse possession: "In most of the cases asserting [the requirement of a claim of right], it means no more than that possession must be hostile, which in turn means only that the owner has not expressly consented to it by lease or license or has not been led into acquiescing in it by the denial of adverse claim on the part of the possessor." (3 Casner, American Law of Property (1952) Title by Adverse Possession, § 5.4, p. 776.)... Enloe testified that he had no discussion with the bank about deliveries being made over its property. The jury could reasonably conclude the Enloes used the bank's property without its permission. Thus they used it under a claim of right.

The Sonis attempt to make much of the fence the bank constructed between the properties and Enloe's request to put in a gate. But Enloe was uncertain when the fence and gate were constructed. The Sonis' attorney argued it was constructed in January of 1988. The jury could reasonably conclude that by then the prescriptive easement had been established.

The Sonis argue the gate shows the use of their property was not hostile. They cite *Myran v. Smith* (1931) 117 Cal.App. 355, 362, 4 P.2d 219, for the proposition that to effect a prescriptive easement the adverse user "... must unfurl his flag on the land, and keep it flying, so that the owner may see, if he will, that an enemy has invaded his domains, and planted the standard of conquest."

But *Myran* made the statement in the context of what is necessary to create a prescriptive easement. Here, as we have said, the jury could reasonably conclude the prescriptive easement was established prior to the erection of the fence and gate. The Sonis cite no authority for the proposition that even after the easement is created, the user must keep the flag of hostility flying. To the contrary, once the easement is created, the use continues as a matter of legal right, and it is irrelevant whether the owner of the servient estate purports to grant permission for its continuance....

Notes

1. **Fiction of the lost grant.** *Felgenhauer* refers to the fiction of the lost grant. The principle traces back to English law. 4-34 POWELL ON REAL PROPERTY § 34.10 ("In early England the enjoyment had to have been 'from time immemorial,' and this date came to be fixed by statute as the year 1189. Towards the close of the medieval period, this theory was rephrased and an easement of this type was said to arise from a grant, presumably made in favor of the claimant before the time of legal memory, but since lost."). The usual American approach is to ignore the fiction and simply apply rules of prescription that largely track those of adverse possession. *See id.*

2. How do the elements of a prescriptive easement differ from the elements of adverse possession? Why do you think they differ in this way? How do the resulting interests differ?

3. **Easements acquired by the public.** What happens if city pedestrians routinely cut across a private parking lot? May an easement by prescription be claimed by the public at large? Does it matter that the right asserted is not in the hands of any one person? Here, too, the fiction of the lost grant may play a role in the willingness of courts to entertain the possibility.

> There is a split of authority as to whether a public highway may be created by prescription. A number of older cases hold that the public cannot acquire a road by prescription because the doctrine of prescription is based on the theory of a lost grant, and such a grant cannot be made to a large and indefinite body such as the public. See II American Law of Property § 9.50 (J. Casner ed.1952). The lost grant theory, however, has been discarded. W. Burby, Real

Property § 31, at 77 (1965). In its place, courts have resorted to the justifications that underlie statutes of limitations: "[The] functional utility in helping to cause prompt termination of controversies before the possible loss of evidence and in stabilizing long continued property uses." 3 R. Powell, supra note 5, ¶ 413, at 34–103–04; W. Burby, supra, § 31, at 77; Restatement of Property ch. 38, Introductory Note, at 2923 (1944). These reasons apply equally to the acquisition of prescriptive easements by public use. The majority view now is that a public easement may be acquired by prescription. 2 J. Grimes, Thompson on Real Property § 342, at 209 (1980).

Dillingham Commercial Co. v. City of Dillingham, 705 P.2d 410, 416 (Alaska 1985).

What then should the owner of a publicly accessible location do? The owners of Rockefeller Center reportedly block off its streets one day per year in order to prevent the loss of any rights to exclude. David W. Dunlap, "Closing for a Spell, Just to Prove It's Ours," *New York Times* (Oct. 28, 2011), available at http://www.nytimes.com/2011/10/30/nyregion/lever-house-closes-once-a-year-to-maintain-its-ownership-rights.html?_r=0 ("But there is another significant hybrid: purely private space to which the public is customarily welcome, at the owners' implicit discretion. These spaces include Lever House, Rockefeller Plaza and College Walk at Columbia University, which close for part of one day every year."). Another option is to post a sign granting permission to enter (thus negating any element of adversity). Some states approve this approach by statute. Cal. Civ. Code § 1008 ("No use by any person or persons, no matter how long continued, of any land, shall ever ripen into an easement by prescription, if the owner of such property posts at each entrance to the property or at intervals of not more than 200 feet along the boundary a sign reading substantially as follows: 'Right to pass by permission, and subject to control, of owner: Section 1008, Civil Code.'").

4.   Irrevocable Licenses

An easement is distinct from a **license**. A license is permission from the owner to enter the land. Because it is permissive, it is revocable. Many difficulties with distinguishing easements from licenses arise when parties fail to clearly bargain over the right to use land. *See, e.g.*, Willow Tex, Inc. v. Dimacopoulos, 503 N.E.2d 99, 100 (N.Y. 1986) ("The writing must establish unequivocally the grantor's intent to give for all time to come a use of the servient estate to the dominant estate. The policy of the law favoring unrestricted use of realty requires that where there is any ambiguity as to the permanence of the restriction to be imposed on the servient estate, the right of use should be deemed a license, revocable at will by the grantor, rather than an easement.").

Under the right circumstances, a license may become irrevocable.

Richardson v. Franc
182 Cal.Rptr.3d 853 (Cal. App. 2015)

RUVOLO, P.J.

In order to access their home in Novato, California, James Scott Richardson and Lisa Donetti (respondents) had to traverse land belonging to their neighbors, Greg and Terrie Franc (appellants) on a 150–foot long road which was authorized by an easement for "access and public utility purposes." Over a 20–year period, both respondents and their predecessors-in-interest maintained landscaping, irrigation, and lighting appurtenant to both sides of the road within the easement area without any objection. Six years after purchasing the property burdened by the easement, appellants demanded that respondents remove the landscaping, irrigation, and lighting on the ground that respondents' rights in the easement area were expressly limited to access and utility purposes, and the landscaping and other improvements exceeded the purpose for which the easement was granted. Respondents brought this lawsuit seeking, among other things, to establish their right to an irrevocable license which would grant them an uninterrupted right to continue to maintain the landscaping and other improvements....

.... In 1989, Karen and Tom Poksay began building their home on undeveloped property at 2513 Laguna Vista Drive in Novato, California. The project included constructing and landscaping a 150–foot long driveway within the 30–foot wide easement running down to the site of their new home, which was hidden from the street. The driveway was constructed pursuant to an easement over 2515 Laguna Vista Drive, which was then owned by [appellants' predecessors in interest]. The easement was for access and utility purposes only.

Landscaping along the driveway was important to the Poksays.... They hired a landscaper, who dug holes for plants and trees. Ms. Poksay then added plants and trees along both sides of the driveway in the easement area—hawthorn trees, Australian tea trees, daylilies, Mexican sage, breath of heaven, flowering pear trees, and evergreen shrubs.

The landscaper installed a drip irrigation system.... Water fixtures were also installed along the driveway for fire safety. The Poksays also added electrical lighting along the driveway, later replacing the electrical lighting with solar lighting.

During the decade that the Poksays resided at the property Ms. Poksay regularly tended to the landscaped area, including trimming and weeding, ensuring the irrigation system was working properly, and replacing plants and trees as necessary. In addition to Ms. Poskay's own labor, the Poksays paid their landscaper to perform general maintenance ....

Respondents purchased the property in late 2000.... Over the years, respondents added new plants and trees, including oleanders, an evergreen tree, another tea tree, Mexican sage, lavender, rosemary, and a potato bush. Respondent Donetti testified that landscapers came weekly or every other week, and the landscapers spent 40 to 50 percent of their time in the easement area.... During her testimony, respondent Donetti explained, "we've paid a lot of money to nurture it and grow it. It's beautiful. It has privacy. It's absolutely tied to our house value. It's our curb appeal."

Appellants purchased 2515 Laguna Vista Drive in 2004. [Appellant Greg Franc admitted he knew about the landscaping in the easement area, as well as the hiring of landscapers.] He even admitted that the trees were "beautiful and provide a lot of color and [were] just all-around attractive." From 2004 to August 2010, appellants and respondents lived in relative harmony .... It was not until late 2010—approximately six years after appellants bought the property and two decades after the landscaping and other improvements began—that appellants first raised a concern about the landscaping and other improvements. Prior to that date, no one had ever objected.

In late September or early October 2010, without any notice, appellant Greg Franc cut the irrigation and electrical lines on both sides of the driveway. He cut not only the lines irrigating the landscaping on the easement, but also those irrigating respondents' own property. The water valve pumps leading to the irrigation lines were disassembled as well. As part of these proceedings, the trial court granted respondents' motion for preliminary injunction and the irrigation system was restored.... Following a bench trial and an on-site visit to the property, the court .... granted respondents' request for an irrevocable license . ...

.... [A]s appellants acknowledge, the grant of an irrevocable license is "based in equity." After the trial court has exercised its equitable powers, the appellate court reviews the judgment under the abuse of discretion standard....

Before we address the specific issues appellants raise on appeal, it is helpful to review the law governing the grant of an irrevocable license. "A license gives authority to a licensee to perform an act or acts on the property of another pursuant to the express or implied permission of the owner." (6 Miller & Starr, Cal. Real Estate (3d ed. 2000) Easements, § 15:2, p. 15–10.) "A licensor generally can revoke a license at any time without excuse or without consideration to the licensee. In addition, a conveyance of the property burdened with a license revokes the license...." (*Id.* at pp 15–10–15–11, fns. omitted.)

However, a license may become irrevocable when a landowner knowingly permits another to repeatedly perform acts on his or her land, and the licensee, in reasonable reliance on the continuation of the license, has expended time and a substantial amount of money on improvements with the licensor's knowledge. Under such circumstances, it would be inequitable to terminate the license. In that case, the licensor is said to be estopped from revoking the license, and the license becomes the equivalent of an easement, commensurate in its extent and duration with the right to be enjoyed. A trial court's factual finding that a license is irrevocable is reviewed for substantial evidence.

In the paradigmatic case, a landowner allows his neighbor the right to use some portion of his property—often a right of way or water from a creek—knowing that the neighbor needs the right to develop his property. The neighbor then builds a house, digs an irrigation ditch, paves the right of way, plants an orchard, or farms the land in reliance on the landowner's acquiescence. Later, after failing to make a timely objection, the landowner or his successor suddenly raises legal objections and seeks to revoke the neighbor's permissive usage....

In the instant case .... the statement of decision states: "Because [respondents] adduced sufficient evidence at trial concerning their substantial expenditures in the easement area for landscaping, maintenance, care, and physical labor, and because sufficient evidence was presented at trial to support that [respondents'] predecessor-in-interest, Ms. Poksay, also expended substantial sums in the easement area for landscaping, maintenance, care, and physical labor, and because, as the evidence and testimony at trial showed, that no objection was made to any of this by either [appellants] or [appellants'] predecessor-in-interest, Mr. Schaefer, over the course of more than 20 years, [respondents] have sufficiently met the requirements for an irrevocable parol license for both [respondents], and [respondents'] successors-in-interest. Both law and equity dictate this result."

....[Appellants] contend the trial court erred in finding the evidence supported the creation of an irrevocable license because respondents' reliance on continued permission to landscape and make other improvements in the easement area was not reasonable as a matter of law.

Appellants point out the evidence at trial revealed that throughout the history of the ownership of the property, there was never an actual request for permission to make and maintain these improvements and express consent was never given. In essence, appellants contend that tacit permission by silence is insufficient to create an irrevocable license and that respondents were required to show an express grant of permission induced them into undertaking the improvements within the easement area.

Permission sufficient to establish a license can be express or implied.... A license may also arise by implication from the acts of the parties, from their relations, or from custom. When a landowner knowingly permits another to perform acts on his land, a license may be implied from his failure to object....

.... Here, the undisputed evidence revealed appellants failed to object to the landscaping and other improvements for *6 years* before appellants first made their demand that the landscaping and other improvements be removed. Thus, with full knowledge that the road providing ingress and egress to respondents' property was landscaped, irrigated, and lit, and with full knowledge that respondents were maintaining these improvements on an ongoing basis, appellants said nothing to respondents. When coupled with the previous 14 years appellants' predecessors-in-interest acquiesced in these improvements, this constituted a total of *20 years* of uninterrupted permissive use of the easement area for the landscaping and other improvements. Therefore, we find the court had ample evidence to conclude that adequate and sufficient permission was granted to respondents by appellants to maintain the extensive landscaping improvements on either side of the roadway.

Appellants next stress that for the license to be irrevocable, there must be substantial expenditures in reliance on the license. In this regard, the trial court made the necessary findings that respondents "have expended substantial monetary sums to improve, maintain, landscape, and care for the easement area, including the retention of professional landscapers on a regular basis...."

Appellants next challenge "the unlimited physical scope and duration of the license" granted by the trial court. They claim "the trial court, in derogation of equity and the law, decided that [r]espondents ... should have sole and absolute discretion to decide what will happen on property that is owned by [appellants]." In making this argument, appellants ignore the fact that the trial court was vested with broad discretion in framing an equitable result under the facts of this case.... As it was empowered to do, the trial court exercised its broad equitable discretion and fashioned relief to fit the specific facts of this case. The court found "by a preponderance of the evidence that [respondents] hold an irrevocable parol license for themselves and their successors-in-interest to maintain and improve landscaping, irrigation, and lighting within the 30' wide and 150' long easement."

Appellants assert "it is wholly erroneous and grossly unfair to make the license *irrevocable in perpetuity*." (Original italics.) Appellants argue that a proper ruling in this case would be to grant respondents an irrevocable license but "with the license to landscape and garden limited in duration until [respondents] transfer title to anyone else or no longer reside on the property...."

The principles relating to the duration of an irrevocable license were stated by our Supreme Court over a century ago, and these principles are still valid today. An otherwise revocable license becomes irrevocable when the licensee, acting in reasonable reliance either on the licensor's representations or on the terms of the license, makes substantial expenditures of money or labor in the execution of the license; and the license will continue "for so long a time as the nature of it calls for." As explained in a leading treatise, "A license remains irrevocable for a period sufficient to enable the licensee to capitalize on his or her investment. He can continue to use it only as long as justice and equity require its use." (6 Miller & Starr, *supra,* § 15:2, p. 15–15.)

The evidence adduced at trial indicates respondents and their predecessors in interest expended significant money and labor when they planted and nurtured the landscaping abutting the roadway, installed sophisticated irrigation equipment throughout the easement area, and constructed lighting along the roadway. Under such circumstances the trial court did not abuse its discretion in concluding it would be inequitable to require respondents to remove these improvements when the property is transferred, given the substantial investment in time and money and the permanent nature of these improvements....

Lastly, we reject appellants' hyperbolic claim that in fashioning the scope and duration of the irrevocable license granted in this case, "the trial court, without exercising caution, took property that rightfully belonged to [appellants] and ceded it to [r]espondents—and their successors—forever."

This argument ignores that a license does not create or convey any interest in the real property; it merely makes lawful an act that otherwise would constitute a trespass.... Far from granting respondents "an exclusive easement amounting to fee title" as appellants' claim, the court's decision simply maintains the status quo that has existed for over 20 years and was obvious to appellants when they purchased the property a decade ago.

Notes and Questions

1. The Restatement characterizes irrevocable license situations as a servitude created by estoppel. Restatement § 2.10. Is there any difference, then, between an irrevocable license and an easement by prescription? Is there any reason to treat them differently?

2. Is landscaping important enough to justify the intrusion into property ownership interests? What do you think would have happened had the appellants won?

3. How well does *Richardson* track your intuitions about everyday behavior? Would you ask permission before engaging in the landscaping at issue here? Would you advise a client to? Suppose you asked your neighbor for an easement of way to enable you to build on an adjoining property? You're friends, and he says yes. But you know a thing or two about the law, so you know that if your relations turn sour you would have to rely on an irrevocable license claim. Would you push for a formal grant in writing? Is that a neighborly thing to do? For one view, *see* Shepard v. Purvine, 248 P.2d 352, 361-62 (Or. 1952) ("Under the circumstances, for plaintiffs to have insisted upon a deed would have been embarrassing; in effect, it would have been expressing a doubt as to their friend's integrity."). Does it make a difference that you know to ask? What about those without legal training? Should the law accommodate private ordering or funnel property holders into formal arrangements? Do the interests of third parties, including possible future purchasers of each of the affected properties, matter to your analysis?

C. Altering Easements

Brown v. Voss
715 P.2d 514 (Wash. 1986)

BRACHTENBACH, Justice.
The question posed is to what extent, if any, the holder of a private road easement can traverse the servient estate to reach not only the original dominant estate, but a subsequently acquired parcel when those two combined parcels are used in such a way that there is no increase in the

burden on the servient estate. The trial court denied the injunction sought by the owners of the servient estate. The Court of Appeals reversed. We reverse the Court of Appeals and reinstate the judgment of the trial court.

A portion of an exhibit depicts the involved parcels.

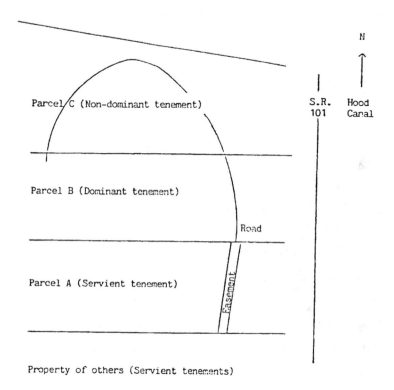

In 1952 the predecessors in title of parcel A granted to the predecessor owners of parcel B a private road easement across parcel A for "ingress to and egress from" parcel B. Defendants acquired parcel A in 1973. Plaintiffs bought parcel B on April 1, 1977 and parcel C on July 31, 1977, but from two different owners. Apparently the previous owners of parcel C were not parties to the easement grant.

When plaintiffs acquired parcel B a single family dwelling was situated thereon. They intended to remove that residence and replace it with a single family dwelling which would straddle the boundary line common to parcels B and C.

Plaintiffs began clearing both parcels B and C and moving fill materials in November 1977. Defendants first sought to bar plaintiff's use of the easement in April 1979 by which time plaintiffs had spent more than $11,000 in developing their property for building.

Defendants placed logs, a concrete sump and a chain link fence within the easement. Plaintiffs sued for removal of the obstructions, an injunction against defendant's interference with their use of the easement and damages. Defendants counterclaimed for damages and an injunction against plaintiffs using the easement other than for parcel B.

The trial court awarded each party $1 in damages. The award against the plaintiffs was for a slight inadvertent trespass outside the easement.

The trial court made the following findings of fact:

VI

> The plaintiffs have made no unreasonable use of the easement in the development of their property. There have been no complaints of unreasonable use of the roadway to the south of the properties of the parties by other neighbors who grant easements to the parties to this action to cross their properties to gain access to the property of the plaintiffs. Other than the trespass there is no evidence of any damage to the defendants as a result of the use of the easement by the plaintiffs. There has been no increase in volume of travel on the easement to reach a single family dwelling whether built on tract B or on Tacts [sic] B and C. There is no evidence of any increase in the burden on the subservient estate from the use of the easement by the plaintiffs for access to parcel C.

VIII

If an injunction were granted to bar plaintiffs access to tract C across the easement to a single family residence, Parcel C would become landlocked; plaintiffs would not be able to make use of their property; they would not be able to build their single family residence in a manner to properly enjoy the view of the Hood Canal and the surrounding area as originally anticipated at the time of their purchase and even if the single family residence were constructed on parcel B, if the injunction were granted, plaintiffs would not be able to use the balance of their property in parcel C as a yard or for any other use of their property in conjunction with their home. Conversely, there is and will be no appreciable hardship or damage to the defendants if the injunction is denied.

IX

If an injunction were to be granted to bar the plaintiffs access to tract C, the framing and enforcing of such an order would be impractical. Any violation of the order would result in the parties back in court at great cost but with little or no damages being involved.

X

Plaintiffs have acted reasonable [sic] in the development of their property. Their trespass over a "little" corner of the defendants' property was inadvertent, and de minimis. The fact that the defendants counter claim seeking an injunction to bar plaintiffs access to parcel C was filed as leverage against the original plaintiffs' claim for an interruption of their easement rights, may be considered in determining whether equitable relief by way of an injunction should be granted.

Relying upon these findings of fact, the court denied defendant's request for an injunction and granted the plaintiffs the right to use the easement for access to parcels B & C "as long as plaintiffs [sic] properties (B and C) are developed and used solely for the purpose of a single family residence."

The Court of Appeals reversed ....

The easement in this case was created by express grant. Accordingly, the extent of the right acquired is to be determined from the terms of the grant properly construed to give effect to the intention of the parties. By the express terms of the 1952 grant, the predecessor owners of parcel B acquired a private road easement across parcel A and the right to use the easement for ingress to and egress from parcel B. Both plaintiffs and defendants agree that the 1952 grant created an easement appurtenant to parcel B as the dominant estate. Thus, plaintiffs, as owners of the dominant estate, acquired rights in the use of the easement for ingress to and egress from parcel B.

However, plaintiffs have no such easement rights in connection with their ownership of parcel C, which was not a part of the original dominant estate under the terms of the 1952 grant. As a general rule, an easement appurtenant to one parcel of land may not be extended by the owner of the dominant estate to other parcels owned by him, whether adjoining or distinct tracts, to which the easement is not appurtenant.

Plaintiffs, nonetheless, contend that extension of the use of the easement for the benefit of nondominant property does not constitute a misuse of the easement, where as here, there is no evidence of an increase in the burden on the servient estate. We do not agree. If an easement is appurtenant to a particular parcel of land, any extension thereof to other parcels is a misuse of the easement.... Under the express language of the 1952 grant, plaintiffs only have rights in the use of the easement for the benefit of parcel B. Although, as plaintiffs contend, their planned use of the easement to gain access to a single family residence located partially on parcel B and partially on parcel C is perhaps no more than technical misuse of the easement, we conclude that it is misuse nonetheless.

However, it does not follow from this conclusion alone that defendants are entitled to injunctive relief. Since the awards of $1 in damages were not appealed, only the denial of an injunction to defendants is in issue. Some fundamental principles applicable to a request for an injunction must be considered. (1) The proceeding is equitable and addressed to the sound discretion of the trial court. (2) The trial court is vested with a broad discretionary power to shape and fashion injunctive relief to fit the *particular facts, circumstances, and equities of the case before it.* Appellate courts give great weight to the trial court's exercise of that discretion. (3) One of the essential criteria for injunctive relief is actual and substantial injury sustained by the person seeking the injunction.

The trial court found as facts, upon substantial evidence, that plaintiffs have acted reasonably in the development of their property, that there is and was no damage to the defendants from plaintiffs' use of the easement, that there was no increase in the volume of travel on the easement, that there was no increase in the burden on the servient estate, that defendants sat by for more than a year while plaintiffs expended more than $11,000 on their project, and that defendants' counterclaim was an effort to gain "leverage" against plaintiffs' claim. In addition, the court found from the evidence that plaintiffs would suffer considerable hardship if the injunction were granted whereas no appreciable hardship or damages would flow to defendants from its denial. Finally, the court limited plaintiffs' use of the combined parcels solely to the same purpose for which the original parcel was used—*i.e.,* for a single family residence.

.… Based upon the equities of the case, as found by the trial court, we are persuaded that the trial court acted within its discretion. The Court of Appeals is reversed and the trial court is affirmed.

DORE, Justice (dissenting).

The majority correctly finds that an extension of this easement to nondominant property is a misuse of the easement. The majority, nonetheless, holds that the owners of the servient estate are not entitled to injunctive relief. I dissent.

The comments and illustrations found in the Restatement of Property § 478 (1944) address the precise issue before this court. Comment *e* provides in pertinent part that "if one who has an easement of way over Whiteacre appurtenant to Blackacre uses the way with the purpose of going to Greenacre, the use is improper even though he eventually goes to Blackacre rather than to Greenacre." Illustration 6 provides:

> 6. By prescription, A has acquired, as the owner and possessor of Blackacre, an easement of way over an alley leading from Blackacre to the street. He buys Whiteacre, an adjacent lot, to which the way is not appurtenant, and builds a public garage one-fourth of which is located on Blackacre and three-fourths of which is located on Whiteacre. A wishes to use the alley as a means of ingress and egress to and from the garage. He has no privilege to use the alley to go to that part of the garage which is built on Whiteacre, and he may not use the alley until that part of the garage built on Blackacre is so separated from the part built on Whiteacre that uses for the benefit of Blackacre are distinguishable from those which benefit Whiteacre.

The majority grants the privilege to extend the agreement to nondominant property on the basis that the trial court found no appreciable hardship or damage to the servient owners. However, as conceded by the majority, any extension of the use of an easement to benefit a nondominant estate constitutes a misuse of the easement. Misuse of an easement is a trespass. The Brown's use of the easement to benefit parcel C, especially if they build their home as planned, would involve a continuing trespass for which damages would be difficult to measure. Injunctive relief is the appropriate remedy under these circumstances....

The Browns are responsible for the hardship of creating a landlocked parcel. They knew or should have known from the public records that the easement was not appurtenant to parcel C. In encroachment cases this factor is significant....

In addition, an injunction would not interfere with the Brown's right to use the easement as expressly granted, *i.e.*, for access to parcel B. An injunction would merely require the Browns to acquire access to parcel C if they want to build a home that straddles parcels B and C. One possibility would be to condemn a private way of necessity over their existing easement in an action under RCW 8.24.010. *See Brown v. McAnally*, 97 Wash.2d 360, 644 P.2d 1153 (1982)....

Notes and Questions

1. What do you make of the reasoning in *Brown*? What is the point of taking a strict view of the modification of easements if the majority has no intention of following it through to its logical consequence? Would it be better to be more flexible about easement law? Or is the dissent's approach preferable?

2. It turns out that the facts in *Brown* were a good deal less straightforward than the majority indicates. Elizabeth J. Samuels, *Stories Out of School: Teaching the Case of Brown v. Voss*, 16 CARDOZO L. REV. 1445, 1451 (1995) ("What I discovered from the record in the case, related land and other court records, and interviews with the parties was predictable in some ways and startling in others. As the reader of the opinion suspects, the conflict between the neighbors had a dark and bitter emotional history. As one cannot easily suspect, the physical aspects of the property differ in legally

significant ways from the court's description and understanding. When the supreme court of Washington decided the case, the controversy, unbeknownst to the court, was moot. And the party who appears to be the loser in the opinion was in reality the winner." (footnotes omitted)).

3. Can you reconcile this case with *Jacque v. Steenberg Homes?*

4. Note the range of possible outcomes in easement disputes. It is not so simple as saying the property owner has the right to block the would-be easement holder or not. Cases like *Brown* honor the property interests of the landowner, but by requiring the payment of damages rather than granting an injunction. In other words, the trespasser gets to choose whether or not to continue using the land. Likewise, the right-of-way statutes discussed above allow passage with payment. Recall similar remedies in the adverse possession setting in cases of innocent encroachments. What do you think motivates courts to elect payment remedies in these situations? Why do you think they are not the norm in property law?

M.P.M. Builders, LLC v. Dwyer
809 N.E.2d 1053 (Mass. 2004)

COWIN, J.

We are asked to decide whether the owner of a servient estate may change the location of an easement without the consent of the easement holder. We conclude that, subject to certain limitations, described below, the servient estate owner may do so.

1. *Facts.* The essential facts are not in dispute. The defendant, Leslie Dwyer, owns a parcel of land in Raynham abutting property owned by the plaintiff, M.P.M. Builders, L.L.C. (M.P.M.). Dwyer purchased his parcel in 1941, and, in the deed, he was also conveyed an easement, a "right of

way along the cartway to Pine Street," across M.P.M.'s land. The cartway branches so that it provides Dwyer access to his property at three separate points. The deed describes the location of the easement and contains no language concerning its relocation.

In July, 2002, M.P.M. received municipal approval for a plan to subdivide and develop its property into seven house lots. Because Dwyer's easement cuts across and interferes with construction on three of M.P.M.'s planned lots, M.P.M. offered to construct two new access easements to Dwyer's property. The proposed easements would continue to provide unrestricted access from the public street (Pine Street) to Dwyer's parcel in the same general areas as the existing cartway. The relocation of the easement would allow unimpeded construction by M.P.M. on its three house lots. M.P.M. has agreed to clear and construct the new access ways, at its own expense, so "that they are as convenient [for the defendant] as the existing cartway[ ]." Dwyer objected to the proposed easement relocation, "preferring to maintain [his] right of way in the same place that it has been and has been used by [him] for the past 62 years."

2. *Procedural history.* M.P.M. sought a declaration, pursuant to G.L. c. 231A, that it has a right unilaterally to relocate Dwyer's easement. When M.P.M. moved for summary judgment, a Land Court judge found that there were no material issues of fact in dispute, denied M.P.M.'s motion for summary judgment, entered summary judgment against M.P.M., and dismissed the case.

The judge recognized that this case was "a clear example of an increasingly common situation where a dominant tenant is able to block development on the servient land because of the common-law rule which ... may well be the result of unreflective repetition of a misapplied rationale." He noted that the rule conflicts with the "right of a servient tenant to use his land in any lawful manner that does not interfere with the purpose of the easement." Nevertheless, he concluded that under the "settled" common law, once the location of an easement has been fixed it cannot be changed except by agreement of the estate owners. The judge concluded that, unless this court decides "to dispel the uncertainty that now exists and adapt the common law to present-day circumstances," he was bound to apply the law currently in effect. We granted M.P.M.'s application for direct appellate review to decide whether our law should permit the owner of a servient estate to change the location of an easement without the easement holder's consent.

3. *Discussion.* …

The parties disagree whether our common law permits the servient estate owner to relocate an easement without the easement holder's consent. Dwyer, citing language in our cases, contends that, once the location of an easement has been defined, it cannot be changed except by agreement of the parties. … M.P.M. claims that our common law permits the servient estate owner to relocate an easement as long as such relocation would not materially increase the cost of, or inconvenience to, the easement holder's use of the easement for its intended purpose. M.P.M. urges us to clarify the law by expressly adopting the modern rule proposed by the American Law Institute in the Restatement (Third) of Property (Servitudes) § 4.8(3) (2000).

This section provides that:

> "Unless expressly denied by the terms of an easement, as defined in § 1.2, the owner of the servient estate is entitled to make reasonable changes in the location or dimensions of an easement, at the servient owner's expense, to permit normal use or development of the servient estate, but only if the changes do not (a) significantly lessen the utility of the easement, (b) increase the burdens on the owner of the easement in its use and enjoyment, or (c) frustrate the purpose for which the easement was created."

Section 4.8(3) is a default rule, to apply only in the absence of an express prohibition against relocation in the instrument creating the easement and only to changes made by the servient, not the dominant, estate owner.[4] It "is designed to permit development of the servient estate to the extent it can be accomplished without unduly interfering with the legitimate interests of the easement holder." *Id.* at comment f, at 563. Section 4.8(3) maximizes the over-all property utility by increasing the value of the servient estate without diminishing the value of the dominant estate; minimizes the cost associated with an easement by reducing the risk that the easement will prevent future beneficial development of the servient estate; and encourages the use of easements. Regardless of what heretofore has been the common law, we conclude that § 4.8(3) of the Restatement is a sensible development in the law and now adopt it as the law of the Commonwealth.

We are persuaded that § 4.8(3) strikes an appropriate balance between the interests of the respective estate owners by permitting the servient owner to develop his land without unreasonably interfering with the easement holder's rights. The rule permits the servient owner to relocate the easement subject to the stated limitations as a "fair tradeoff for the vulnerability of the servient estate to increased use of the easement to accommodate changes in technology and development of the dominant estate." Restatement (Third) of Property (Servitudes), *supra* at comment f, at 563. Therefore, under § 4.8(3), the owner of the servient estate is "able to make the fullest use of his or her property allowed by law, subject only to the requirement that he or she not damage other vested rights holders." *Roaring Fork Club, L.P. v. St. Jude's Co.,* [36 P.3d 1229,] 1237 [(Colo. 2001)].

---

[4] We previously have concluded that the dominant estate owner, that is, the easement holder, may not unilaterally relocate an easement. According to the Restatement, many jurisdictions have erroneously expanded that sensible restriction into one that prevents the owner of the servient estate from relocating the easement without the consent of the easement holder. Restatement (Third) of Property (Servitudes) § 4.8(3) comment f, at 563 (2000).

It is a long-established rule in the Commonwealth that the owner of real estate may make any and all beneficial uses of his property consistent with the easement.... We conclude that § 4.8(3) is consistent with these principles in its protection of the interests of the easement holder: a change may not significantly lessen the utility of the easement, increase the burden on the use and enjoyment by the owner of the easement, or frustrate the purpose for which the easement was created. The servient owner must bear the entire expense of the changes in the easement.

Dwyer urges us to reject the Restatement approach. He argues that adoption of § 4.8(3) will devalue easements, create uncertainty in property interests, and lead to an increase in litigation over property rights. Our adoption of § 4.8(3) will neither devalue easements nor place property interests in an uncertain status. An easement is by definition a limited, nonpossessory interest in realty.... An easement is created to serve a particular objective, not to grant the easement holder the power to veto other uses of the servient estate that do not interfere with that purpose.

The limitations embodied in § 4.8(3) ensure a relocated easement will continue to serve the purpose for which it was created. So long as the easement continues to serve its intended purpose, reasonably altering the location of the easement does not destroy the value of it. For the same reason, a relocated easement is not any less certain as a property interest. The only uncertainty generated by § 4.8(3) is in the easement's location. A rule that permits the easement holder to prevent any reasonable changes in the location of an easement would render an access easement virtually a possessory interest rather than what it is, merely a right of way. Finally, parties retain the freedom to contract for greater certainty as to the easement's location by incorporating consent requirements into their agreement.

"Clearly, the best course is for the [owners] to agree to alterations that would accommodate both parties' use of their respective properties to the fullest extent possible." *Roaring Fork Club, L.P. v. St. Jude's Co., supra* at 1237. In some cases, the parties will be unable to reach a meeting of the minds on the location of an easement. In the absence of agreement between the owners of the dominant and servient estates concerning the relocation of an easement, the servient estate owner should seek a declaration from the court that the proposed changes meet the criteria in § 4.8(3). Such an action gives the servient owner an opportunity to demonstrate that relocation comports with the Restatement requirements and the dominant owner an opportunity to demonstrate that the proposed alterations will cause damage. The servient owner may not resort to self-help remedies, and, as M.P.M. did here, should obtain a declaratory judgment before making any alterations.

Although Dwyer may be correct that increased litigation could result as a consequence of adopting § 4.8(3), we do not reject desirable developments in the law solely because such developments may result in disputes spurring litigation. Section 4.8(3) "imposes upon the easement holder the burden and risk of bringing suit against an unreasonable relocation," but this "far surpasses in utility and fairness the traditional rule that left the servient land owner remediless against an unreasonable easement holder." *Roaring Fork Club, L.P. v. St. Jude's Co., supra* at 1237, quoting Note, Balancing the Equities: Is Missouri Adopting a Progressive Rule for Relocation of Easements?, 61 Mo. L.Rev. 1039, 1060 (1996). We trust that, over time, uncertainties will diminish and litigation will subside as easement holders realize that in some circumstances unilateral changes to an easement, paid for by the servient estate owner, will be enforced by courts. Dominant and servient estate owners will have an incentive to negotiate a result rather than having a court impose one on them.

We return to the facts of this case. The Land Court judge ruled correctly under existing law. But we conclude that § 4.8(3) of the Restatement best complies with present-day realities. The deed creating Dwyer's easement does not expressly prohibit relocation. Therefore, M.P.M. may relocate the easement at its own expense if the proposed change in location does not significantly lessen the utility of the easement, increase the burdens on Dwyer's use and enjoyment of the easement, or frustrate the purpose for which the easement was created. M.P.M. shall pay for all the costs of relocating the easement.

Because we cannot determine from the present record whether the proposed relocation of the easement meets the aforementioned criteria, we vacate the judgment and remand the case to the Land Court for further proceedings consistent with this opinion.

Note

The ability to adapt long-term easements to new uses often depends on formal labels. Suppose a railroad acquires the right to conduct rail service over a stretch of land. Decades pass, and the railroad seeks to abandon the line and turn the tracks over to a local government that will tear them out and create a system of nature trails. Can it? If the railroad had acquired a fee simple, sure. But if it only had an easement of way for railroad operations, the change would exceed the easement's scope, giving the owner of the underlying land a claim. Restatement (First) of Property § 482 (1944) ("The extent of an easement created by a conveyance is fixed by the conveyance."). This is so even if the easement gave the railroad exclusive access to the land in question while the easement was active. *See, e.g.*, Preseault v. U.S., 100 F.3d 1525 (Fed. Cir. 1996).

D.   Transferring Easements

Easements appurtenant. Transferring easements appurtenant is simple; when the dominant estate is conveyed, the rights of the easement come along. This is a natural consequence of the principle that servitudes (such as easements) run with the land. A more complicated problem concerns the division of the dominant estate into smaller parcels. The default approach is to allow each parcel to enjoy the benefit of the easement.

Restatement (First) of Property § 488 (1944) ("Except as limited by the terms of its transfer, or by the manner or terms of the creation of the easement appurtenant, those who succeed to the possession of each of the parts into which a dominant tenement may be subdivided thereby succeed to the privileges of use of the servient tenement authorized by the easement."). Here, however, foreseeability and the extent of the added burden matters. *See generally* R. W. Gascoyne, *Right of owners of parcels into which dominant tenement is or will be divided to use right of way,* 10 A.L.R.3d 960 (Originally published in 1966) (collecting cases).

Easements in gross. The modern view is that easements in gross are transferable, assuming no contrary intent in their creation (e.g., that the benefit was intended to be personal to the recipient). *Restatement (Third) of Property (Servitudes)* § 4.6 cmt. (2000) ("Although historically courts have often stated that benefits in gross are not transferable, American courts have long carved out an exception for profits and easements in gross that serve commercial purposes. Under the rule stated in this section, the exception has now become the rule."); Restatement (First) of Property § 489 (1944) (commercial easements in gross, as distinct from easements for personal satisfaction, are transferable); § 491 (noncommercial easements in gross "determined by the manner or the terms of their creation").

Another issue concerns the divisibility of an easement in gross. Here, too, the danger is that divisibility may lead to excessive burdens on the servient estate. Section 493 of the First Restatement of Property provides that whether divisibility is permitted depends on the circumstances surrounding the easement's creation. The facts giving rise to a prescriptive easement, for example, may give a landowner fair notice that a single trespasser may acquire an easement, but not that the easement may then be shared by many others once the prescription period passes. In contrast, an exclusive easement might lead to a presumption of divisibilty, for "the fact that [the owner of the servient tenement] is excluded from making the use authorized by the easement, plus the fact that apportionability increases the value of the easement to its owner, tends to the inference in the usual case that the easement was intended in its creation to be apportionable." *Id.* cmt. c. Where the grant is non-exclusive a clearer indication of intended divisibility may be required. *Id.* cmt. d. Section 5.9 of the modern Restatement goes further by making divisibility the default assumption unless contrary to the parties intent or where divisibility would place unreasonable burdens on the servient estate.

E. Terminating Easements

Easements can be terminated in a variety of ways.

1. **Unity of ownership.** When the dominant and servient estates of an easement appurtenant unite under one owner, the easement ends. Likewise an easement in gross ends if the owner acquires an interest in the servient tenement that would have provided independent authority to exercise the rights of the easement.

2. **Release by the easement holder.** The First Restatement would require a written instrument under seal for an inter vivos release, while the modern Restatement simply requires compliance with the Statute of Frauds.

3. **Abandonment.** Abandonment resembles a release. The First Restatement treats them separately, however, and distinguishes the two by describing abandonment as intent by the easement holder to give up the easement, while a release is an act done on behalf of the owner of the burdened property. Abandonment may be inferred by actions. Restatement (First) of Property § 504 (1944).

4. **Estoppel.** Estoppel may terminate an easement when 1) the owner of the servient tenement acts in a manner that is inconsistent with the easement's continuation; 2) the acts are in foreseeable reasonable reliance on conduct by the easement holder; and 3) allowing the easement to continue would work an unreasonable harm to the owner of the servient property. *Id.* § 505.

5. **Prescription.** Just as an easement may be gained by prescription, so too may it be lost by open and notorious adverse acts by the owner of the servient tenement that interrupt the exercise of the easement for the prescription period.

6. **Condemnation.** The exercise of the eminent domain power to take the servient estate creates the possibility of compensation for the easement owner.

7. **A tax deed.** Section 509 of the First Restatement provides that a tax deed will extinguish an easement in gross, but not an easement appurtenant.

8. **Expiration**, if the interest was for a particular time.

9. **Recording Acts.** Being property interests, easements are subject to the recording acts, and unrecorded interests may be defeated by transferees without notice. The modern restatement provides for exceptions for certain easements not subject to the Statute of Frauds and generally for servitudes that "would be discovered by reasonable inspection or inquiry." Restatement (Third) of Property (Servitudes) § 7.14 (2000).

F.   Negative Easements/Conservation Easements

In the United States, most of the work that could have been done by negative easements is largely performed by real covenants or equitable servitudes, which we take up in a future reading. *See Restatement (Third) of Property (Servitudes)* § 1.2 ("A 'negative' easement, the obligation not to use land in one's possession in specified ways, has become indistinguishable from a restrictive covenant, and is treated as such in this Restatement."). Nineteenth century English law gave negative easements a narrow domain. They were available only to prevent the servient estate from restricting light, air, support, or the flow of water of an artificial stream to the dominant estate. *Id.* § 1.2 cmt. h. Such easements were likewise not widely embraced in the United States, where equitably enforced negative covenants held in gross were disfavored.

For the most part, negative easements only arise by agreement or grant. U.S. courts therefore consistently reject the English "doctrine of ancient lights," which recognizes a right to light from a neighbor's land after the passage of time under certain circumstances. 4-34 POWELL ON REAL PROPERTY § 34.11.

The limitations of negative easements complicated efforts to create conservation and preservation easements. Such easements tend to be held in gross (e.g., by a conservation organization), and the common law prohibited equitable enforcement of negative covenants held in gross. The law likewise was skeptical about expanding the categories for which negative easements were available. Restatement (Third) of Property (Servitudes) § 1.6 cmt. a (2000). The problem was addressed by the Uniform Conservation Easement Act, which has now been adopted by every state. 4-34A POWELL ON REAL PROPERTY § 34A.01.

Restrictive Covenants

A.   Introduction

The historical antipathy of English law toward *negative* easements—the right of a landowner to *prevent* particular uses of *someone else's* land—made private ordering over conflicting land uses somewhat difficult. The basic problem is relatively easy to understand. Suppose Abigail pays her neighbor Beatrice $1000 in exchange for a promise that Beatrice will use her land only for residential purposes, because Abigail does not want to live next door to a busy commercial or industrial facility. Suppose that Beatrice then begins to construct a factory on her land. Abigail could sue for breach of contract and obtain appropriate remedies—perhaps including injunctive relief barring Beatrice from building the factory.

But now suppose that instead of building a factory herself, Beatrice sells her land to Clara, who intends to build a factory on the land. Clara didn't promise Abigail anything, and Abigail gave Clara no consideration—they are not in privity of contract. We might therefore conclude that Abigail is out of luck: she cannot enforce a contract against someone who didn't agree to be bound by it. But if that is our conclusion, there is now a huge obstacle to Abigail and Beatrice ever reaching their agreement in the first place: how could Abigail ever trust that her consideration is worth paying if Beatrice can deprive Abigail of the benefit of the bargain by selling her (Beatrice's) land? More generally, if a promise to *refrain* from certain uses will not "run with the land," can private parties ever effectively resolve their disputes over competing land uses by agreement?

Notwithstanding this concern, English courts were historically quite resistant to enforcing such restrictions against successors to the promisor's property interest. As you've already learned, only a very small number of negative easements were recognized. Furthermore, actions at law—seeking the remedy of money damages—for breach of a covenant restricting the use of land were available only in quite limited circumstances, in cases involving landlord-tenant relationships. Early American courts were more willing to enforce such covenants outside of the landlord-tenant context, but still required quite strict chains of privity of estate—voluntary transfers of title by written instruments—before they would enforce such covenants by an action for money damages. Of course, where the dispute is over competing uses of neighboring land, perhaps money damages are not the appropriate—or even the desired— remedy. And herein was the key to substantial liberalization of the enforcement of restrictive covenants. Eventually, landowners with an interest in enforcing such covenants found a workaround.

Tulk v. Moxhay
[1845] 47 Eng. Rep. 1345

Leicester Square in the 18th Century.
Source: JOHN HOLLINGSHEAD, THE STORY OF LEICESTER SQUARE 19 (1892), *available at* British
Library Online: http://access.bl.uk/item/pdf/lsidyv3c48bb3a

This was a motion by way of appeal from the Master of the Rolls to dissolve an injunction.

In the month of July 1808, the Plaintiff was seised in fee-simple not only of the piece of ground which formed the open space or garden in Leicester Square, but also of several houses situated in that square.

By an indenture of release, dated the 15th of July 1808, and made between the Plaintiff, of the one part, and Charles Elms, of the other part, after reciting that the Plaintiff was seised of that piece of land in fee-simple, and had contracted to sell it to Elms, but not reciting that that contract was made subject to any condition, in consideration of £210, the Plaintiff conveyed to Elms, in fee-simple, "all that piece or parcel of land, commonly called Leicester Square Garden or pleasure-ground, with the equestrian statue then standing in the centre thereof, and the iron railings and stone- work round the garden, and all easements or ways, &c., to hold the same to Elms, his heirs and assigns for ever." And in that indenture there was contained a covenant by Elms, in the words following:— "And the said Charles Elms, for himself, his heirs, executors, administrators, and assigns, doth covenant, promise, and agree to and with the said Charles Augustus Tulk, his heirs, executors, and administrators, in manner following—that is to say, that he, the said Charles Elms, his heirs and assigns, shall and will, from time to time, and at all times for ever hereafter, at his and their own proper costs and charges, keep and maintain the said piece or parcel of ground and square garden, and the iron railing round the same, in its present form, and in sufficient and proper repair as a square garden and pleasure-ground, in an open state, uncovered with any buildings, in a neat and ornamental order; and shall not nor will take down, nor permit or suffer to be taken down or defaced, at any time or times hereafter, the equestrian statue now standing or being in the centre of the said square garden, but shall and will continue and keep the same in its present situation, as it now is; and also, that it shall be lawful to and for the inhabitants of Leicester Square aforesaid, tenants of the said Charles Augustus Tulk, and of John Augustus Tulk, Esq., his father, their heirs and assigns, as well as the said Charles Augustus Tulk and John Augustus Tulk, their heirs and assigns, on payment of a reasonable rent for the same, to have keys (at their own expense), and the privilege of admission therewith annually, at any time or times, into the said square garden and pleasure-ground."

The bill then stated, that ... the Defendant had become the owner of that piece of ground by Virtue of a title derived from Elms [through several successive conveyances]; and that he had formed a plan, or scheme for erecting certain lines of shops and buildings thereon; but that the Plaintiff objected to such scheme, as being contrary to the aforesaid covenant, and injurious to the Plaintiff's houses in the square; that the Defendant had, nevertheless, proceeded to cut down several of the trees and shrubs, and had pulled down part of the iron railing, and had erected a hoarding or boards across the said piece of ground.

The bill charged, that, at the time when the Defendant purchased the piece of ground, and also when he took possession thereof, and also when he committed the acts complained of, he had notice of the covenant.

The bill prayed, that the Defendant, and his agents and workmen, might be restrained from … doing or committing, or permitting or suffering to be done or committed, any waste, spoil, destruction, or nuisance to be in or upon the said piece of garden ground.

An *ex parte* injunction was obtained from the Master of the Rolls, and the Defendant … by his answer, stated, that the inhabitants of Leicester Square and of the Plaintiff's houses had entirely ceased to use this piece of ground as a garden and pleasure-ground, or to pay any sum for the privilege of admission; and that, for many years before the Defendant purchased it, it had been in a ruinous condition, and not in an ornamental state, but altogether out of repair; that Tulk never took any steps to enforce the covenant, or to have the site of the ground improved; that the square was no longer a quiet place of residence, but that a thoroughfare had lately been made through it from Long Acre to Piccadilly; that he proposed to open two footpaths diagonally across the square, putting up gates and fences; that he had not yet fixed on any plan for building on it; or as to the ultimate use he should make of it; but he reserved by his answer the right to make all such use of the land as he might thereafter think fit, and lawfully could do; and he also submitted to the Court, that the covenant did not run with the land, and did not bind him as assignee.

The Defendant applied to the Master of the Rolls to dissolve the injunction, which his Lordship refused to do…. The effect of the injunction, as varied, was to restrain the Defendant, his workmen, &c., from converting or using the piece of ground and square garden in the bill mentioned, and the iron railing round the same, to or for any other purpose than as a square garden and pleasure-ground, in an open state, uncovered with buildings, until the hearing of this cause, or the further order of this Court.

The motion to dissolve the injunction was now renewed before the Lord Chancellor….

THE LORD CHANCELLOR [COTTENHAM].
… It is not disputed that a party selling land may, by some means or other, provide that the party to whom he sells it shall conform to certain rules, which the parties may think proper to lay down as between themselves. They may so contract as to bind the party purchasing to deal with the land according to the stipulation between him and the vendor…. Here, then, upon the face of the instrument, and in a manner free from doubt … the owner of the houses sells and disposes of land adjoining to those houses with an express covenant on the part of the purchaser, his heirs and assigns, that there shall be no buildings erected upon that land. It is now contended, not that Elms, the vendee, could violate that contract—not that he could build immediately after he had covenanted not to build, or that this Court could have had any difficulty, if he had made that attempt, to prevent him from building—but that he might sell that piece of land as if it were not incumbered with that covenant; and that the person to whom he sold it might at once, without the risk of the interference of this Court, violate the covenant of the party from whom he purchased it.

Now, I do not apprehend that the jurisdiction of this Court is fettered by the question, whether the covenant runs with the land or not. The question is, whether a party taking property with a stipulation to use it in a particular manner—that stipulation being imposed on him by the vendor in such a manner as to be binding by the law and principles of this Court—will be permitted by this Court to use it in a way diametrically opposite to that which the party has stipulated for.... Of course, the party purchasing the property, which is under such restriction, gives less for it than he would have given if he had bought it unincumbered. Can there, then, be anything much more inequitable or contrary to good conscience, than that a party, who takes property at a less price because it is subject to a restriction, should receive the full value from a third party, and that such third party should then hold it unfettered by the restriction under which it was granted? That would be most inequitable, most unjust, and most unconscientious; and, as far as I am informed, this Court never would sanction any such course of proceeding; but, on the contrary, it has always acted upon this principle, that you, who have the property, are bound by the principles and law of this Court to submit to the contract you have entered into; and you will not be permitted to hand over that property, and give to your assignee or your vendee a higher title, with regard to interest as between yourself and your vendor, than you yourself possess.

That is quite unconnected with the doctrine of a covenant running with the land. ...There is no question about the legal liability, which is best proved by this: that if there be a merely legal agreement, and no covenant—no question about the covenant running with the land—the party who takes the land takes it subject to the equity which the owner of the property has created: and if he takes it, subject to that equity, created by those through whom he has derived a title to it, is it not the rule of this Court, that the party, who has taken the property with knowledge of the equity, is liable to the equity? Is not this an equity attached to the property, by the party who is competent to bind the property? If a party enters into an agreement for a lease, and then sells the property which was to be demised, the purchaser of that property, with knowledge of the agreement, cannot set up his title against the party claiming the benefit of that contract; because, if there had been an equity attaching to the property in the owner, the owner is not permitted to give a better title to the purchaser with notice than he himself possesses. The other party is entitled to the benefit of the contract, and to have it exercised and carried into effect against the person who is in possession, unless that person can shew he purchased it without notice. Here there is a clear, distinct, and admitted equity in the vendor, as against Mr. Elms; and as to the party now sought to be affected by it, it is not in dispute that he took the land with notice of the covenant: indeed, it appears on the face of the instrument which is the foundation of his title. It seems to me to be the simplest case that a Court of Equity ever acted upon, that a purchaser cannot have a better title than the party under whom he claims.

Without adverting to any question about a covenant running with land or not, I consider that this piece of land is purchased subject to an equity created by a party competent to create it; that the present Defendant took it with distinct knowledge of such equity existing; and that such equity ought to be enforced against him, as it would have been against the party who originally took the land from Mr. Tulk.

...I think, therefore, that the Master of the Rolls is quite right ... and that this motion must be refused, with costs.

Notes and Questions

1. Is the result in *Tulk* attributable to a difference in the willingness of courts of equity (as compared to courts of law) to find a covenant will "run with the land"? To the principle of *nemo dat?* To the rules regarding good-faith purchasers? To something else?

2. Is the result in *Tulk* consistent with the principle of *numerus clausus?* With the common-law policy against restraints on alienation?

3. *Tulk v. Moxhay* represented a new opening for private ordering regarding competing land uses, which hinged on the distinction

between law and equity. In the end, the equitable exception swallowed the legal rule against restrictive covenants running with land. As one court explained:

> In the past, some courts . . . have distinguished between a "real covenant" that runs with the land and an "equitable covenant" (sometimes called an "equitable servitude" or "equitable restriction") that runs with the land. Today however, the *Restatement* [*(Third), Property (Servitudes)*] sensibly explains:

> [T]he differences between covenants that historically could be enforced at law and those enforceable in equity ... have all but disappeared in modern law. Continuing use of the dual terminology of real covenant and equitable servitude is confusing because it suggests the continued existence of two separate servitude categories with important differences. In fact, however, in modern law there are no significant differences. Valid covenants, like other contracts and property interests, can be enforced and protected by both legal and equitable remedies as appropriate, without regard to the form of the transaction that created the servitude.

Lake Limerick Country Club v. Hunt Mfg. Homes, Inc., 120 Wash. App. 246, 253-54, 84 P.3d 295, 298-99 (2004) (footnotes omitted).

4. It is worth noting again that the Third Restatement, quoted in *Lake Limerick Country Club*, is somewhat unique in not simply restating the law but also pushing it in a particular direction. Many jurisdictions have yet to adopt its more modern approach on merging the various servitudes, or on other important issues. As always in property law, it is important to consult the relevant

authorities in your jurisdiction in order to determine whether courts there still follow more traditional rules regarding the creation, enforcement, modification, and termination of restrictive covenants.

5. **Coase Revisited.** Which way do the equities really cut in *Tulk*? Lord Chancellor Cottenham concluded that it was unfair for Moxhay to deprive Tulk of the benefit of his bargain with Elms. Couldn't we just as easily say it is unfair for Tulk to interfere with Moxhay's use of the land he purchased? Indeed, given that English law courts of the time typically refused to hold that restrictive covenants would run with the land, doesn't Moxhay have the stronger equitable case? Wasn't it unreasonable for Tulk to expect he could obtain an enforceable covenant *from Elms alone* on behalf of Elms's "heirs, executors, administrators, and assigns"?

6. Put another way, isn't the problem here *reciprocal* in that the parties simply have incompatible land use preferences? Thus, when Lord Cottenham rhetorically asks, "Is not this an equity attached to the property, by the party who is competent to bind the property?" is he merely assuming the initial allocation of the relevant entitlement to the party that was there first? If so, is the application of a restrictive covenant to successors a circumstance in which the parties could effectively bargain to reach the efficient result?

7. Recall the dispute between Abigail, Beatrice, and Clara. Does the principle of "first in time is first in right" provide any reason to privilege Abigail's preferred use of Clara's land over Clara's preferred use? Does the fact that Abigail and Beatrice reached their agreement *before* Clara became involved suggest that, as a matter of general property law principles, later comers will have to either abide by that agreement or obtain *both parties'* consent to abrogate

it? Is such a rule necessary to protect Abigail's legitimate expectations with respect to the use and enjoyment of her own property?

8. More generally, are the arguments supporting the principle of priority in time persuasive when applied to land *use* conflicts (as opposed to disputes over *title* or *possession*)? Conversely, if we *do* allow agreements like the one Abigail and Beatrice to run with the land, are we giving past owners too much control over the ability of present and future owners to adapt their land uses to changing circumstances?

B. Creation of an Enforceable Restrictive Covenant

As courts became more amenable to the enforcement of restrictive covenants by and against successors to the property interests of the original covenanting parties, they developed a set of requirements for such covenants to run with the land. As one court described these requirements:

> The prerequisites for a covenant to "run with the land" are these: (1) the covenants must have been enforceable between the original parties, such enforceability being a question of contract law except insofar as the covenant must satisfy the statute of frauds; (2) the covenant must "touch and concern" both the land to be benefitted and the land to be burdened; (3) the covenanting parties must have intended to bind their successors-in-interest; (4) there must be vertical privity of estate, i.e., privity between the original parties to the covenant and the present disputants; and (5) there must be horizontal privity of estate, or privity between the original parties.

Leighton v. Leonard, 589 P.2d 279, 281 (Ct. App. Wash. Div. 1 1978). A further requirement is that a restrictive covenant is enforceable only against parties who are on actual or constructive notice of it. *See id.* at 281-

282; *accord* Inwood N. Homeowners' Ass'n, Inc. v. Harris, 736 S.W.2d 632, 635 (Tex. 1987).

The Third Restatement, following general trends in the caselaw, significantly relaxes this approach. Section 2.1 of the Restatement provides in relevant part:

> A servitude is created
>
> (1) if the owner of the property to be burdened
>
>> (a) enters into a contract or makes a conveyance intended to create a servitude that complies with … [the] Statute of Frauds … or … [a recognized e]xception to the Statute of Frauds…; or
>>
>> (b) conveys a lot or unit in a general-plan development or common-interest community subject to a recorded declaration of servitudes for the development or community; or
>
> (2) if the requirements for creation of a servitude by estoppel, implication, necessity, or prescription … are met….

A few features of the Restatement approach are worth noting. The first is that the common law's requirement of "horizontal privity of estate"—that the covenant be created in an instrument that conveys some interest in real property between the original covenantor and the original covenantee[24]—is eliminated. Under the Restatement view, a contract

---

[24] Thus, at common-law, if B promised to use her land only for residential purposes *in a deed from A to B*, A and B would be in horizontal privity of estate with one another. However, if A and B simply entered into a *contract* whereby A paid B a sum of money in exchange for B's

containing the covenant is sufficient to bind successors, even if it passes no *other* property interest, so long as the parties intended the covenant to run with the land. (Under this view, a covenant intended to bind successors is *itself* a sufficient interest in land.) Second, there is a deep connection between covenants that run with the land and "common-interest communities"—a property law institution that we will investigate further in a later chapter. Third, the Restatement elsewhere treats the common law requirement of notice as essentially a matter for the recording system, making the unenforceability of covenants for want of notice subject to the same rules as any other property interest. See Restatement §7.14.

Finally, the Restatement rejects, with heavy criticism, the common law requirement that a restrictive covenant "touch or concern" land. *Restatement* § 3.1 cmt. a. Nevertheless, many jurisdictions continue to apply touch-and-concern doctrine, sometimes explicitly declining to follow the Restatement approach. *See Note: Touch and Concern, the Restatement (Third) of Property: Servitudes, and a Proposal,* 122 HARV. L. REV. 938, 942-45 (2009)). It is worth comparing the two approaches.

Neponsit Prop. Owners' Ass'n v. Emigrant Indus. Sav. Bank
15 N.E.2d 793 (N.Y. 1938)

LEHMAN, Judge.

The plaintiff, as assignee of Neponsit Realty Company, has brought this action to foreclose a lien upon land which the defendant owns. The lien, it is alleged, arises from a covenant, condition or charge contained in a deed of conveyance of the land from Neponsit Realty Company to a predecessor in title of the defendant. The defendant purchased the land at a judicial sale. The referee's deed to the defendant and every deed in the defendant's chain of title since the conveyance of the land by Neponsit

---

promise to use her land only for residential purposes, they would not be in horizontal privity of estate—because no interest in real property passed under the contract.

Realty Company purports to convey the property subject to the covenant, condition or charge contained in the original deed….

Upon this appeal the defendant contends that the land which it owns is not subject to any lien or charge which the plaintiff may enforce. Its arguments are confined to serious questions of law. …On this appeal we may confine our consideration to the merits of these questions, and, in our statement of facts, we drew indiscriminately from the allegations of the complaint and the allegations of the answer.

It appears that in January, 1911, Neponsit Realty Company, as owner of a tract of land in Queens county, caused to be filed in the office of the clerk of the county a map of the land. The tract was developed for a strictly residential community, and Neponsit Realty Company conveyed lots in the tract to purchasers, describing such lots by reference to the filed map and to roads and streets shown thereon. In 1917, Neponsit Realty Company conveyed the land now owned by the defendant to Robert Oldner Deyer and his wife by deed which contained the covenant upon which the plaintiff's cause of action is based.

That covenant provides:

> 'And the party of the second part for the party of the second part and the heirs, successors and assigns of the party of the second part further covenants that the property conveyed by this deed shall be subject to an annual charge in such an amount as will be fixed by the party of the first part, its successors and assigns, not, however exceeding in any year the sum of four ($4.00) Dollars per lot 20x100 feet. The assigns of the party of the first part may include a Property Owners' Association which may hereafter be organized for the purposes referred to in this paragraph, and in case such association is organized the sums in this paragraph provided for shall be payable to such association. The party of the

second part for the party of the second part and the heirs, successors and assigns of the party of the second part covenants that they will pay this charge to the party of the first part, its successors and assigns on the first day of May in each and every year, and further covenants that said charge shall on said date in each year become a lien on the land and shall continue to be such lien until fully paid. Such charge shall be payable to the party of the first part or its successors or assigns, and shall be devoted to the maintenance of the roads, paths, parks, beach, sewers and such other public purposes as shall from time to time be determined by the party of the first part, its successors or assigns. And the party of the second part by the acceptance of this deed hereby expressly vests in the party of the first part, its successors and assigns, the right and power to bring all actions against the owner of the premises hereby conveyed or any part thereof for the collection of such charge and to enforce the aforesaid lien therefor.

'These covenants shall run with the land and shall be construed as real covenants running with the land until January 31st, 1940, when they shall cease and determine.'

Every subsequent deed of conveyance of the property in the defendant's chain of title, including the deed from the referee to the defendant, contained, as we have said, a provision that they were made subject to covenants and restrictions of former deeds of record.

There can be no doubt that Neponsit Realty Company intended that the covenant should run with the land and should be enforceable by a property owners association against every owner of property in the residential tract which the realty company was then developing. The language of the covenant admits of no other construction. Regardless of the intention of the parties, a covenant will run with the land and will be enforceable against a subsequent purchaser of the land at the suit of one who claims the benefit of the covenant, only if the covenant complies with certain legal requirements. These requirements rest upon ancient rules and precedents. The age-old essentials of a real covenant, aside from the form of the covenant, may be summarily formulated as follows: (1) It must appear that grantor and grantee intended that the covenant should run with the land; (2) it must appear that the covenant is one 'touching' or 'concerning' the land with which it runs; (3) it must appear that there is 'privity of estate' between the promisee or party claiming the benefit of the covenant and the right to enforce it, and the promisor or party who rests under the burden of the covenant....

The covenant in this case is intended to create a charge or obligation to pay a fixed sum of money to be 'devoted to the maintenance of the roads, paths, parks, beach, sewers and such other public purposes as shall from time to time be determined by the party of the first part [the grantor], its successors or assigns.' It is an affirmative covenant to pay money for use in connection with, but not upon, the land which it is said is subject to the burden of the covenant. Does such a covenant 'touch' or 'concern' the land? ...In truth such a description or test so formulated is too vague to be of much assistance and judges and academic scholars alike have struggled, not with entire success, to formulate a test at once more satisfactory and more accurate. 'It has been found impossible to state any absolute tests to determine what covenants touch and concern land and what do not. The question is one for the court to determine in the exercise of its best judgment upon the facts of each case.' Clark, op. cit. p. 76.

Even though that be true, a determination by a court in one case upon particular facts will often serve to point the way to correct decision in other cases upon analogous facts. Such guideposts may not be disregarded. It has been often said that a covenant to pay a sum of money is a personal affirmative covenant which usually does not concern or touch the land. Such statements are based upon English decisions which hold in effect that only covenants, which compel the covenanter to submit to some *restriction on the use* of his property, touch or concern the land, and that the burden of a covenant which requires the covenanter to do an affirmative act, even on his own land, for the benefit of the owner of a 'dominant' estate, does not run with his land. ... [Nevertheless s]ome promises to pay money have been enforced, as covenants running with the land, against subsequent holders of the land who took with notice of the covenant. ...[T]hough it may be inexpedient and perhaps impossible to formulate a rigid test or definition which will be entirely satisfactory or which can be applied mechanically in all cases, we should at least be able to state the problem and find a reasonable method of approach to it. It has been suggested that a covenant which runs with the land must affect the legal relations—the advantages and the burdens—of the parties to the covenant, as owners of particular parcels of land and not merely as members of the community in general, such as taxpayers or owners of other land. That method of approach has the merit of realism. The test is based on the effect of the covenant rather than on technical distinctions. Does the covenant impose, on the one hand, a burden upon an interest in land, which on the other hand increases the value of a different interest in the same or related land?

Even though we accept that approach and test, it still remains true that whether a particular covenant is sufficiently connected with the use of land to run with the land, must be in many cases a question of degree. A promise to pay for something to be done in connection with the promisor's land does not differ essentially from a promise by the promisor to do the thing himself, and both promises constitute, in a substantial sense, a restriction upon the owner's right to use the land, and a burden upon the legal interest of the owner. On the other hand, a covenant to perform or pay for the performance of an affirmative act disconnected with the use of the land cannot ordinarily touch or concern the land in any substantial degree. Thus, unless we exalt technical form over substance, the distinction between covenants which run with land and covenants which are personal, must depend upon the effect of the covenant on the legal rights which otherwise would flow from ownership of land and which are connected with the land. The problem then is: Does the covenant in purpose and effect substantially alter these rights?

...Looking at the problem presented in this case ... and stressing the intent and substantial effect of the covenant rather than its form, it seems clear that the covenant may properly be said to touch and concern the land of the defendant and its burden should run with the land. True, it calls for payment of a sum of money to be expended for 'public purposes' upon land other than the land conveyed by Neponsit Realty Company to plaintiff's predecessor in title. By that conveyance the grantee, however, obtained not only title to particular lots, but an easement or right of common enjoyment with other property owners in roads, beaches, public parks or spaces and improvements in the same tract. For full enjoyment in common by the defendant and other property owners of these easements or rights, the roads and public places must be maintained. In order that the burden of maintaining public improvements should rest upon the land benefited by the improvements, the grantor exacted from the grantee of the land with its appurtenant easement or right of enjoyment a covenant that the burden of paying the cost should be inseparably attached to the land which enjoys the benefit. It is plain that any distinction or definition which would exclude such a covenant from the classification of covenants which 'touch' or 'concern' the land would be based on form and not on substance....

... Another difficulty remains. Though between the grantor and the grantee there was privity of estate, the covenant provides that its benefit shall run to the assigns of the grantor who 'may include a Property Owners' Association which may hereafter be organized for the purposes referred to in this paragraph.' The plaintiff has been organized to receive the sums payable by the property owners and to expend them for the benefit of such owners. Various definitions have been formulated of 'privity of estate' in connection with covenants that run with the land, but none of such definitions seems to cover the relationship between the plaintiff and the defendant in this case. The plaintiff has not succeeded to the ownership of any property of the grantor. It does not appear that it ever had title to the streets or public places upon which charges which are payable to it must be expended. It does not appear that it owns any other property in the residential tract to which any easement or right of enjoyment in such property is appurtenant. It is created solely to act as the assignee of the benefit of the covenant, and it has no interest of its own in the enforcement of the covenant.

The arguments that under such circumstances the plaintiff has no right of action to enforce a covenant running with the land are all based upon a distinction between the corporate property owners association and the property owners for whose benefit the association has been formed. If that distinction may be ignored, then the basis of the arguments is destroyed. How far privity of estate in technical form is necessary to enforce in equity a restrictive covenant upon the use of land, presents an interesting question. Enforcement of such covenants rests upon equitable principles, and at times, at least, the violation 'of the restrictive covenant may be restrained at the suit of one who owns property or for whose benefit the restriction was established, irrespective of whether there were privity either of estate or of contract between the parties, or whether an action at law were maintainable.' Chesebro v. Moers, 233 N.Y. 75, 80, 134 N.E. 842, 843, 21 A.L.R. 1270. ... We do not attempt ... to formulate a definite rule as to when, or even whether, covenants in a deed will be enforced, upon equitable principles, against subsequent purchasers with notice, at the suit of a party without privity of contract or estate. There is no need to resort to such a rule if the courts may look behind the corporate form of the plaintiff.

The corporate plaintiff has been formed as a convenient instrument by which the property owners may advance their common interests. We do not ignore the corporate form when we recognize that the Neponsit

Property Owners' Association, Inc., is acting as the agent or representative of the Neponsit property owners. As we have said in another case: when Neponsit Property Owners' Association, Inc., 'was formed, the property owners were expected to, and have looked to that organization as the medium through which enjoyment of their common right might be preserved equally for all.' Matter of City of New York, Public Beach, Borough of Queens, 269 N.Y. 64, 75, 199 N.E. 5, 9. Under the conditions thus presented we said: 'It may be difficult, or even impossible to classify into recognized categories the nature of the interest of the membership corporation and its members in the land. The corporate entity cannot be disregarded, nor can the separate interests of the members of the corporation' (page 73, 199 N.E. page 8). Only blind adherence to an ancient formula devised to meet entirely different conditions could constrain the court to hold that a corporation formed as a medium for the enjoyment of common rights of property owners owns no property which would benefit by enforcement of common rights and has no cause of action in equity to enforce the covenant upon which such common rights depend. Every reason which in other circumstances may justify the ancient formula may be urged in support of the conclusion that the formula should not be applied in this case. In substance if not in form the covenant is a restrictive covenant which touches and concerns the defendant's land, and in substance, if not in form, there is privity of estate between the plaintiff and the defendant....

Notes and Questions

1. Does the touch-and-concern requirement lessen the potential for conflict between the law of restrictive covenants and the common-law doctrines designed to preserve marketability of land, such as *numerus clausus* and the rule against restraints on alienation?

2. Is the court's resolution of the privity-of-estate issue consistent with what you've learned about corporate property? With the later New York case of *Walkovszky v. Carlton?*

3. As with easements, restrictive covenants may be implied in particular circumstances, and they may arise by estoppel. The most common context for such a covenant by implication is a common-scheme development, where purchasers acquire an interest in a parcel that is part of a community that appears to have commonly planned features—such as residential uses of particular size and density. Such purchasers may be charged with notice of an implied reciprocal covenant restricting their parcels to uses consistent with the common scheme or plan. *See* Sanborn v. McLean, 206 N.W. 496 (Mich. 1925); Restatement §§ 2.11 & illus. 7; § 2.14. Conversely, where the seller touts the benefits of such features to purchasers who buy in reliance on the seller's representations, the seller and his successors may be estopped from using the seller's retained land in a manner inconsistent with those uses. Indeed, such an estoppel may even serve as an acceptable substitute for the writing required under the Statute of Frauds. Restatement §§ 2.9-2.10.

4. A historical note in the Third Restatement explains:

> At the beginning of the 20th century, four doctrines peculiar to servitudes law constrained landowners in the creation of servitudes: the horizontal-privity doctrine, the prohibition on creating benefits in gross, the prohibition on imposing affirmative burdens on fee owners, and the touch-or-concern doctrine. At the end of the century, little remains of those doctrines, which have gradually been displaced by doctrines that more specifically target the harms that may be caused by servitudes.

Restatement § 3.1, cmt. a. The touch-and-concern doctrine comes in for particular criticism in the Restatement, which attacks the doctrine's "vagueness, its obscurity, its intent-defeating character, and its growing redundancy." *Id.* § 3.2 cmt. b. Accordingly, the Restatement adopts a very different approach to the question of enforceability of restrictive covenants:

Restatement (Third) of Property (Servitudes)
§ 3.1 Validity Of Servitudes: General Rule

A servitude … is valid unless it is illegal or unconstitutional or violates public policy.

Servitudes that are invalid because they violate public policy include, but are not limited to:

(1) a servitude that is arbitrary, spiteful, or capricious;

(2) a servitude that unreasonably burdens a fundamental constitutional right;

(3) a servitude that imposes an unreasonable restraint on alienation…;

(4) a servitude that imposes an unreasonable restraint on trade or competition …; and

(5) a servitude that is unconscionable….

Notes and Questions

1. Is the rationale of the touch-and-concern requirement discussed in *Neponsit* reflected in Section 3.1 of the Restatement? If not, are there other features of Section 3.1 that serve the common-law rules designed to ensure marketability of real property?

2. The Restatement's invalidation of servitudes that impose "an unreasonable restraint on alienation" draws further distinctions between "direct" and "indirect" restraints. "Direct" restraints—

including overt prohibitions on lease or transfer, rights to withhold consent, options to purchase, and rights of first refusal—are valid if "reasonable," with reasonableness being determined "by weighing the utility of the restraint against the injurious consequences of enforcing the restraint." *Restatement* § 3.4. An "indirect" restraint is any other restriction on use that might incidentally "limit[] the numbers of potential buyers or … reduc[e] the amount the owner might otherwise realize on a sale of the property," and such a covenant is valid unless it "lacks a rational justification." *Id.* § 3.5 & cmt. a.

3. In the late 2000s, as the financial crisis and the collapse of the housing market dealt crippling blows to the construction industry, one firm came up with what it thought was a clever solution that built on the same securitization model that powered the mortgage market in the run-up to the collapse. The firm, Freehold Capital Partners, advised real estate developers to insert a covenant in all the deeds to lots in their new housing subdivisions that would require the purchaser and their successors to pay a portion of the resale price *to the developer* on every subsequent transfer of the property. *See* Robbie Whelan, *Home-Resale Fees Under Attack*, WALL ST. J. (July 30, 2010), available at http://www.wsj.com/articles/SB10001424052748703314904575 399290511802382. The plan was to securitize these "private transfer fee" payments: sell off slices of the right to the income stream from the transfer fees, and use the sale price of the securities to finance the construction of the homes that would be encumbered by the private transfer fee covenants. The scheme as conceived would not necessarily require the developer to retain title to any real property in the developments bound by these covenants.

Realtors, title search agencies, legislators, and eventually the federal government mobilized against this business model. Many states passed statutes prohibiting or seriously restricting these private fee transfer covenants. *See, e.g.,* Tex. Prop. Code § 5.202 (effective June 17, 2011). As of March 16, 2012, the Federal agencies that repurchase or otherwise backstop many American residential mortgages will not deal in mortgages on properties encumbered by such covenants.

Was all this legislative and regulatory action necessary? Would Freehold Capital Partners' private transfer fee covenants be enforceable under the common law of restrictive covenants as set forth in *Neponsit*? Under the Restatement?

4. What other types of covenants might offend public policy? And how far will public policy intrude on private ordering of property rights? Consider the following case.

Shelley v. Kraemer
334 U.S. 1 (1948)

Mr. Chief Justice VINSON delivered the opinion of the Court.

These cases present for our consideration questions relating to the validity of court enforcement of private agreements, generally described as restrictive covenants, which have as their purpose the exclusion of persons of designated race or color from the ownership or occupancy of real property. Basic constitutional issues of obvious importance have been raised.

The first of these cases comes to this Court on certiorari to the Supreme Court of Missouri. On February 16, 1911, thirty out of a total of thirty-nine owners of property fronting both sides of Labadie Avenue between Taylor Avenue and Cora Avenue in the city of St. Louis, signed an agreement, which was subsequently recorded, providing in part:

'* * * the said property is hereby restricted to the use and occupancy for the term of Fifty (50) years from this date, so that it shall be a condition all the time and whether recited and referred to as (sic) not in subsequent conveyances and shall attach to the land, as a condition precedent to the sale of the same, that hereafter no part of said property or any portion thereof shall be, for said term of Fifty-years, occupied by any person not of the Caucasian race, it being intended hereby to restrict the use of said property for said period of time against the occupancy as owners or tenants of any portion of said property for resident or other purpose by people of the Negro or Mongolian Race.'

…On August 11, 1945, pursuant to a contract of sale, petitioners Shelley, who are Negroes, for valuable consideration received from one Fitzgerald a warranty deed to the parcel in question. The trial court found that petitioners had no actual knowledge of the restrictive agreement at the time of the purchase.

On October 9, 1945, respondents, as owners of other property subject to the terms of the restrictive covenant, brought suit in Circuit Court of the city of St. Louis praying that petitioners Shelley be restrained from taking possession of the property and that judgment be entered divesting title out of petitioners Shelley and revesting title in the immediate grantor or in such other person as the court should direct. The trial court denied the requested relief on the ground that the restrictive agreement, upon which respondents based their action, had never become final and complete because it was the intention of the parties to that agreement that it was not to become effective until signed by all property owners in the district, and signatures of all the owners had never been obtained.

The Supreme Court of Missouri sitting en banc reversed and directed the trial court to grant the relief for which respondents had prayed. That court held the agreement effective and concluded that enforcement of its

provisions violated no rights guaranteed to petitioners by the Federal
Constitution. At the time the court rendered its decision, petitioners were
occupying the property in question.

…Petitioners have placed primary reliance on their contentions, first
raised in the state courts, that judicial enforcement of the restrictive
agreements in these cases has violated rights guaranteed to petitioners by
the Fourteenth Amendment of the Federal Constitution and Acts of
Congress passed pursuant to that Amendment. Specifically, petitioners
urge that they have been denied the equal protection of the laws, deprived
of property without due process of law, and have been denied privileges
and immunities of citizens of the United States. We pass to a
consideration of those issues.

I.

Whether the equal protection clause of the Fourteenth Amendment
inhibits judicial enforcement by state courts of restrictive covenants based
on race or color is a question which this Court has not heretofore been
called upon to consider.

… It should be observed that these covenants do not seek to proscribe
any particular use of the affected properties. Use of the properties for
residential occupancy, as such, is not forbidden. The restrictions of these
agreements, rather, are directed toward a designated class of persons and
seek to determine who may and who may not own or make use of the
properties for residential purposes. The excluded class is defined wholly
in terms of race or color; 'simply that and nothing more.'

It cannot be doubted that among the civil rights intended to be protected
from discriminatory state action by the Fourteenth Amendment are the
rights to acquire, enjoy, own and dispose of property. Equality in the
enjoyment of property rights was regarded by the framers of that
Amendment as an essential pre-condition to the realization of other basic

civil rights and liberties which the Amendment was intended to guarantee.[7] Thus, § 1978 of the Revised Statutes, derived from § 1 of the Civil Rights Act of 1866 which was enacted by Congress while the Fourteenth Amendment was also under consideration, provides:

> 'All citizens of the United States shall have the same right, in every State and Territory, as is enjoyed by white citizens thereof to inherit, purchase, lease, sell, hold, and convey real and personal property.'[9]

This Court has given specific recognition to the same principle.

It is likewise clear that restrictions on the right of occupancy of the sort sought to be created by the private agreements in these cases could not be squared with the requirements of the Fourteenth Amendment if imposed by state statute or local ordinance. We do not understand respondents to urge the contrary.

… But the present cases … do not involve action by state legislatures or city councils. Here the particular patterns of discrimination and the areas in which the restrictions are to operate, are determined, in the first instance, by the terms of agreements among private individuals. Participation of the State consists in the enforcement of the restrictions so defined. The crucial issue with which we are here confronted is whether this distinction removes these cases from the operation of the prohibitory provisions of the Fourteenth Amendment.

Since the decision of this Court in the Civil Rights Cases, 1883, 109 U.S. 3, 3 S.Ct. 18, 27 L.Ed. 835, the principle has become firmly embedded in our constitutional law that the action inhibited by the first section of the Fourteenth Amendment is only such action as may fairly be said to be that of the States. That Amendment erects no shield against merely private conduct, however discriminatory or wrongful.

We conclude, therefore, that the restrictive agreements standing alone cannot be regarded as a violation of any rights guaranteed to petitioners by the Fourteenth Amendment. So long as the purposes of those agreements are effectuated by voluntary adherence to their terms, it would appear clear that there has been no action by the State and the provisions of the Amendment have not been violated.

But here there was more. These are cases in which the purposes of the agreements were secured only by judicial enforcement by state courts of the restrictive terms of the agreements. The respondents urge that judicial enforcement of private agreements does not amount to state action; or, in any event, the participation of the State is so attenuated in character as not to amount to state action within the meaning of the Fourteenth Amendment. Finally, it is suggested, even if the States in these cases may be deemed to have acted in the constitutional sense, their action did not deprive petitioners of rights guaranteed by the Fourteenth Amendment. We move to a consideration of these matters....

III

...We have no doubt that there has been state action in these cases in the full and complete sense of the phrase. The undisputed facts disclose that petitioners were willing purchasers of properties upon which they desired to establish homes. The owners of the properties were willing sellers; and contracts of sale were accordingly consummated. It is clear that but for the active intervention of the state courts, supported by the full panoply of state power, petitioners would have been free to occupy the properties in question without restraint.

These are not cases, as has been suggested, in which the States have merely abstained from action, leaving private individuals free to impose such discriminations as they see fit. Rather, these are cases in which the States have made available to such individuals the full coercive power of government to deny to petitioners, on the grounds of race or color, the enjoyment of property rights in premises which petitioners are willing and financially able to acquire and which the grantors are willing to sell. The difference between judicial enforcement and nonenforcement of the restrictive covenants is the difference to petitioners between being denied rights of property available to other members of the community and being accorded full enjoyment of those rights on an equal footing.

The enforcement of the restrictive agreements by the state courts in these cases was directed pursuant to the common-law policy of the States as formulated by those courts in earlier decisions. In the Missouri case, enforcement of the covenant was directed in the first instance by the highest court of the State…. The judicial action in each case bears the clear and unmistakable imprimatur of the State. We have noted that previous decisions of this Court have established the proposition that judicial action is not immunized from the operation of the Fourteenth Amendment simply because it is taken pursuant to the state's common-law policy. Nor is the Amendment ineffective simply because the particular pattern of discrimination, which the State has enforced, was defined initially by the terms of a private agreement. State action, as that phrase is understood for the purposes of the Fourteenth Amendment, refers to exertions of state power in all forms. And when the effect of that action is to deny rights subject to the protection of the Fourteenth Amendment, it is the obligation of this Court to enforce the constitutional commands.

We hold that in granting judicial enforcement of the restrictive agreements in these cases, the States have denied petitioners the equal protection of the laws and that, therefore, the action of the state courts cannot stand. We have noted that freedom from discrimination by the States in the enjoyment of property rights was among the basic objectives sought to be effectuated by the framers of the Fourteenth Amendment. That such discrimination has occurred in these cases is clear. Because of the race or color of these petitioners they have been denied rights of ownership or occupancy enjoyed as a matter of course by other citizens of different race or color....

The historical context in which the Fourteenth Amendment became a part of the Constitution should not be forgotten. Whatever else the framers sought to achieve, it is clear that the matter of primary concern was the establishment of equality in the enjoyment of basic civil and political rights and the preservation of those rights from discriminatory action on the part of the States based on considerations of race or color. Seventy-five years ago this Court announced that the provisions of the Amendment are to be construed with this fundamental purpose in mind. Upon full consideration, we have concluded that in these cases the States have acted to deny petitioners the equal protection of the laws guaranteed by the Fourteenth Amendment. Having so decided, we find it unnecessary to consider whether petitioners have also been deprived of property without due process of law or denied privileges and immunities of citizens of the United States.

For the reasons stated, the judgment of the Supreme Court of Missouri and the judgment of the Supreme Court of Michigan must be reversed. Reversed.

Mr. Justice REED, Mr. Justice JACKSON, and Mr. Justice RUTLEDGE took no part in the consideration or decision of these cases.

Notes and Questions

1. Racially restrictive covenants were widespread in the United States in the first half of the twentieth century. *See generally* Michael Jones-Correa, *The Origins and Diffusion of Racial Restrictive Covenants*, 115 POL. SCI. Q. 541 (2001). Indeed, just two decades prior to its decision in *Shelley*, in the case of *Corrigan v. Buckley*, 271 U.S. 323 (1926), the Supreme Court had affirmed the enforcement of such

a covenant (against the original covenantor) in the District of Columbia (on grounds that the Equal Protection Clause of the 14th Amendment was inapplicable to the federal government—a proposition the Court retreated from in *Bolling v. Sharpe*, 347 U.S. 497 (1954)).

Note that three justices recused themselves from consideration of *Shelley*. Justice John Paul Stevens, in his memoir, surmises that they had to do so because they owned homes burdened (and, in the view of many white Americans of the day, benefited) by racially restrictive covenants. JUSTICE JOHN PAUL STEVENS, FIVE CHIEFS: A SUPREME COURT MEMOIR 69 (2011).

2. Does *Shelley* provide useful guidance on what types of privately agreed restrictions will be enforced and what types will go unenforced on constitutional or public policy grounds? Does the Restatement do any better?

3. Like racism, racially restrictive covenants have not gone away. Though unenforceable in court, they remain in the chain of title of much residential real estate today. In the wake of white supremacist violence in Charlottesville, Virginia, in August of 2017, Charlottesville resident and legal commentator Dahlia Lithwick recounted:

> "Our lawyer once told us, when we purchased our home in Charlottesville, that the house to this day carries a racially restrictive covenant. No blacks, no Jews. That covenant is illegal and unenforceable. And so I have a house in Charlottesville that could once have been taken from me by the force of law."

Dahlia Lithwick, *They Will Not Replace* Us, SLATE (Aug. 13, 2017), http://www.slate.com/articles/news_and_politics/politics/2017/08/dahlia_lithwick_on_the_nazis_in_charlottesville.html. Because they remain on the books, these types of discriminatory covenants still occasionally lead to disputes, particularly where residents continue to believe they are a good idea. *See* Nicholas Casey, *Buyers' Rule in L.I. Town Is Relic of Its Nazi Past*, N.Y. TIMES (Oct. 20, 2015) at A1, available at https://nyti.ms/2ktUqEW; Settlement Agreement and Order, Long Island Housing Servs., Inc. v. German-American Settlement League, Inc., Case No. 15-CV-05987 (E.D.N.Y. Jan. 13, 2016), available at https://www.dropbox.com/s/6prgixwmftosqy2/Yaphank.pdf.

C.   Modification and Termination of Covenants

Restrictive covenants, like easements, can be modified or terminated in many ways. The Restatement mostly does not draw a distinction between these two types of servitudes with respect to modification or termination, meaning that the grounds for termination discussed in our unit on Easements—merger, agreement, abandonment, etc.—apply with equal force to restrictive covenants.

One basis for modification or termination that is perhaps more likely to arise with respect to restrictive covenants than it is for easements is that conditions of the land have changed to such an extent that continued enforcement is inappropriate. This is particularly so where the restrictive covenants are part of a common scheme or plan for a community. In such a community, what types of changes to "facts on the ground" should justify terminating the covenants shaping the community's land uses?

El Di, Inc. v. Town of Bethany Beach
477 A.2d 1066 (Del. 1984)

HERRMANN, Chief Justice for the majority:

This is an appeal from a permanent injunction granted by the Court of Chancery upon the petition of the plaintiffs, The Town of Bethany Beach, et al., prohibiting the defendant, El Di, Inc. ("El Di") from selling alcoholic beverages at Holiday House, a restaurant in Bethany Beach owned and operated by El Di.

I.

The pertinent facts are as follows:

El Di purchased the Holiday House in 1969. In December 1981, El Di filed an application with the State Alcoholic Beverage Control Commission (the "Commission") for a license to sell alcoholic beverages at the Holiday House. On April 15, 1982, finding "public need and convenience," the Commission granted the Holiday House an on-premises license. The sale of alcoholic beverages at Holiday House began within 10 days of the Commission's approval. Plaintiffs subsequently filed suit to permanently enjoin the sale of alcoholic beverages under the license.

On appeal it is undisputed that the chain of title for the Holiday House lot included restrictive covenants prohibiting both the sale of alcoholic beverages on the property and nonresidential construction.[25] The same

---

[25] The restrictive covenant stated:

"This covenant is made expressly subject to and upon the following conditions: viz; That no intoxicating liquors shall ever be sold on the said lot, that no other than dwelling or cottage shall be erected thereon and but one to each lot, which must be of full size according to the said plan ... a breach of which said conditions, or any of them, shall cause said lot to revert to and become again the property of the grantor, his heirs and assigns; and upon such breach of said conditions or restrictions, the same may be

restriction was placed on property in Bethany Beach as early as 1900 and 1901 when the area was first under development.

As originally conceived, Bethany Beach was to be a quiet beach community. The site was selected at the end of the nineteenth-century by the Christian Missionary Society of Washington, D.C. In 1900, the Bethany Beach Improvement Company ("BBIC") was formed. The BBIC purchased lands, laid out a development and began selling lots. To insure the quiet character of the community, the BBIC placed restrictive covenants on many plots, prohibiting the sale of alcohol and restricting construction to residential cottages. Of the original 180 acre development, however, approximately ⅓ was unrestricted.

The Town of Bethany Beach was officially incorporated in 1909. The municipal limits consisted of 750 acres including the original BBIC land (hereafter the original or "old-Town"), but expanded far beyond the 180 acre BBIC development. The expanded acreage of the newly incorporated Town, combined with the unrestricted plots in the original Town, left only 15 percent of the new Town subject to the restrictive covenants.

Despite the restriction prohibiting commercial building ("no other than a dwelling or cottage shall be erected ..."), commercial development began in the 1920's on property subject to the covenants. This development included numerous inns, restaurants, drug stores, a bank, motels, a town hall, shops selling various items including food, clothing, gifts and novelties and other commercial businesses. Of the 34 commercial buildings presently within the Town limits, 29 are located in the old-Town originally developed by BBIC. Today, Bethany Beach has a permanent population of some 330 residents. In the summer months the population increases to approximately 10,000 people within the corporate limits and

---

restrained or enjoined in equity by the grantor, his heirs or assigns, or by any co-lot owner in said plan or other party injured by such breach."

to some 48,000 people within a 4 mile radius. In 1952, the Town enacted a zoning ordinance which established a central commercial district designated C-1 located in the old-Town section. Holiday House is located in this district.

Since El Di purchased Holiday House in 1969, patrons have been permitted to carry their own alcoholic beverages with them into the restaurant to consume with their meals. This "brown-bagging" practice occurred at Holiday House prior to El Di's ownership and at other restaurants in the Town. El Di applied for a license to sell liquor at Holiday House in response to the increased number of customers who were engaging in "brown-bagging" and in the belief that the license would permit restaurant management to control excessive use of alcohol and use by minors. Prior to the time El Di sought a license, alcoholic beverages had been and continue to be readily available for sale at nearby licensed establishments including: one restaurant ½ mile outside the Town limits, 3 restaurants within a 4 mile radius of the Town, and a package store some 200-300 yards from the Holiday House.

The Trial Court granted a stay pending the outcome of this appeal.

II.

In granting plaintiffs' motion for a permanent injunction, the Court of Chancery rejected defendant's argument that changed conditions in Bethany Beach rendered the restrictive covenants unreasonable and therefore unenforceable. The Chancery Court found that although the evidence showed a considerable growth since 1900 in both population and the number of buildings in Bethany Beach, "the basic nature of Bethany Beach as a quiet, family oriented resort has not changed." The Court also found that there had been development of commercial activity since 1900, but that this "activity is limited to a small area of Bethany Beach and consists mainly of activities for the convenience and patronage of the residents of Bethany Beach."

The Trial Court also rejected defendant's contention that plaintiffs' acquiescence and abandonment rendered the covenants unenforceable. In this connection, the Court concluded that the practice of "brown-bagging" was not a sale of alcoholic beverages and that, therefore, any failure to enforce the restriction as against the practice did not constitute abandonment or waiver of the restriction.

III.

We find that the Trial Court erred in holding that the change of conditions was insufficient to negate the restrictive covenant.

A court will not enforce a restrictive covenant where a fundamental change has occurred in the intended character of the neighborhood that renders the benefits underlying imposition of the restrictions incapable of enjoyment. Review of all the facts and circumstances convinces us that the change, since 1901, in the character of that area of the old-Town section now zoned C-1 is so substantial as to justify modification of the deed restriction. We need not determine a change in character of the entire restricted area in order to assess the continued applicability of the covenant to a portion thereof.

It is uncontradicted that one of the purposes underlying the covenant prohibiting the sale of intoxicating liquors was to maintain a quiet, residential atmosphere in the restricted area. Each of the additional covenants reinforces this objective, including the covenant restricting construction to residential dwellings. The covenants read as a whole evince an intention on the part of the grantor to maintain the residential, seaside character of the community.

But time has not left Bethany Beach the same community its grantors envisioned in 1901. The Town has changed from a church-affiliated residential community to a summer resort visited annually by thousands of tourists. Nowhere is the resultant change in character more evident than in the C-1 section of the old-Town. Plaintiffs argue that this is a relative change only and that there is sufficient evidence to support the Trial Court's findings that the residential character of the community has been maintained and that the covenants continue to benefit the other lot owners. We cannot agree.

In 1909, the 180 acre restricted old-Town section became part of a 750 acre incorporated municipality. Even prior to the Town's incorporation, the BBIC deeded out lots free of the restrictive covenants. After incorporation and partly due to the unrestricted lots deeded out by the BBIC, 85 percent of the land area within the Town was not subject to the restrictions. Significantly, nonresidential uses quickly appeared in the restricted area and today the old-Town section contains almost all of the commercial businesses within the entire Town.

The change in conditions is also reflected in the Town's decision in 1952 to zone restricted property, including the lot on which the Holiday House is located, specifically for commercial use. Although a change in zoning is not dispositive as against a private covenant, it is additional evidence of changed community conditions.

Time has relaxed not only the strictly residential character of the area, but the pattern of alcohol use and consumption as well. The practice of "brown-bagging" has continued unchallenged for at least twenty years at commercial establishments located on restricted property in the Town. On appeal, plaintiffs rely on the Trial Court finding that the "brown-bagging" practice is irrelevant as evidence of waiver inasmuch as the practice does not involve the sale of intoxicating liquors prohibited by the covenant. We find the "brown-bagging" practice evidence of a significant change in conditions in the community since its inception at the turn of the century. Such consumption of alcohol in public places is now generally tolerated by owners of similarly restricted lots. The license issued to the Holiday House establishment permits the El Di management to better control the availability and consumption of intoxicating liquors on its premises. In view of both the ready availability of alcoholic beverages in the area surrounding the Holiday House and the long-tolerated and increasing use of "brown-bagging" enforcement of the restrictive covenant at this time would only serve to subvert the public interest in the control of the availability and consumption of alcoholic liquors.

…In view of the change in conditions in the C-1 district of Bethany Beach, we find it unreasonable and inequitable now to enforce the restrictive covenant. To permit unlimited "brown-bagging" but to prohibit licensed sales of alcoholic liquor, under the circumstances of this case, is inconsistent with any reasonable application of the restriction and contrary to public policy.

We emphasize that our judgment is confined to the area of the old-Town section zoned C-1. The restrictions in the neighboring residential area are unaffected by the conclusion we reach herein.

Reversed.

CHRISTIE, Justice, with whom MOORE, Justice, joins, dissenting:
I respectfully disagree with the majority.

I think the evidence supports the conclusion of the Chancellor, as finder of fact, that the basic nature of the community of Bethany Beach has not changed in such a way as to invalidate those restrictions which have continued to protect this community through the years as it has grown. Although some of the restrictions have been ignored and a portion of the community is now used for limited commercial purposes, the evidence shows that Bethany Beach remains a quiet, family-oriented resort where no liquor is sold. I think the conditions of the community are still consistent with the enforcement of a restrictive covenant forbidding the sale of intoxicating beverages.

In my opinion, the toleration of the practice of "brown bagging" does not constitute the abandonment of a longstanding restriction against the sale of alcoholic beverages. The restriction against sales has, in fact, remained intact for more than eighty years and any violations thereof have been short-lived. The fact that alcoholic beverages may be purchased right outside the town is not inconsistent with my view that the quiet-town atmosphere in this small area has not broken down, and that it can and should be preserved. Those who choose to buy land subject to the restrictions should be required to continue to abide by the restrictions.

I think the only real beneficiaries of the failure of the courts to enforce the restrictions would be those who plan to benefit commercially.

I also question the propriety of the issuance of a liquor license for the sale of liquor on property which is subject to a specific restrictive covenant against such sales.

I think that restrictive covenants play a vital part in the preservation of neighborhood schemes all over the State, and that a much more complete breakdown of the neighborhood scheme should be required before a court declares that a restriction has become unenforceable.

I would affirm the Chancellor.

Notes and Questions

1. Several types of events may constitute "changed conditions" sufficient to at least trigger an inquiry whether a covenant ought still to be enforceable. Typical examples include condemnation of the burdened parcel through the power of eminent domain (typically bringing with it dedication to some purpose outside the scope of the covenant); zoning or rezoning (which may make the land incapable of legal use within the scope of the covenant); and nearby redevelopment that otherwise frustrates the purpose of the covenant.

2. The rule of *El Di* would hold covenants unenforceable for changed conditions if those conditions "render[] the benefits underlying imposition of the restrictions incapable of enjoyment." Do residents really derive *no* benefit from a limit on the available venues for the sale of alcoholic beverages in their family vacation town? Does anyone else derive a benefit from such limits? If so, are they the kind of benefits that are enforceable as a matter of the law of servitudes?

3. There are subtle differences in the framing of the test courts apply under the doctrine of changed conditions, particularly in the context of the covenants governing a common-interest community. As the Third Restatement puts it:

    > The test for finding changed conditions sufficient to warrant termination of reciprocal-subdivision servitudes is often said to be whether there has been such a radical change in conditions since creation of the servitudes that perpetuation of the servitude would be of no substantial benefit to the dominant estate. However, the test is not whether the servitude retains value, but whether it can continue to serve the purposes for which it was created.

    Restatement § 7.10, cmt. c. Do you think the difference between these two tests is likely to make a difference in the resolution of disputes? Which (if either) did the court apply in *El Di*? If *El Di* had applied the other test, would the outcome have been any different?

4. Does the mere fact of the disagreement between the majority and the dissent in *El Di* have any implications for the soundness of the doctrine of changed conditions? If reasonable minds can differ as

to whether a covenant can still serve its purpose or still provides some benefit to the dominant owner, might that in itself be a reason to continue enforcing the parties' private agreement? How does the answer to this question relate to the public policy limits on enforceability of restrictive covenants? On the danger of dead-hand control discussed in the notes following *Tulk v. Moxhay?*

Common-Interest Communities

A.   In General

As you have already seen, one prevalent application of restrictive covenants is in real estate development schemes that purport to subject many disparately held parcels within a community to a common scheme or plan. Neponsit and Bethany Beach are both communities that were initially developed under such a common scheme. Like zoning ordinances, the restrictive covenants that burden privately owned land within such developments may serve to quite comprehensively regulate the uses of land by members of the community.

Indeed, one major American city—Houston—relies largely (though not exclusively) on restrictive covenants to do the work that most other municipalities achieve by zoning. When zoning swept the nation in the 1920s, Houston was a growing, libertarian city, and sometimes-overheated rhetoric led Houstonians to reject zoning as communistic government interference with liberty. Later attempts to introduce zoning also failed due to the persistence of anti-zoning movements. *See* Barry J. Kaplan, *Urban Development, Economic Growth, and Personal Liberty: The Rhetoric of the Houston Anti-Zoning Movements, 1947-1962*, 84 SOUTHWESTERN HISTORICAL Q. 133 (1980); *see also* Houstonians for Responsible Growth, How Houston "Got It Right": The World Takes Notice (n.d) (collecting numerous encomiums to Houston's freedom and prosperity as the result of lack of zoning). The absence of zoning doesn't mean that land use in Houston is unregulated—the city code imposes minimum lot size and parking restrictions that have made the city the most sprawling American metropolis, and the most heavily dependent on privately-owned automobiles for transportation. But more detailed restrictions are often the work of private covenants.

Private covenants are common in Houston, replicating many of the standard functions of zoning, particularly separation of uses. Houston encourages covenant creation by allowing their creation by a majority vote of subdivision residents. Houstonians separate homes from businesses through restrictive covenants that specify the appropriate use for each lot in a subdivision, and enable every lot owner individually to sue. This regime works most effectively in wealthy neighborhoods. Houston's city code, unlike that of most American cities, also allows the city attorney to sue to enforce restrictive covenants. The city may seek civil penalties of up to $1000 per day for a violation, and the city prioritizes enforcement of use restrictions, rather than other covenants such as aesthetic rules. In essence, the city has recreated "single use zoning" as covenant enforcement.

Both within and outside of Houston, such uses of restrictive covenants may allow—like the covenants in *Neponsit*—for centralized *private* authority to administer and enforce the covenants through a corporation or association constituted from among the property owners in the community. This kind of collective governance of land uses via restrictive covenants is what the Third Restatement refers to as a **common-interest community**. There are three primary types of common-interest community in the United States: the **homeowners association** (or **"HOA"**), the **condominium** (or **"condo"**), and the **cooperative** (or **"co-op"**). State statutes provide for the creation of these legal entities. According to the Community Associations Institute—an international research, education, and advocacy nonprofit organization that promotes and supports common-interest communities—there were over 330,000 common-interest communities in the United States in 2014, encompassing 26.7 million housing units and 66.7 million residents. COMMUNITY ASSOCIATIONS INSTITUTE STATISTICAL REVIEW FOR 2014, at 1, available at http://www.cairf.org/research/factbook/2014_statistical_review.pdf.

1.   Homeowners Associations

The homeowners association is the most common type of common-interest community in the United States—over half of all common interest communities in the United States are HOAs. *Id.* In an HOA, the creation of community-wide restrictive covenants typically happens at the planning stage: a real estate developer plans out a subdivision of a contiguous parcel of undeveloped or underdeveloped land, and files with the local clerk or register of deeds a **subdivision plat** mapping out a survey of the separate lots of the planned community and a **declaration of covenants, conditions, and restrictions** ("**CC&Rs**") to bind each of those lots as restrictive covenants. When the subdivided lots are initially sold, the developer writes the same covenants into the deed to every lot, either explicitly or incorporating the CC&Rs of the declaration by reference. The CC&Rs will typically delegate enforcement to a homeowners association—a legal entity that is incorporated or otherwise created for the purpose of managing the common-interest community (as with the property owners' association in *Neponsit*). The association's membership is comprised of all owners of real property in the subdivision. These members are entitled to elect a board of managers to act on behalf of the association, though votes are usually not equally distributed to all residents; typically votes are allocated according to some proxy for property value, such as lot size.

The association itself may hold title to real property in common areas of the subdivision—such as private roads, parks and other recreational facilities, and common utilities. It may also contract on behalf of the community for common services, such as professional security guards. But its main function is to administer, modify as necessary, and enforce the restrictive covenants that bind the real property in the subdivision. This includes the collection of HOA dues—such as the fees that were at issue in *Neponsit*—that go toward the maintenance of the subdivision and other expenses incurred by the association (for example, professional fees for attorneys, accountants, etc.). The association is typically also empowered to levy special assessments against property owners in the subdivision as it deems necessary. *See* Restatement, § 6.5. The authority of the association to act is governed both by the CC&Rs and by a set of bylaws—like the bylaws of any other corporation—that set forth in detail what actions the managers may take according to what procedures, what actions require a vote of all members of the association, and whether there is any supermajority requirement for certain actions. As we will see, the association may also enact regulations regarding use and maintenance of privately owned property in the subdivision that go beyond the CC&Rs.

2.   Condominiums

A **condominium** is very similar to a homeowners association, except it typically covers either a single multi-unit structure or several structures comprising attached residences on a single contiguous lot. Like a homeowners association, a condominium is established by filing with the appropriate public official a **condominium declaration**, which like the homeowners association declaration will contain the CC&Rs that will govern the condominium, and will provide for a condominium association to administer the CC&Rs and otherwise act on behalf of the community. State statutes typically impose a bit more regulation on condominiums than on subdivision HOAs, sometimes setting forth substantive rules limiting the powers of condominium associations or subjecting them to certain procedural requirements. But condominium associations typically have the same types of powers as HOAs, including the power to assess dues and special assessments from individual owner/members.

One important distinction between condominiums and homeowners associations has to do with how title to property is held in each. In a condominium, each unit owner holds title to their individual unit in fee simple, but the individual unit owners collectively own all common areas of the condominium property (hallways, common outdoor spaces, lobbies, recreation areas, etc.) as tenants in common. State statutes prohibit condominium owners from seeking partition of these commonly owned spaces. As with voting rights in the condominium association, each owner's fractional share in this tenancy in common is typically determined by some proxy for the value of the owner's particular unit, such as square footage.

3. Cooperatives

By far the least common form of common-interest community is the **cooperative**. In a cooperative, title to all real property in the community (typically an apartment building) is held by a cooperative corporation, whose shareholders are the residents of individual units. As with the other common-interest communities, the number of shares each individual unit owner holds is typically proportional to some proxy for the value of their residence—such as square footage. Each resident's shares are "appurtenant" (i.e., connected) to a **proprietary lease** for a particular unit—a lease whose term is tied to the resident's ownership of their shares in the cooperative. Co-op owners therefore have a dual relationship with their common-interest community: they are formally tenants, but at the same time they are shareholders of the (corporate) landlord. The proprietary lease typically plays the role that CC&Rs serve in HOAs and condominiums: it contains the covenants restricting residents' use of their own unit and any common spaces, and in lieu of rent it obliges residents to pay maintenance fees—which typically represent a fractional share of both operating expenses and carrying costs of the entire property (such as mortgage payments and property taxes).

The board of directors of a cooperative corporation typically wields significant power over the property and its residents. In addition to administering and enforcing the terms of the proprietary lease and managing the property on behalf of all the residents, co-op boards are typically empowered to create and enforce additional rules to govern the community via their own by-laws and, sometimes, separate and potentially quite intrusive "house rules." Beyond this, the governing documents of most co-operatives reserve to the board a right to withhold consent to any transfer of shares in the corporation (and, thus, of the proprietary lease to any unit in the cooperative). Absent violation of the anti-discrimination laws, boards are generally free to arbitrarily withhold such consent. One justification for this power is that residents of a co-operative depend on one another for the financial stability of their homes: a shareholder who fails to pay maintenance on time could threaten not only themselves but the entire community with foreclosure of a mortgage or a tax lien, and the board therefore has an interest in screening new shareholders for financial wherewithal and reliability. But another theory justifying such power is that a cooperative is, as its name implies, a form of collective governance of an intimate residential community, which limits the appropriate degree of outside legal interference. As the New York Court of Appeals put it: "there is no reason why the owners of the co-operative apartment house could not decide for themselves with whom they wish to share their elevators, their common halls and facilities, their stockholders' meetings, their management problems and responsibilities and their homes." Weisner v. 791 Park Ave. Corp., 160 N.E.2d 720, 724 (N.Y. 1959).

Cooperatives exist almost exclusively in New York City, where they account for the majority of owner-occupied apartments in Manhattan. Given the tremendous power co-operative boards can exercise over admission of new shareholders, it is perhaps unsurprising that co-ops constitute the form of ownership for many of the city's most exclusive residential apartment buildings. Tom Wolfe famously profiled these co-ops in the heady days of the 1980s bull market:

> These so-called Good Buildings are forty-two cooperative apartment houses built more than half a century ago. Thirty-seven

of them are located in a small wedge of Manhattan's Upper East Side known as the Triangle[,]... an area defined by Fifty-seventh Street from Sutton Place to Fifth Avenue on the south, Fifth [Avenue] to Ninety-eighth Street on the west, and a diagonal back down to Sutton on the east.... The term Good Building was originally uttered sotto voce. Before the First World War it was code for "restricted to Protestants of northern European stock".... Today Good certainly doesn't mean democratic, but it does pertain to attributes that are at least more broadly available than Protestant grandparents: namely, decorous demeanor, dignified behavior, business and social connections, and sheer wealth. In short, bourgeois respectability. The co-op boards want quiet, conservatively dressed families, although not with too many children. Children tie up the elevators and make noise in the lobby.... The boards raise and lower their financial requirements, as well as their social requirements, with the temperature of the market.... The first requirement is that the buyer be able to pay for the apartment in cash.... The second, in many buildings, is that he not be dependent on his job or profession to pay for his monthly maintenance fees and keep up appearances.... The prospects and their families are also expected to drop by the building for "cocktails," which is an inspection of dress and deportment.... The stiffest known financial requirements are at a Good Building on Park Avenue in the seventies, where the board asks that a purchaser of an apartment demonstrate a net worth of at least $30 million.[26]

Tom Wolfe, *Proper Places*, ESQUIRE (June 1985), at 194, 196-200.

---

[26] [*Eds.:* This would be over $66 million in 2015 dollars.]

B.   Rulemaking Authority

As noted above, the governing documents of a common-interest community can significantly regulate the lives of its residents, and the governing bodies of the community are usually empowered to impose additional regulations. How expansive is this rulemaking authority?

Hidden Harbour Estates, Inc. v. Norman
309 So. 2d 180 (Fla. Dist. Ct. App. 1975)

DOWNEY, Judge.

The question presented on this appeal is whether the board of directors of a condominium association may adopt a rule or regulation prohibiting the use of alcoholic beverages in certain areas of the common elements of the condominium.

Appellant is the condominium association formed, pursuant to a Declaration of Condominium, to operate a 202 unit condominium known as Hidden Harbour. Article 3.3(f) of appellant's articles of incorporation provides, inter alia, that the association shall have the power 'to make and amend reasonable rules and regulations respecting the use of the condominium property.' A similar provision is contained in the Declaration of Condominium.

Among the common elements of the condominium is a club house used for social occasions. Pursuant to the association's rule making power the directors of the association adopted a rule prohibiting the use of alcoholic beverages in the club house and adjacent areas. Appellees, as the owners of one condominium unit, objected to the rule, which incidentally had been approved by the condominium owners voting by a margin of 2 to 1 (126 to 63). Being dissatisfied with the association's action, appellees brought this injunction suit to prohibit the enforcement of the rule. After a trial on the merits at which appellees showed there had been no untoward incidents occurring in the club house during social events when alcoholic beverages were consumed, the trial court granted a permanent injunction against enforcement of said rule. The trial court was of the view that rules and regulations adopted in pursuance of the management and operation of the condominium 'must have some reasonable relationship to the protection of life, property or the general welfare of the residents of the condominium in order for it to be valid and enforceable.' In its final judgment the trial court further held that any resident of the condominium might engage in any lawful action in the club house or on any common condominium property unless such action was engaged in or carried on in such a manner as to constitute a nuisance.

With all due respect to the veteran trial judge, we disagree. It appears to us that inherent in the condominium concept is the principle that to promote the health, happiness, and peace of mind of the majority of the unit owners since they are living in such close proximity and using facilities in common, each unit owner must give up a certain degree of freedom of choice which he might otherwise enjoy in separate, privately owned property. Condominium unit owners comprise a little democratic sub society of necessity more restrictive as it pertains to use of condominium property than may be existent outside the condominium organization. The Declaration of Condominium involved herein is replete with examples of the curtailment of individual rights usually associated with the private ownership of property. It provides, for example, that no sale may be effectuated without approval; no minors may be permanent residents; no pets are allowed.

Certainly, the association is not at liberty to adopt arbitrary or capricious rules bearing no relationship to the health, happiness and enjoyment of life of the various unit owners. On the contrary, we believe the test is reasonableness. If a rule is reasonable the association can adopt it; if not, it cannot. It is not necessary that conduct be so offensive as to constitute a nuisance in order to justify regulation thereof. Of course, this means that each case must be considered upon the peculiar facts and circumstances thereto appertaining.

Finally, restrictions on the use of alcoholic beverages are widespread throughout both governmental and private sectors; there is nothing unreasonable or unusual about a group of people electing to prohibit their use in commonly owned areas.

Accordingly, the judgment appealed from is reversed and the cause is remanded with directions to enter judgment for the appellant.

Notes and Questions

1. What is the difference between the standard applied by the trial judge and that applied by the Court of Appeal in *Norman*? Don't both merely require rules promulgated by an association to be "reasonable"?

2. The Hidden Harbour development was back before the Florida District Court of Appeal six years later over a different dispute involving a resident's private well. In Hidden Harbour Estates, Inc. v. Basso, 393 So.2d 637 (Fla. Dist. Ct. App. 1981), the court opined:

> There are essentially two categories of cases in which a condominium association attempts to enforce rules of restrictive uses. The first category is that dealing with the validity of restrictions found in the declaration of condominium itself. The second category of cases involves the validity of rules promulgated by the association's board of directors or the refusal of the board of directors to allow a particular use when the board is invested with the power to grant or deny a particular use.

In the first category, the restrictions are clothed with a very strong presumption of validity which arises from the fact that each individual unit owner purchases his unit knowing of and accepting the restrictions to be imposed. Such restrictions are very much in the nature of covenants running with the land and they will not be invalidated absent a showing that they are wholly arbitrary in their application, in violation of public policy, or that they abrogate some fundamental constitutional right. Thus, although case law has applied the word "reasonable" to determine whether such restrictions are valid, this is not the appropriate test....

The rule to be applied in the second category of cases, however, is different. In those cases where a use restriction is not mandated by the declaration of condominium per se, but is instead created by the board of directors of the condominium association, the rule of reasonableness comes into vogue. The requirement of "reasonableness" in these instances is designed to somewhat fetter the discretion of the board of directors. By imposing such a standard, the board is required to enact rules and make decisions that are reasonably related to the promotion of the health, happiness and peace of mind of the unit owners. In cases like the present one where the decision to allow a particular use is within the discretion of the board, the board must allow the use unless the use is demonstrably antagonistic to the legitimate objectives of the condominium association, i.e., the health, happiness and peace of mind of the individual unit owners.

The Restatement draws the same distinction between the standard for validity of covenants set forth in the CC&Rs of a declaration and the standard for validity of rules enacted by the governing body of a common-interest community. Thus, restrictions in a condominium declaration are valid—even if unreasonable—unless they are illegal, unconstitutional, or against public policy, (Restatement § 3.1), while house rules and their enforcement are subject to a reasonableness standard (Restatement § 6.7 & Reporter's Note).

Does this distinction make sense? The court in *Basso* notes that "house rules," unlike CC&Rs, may be adopted *after* a resident acquires their property and thus without the notice that recording of the declaration provides before a resident invests in the community.* Does that distinction justify the diverging standards for validity? Is such a justification consistent with the reasoning of *Norman*?

3. Not all jurisdictions follow the distinction drawn by *Basso* and the Restatement. Consider the following case.

Nahrstedt v. Lakeside Village Condominium Assoc., Inc.
878 P.2d 1275 (Cal. 1994)

KENNARD, Justice.

A homeowner in a 530–unit condominium complex sued to prevent the homeowners association from enforcing a restriction against keeping cats, dogs, and other animals in the condominium development. The owner asserted that the restriction, which was contained in the project's declaration recorded by the condominium project's developer, was "unreasonable" as applied to her because she kept her three cats indoors and because her cats were "noiseless" and "created no nuisance." Agreeing with the premise underlying the owner's complaint, the Court

---

* Typically, either under state law or by a declaration's own terms (or both), the CC&Rs in a declaration may only be amended by a supermajority vote of all members of the association.

of Appeal concluded that the homeowners association could enforce the restriction only upon proof that plaintiff's cats would be likely to interfere with the right of other homeowners "to the peaceful and quiet enjoyment of their property."

Those of us who have cats or dogs can attest to their wonderful companionship and affection. Not surprisingly, studies have confirmed this effect.... But the issue before us is not whether in the abstract pets can have a beneficial effect on humans. Rather, the narrow issue here is whether a pet restriction that is contained in the recorded declaration of a condominium complex is enforceable against the challenge of a homeowner. As we shall explain, the Legislature, in Civil Code section 1354, has required that courts enforce the covenants, conditions and restrictions contained in the recorded declaration of a common interest development "unless unreasonable."

Because a stable and predictable living environment is crucial to the success of condominiums and other common interest residential developments, and because recorded use restrictions are a primary means of ensuring this stability and predictability, the Legislature in section 1354 has afforded such restrictions a presumption of validity and has required of challengers that they demonstrate the restriction's "unreasonableness" by the deferential standard applicable to equitable servitudes. Under this standard established by the Legislature, enforcement of a restriction does not depend upon the conduct of a particular condominium owner. Rather, the restriction must be uniformly enforced in the condominium development to which it was intended to apply unless the plaintiff owner can show that the burdens it imposes on affected properties so substantially outweigh the benefits of the restriction that it should not be enforced against any owner. Here, the Court of Appeal did not apply this standard in deciding that plaintiff had stated a claim for declaratory relief. Accordingly, we reverse the judgment of the Court of Appeal and remand for further proceedings consistent with the views expressed in this opinion.

I

Lakeside Village is a large condominium development in Culver City, Los Angeles County. It consists of 530 units spread throughout 12 separate 3–story buildings. The residents share common lobbies and hallways, in addition to laundry and trash facilities.

The Lakeside Village project is subject to certain covenants, conditions and restrictions (hereafter CC & R's) that were included in the developer's declaration recorded with the Los Angeles County Recorder on April 17, 1978, at the inception of the development project. Ownership of a unit includes membership in the project's homeowners association, the Lakeside Village Condominium Association (hereafter Association), the body that enforces the project's CC & R's, including the pet restriction, which provides in relevant part: "No animals (which shall mean dogs and cats), livestock, reptiles or poultry shall be kept in any unit."[3]

In January 1988, plaintiff Natore Nahrstedt purchased a Lakeside Village condominium and moved in with her three cats. When the Association learned of the cats' presence, it demanded their removal and assessed fines against Nahrstedt for each successive month that she remained in violation of the condominium project's pet restriction.

Nahrstedt then brought this lawsuit against the Association, its officers, and two of its employees, asking the trial court to invalidate the assessments, to enjoin future assessments, to award damages for violation of her privacy when the Association "peered" into her condominium unit, to award damages for infliction of emotional distress, and to declare the pet restriction "unreasonable" as applied to indoor cats (such as hers) that

---

[3] The CC & R's permit residents to keep "domestic fish and birds."

are not allowed free run of the project's common areas. Nahrstedt also alleged she did not know of the pet restriction when she bought her condominium....

The Association demurred to the complaint. In its supporting points and authorities, the Association argued that the pet restriction furthers the collective "health, happiness and peace of mind" of persons living in close proximity within the Lakeside Village condominium development, and therefore is reasonable as a matter of law. The trial court sustained the demurrer as to each cause of action and dismissed Nahrstedt's complaint. Nahrstedt appealed.

A divided Court of Appeal reversed the trial court's judgment of dismissal.... On the Association's petition, we granted review to decide when a condominium owner can prevent enforcement of a use restriction that the project's developer has included in the recorded declaration of CC & R's....

II

Today, condominiums, cooperatives, and planned-unit developments with homeowners associations have become a widely accepted form of real property ownership. These ownership arrangements are known as "common interest" developments. ...Use restrictions are an inherent part of any common interest development and are crucial to the stable, planned environment of any shared ownership arrangement.... The restrictions on the use of property in any common interest development may limit activities conducted in the common areas as well as in the confines of the home itself. Commonly, use restrictions preclude alteration of building exteriors, limit the number of persons that can occupy each unit, and place limitations on—or prohibit altogether—the keeping of pets.

Restrictions on property use are not the only characteristic of common interest ownership. Ordinarily, such ownership also entails mandatory membership in an owners association, which, through an elected board of directors, is empowered to enforce any use restrictions contained in the project's declaration or master deed and to enact new rules governing the use and occupancy of property within the project. Because of its considerable power in managing and regulating a common interest development, the governing board of an owners association must guard against the potential for the abuse of that power. As Professor Natelson observes, owners associations "can be a powerful force for good or for ill" in their members' lives. Therefore, anyone who buys a unit in a common interest development with knowledge of its owners association's discretionary power accepts "the risk that the power may be used in a way that benefits the commonality but harms the individual." Generally, courts will uphold decisions made by the governing board of an owners association so long as they represent good faith efforts to further the purposes of the common interest development, are consistent with the development's governing documents, and comply with public policy.

Thus, subordination of individual property rights to the collective judgment of the owners association together with restrictions on the use of real property comprise the chief attributes of owning property in a common interest development....

Notwithstanding the limitations on personal autonomy that are inherent in the concept of shared ownership of residential property, common interest developments have increased in popularity in recent years, in part because they generally provide a more affordable alternative to ownership of a single-family home....

...When restrictions limiting the use of property within a common interest development satisfy the requirements of covenants running with the land or of equitable servitudes, what standard or test governs their enforceability? In California, as we explained at the outset, our Legislature has made common interest development use restrictions contained in a project's recorded declaration "enforceable ... *unless unreasonable.*" (§ 1354, subd. (a), italics added.) ...In other words, such restrictions should be enforced unless they are wholly arbitrary, violate a fundamental public policy, or impose a burden on the use of affected land that far outweighs any benefit.

This interpretation of section 1354 is consistent with the views of legal commentators as well as judicial decisions in other jurisdictions that have applied a presumption of validity to the recorded land use restrictions of a common interest development. As these authorities point out, and as we discussed previously, recorded CC & R's are the primary means of achieving the stability and predictability so essential to the success of a shared ownership housing development.... When courts accord a presumption of validity to all such recorded use restrictions and measure them against deferential standards of equitable servitude law, it discourages lawsuits by owners of individual units seeking personal exemptions from the restrictions. This also promotes stability and predictability in two ways. It provides substantial assurance to prospective condominium purchasers that they may rely with confidence on the promises embodied in the project's recorded CC & R's. And it protects all owners in the planned development from unanticipated increases in association fees to fund the defense of legal challenges to recorded restrictions.

How courts enforce recorded use restrictions affects not only those who have made their homes in planned developments, but also the owners associations charged with the fiduciary obligation to enforce those restrictions. When courts treat recorded use restrictions as presumptively valid, and place on the challenger the burden of proving the restriction "unreasonable" under the deferential standards applicable to equitable servitudes, associations can proceed to enforce reasonable restrictive covenants without fear that their actions will embroil them in costly and prolonged legal proceedings. Of course, when an association determines that a unit owner has violated a use restriction, the association must do so in good faith, not in an arbitrary or capricious manner, and its enforcement procedures must be fair and applied uniformly.

There is an additional beneficiary of legal rules that are protective of recorded use restrictions: the judicial system. Fewer lawsuits challenging such restrictions will be brought, and those that are filed may be disposed of more expeditiously, if the rules courts use in evaluating such restrictions are clear, simple, and not subject to exceptions based on the peculiar circumstances or hardships of individual residents in condominiums and other shared-ownership developments.

...Refusing to enforce the CC & R's contained in a recorded declaration, or enforcing them only after protracted litigation that would require justification of their application on a case-by-case basis, would impose great strain on the social fabric of the common interest development. It would frustrate owners who had purchased their units in reliance on the CC & R's. It would put the owners and the homeowners association in the difficult and divisive position of deciding whether particular CC & R's should be applied to a particular owner. Here, for example, deciding whether a particular animal is "confined to an owner's unit and create[s] no noise, odor, or nuisance" is a fact-intensive determination that can only be made by examining in detail the behavior of the particular animal and the behavior of the particular owner. Homeowners associations are ill-equipped to make such investigations, and any decision they might make in a particular case could be divisive or subject to claims of partiality.

Enforcing the CC & R's contained in a recorded declaration only after protracted case-by-case litigation would impose substantial litigation costs on the owners through their homeowners association, which would have to defend not only against owners contesting the application of the CC &

R's to them, but also against owners contesting any case-by-case exceptions the homeowners association might make. In short, it is difficult to imagine what could more disrupt the harmony of a common interest development....

Under the holding we adopt today, the reasonableness or unreasonableness of a condominium use restriction that the Legislature has made subject to section 1354 is to be determined *not* by reference to facts that are specific to the objecting homeowner, but by reference to the common interest development as a whole. As we have explained, when, as here, a restriction is contained in the declaration of the common interest development and is recorded with the county recorder, the restriction is presumed to be reasonable and will be enforced uniformly against all residents of the common interest development *unless* the restriction is arbitrary, imposes burdens on the use of lands it affects that substantially outweigh the restriction's benefits to the development's residents, or violates a fundamental public policy.

Accordingly, here Nahrstedt could prevent enforcement of the Lakeside Village pet restriction by proving that the restriction is arbitrary, that it is substantially more burdensome than beneficial to the affected properties, or that it violates a fundamental public policy. For the reasons set forth below, Nahrstedt's complaint fails to adequately allege any of these three grounds of unreasonableness.

We conclude, as a matter of law, that the recorded pet restriction of the Lakeside Village condominium development prohibiting cats or dogs but allowing some other pets is not arbitrary, but is rationally related to health, sanitation and noise concerns legitimately held by residents of a high-density condominium project such as Lakeside Village, which includes 530 units in 12 separate 3–story buildings.

Nahrstedt's complaint alleges no facts that could possibly support a finding that the burden of the restriction on the affected property is so disproportionate to its benefit that the restriction is unreasonable and should not be enforced. Also, the complaint's allegations center on Nahrstedt and her cats (that she keeps them inside her condominium unit and that they do not bother her neighbors), without any reference to the effect on the condominium development as a whole, thus rendering the allegations legally insufficient to overcome section 1354's presumption of the restriction's validity....

LUCAS, C.J., and MOSK, BAXTER, GEORGE and WERDEGAR, JJ., concur.

ARABIAN, Justice, dissenting.
"There are two means of refuge from the misery of life: music and cats."[1]

I respectfully dissent. While technical merit may commend the majority's analysis,[2] its application to the facts presented reflects a narrow, indeed chary, view of the law that eschews the human spirit in favor of arbitrary efficiency. In my view, the resolution of this case well illustrates the conventional wisdom, and fundamental truth, of the Spanish proverb, "It is better to be a mouse in a cat's mouth than a man in a lawyer's hands."

As explained below, I find the provision known as the "pet restriction" contained in the covenants, conditions, and restrictions (CC & R's) governing the Lakeside Village project patently arbitrary and unreasonable within the meaning of Civil Code section 1354. Beyond dispute, human beings have long enjoyed an abiding and cherished association with their household animals. Given the substantial benefits derived from pet ownership, the undue burden on the use of property imposed on condominium owners who can maintain pets within the confines of their units without creating a nuisance or disturbing the quiet enjoyment of others substantially outweighs whatever meager utility the restriction may serve in the abstract. It certainly does not promote "health, happiness [or]

---

[1] Albert Schweitzer.

peace of mind" commensurate with its tariff on the quality of life for those who value the companionship of animals. Worse, it contributes to the fraying of our social fabric.

…Generically stated, plaintiff challenges this restriction to the extent it precludes not only her but anyone else living in Lakeside Village from enjoying the substantial pleasures of pet ownership while affording no discernible benefit to other unit owners if the animals are maintained without any detriment to the latter's quiet enjoyment of their own space and the common areas. In essence, she avers that when pets are kept out of sight, do not make noise, do not generate odors, and do not otherwise create a nuisance, reasonable expectations as to the quality of life within the condominium project are not impaired. At the same time, taking into consideration the well-established and long-standing historical and cultural relationship between human beings and their pets and the value they impart[,] enforcement of the restriction significantly and unduly burdens the use of land for those deprived of their companionship. Considered from this perspective, I find plaintiff's complaint states a cause of action for declaratory relief.

…Our true task in this turmoil is to strike a balance between the governing rights accorded a condominium association and the individual freedom of its members…. Pet ownership substantially enhances the quality of life for those who desire it. When others are not only undisturbed by, but *completely unaware of,* the presence of pets being enjoyed by their neighbors, the balance of benefit and burden is rendered disproportionate and unreasonable, rebutting any presumption of validity….

I would affirm the judgment of the Court of Appeal.

Notes and Questions

1. A few years after *Nahrstedt* was decided, the California legislature later enacted a statute providing that common-interest community governing documents cannot prohibit the keeping of "at least one pet." Cal. Civ. Code § 4715.

2. Did Natore Nahrstedt lose because the pet restriction is reasonable in general, because the restriction is reasonable as applied to indoor cats, or because the fines levied by the board were a reasonable means of enforcing the restriction?

3. Is the reasonableness standard applied in *Nahrstedt* the same standard applied by the court in *Norman* and *Basso*? If not, how do the standards differ? How does the reasonableness standard of *Nahrstedt* differ from the standard Florida applies to CC&Rs?

C. Enforcement of Rules and Covenants by Common-Interest Communities

What happens if a resident of a common interest community breaches a covenant? How can the governing body of the community—the HOA managers, the condo board, or the co-op board—enforce the rules laid down in the restrictive covenants against breaching community members? *Neponsit* provides one answer: the breach of a covenant to pay money— such as dues and assessments—will serve as an equitable lien on the breaching resident's property in the community. This lien could be foreclosed, or more commonly the threat of foreclosure and the encumbrance of the lien can be used to leverage payment if and when the resident ever tries to sell her home. The governing body could also sue to recover unpaid sums, but because this involves significant additional expense it is typically an unattractive option reserved as a last resort.

But what about covenants that restrict use of property in the community—or rules that govern the conduct of residents on the community's property? The Restatement suggests that the governing bodies of common-interest communities enjoy wide latitude to enforce the restrictions in governing documents. Section 6.8 provides: "In addition to seeking court enforcement, the association may adopt reasonable rules and procedures to encourage compliance and deter violations, including the imposition of fines, penalties, late fees, and the withdrawal of privileges to use common recreational and social facilities." Typically the governing documents will empower the association or board to levy fines against residents for their breach of such rules of conduct or use. Those fines, like unpaid dues or assessments, can also become an equitable lien on the resident's property if state law and/or the declaration so provide.

How should we assess the "reasonableness" of any particular enforcement action? And how searching a review should courts take of such actions if and when they are challenged by aggrieved members of the common-interest community?

40 West 67th Street v. Pullman
790 N.E.2d 1174 (N.Y. 2003)

ROSENBLATT, J.

In *Matter of Levandusky v. One Fifth Ave. Apt. Corp.*, 75 N.Y.2d 530, 554 N.Y.S.2d 807, 553 N.E.2d 1317 [1990] we held that the business judgment rule is the proper standard of judicial review when evaluating decisions made by residential cooperative corporations. In the case before us, defendant is a shareholder-tenant in the plaintiff cooperative building. The relationship between defendant and the cooperative, including the conditions under which a shareholder's tenancy may be terminated, is governed by the shareholder's lease agreement. The cooperative terminated defendant's tenancy in accordance with a provision in the lease that authorized it to do so based on a tenant's "objectionable" conduct....

I.

Plaintiff cooperative owns the building located at 40 West 67th Street in Manhattan, which contains 38 apartments. In 1998, defendant bought into the cooperative and acquired 80 shares of stock appurtenant to his proprietary lease for apartment 7B.

Soon after moving in, defendant engaged in a course of behavior that, in the view of the cooperative, began as demanding, grew increasingly disruptive and ultimately became intolerable. After several points of friction between defendant and the cooperative,[1] defendant started complaining about his elderly upstairs neighbors, a retired college professor and his wife who had occupied apartment 8B for over two decades. In a stream of vituperative letters to the cooperative—16 letters in the month of October 1999 alone—he accused the couple of playing their television set and stereo at high volumes late into the night, and claimed they were running a loud and illegal bookbinding business in their apartment. Defendant further charged that the couple stored toxic chemicals in their apartment for use in their "dangerous and illegal" business. Upon investigation, the cooperative's Board determined that the couple did not possess a television set or stereo and that there was no evidence of a bookbinding business or any other commercial enterprise in their apartment.

Hostilities escalated, resulting in a physical altercation between defendant and the retired professor.[2] Following the altercation, defendant

---

[1] Initially, defendant sought changes in the building services, such as the installation of video surveillance, 24-hour door service and replacement of the lobby mailboxes. After investigation, the Board deemed these proposed changes inadvisable or infeasible.

[2] Defendant brought charges against the professor which resulted in the professor's arrest. Eventually, the charges were adjourned in contemplation of dismissal.

distributed flyers to the cooperative residents in which he referred to the professor, by name, as a potential "psychopath in our midst" and accused him of cutting defendant's telephone lines. In another flyer, defendant described the professor's wife and the wife of the Board president as having close "intimate personal relations." Defendant also claimed that the previous occupants of his apartment revealed that the upstairs couple have "historically made excessive noise." The former occupants, however, submitted an affidavit that denied making any complaints about noise from the upstairs apartment and proclaimed that defendant's assertions to the contrary were "completely false."

Furthermore, defendant made alterations to his apartment without Board approval, had construction work performed on the weekend in violation of house rules, and would not respond to Board requests to correct these conditions or to allow a mutual inspection of his apartment and the upstairs apartment belonging to the elderly couple. Finally, defendant commenced four lawsuits against the upstairs couple, the president of the cooperative and the cooperative management, and tried to commence three more.

In reaction to defendant's behavior, the cooperative called a special meeting pursuant to article III (First) (f) of the lease agreement, which provides for termination of the tenancy if the cooperative by a two-thirds vote determines that "because of objectionable conduct on the part of the Lessee * * * the tenancy of the Lessee is undesirable."[3] The cooperative informed the shareholders that the purpose of the meeting was to determine whether defendant "engaged in repeated actions inimical to

---

[3] The full provision authorizes termination "if at any time the Lessor shall determine, upon the affirmative vote of the holders of record of at least two-thirds of that part of its capital stock which is then owned by Lessees under proprietary leases then in force, at a meeting of such stockholders duly called to take action on the subject, that because of objectionable conduct on the part of the Lessee, or of a person dwelling in or visiting the apartment, the tenancy of the Lessee is undesirable."

cooperative living and objectionable to the Corporation and its stockholders that make his continued tenancy undesirable."

Timely notice of the meeting was sent to all shareholders in the cooperative, including defendant. At the ensuing meeting, held in June 2000, owners of more than 75% of the outstanding shares in the cooperative were present. Defendant chose not attend. By a vote of 2,048 shares to 0, the shareholders in attendance passed a resolution declaring defendant's conduct "objectionable" and directing the Board to terminate his proprietary lease and cancel his shares. The resolution contained the findings upon which the shareholders concluded that defendant's behavior was inimical to cooperative living. Pursuant to the resolution, the Board sent defendant a notice of termination requiring him to vacate his apartment by August 31, 2000. Ignoring the notice, defendant remained in the apartment, prompting the cooperative to bring this suit for possession and ejectment, a declaratory judgment cancelling defendant's stock, and a money judgment for use and occupancy, along with attorneys' fees and costs....

II. THE *LEVANDUSKY* BUSINESS JUDGMENT RULE

The heart of this dispute is the parties' disagreement over the proper standard of review to be applied when a cooperative exercises its agreed-upon right to terminate a tenancy based on a shareholder-tenant's objectionable conduct. In the agreement establishing the rights and duties of the parties, the cooperative reserved to itself the authority to determine whether a member's conduct was objectionable and to terminate the tenancy on that basis. The cooperative argues that its decision to do so should be reviewed in accordance with *Levandusky*'s business judgment rule. Defendant contends that the business judgment rule has no application under these circumstances and that RPAPL 711 requires a court to make its own evaluation of the Board's conduct based on a judicial standard of reasonableness.

Levandusky established a standard of review analogous to the corporate business judgment rule for a shareholder-tenant challenge to a decision of a residential cooperative corporation. The business judgment rule is a common-law doctrine by which courts exercise restraint and defer to good faith decisions made by boards of directors in business settings. The rule has been long recognized in New York. In *Levandusky*, the cooperative board issued a stop work order for a shareholder-tenant's renovations that violated the proprietary lease. The shareholder-tenant brought a CPLR article 78 proceeding to set aside the stop work order. The Court upheld the Board's action, and concluded that the business judgment rule "best balances the individual and collective interests at stake" in the residential cooperative setting (*Levandusky*, 75 N.Y.2d at 537, 554 N.Y.S.2d 807, 553 N.E.2d 1317).

In the context of cooperative dwellings, the business judgment rule provides that a court should defer to a cooperative board's determination "[s]o long as the board acts for the purposes of the cooperative, within the scope of its authority and in good faith" (*id.* at 538, 554 N.Y.S.2d 807, 553 N.E.2d 1317). In adopting this rule, we recognized that a cooperative board's broad powers could lead to abuse through arbitrary or malicious decisionmaking, unlawful discrimination or the like. However, we also aimed to avoid impairing "the purposes for which the residential community and its governing structure were formed: protection of the interest of the entire community of residents in an environment managed by the board for the common benefit" (*id.* at 537, 554 N.Y.S.2d 807, 553 N.E.2d 1317). The Court concluded that the business judgment rule best balances these competing interests and also noted that the limited judicial review afforded by the rule protects the cooperative's decisions against "undue court involvement and judicial second-guessing" (*id.* at 540, 554 N.Y.S.2d 807, 553 N.E.2d 1317).

Although we applied the business judgment rule in *Levandusky*, we did not attempt to fix its boundaries, recognizing that this corporate concept may not necessarily comport with every situation encountered by a cooperative and its shareholder-tenants. Defendant argues that when it comes to terminations, the business judgment rule conflicts with RPAPL 711(1) and is therefore inoperative.[5] We see no such conflict. In the realm of cooperative governance and in the lease provision before us, the cooperative's determination as to the tenant's objectionable behavior stands as competent evidence necessary to sustain the cooperative's determination. If that were not so, the contract provision for termination of the lease-to which defendant agreed-would be meaningless.

We reject the cooperative's argument that RPAPL 711(1) is irrelevant to these proceedings, but conclude that the business judgment rule may be applied consistently with the statute. Procedurally, the business judgment standard will be applied across the cases, but the manner in which it presents itself varies with the form of the lawsuit. *Levandusky*, for example, was framed as a CPLR article 78 proceeding, but we applied the business judgment rule as a concurrent form of "rationality" and "reasonableness" to determine whether the decision was "arbitrary and capricious" pursuant to CPLR 7803(3).

Similarly, the procedural vehicle driving this case is RPAPL 711(1), which requires "competent evidence" to show that a tenant is objectionable. Thus, in this context, the competent evidence that is the basis for the shareholder vote will be reviewed under the business judgment rule, which means courts will normally defer to that vote and the shareholders' stated findings as competent evidence that the tenant is indeed objectionable under the statute. As we stated in *Levandusky*, a single standard of review for cooperatives is preferable, and "we see no purpose

---

[5] RPAPL 711(1), in pertinent part, states: "A proceeding seeking to recover possession of real property by reason of the termination of the term fixed in the lease pursuant to a provision contained therein giving the landlord the right to terminate the time fixed for occupancy under such agreement if he deem the tenant objectionable, shall not be maintainable unless the landlord shall by competent evidence establish to the satisfaction of the court that the tenant is objectionable."

in allowing the form of the action to dictate the substance of the standard by which the legitimacy of corporate action is to be measured" (id. at 541, 554 N.Y.S.2d 807, 553 N.E.2d 1317).

Despite this deferential standard, there are instances when courts should undertake review of board decisions. To trigger further judicial scrutiny, an aggrieved shareholder-tenant must make a showing that the board acted (1) outside the scope of its authority, (2) in a way that did not legitimately further the corporate purpose or (3) in bad faith.

III.

A. The Cooperative's Scope of Authority

Pursuant to its bylaws, the cooperative was authorized (through its Board) to adopt a form of proprietary lease to be used for all shareholder-tenants. Based on this authorization, defendant and other members of the cooperative voluntarily entered into lease agreements containing the termination provision before us. The cooperative does not contend that it has the power to terminate the lease absent the termination provision. Indeed, it recognizes, correctly, that if there were no such provision, termination could proceed only pursuant to RPAPL 711(1).

The cooperative unfailingly followed the procedures contained in the lease when acting to terminate defendant's tenancy. In accordance with the bylaws, the Board called a special meeting, and notified all shareholder-tenants of its time, place and purpose. Defendant thus had notice and the opportunity to be heard. In accordance with the agreement, the cooperative acted on a supermajority vote after properly fashioning the issue and the question to be addressed by resolution. The resolution specified the basis for the action, setting forth a list of specific findings as to defendant's objectionable behavior. By not appearing or presenting evidence personally or by counsel, defendant failed to challenge the findings and has not otherwise satisfied us that the Board has in any way acted ultra vires. In all, defendant has failed to demonstrate that the cooperative acted outside the scope of its authority in terminating the tenancy.

B. Furthering the Corporate Purpose

Levandusky also recognizes that the business judgment rule prohibits judicial inquiry into Board actions that, presupposing good faith, are taken in legitimate furtherance of corporate purposes. Specifically, there must be a legitimate relationship between the Board's action and the welfare of the cooperative. Here, by the unanimous vote of everyone present at the meeting, the cooperative resoundingly expressed its collective will, directing the Board to terminate defendant's tenancy after finding that his behavior was more than its shareholders could bear. The Board was under a fiduciary duty to further the collective interests of the cooperative. By terminating the tenancy, the Board's action thus bore an obvious and legitimate relation to the cooperative's avowed ends.

There is, however, an additional dimension to corporate purpose that *Levandusky* contemplates, notably, the legitimacy of purpose—a feature closely related to good faith. Put differently, all the shareholders of a cooperative may agree on an objective, and the Board may pursue that objective zealously, but that does not necessarily mean the objective is lawful or legitimate. Defendant, however, has not shown that the Board's purpose was anything other than furthering the over-all welfare of a cooperative that found it could no longer abide defendant's behavior.

C. Good Faith, in the Exercise of Honest Judgment

Finally, defendant has not shown the slightest indication of any bad faith, arbitrariness, favoritism, discrimination or malice on the cooperative's part, and the record reveals none. Though defendant contends that he raised sufficient facts in this regard, we agree with the Appellate Division majority that defendant has provided no factual support for his conclusory assertions that he was evicted based upon illegal or impermissible considerations. Moreover, as the Appellate Division noted, the cooperative emphasized that upon the sale of the apartment it "will 'turn over [to the defendant] all proceeds after deduction of unpaid use and occupancy, costs of sale and litigation expenses incurred in this dispute'". Defendant does not contend otherwise.

Levandusky cautions that the broad powers of cooperative governance carry the potential for abuse when a board singles out a person for harmful treatment or engages in unlawful discrimination, vendetta, arbitrary decisionmaking or favoritism. We reaffirm that admonition and stress that those types of abuses are incompatible with good faith and the exercise of honest judgment. While deferential, the *Levandusky* standard should not serve as a rubber stamp for cooperative board actions, particularly those involving tenancy terminations. We note that since *Levandusky* was decided, the lower courts have in most instances deferred to the business judgment of cooperative boards but in a number of cases have withheld deference in the face of evidence that the board acted illegitimately.[8]

The very concept of cooperative living entails a voluntary, shared control over rules, maintenance and the composition of the community. Indeed,

---

[8] *See e.g. Abrons Found. v. 29 E. 64th St. Corp.*, 297 A.D.2d 258, 746 N.Y.S.2d 482 [1st Dept.2002] [tenant raised genuine issues of material fact as to whether board acted in bad faith in imposing sublet fee meant solely to impact one tenant]; *Greenberg v Board of Mgrs. of Parkridge Condominiums*, 294 A.D.2d 467, 742 N.Y.S.2d 560 [2d Dept.2002] [affirming injunction against board because it acted outside scope of authority in prohibiting tenant from erecting a succah on balcony]; *Dinicu v. Groff Studios Corp.*, 257 A.D.2d 218, 690 N.Y.S.2d 220 [1st Dept.1999] [business judgment rule does not protect cooperative board from its own breach of contract]; *Matter of Vacca v Board of Mgrs. of Primrose Lane Condominium*, 251 A.D.2d 674, 676 N.Y.S.2d 188 [2d Dept.1998] [board acted in bad faith in prohibiting tenant from displaying religious statue in yard]; *Johar v 82-04 Lefferts Tenants Corp.*, 234 A.D.2d 516, 651 N.Y.S.2d 914 [2d Dept.1996] [board vote amending bylaws to declare plaintiff tenant ineligible to sit on cooperative board not shielded by business judgment rule]. While we do not undertake to address the correctness of the rulings in all of these cases, we list them as illustrative.

as we observed in *Levandusky*, a shareholder-tenant voluntarily agrees to submit to the authority of a cooperative board, and consequently the board "may significantly restrict the bundle of rights a property owner normally enjoys" (75 N.Y.2d at 536, 554 N.Y.S.2d 807, 553 N.E.2d 1317). When dealing, however, with termination, courts must exercise a heightened vigilance in examining whether the board's action meets the *Levandusky* test....

Notes and Questions

1. For further background on this dispute, including quotes from David Pullman himself, see Dan Barry, *Sleepless and Litigious in 7B: A Co-op War Ends in Court*, N.Y. TIMES (June 7, 2003), available at https://nyti.ms/2leMd9c.

2. What aspect of the Court of Appeals' analysis constitutes "heightened vigilance"?

3. The Restatement does not adopt the business judgment rule for review of board actions, instead applying a "reasonableness" standard. The Reporter's comments suggest that the reasonableness of an enforcement action will depend on any number of factors, including its proportionality to the resident's offensive conduct (*e.g.*, no $1,000 fines for a single instance of failing to sort an aluminum can for recycling), the logical relationship between the offensive conduct and the remedy (*e.g.*, no revocation of parking privileges for breach of a pet restriction), and whether the resident was provided with sufficient notice and opportunity to respond to the managers' complaint before any enforcement action was taken. *See* Restatement § 6.8 & cmt. b. Elsewhere the Restatement states that board members and officers have duties of care, prudence, and fairness toward members of the

community. *Id.* § 6.13 & cmt. b. Is the Restatement position consistent with *Pullman?* If not, how does it differ?

4. The Court of Appeals did not consider the question whether the provision in Pullman's proprietary lease allowing the cooperative to kick him out on grounds that he was "objectionable" should be enforceable as a general matter. If it had, what do you think would have been the result? Does it matter which standard—reasonableness or the more permissive standard applicable to CC&Rs—applies? Which do you think ought to apply to the covenants in the proprietary leases of a cooperative?

5. Say you live in a residential neighborhood unencumbered by any restrictive covenants. Could you and your neighbors come together and decide to sell an unfriendly neighbor's house over his objection? If not, what additional facts make it possible for the residents of 40 West 67th Street (a tudor-style luxury pre-war apartment building half a tree-lined block from Central Park) to vote Pullman out of the apartment he bought in their building?

6. Common-interest communities are sometimes likened to miniature private governments. (Recall *Norman's* description of condominium owners as "a little democratic sub society.") The analogy holds up somewhat: they hold elections, the elected leaders can pass rules that all are bound to follow; they can assess fines for breaking the rules; they can levy the equivalent of taxes to fund common services. There are, of course, important differences—not least failure to adhere to the principle of one-person-one-vote. But *Pullman* suggests another distinction: could any government officer or entity in the United States do to one of its citizens what Pullman's neighbors did to him? If not, what are the limits on government authority that would prevent such action, and what are the justifications for those limits? Do these

justifications carry less force in the context of the enforcement of servitudes by the managers of a common-interest-community?

Made in the USA
Middletown, DE
09 January 2020